Towards a Refugee Oriented Right of Asylum

LAURA WESTRA
University of Windsor, Canada

SATVINDER JUSS
King's College London, UK

TULLIO SCOVAZZI
University of Milano-Bicocca, Italy

Routledge
Taylor & Francis Group
LONDON AND NEW YORK

First published 2015 by Ashgate Publishing

2 Park Square, Milton Park, Abingdon, Oxon OX14 4RN
711 Third Avenue, New York, NY 10017, USA

Routledge is an imprint of the Taylor & Francis Group, an informa business

First issued in paperback 2017

British Library Cataloguing in Publication Data
A catalogue record for this book is available from the British Library

The Library of Congress has cataloged the printed edition as follows:
Towards a refugee oriented right of asylum / by Laura Westra, Satvinder Juss and Tullio Scovazzi.
pages cm. -- (Law and migration)
Includes bibliographical references and index.
ISBN 978-1-4724-5778-3 (hardback)
1. Asylum, Right of. 2. Refugees--Legal status, laws, etc. I. Juss, Satvinder S. (Satvinder Singh), author, editor. II. Scovazzi, Tullio, author, editor. III. Westra, Laura, author, editor.
K3268.3.T69 2015
342.08'3--dc23

2015002544

ISBN 978-1-4724-5778-3 (hbk)
ISBN 978-1-138-73211-7 (pbk)

TOWARDS A REFUGEE ORIENTED RIGHT OF ASYLUM

The ever-increasing number of displaced people and the growing resistance of states to grant them asylum is an unfolding human tragedy of the highest order. The plight of millions of people raises fundamental questions about state sovereignty, citizenship and human rights. This book offers thorough analysis and practical solutions. Written by eminent scholars, a convincing case is made for legal reforms based on human rights and global responsibilities.

Klaus Bosselmann, University of Auckland, New Zealand

This very timely book dares to ask the hard questions about causes and conditions of mass migrations that potential receiving states, through their politicians, refuse to confront. The authors probe the increasingly serious problems faced by spiralling numbers of refugees, displaced persons or asylum seekers produced by trafficking, climate change, wars, or terrorism, and the woefully inadequate laws available to protect them or give them refuge.

The authors examine the principles underlying policies of closed borders and exclusion, challenging the cynicism of 'border imperialism' and arbitrary treatment of asylum seekers by those who simultaneously espouse fidelity to principles of human rights and humanitarian law. They make concrete suggestions, from re-defining 'refugee' to include a far broader range of migrants, to re-configuring international refugee law to be as much a compensatory scheme as a human rights one based on the fundamental legal principle that those who cause harm to others through their deliberate or negligent acts must pay for them.

This book is a voice for reform, for moral and ethical leadership and for states to take responsibility for their role in causing the unbearable conditions leading to mass movements of the most vulnerable and destitute people in the world. Anyone interested in this most critical issue of our time, should read this book.

Kathleen Mahoney QC, FRSC, University of Calgary, Canada

Law and Migration

Series Editor
Satvinder S. Juss, King's College London, UK

Migration and its subsets of refugee and asylum policy are rising up the policy agenda at national and international level. Current controversies underline the need for rational and informed debate of this widely misrepresented and little understood area.

Law and Migration contributes to this debate by establishing a monograph series to encourage discussion and help to inform policy in this area. The series provides a forum for leading new research principally from the Law and Legal Studies area but also from related social sciences. The series is broad in scope, covering a wide range of subjects and perspectives.

Other titles in this series:

The Integration and Protection of Immigrants
Canadian and Scandinavian Critiques
Edited by Paul Van Aerschot and Patricia Daenzer
978-1-4724-3654-2

Asylum – A Right Denied
A Critical Analysis of European Asylum Policy
Helen O'Nions
978-1-4094-0409-5

Regional Approaches to the Protection of Asylum Seekers
An International Legal Perspective
Edited by Ademola Abass and Francesca Ippolito
978-1-4094-4297-4

Immigration, Integration and the Law
The Intersection of Domestic, EU and International Legal Regimes
Clíodhna Murphy
978-1-4094-6251-4

Contents

PART III: THE CASE FOR THE SUPPORT OF ASYLUM SEEKERS

Foreword

Erika Feller, University of Melbourne

This is a scholarly, well researched and articulately presented assault on the conscience of those who vilify asylum-seeking and respond by turning their backs and foregoing their responsibilities. It comes at a time when new voices do need to be heard on this issue of global concern, as the responses by states and communities become ever more mired in polemics, populist politics and a bewildering mass of misinformation. There is a need to bring order into the discussion in a balanced way, to offset fears, offer new directions for thinking and action, and reinstate the core values and principles at its centre.

Assisting and protecting asylum-seekers and refugees should proceed within an apolitical and law-based framework. At the heart of this framework is the 1951 Convention relating to the Status of Refugees, together with the broad body of human rights texts and other legal and soft law instruments that collectively bear on the rights of affected peoples and the duties of states to them.

The 1951 Convention is the cornerstone text. One hears with alarming frequency the rationale for ever tougher government approaches being linked to perceived inadequacies of the Convention. It is said that the Convention is an outdated relic of the Cold War era, a text out of step with the displacement challenges of the times. Such commentary is at best ill-informed, as this volume brings out. The Convention is not responsible for the policy failures of governments. It is a rights protection instrument. It was never drafted as a migration regulatory instrument, and should not be held to account for alleged failures on this score. Anyone who has ever worked with refugees will know how singularly important the Convention is as often the only barrier lying between many helpless people and the whims and vagaries of state discretion. It is, though, not a perfect text. If the Convention is clear in terms of the rights, it is not so when it comes to which state actually has the responsibility to protect these rights in any given case. It rests on concepts of burden and responsibility-sharing, but without sufficient guidance, definitions or indicators to help the apportionment. It takes an approach to protection which has individuals at its centre, when many situations involve mass arrivals. It was drafted in an era before certain of the forms of persecution had even a name, much less attracted global recognition, such as ethnic cleansing or gender crimes. Important elements of this framework are the subject of careful analysis and scrutiny in the various chapters of this volume, which brings out both the resilience of the basic rules, together with the minefield of legal and policy issues involved in their actual application.

The international refugee law framework has to operate, or be allowed to operate, in the particular and highly political working context of modern displacement problems. Acquiring refugee status is but the first of many hurdles asylum-seekers who are refugees have to overcome to access and enjoy their right to asylum. Practical realities on the ground, not so much the rules themselves, can in practice constitute insurmountable hurdles to ensuring other than the most basic of refugee rights are actually able to be protected and enjoyed.

The world is currently witnessing the highest amount of forced displacement since the Second World War. Some of it is very visible and kept to the fore through intense and constant media focus. Events in Syria, Iraq, Afghanistan and the Ukraine collectively have forced millions to leave their homes and find sanctuary in or outside their countries of origin. There are, though, also very large numbers of persons seeking protection and assistance – refugees, the internally displaced, stateless persons, asylum-seekers – who exist in the shadows of global consciousness. Central African Republic, Sudan and Somalia remain consistently and violently part of those countries contributing to the some 46 million persons of direct concern to the United Nations High Commissioner for Refugees.

Forced displacement affects more people for longer periods than a decade ago and is growing in cost and complexity. One measure of just how costly is the burgeoning budget of UNHCR, which has grown exponentially over recent years, topping $6 billion for 2015. With more than 85 percent of the world's displaced hosted in developing countries, underfunding against needs is a perennial problem and a barrier to rights access. It is not the only one.

Conflicts today generate the highest level of forced displacement, outside natural disasters. They are ever more difficult, unpredictable and dangerous working environments over which the humanitarian agencies have little or no leverage or control. They tend to engage a multiplicity of actors, many of whom have no respect for the fundamental principles of humanitarian law or human rights law. Many of these actors – from paramilitaries, to militias, from mercenaries to ad hoc vigilantes – operate outside any regular political structures, have unclear or diffuse chains of command within and act in a climate of full impunity. There is scant regard for the lives of civilians or for the safety of humanitarian staff, both of whom increasingly are implicated in the strategies of the conflict. Aid being provided to victims and survivors may become part of the strategies and the economy of warring parties.

Refugees often arrive in remote parts of poor countries where the rule of law may take on a very local or traditional character. Hosting facilities will often be limited, with competition between refugees and host communities for scarce resources like water, food, firewood or grazing land, or for such education, health and infrastructure services as may exist. Delicate environments may sustain important damage. Should the refugees move in sizeable numbers to towns or urban settlements, they can swell the ranks of the marginalized, urban poor. Refugee camps may become militarized and hosting them can become a security threat. Such concerns have proved a significant challenge to the realization of other than the very basic refugee rights.

In a number of countries in the developed world the rights framework is also under serious challenge. Abuse of asylum procedures and difficulties in returning unsuccessful asylum seekers have contributed to a growing negativity about asylum. Protection systems in some countries are groaning under their own costs. Generosity when it comes to receiving and protecting refugees has had to contend, variously, with global economic crises, available jobs in decline, terrorism and transnational crime on the rise, distinctions between refugees and migrants blurring, a heightened sense of general insecurity on the part of civil society in many countries and the accompanying rise of populist politics. Political will has proved rather weak in a number of countries when it comes to insulating and protecting refugee rights in irregular, mixed migration situations. It is of particular concern how international crime and terrorism have impacted the openness of states to receiving refugees. Asylum seekers, many of whom are or may be refugees, can find themselves in a sort of legal limbo where protection of legal rights takes second place to harsh migration controls, outside regular legal scrutiny. An increasing number of 'virtual' or offshore border controls (visa requirements, interception practices, carrier sanctions) is prevalent when it comes to sea borders and these often fall outside national legal frameworks. Detention, periodically arbitrary and often of children, is prevalent in some countries, with possibilities to challenge this not always present. Where detention is resorted to, it is often in a deterrent context so that the conditions are unduly or unacceptably harsh, the duration over-long and the possibilities for oversight review very limited.

Compassion and justice, international obligations and national due process requirements should frame any country's response to those who make a claim to its protection. International burden-sharing and solidarity requires sustained support of efforts by first asylum countries to assist and protect refugees. This though is not enough in this era when refugee producing situations continue to proliferate and many host states approach breaking point. The importance of meaningful asylum being more widely available, beyond the immediate region of the refugee exodus, continues only to grow. Meaningful asylum will only exist when the availability of effective refugee protection does not depend on where an individual seeks asylum; where deterrence based policies and responses remain subject to rigorous review including by the courts; and when functioning and accessible national asylum systems, which respect international law, are genuinely fostered.

Protecting the rights of refugees and asylum seekers in today's displacement situations is heavily dependent on the broad range of factors found at the intersection where law meets politics, security, community dynamics, donor priorities, international capacities and practical realities on the ground. This is not an argument for pragmatism unrestrained by law; if anything, quite the reverse. It gives added meaning to the title of this publication. While asylum in principle should always be refugee oriented, the fact is that in a world where borders are made ever more impenetrable, where the focus has turned to keeping people out and where the refugee concept is being subtly re-defined in a negative direction, this is no longer so self-evident. This all adds up to a strong case for new thinking about refugee law principles and concepts, and how to reinforce and develop them to meet successfully the challenges which beset refugee protection and the institution of asylum in modern times. I believe that this current volume will make an important contribution in this regard.

Acknowledgements

I am very grateful to have been able to include the work of Donald A. Brown for the chapter on climate refugees. His long involvement with the issue of climate change, and with the various US and international government agencies connected with climate change, make his participation invaluable for the volume.

Donald's interest in refugee issues has arisen due to his deep interest in climate change issues. He believes climate change is and will continue to create new challenges for refugee law and that climate refugees create new ethical duties for high-emitting nations and entities around the world. He is Scholar in Residence for Sustainability Ethics and Law and Professor, Widener University School of Law in Harrisburg, Pennsylvania. At Widener he teaches International Environmental Law, Human Rights Law, and Climate Change Law. He is also a part-time professor at Nanjing University, Nanjing, China, where he lectures regularly on climate change ethics. He was also in the past year a visiting professor at Nagoya University School of Law, Nagoya, Japan and a visiting lecturer at Griffith University, Brisbane, Australia. He was also a contributing author to the Intergovernmental Panel on Climate Change (IPCC), 5th Assessment Report. He has written over 150 articles, 15 book chapters and three books on climate change ethics. He is a former environmental lawyer for the US states of New Jersey and Pennsylvania, and Program Manager for United Nations Organizations at the US Environmental Protection Agency, Office of International Affairs.

Thanks are also due to Francesca Mussi, who assisted me with my own research, and to my son Richard Westra, whose suggestions for research helped me place my work, at least in part, within a socialist framework. Finally, thanks are due also to Luc Quenneville of the University of Windsor for his timely technical assistance, without which these chapters could not have been written. Satvinder Juss would also like to thank his family for their support throughout the writing of this book.

Laura Westra
University of Windsor

Introduction to the Question of Asylum Seekers: 'Se Non Ora, Quando?'

Laura Westra, Satvinder Juss and Tullio Scovazzi

> … given today's obsession with so-called irregular movements of people, with smuggling, trafficking, asylum, and the search for refuge, it probably sounds dated to talk of freedom of movement and the right of everyone to leave any country, including their own.
>
> But it is no more contradictory, I suggest, than for governments to talk of their respect for human dignity and human rights, even as they organize programmes of interception, interdiction and the return of people to territories and regimes where such respect is perhaps even less understood.[1]

With the felicitous expression cited in the title of this introductory chapter, Goodwin-Gill raises the question: if not now, when ('se non ora, quando'), are we going to revise the existing laws for the protection of the mounting numbers of refugees, asylum seekers and – more generally – displaced persons? The causes of this mass exodus are many and so are the nationalities of those who escape hoping for a better life, or at least for survival from the latest climatic disaster or illegal conflict, and we will discuss some of these issues below.

There are several common threads uniting all the problems that prompt seeking refuge. One such common thread is the total disinterest on the part of both states and international regulatory bodies in producing any effort to discover the causes for the flights, or to ensure more desirable conditions in the refugees' countries of origin. Almost a decade ago, Satvinder Juss had remarked that even as 'the hysteria over refugees reaches ever more new heights' the fact remains that, 'trained journalists rarely ask refugees what they are fleeing from or why they are seeking asylum' and 'yet, this is surely as important a question as the numbers applying for refugee status'. The omission is fatal to any real, as opposed to an artificial and illusory, discussion of refugee law. 'Never in recent time' as Satvinder Juss wrote then, 'has there been a situation in the democratic world that has more urgently needed brave moral leadership'.[2] In the years since then

1 Goodwin-Gill, Guy S., 2011, 'The Right to Seek Asylum: Interception at Sea and the Principle of Non-refoulement', *International Journal of Refugee Law*, 23, 443–57, p. 443.

2 Juss, Satvinder, 2006, *International Migration and Global Justice* Ashgate, Aldershot, p. ix.

no moral leadership has been forthcoming. Such as there is today comes rather belatedly, as we shall see in the Epilogue, from the Church. This in itself raises the question why it is only the Church and the odd NGO official that raises his or her voice to assail the oppression of refugees that is currently taking place before the world's very eyes, with barely a murmur from democratic governments and their politicians, who would otherwise swear live by the established norms of human rights law and the rule of law. Perhaps the answer lies in the insightful observations of Harsha Walia, who has argued that the main cause of the increases in the numbers of displaced persons lies in the presence of 'border imperialism':

> Border imperialism encapsulates four overlapping and concurrent structurings: first mass displacement of impoverished and colonized communities resulting from asymmetrical relations of global power, and the simultaneous securitization of the border against those migrants whom capitalism and empire have displaced; second, the criminalization of migration with severe punishment and discipline for those deemed 'alien' or 'illegal'; third, the entrenchment of a racialized hierarchy of citizenship by arbitrating who legitimately constitutes the nation-state; and fourth, the state-mediated exploitation of migrant labour, akin to conditions of slavery and servitude, by capitalist interests.[3]

She contends that, although the state's presence is indeed waning in several areas such as the provision of social services to its citizens, 'thousands of kilometers of walls, growing armies of border police, and an increasingly intrusive surveillance apparatus',[4] all indicate that state power and violence is in full force against both migrants and Indigenous peoples. But it is not just migrants and indigenous peoples. What the Wikileaks saga has revealed, in the unmasking of unethical behaviour by governments and institutions, over the last few years is the way in which unaccountable power is held over all of us. Wikileaks is an international journalistic organization which publishes secret information on-line, and its disclosures have included such as the 21 December 2014 disclosure of CIA operations to infiltrate the European Union and the Schengen passport control system.[5] As Slavoj Žižek[6] has explained:

> we face the shameless cynicism of a global order whose agents only imagine that they believe in their ideas of democracy, human rights and so on. Through

3 Walia, Harsha, 2013, *Undoing Border Imperialism*, AK Press and the Institute for Anarchist Studies, Oakland, CA, p. 5.

4 Ibid. pp. 38–9.

5 https://wikileaks.org.

6 Slavoj Žižek, 2011, 'Good Manners in the Age of WikiLeaks', *London Review of Books*, 33, 2 (20 January 2011), pp. 9–10. Available at http://www.lrb.co.uk/v33/n02/slavoj-zizek/good-manners-in-the-age-of-wikileaks (accessed 2 February 2015).

> actions like the WikiLeaks disclosures, the shame – our shame for tolerating such power over us – is made more shameful by being publicised.

Yet, there can be no power so absolute, and so complete, as the power that the richer countries of the world now hold over the poor and distraught in the world who would show the audacity of seeking a better way of life amongst the rich.

Another common thread is the fact that the only existing applicable legal regime, the 1951 Convention on the Status of Refugees[7] and the related 1967 Protocol,[8] are totally inadequate to deal with both the quantity and the quality of asylum seekers. Documents designed to deal primarily with individual asylum seekers with a specific history of persecution, be it religious, ethnic or other, have little to offer to large numbers of asylum seekers intent on escaping situations of unbearable hardship. Their suffering, for the most part, is not the result of deliberate intent, although the knowledge and awareness of the consequences that follow upon state and corporate activities characterize most of the man-made aspects of the disasters that cause each exodus. This is clear from the UNHCR Handbook, which was written in 1979 to provide guidance to states at their specific request as to how they should apply the 1951 Refugee Convention, and which expressly states that, 'Persons compelled to leave their country of origin as a result of international or national armed conflicts are not normally considered refugees under the 1951 Convention or 1967 Protocol'. This is why the European Union had to think of a form of 'subsidiary' protection. This it did pursuant to Article 2 of Directive 2004/83/EC (the Qualification Directive),[9] which acts as a surrogate to refugee status. But to be eligible for 'subsidiary' protection, a person must show 'serious harm'. Article 15 defines this in such a convoluted way as to make it beyond the reach of most applicants. It required proof of risk of 'Serious and individual threat to a civilian life or person by reason of indiscriminate violence in situations of international or internal armed conflict'.[10]

The causes of flight today are varied. They include internal conflicts, localized guerrilla activities and wars; industrial development, especially the side effects of extractive and mining operations; Western globalized industry's well-documented effects on climate events; macroeconomic operations resulting in third world famines; in all cases, the wealthy corporate actors and the complicit states know well the results that will follow upon their actions. Although the latter are not 'planned' specifically to cause disastrous living conditions, the directing and

---

7 CSR (1951) 189 UNTS 150, into force 22 April 1954.

8 Protocol Relating to the Status of Refugees, 606 UNTS 267, in force 22 October 1967.

9 Council Directive 2004/83/EC of 29 April 2004 on minimum standards for the qualification and status of third country nationals or stateless persons as refugees or as persons who otherwise need international protection and the content of the protection granted. *Official Journal of the European Union*, no. L 304 of 30 September 2004.

10 Ibid.

organizing minds behind these activities command the wealthiest R&D departments in the world, so that the ensuing consequences of products and processes are fully understood and accepted.

Before we consider the proximate and distant causes that give rise to the present migrations of asylum seekers, the basic question that must be answered is the status of the principle that supports closed borders and the policies of exclusion and conditional admittance into state territories. Recent writers such as Brad K. Blitz have opened up the ambiguous question of freedom of movement in relation to the restrictions still imposed by national borders and sovereignty, and the difficulties migrants face in turning movement into settlement.[11] But, the question has become acute recently, because of the unprecedented number of asylum seekers attempting to gain admission to states beyond their own borders. The result of this mounting pressure prompts the governments of the 'receiving' countries to do all they can, legal or not, to repel asylum seekers before they reach their borders, hence long before authorities are in a position to properly evaluate their status.[12]

This is a widespread phenomenon, ranging from Australia,[13] to the use of the so-called 'Safe Third Country' agreement between the United States and Canada, which permits the use of 'direct back' policies,[14] or 'return an asylum seeker from one country to the other',[15] to Europe, which is perhaps the first choice of many migrants, given its proximity to many states in North Africa. Hence many migrate to Italy, especially to the island of Lampedusa, a relatively easy to reach target. There is clear evidence now that the so-called Dublin system is a double-edged sword. On the one hand, as the cases decided again Greece and Italy show, front-line states which exist on the periphery of the European continent are forced to shoulder the lion's share of the burden of refugees who are seeking entry into the heart of Europe. On the other hand, because the Dublin system states that responsibility lies with the first Member State with which the asylum applicant establishes contact, in the form of, for example, the issue of a transit visa, the legal presence of a close family member, or in the absence of these, the first physical contact with the territory, the richer countries at the heart of Europe, like Germany, France and Britain, escape liability for burden-sharing, even though they are far better placed to do so. The peripheral countries of Europe, like Greece, Italy or

11 Brad K. Blitz, 2014, *Migration and Freedom* (Mobility, Citizenship and Exclusion) Edward Elgar, Cheltenham.

12 Kritzman-Amir, Tally and Spijerboer, Thomas, 2013, 'On the Morality and Legality of Borders: Border Policies and Asylum Seekers', *Harvard Human Rights Journal*, 26, 1–38.

13 *Plaintiff M70/2011 v. Minister for Immigration and Citizenship* [2011] HCA 32 (Austl).

14 Kritzman-Amir and Spijerboer, 2013: 1.

15 *John Doe et al. v. Canada*, Case 12.586, Inter Am. Comm'n H.R. Report No-24/11, OEA/Ser.L/V/II.141, aoc. 29§2 (2011); see also *Her Majesty the Queen v. Canadian Council for Refugees et al.* [2008] F.C. 229, para. 105 (Can.).

Hungary, may struggle to provide protection as their resources are stretched, but the richer countries of inner-Europe will still require them to readmit individuals transferred on the basis of the Dublin regime because of the assumption of common standards of refugee protection. Recent cases from the European Court of Human Rights have now highlighted that this premise of 'common standards' is flawed. But the 'safe country' notion has still led to the gradual decline in procedural safeguards for asylum seekers. With the recent court cases highlighting the problem has come the realization of the continuous need for reform to tackle the problem of widespread unsatisfactory performance by Member States.

The Italian government was condemned by the European Court of Human Rights in February 2012, as the Italian 'push back' policy was declared illegal.[16] Finally, equally immoral and illegal is the policy of 'hot return' practised by Israel against those who attempt to seek asylum, crossing the border between Egypt and Israel. These refugees, including women and children, are 'returned' to Egypt without any consideration of their status.[17] In all these and many other similar cases, the question is what is the status of the rejected refugees, and whether the state actions can be considered legal.

But the basic question remains unanswered: more than the procedural legalities involved, what are – in general – people's rights?

> The right of every person to be protected trumps competing rights and interests, including state sovereignty, in a way that other rights do not.[18]

Thus the problem harks back to the nature of the human rights involved. Kritzman-Amir and Spijerboer address briefly the difference between relative rights pertaining to the citizens of each country, and 'the right to seek asylum [which] is not limited ... and is not subject to the right of states arbitrarily to refuse to allow the possibility to seek asylum'.[19] Thus it is not the right to asylum that is 'not relative', thus presumably absolute, but simply the right 'to seek asylum' as a qualified refugee. In contrast, Veit Bader states:

> the basic right or need to security is strong enough to outweigh other rights and competing ethico/political, prudential, and realist arguments.[20]

---

16 *Hirsi Jamaa and Others v. Italy*, App. no. 27765/09, paras 9, 13, 40 (Eur. Ct. of HR, 23 Feb. 2012), available at http://hudoc.echr.coe.int/sites/eng/pages/search.aspx?i=001-109231#{%22itemid%22:%5B%22001-109231%22%5D} (accessed 2 February 2015).

17 Kritzman-Amir and Spijerboer, 2013: 2; see also Refugee Rights Forum, 2009, 'Asylum Seekers and Refugees in Israel: February 2009 Update', at www.acri.org.il/pdf/refugees0209en.pdf (accessed 2 February 2015).

18 Kritzman-Amir and Spijerboer, 2013: 7.

19 Ibid.

20 Bader, Veit, 2005, 'The Ethics of Immigration', *Constellations*, 12, 331–61, p. 340.

An additional question is how to access 'human rights', while even 'citizens' rights' are denied:

> Political membership as a national category is today an inherited condition, one experienced as a given rather than as a process of making a rights-bearing subject.[21]

If the rights of citizenship are circumscribed by nationality rights,[22] then clearly, global citizens who can only appeal to universal human rights do not qualify. Sassen views the changes brought about by globalization as 'denationalizing the territorial and institutional organization of state authority: and as fostering the transformation of the institution of citizenship itself'.[23] In that case, and if – at least partially – citizenship is being reinvented, the sharp distinction that is presently claimed between citizen and non-citizen, alien or migrant, cannot remain still valid. Indeed, Article 18 of the Charter of the Fundamental Rights of the European Union now expressly contains the 'Right to Asylum' in terms that: 'The right to asylum shall be guaranteed with due respect for the rules of the Geneva Convention of 28 July 1951 and the Protocol of 31 January 1967 relating to the status of refugees and in accordance with the Treaty on European Union and the Treaty on the Functioning of the European Union (hereinafter referred to as "the Treaties")'.[24] This confirms the right to asylum to be based on the 1951 Refugee Convention itself.[25]

The close connection between state institutions and regulatory regimes on one side, and corporate power on the other, exemplifies the separation between the 'providing state', recipient of citizens' commitment and loyalty, and the dilution of such loyalty, based on the loss of citizens' entitlements, now replaced by corporate business arrangements instead of state-supplied social services.[26] In some sense, the prevalence of large migrations represents the ultimate transformation of citizens

---

21 Sassen, Saskia, 2006, *Territory, Authority, Rights*, Princeton University Press, Princeton, NJ, p. 278.

22 Ibid.: 281.

23 Ibid.: 280.

24 http://eur-lex.europa.eu/legal-content/EN/TXT/?uri=CELEX:12012P/TXT (accessed 2 February 2015).

25 For future possibilities, see Gil-Bazo, Maria-Teresa, 2008, 'The Charter of Fundamental Rights of the European Union and the Right to be Granted Asylum in the Union's Law', *Refugee Survey Quarterly* 27.3, 33–52. Also see European Council on Refugees and Exiles and the Dutch Council for Refugees, October 2014, *The Application of the EU Charter of Fundamental Rights to Asylum Procedural Law*, available at http://ecre.org/component/downloads/downloads/937.html (accessed 2 February 2015).

26 Westra, L., 2013, *The Supranational Corporation*, Brill, Leiden.

into aliens as denationalized citizens could ultimately decouple the concept of citizenship from that of the nation state.[27]

In contrast, as Walia indicates, the alienated migrants pressing at a foreign state's borders are forced to experience the harshest form of militarized imperialism, as the states' residual power can only be demonstrated by the brutal treatment meted out to the weak, the dispossessed and the racially undesirable, in direct conflict with even the limited consideration and acceptance prescribed by international law. In fact, if 'postnational citizenship' is increasingly located 'outside the frame of the national state',[28] then both sharp distinctions and repressive force at the borders would appear to be entirely inappropriate.

Thus far, the discussion has centred on political and moral questions, that is, mainly on large questions that are seldom present or advocated in the legal treatment of aliens and migrants on the part of existing states. But, as we shall see, a consideration of the circumstances relating to state borders in law after the elimination of colonialism[29] may force a reconsideration of the validity and the legality of the forceful defence of borders, as in all cases, Cassese remarks, 'the wishes of the people concerned should always be taken into account',[30] as he cites the *Western Sahara* case:

> As Judge Dillard put it in his separate opinion in the Western Sahara case, 'it is for the people to determine the future of the territory, and not the territory the destiny of the people'.[31]

Of course, migrants are not attempting to establish a new state, but this legal development has and should continue to bring into question the impenetrability of borders, and the unlimited use of force to defend that position. In some sense, however, migrants are intentionally leaving their home country for another, not necessarily the first country of landing. But it seems clear that, by leaving, they ought to acquire, minimally, the universal rights of global citizens.

In order to establish what, if any, are their rights in law, we will need to review in some detail not only the Convention on the Status of Refugees, but also whatever

27 Bosniak, Linda, 2000, 'Universal Citizenship and the Problem of Alienage', *Northwestern University Law Review*, 94.3, 963–84.

28 Sassen, 2006: 305.

29 1960 UN Declaration on the Independence of Colonial Peoples ..., see also Article 1 of both the UN Covenant on Economic, Social and Cultural Rights and the UN Covenant of Civil and Political Rights, which states: 'All peoples have the right of self-determination. By virtue of that right they freely determine their political status and freely pursue their economic, social and cultural development'.

30 Cassese, Antonio, 1995, *Self-Determination of Peoples (A Legal Reappraisal)*, Hersch Lauterpacht Memorial Lectures, Cambridge University Press, Cambridge, p. 189.

31 Ibid., p. 189; see ICJ Reports 1975, p. 122.

international treaties govern the rights of economic refugees,[32] as well as the rights of those displaced by industrial development/globalization and extreme climate events affecting the safety and security of people's habitats, their environment.[33] The chapter by Tullio Scovazzi affords one good example of this here.

But the basic principle for an evaluation of the multiple current aspects of the plight of today's asylum seekers remains the 1948 Universal Declaration of Human Rights, Article 14(1), and the right 'to seek and to enjoy' asylum from persecution:

> The principle of non refoulement, the obligation on states not to send individuals to territories in which they may be persecuted or in which they are at risk of torture or other serious harm may not immediately correlate with the right of everyone to seek asylum, but it does clearly place limits on what states may lawfully do.[34]

Hence we review both the causes and the conditions of asylum seekers, to establish their experiences in order to connect those situations to 'the absolute prohibition of torture, even sharing perhaps in some of the latter's *jus cogens* character'.[35] These conditions and situations are used here to confront the existing domestic/international instruments presumably available to mitigate or correct those conditions. Part I considers the position of asylum seekers, escaping from conflict situations/whether ongoing or terminated, but leaving behind unlivable conditions.

Their plight is discussed against the existing humanitarian and human rights law instruments, an area that perhaps offers more legal regimes and case law than the present for the victims of other 'persecutory' harms, be they economic or environmental.

Part II explores available jurisprudence, especially that originating from the EU and the European Court of Human Rights, which is far more abundant than what is available from North America or Australia.

---

32 Gabor, Francis and Rosenquest, John B. IV, 2006, 'The Unsettled Status of Economic Refugees from the American and International Legal Perspectives: A Proposal for Recognition Under Existing International Law', *Texas International Law Journal*, 41, 275–95; Ramos, Lauren Michelle, 2011, 'A New Standard for Evaluating Claims of Economic Persecution Under the 1951 Convention Relating to the Status of Refugees', *Vanderbilt Journal of Transnational Law*, 44, 499–525; Mathew, Dessi, 2009, 'Claims of Political Asylum Based on Non-Physical Forms of Harm Such as Economic Sanctions and Deprivations', *Pace International Law Review*, 21, 309–34, See also Westra, 2013, ch. 4.

33 Marcs, Carly, 2008–9, 'Spoiling Movi's River: Towards Recognition of Persecutory Environmental Harm Within the Meaning of the Refugee Convention', *American University of International Law Review*, 24, 31–71; Caney, Simon, 2006, 'Cosmopolitan Justice Rights, and Global Climate Change', *Canadian Journal of Law and Jurisprudence*, 19.2, 255–78; see also Westra, L., 2009, *Environmental Justice and the Rights of Ecological Refugees*, Earthscan, London.

34 Goodwin-Gill, 2011: 244.

35 Ibid.: Part I.

Based on existing case law as discussed especially in Part III, and with a clearer understanding of both the existing conditions that force refugee flights, and the *lacunae* in the existing international law, Part III concludes with some proposals about possible solutions regarding all the outstanding issues concerning asylum seekers, including '*non-refoulement*, disembarkation, first asylum, minimum standards of treatment, and resettlement'.[36] We also add some acknowledgment of the illegalities that produce many of the conditions that lead to the urgent flight of refugees, in relation to the responsibilities of state and non-state actors whose practices produce the mounting numbers of asylum seekers.

Laura Westra,
Satvinder Juss,
Tullio Scovazzi
(December 2014)

36 Ibid.: 448.

PART I
Proximate and Distant Causality Affecting Asylum Seekers and Internally Displaced Persons

Chapter 1
The Limitations of the Present International Instruments for the Protection of Refugees

Laura Westra

> Of thirty ways to escape danger, running away is best.
>
> (Old Chinese Proverb)

With these words, Essam El Hinnawi starts his 1985 monograph on the topic of environmental refugees. His starting point is the 1972 Stockholm Conference (Stockholm Declaration of the United Nations Conference for the Human Environment 1972; El Hinnawi 1985); he adds, in his discussion, the concept of 'Ecodevelopment' coined in this document. Like this concept, which has in recent times morphed into the watered down notion of 'sustainable development', the definition of refugee is not totally 'fixed', according to El Hinnawi. He says:

> … environmental refugees are defined as those people who have been forced to leave their traditional habitat, temporarily or permanently, because of a marked environmental disruption (natural or triggered by people) that jeopardizes their existence and/or seriously affected the quality of their life (El Hinnawi 1985: 4).

By adding, 'In a broad sense, all displaced people can be described as environmental refugees', El Hinnawi places environmental refugees in a category that he views as primary or foundational, rather than simply viewing them as 'displaced peoples' instead. These are not accepted as legitimate refuge seekers, according to the 1951 Convention on Refugees (CSR), but rather as IDPs, internally displaced persons, not qualified to claim refugee status.

El Hinnawi's argument is both correct and appropriate. In turn, he defines 'environmental disruption' as:

> … any physical, chemical and/or biological changes in the ecosystem (or the source base) that render it, temporarily or permanently unsuitable to support human life (El Hinnawi 1985: 4).

This is the aspect of the issues confronting environmental refugees that is at the heart of this work: when the resource base, the integrity of the lands where a community resides, is destroyed, indeed it can no longer support human life. That has been the argument proposed by my work since 1994 (Westra 1997; Westra 1998; Pimentel, Westra and Noss 2000; Soskolne, Westra et al. 2007; Westra 2006;

Westra 2007). If ecological integrity is central to human health and survival, as well as to the normal functioning of ecosystems, then its absence represents an attack on both health and survival, as well as ecosystem function.

We are all affected in various measure, as I have argued, but the poor and those who live on the land are indeed the most vulnerable. Whether the flight that ensues is temporary or permanent, for most of these refugees, it is indeed the dangerous circumstances in which they find themselves that defines their status, even when the circumstances are the result of conflicts or other non-environmental situations. But their numbers are often great, and their relocation poses immense problems even in their country of origin. Large migrations, an increasingly common situation today, may well do great damage to the area to which they relocate (El Hinnawi 1985: 5).

The magnitude of the problem cannot be overstated. A Christian Aid Report predicts that, 'given current trends 1 billion people will be forced from their homes between now and 2050' (Christian Aid Report 2007), adding:

> Stranded within their countries and largely ignored by the media, they are the world's forgotten people. The numbered include,
> • 50 million people displaced by conflict and extreme human rights abuse. This assumes a rate of displacement of roughly 1 million people a year, which is conservative;
> • 50 million people displaced by natural disasters. Again this conservatively assumes that around 1 million people will be displaced this way every year;
> • 645 million people displaced by development projects such as dams and mines (at the current rate of 15 million a year);
> • 250 million people permanently displaced by climate change related phenomena, such as floods, droughts, famines and hurricanes;
> • 5 million people will flee their own countries and will be accepted as refugees (Christian Aid Report 2007: 6).

Already in 1994, the 'Almeria Statement on Desertification and Migration' estimated that 'the number of migrants in the world, already at very high levels, nonetheless continues to increase by about 3 million each year' (International Symposium on Desertification and Migration 1994). Norman Myers alerted the world to this emerging crisis already in 1993 (Myers 1993), and in 2005 he 'revised his estimate' (McAdam 2007: 1), suggesting up to 200 million as a possible refugee number (Myers 2005).

However, Sir Nicholas Stern viewed that figure as 'conservative' and Myers has since once again revised his estimate (Stern 2007). The daunting numbers of ecological refugees, that is, the IDPs that comprise climate and other environmental refugees, as well as those displaced by economic oppression and toxic exposures engendered by 'development' and other industrial projects, are grave enough to warrant a thorough re-examination and discussion of present international law.

The main problem with these large migrations lies in the definition of refugee with its strict limits, according to the Convention Relating to the Status of Refugees (adopted 28 July 1951; into force 22 April 1954):

> Article 1. Definition of the Term 'Refugee'
> The term 'refugee shall apply to any person who:
> (1) ...
> (2) As a result of events occurring before 1 January 1951 and owing to well-founded fear of being persecuted for reasons of race, religion, nationality, membership of a particular social group or political opinion, is outside the country of his nationality and is unable or, owing to such fear, is unwilling to avail himself of the protection of that country; or who, not having a nationality and being outside the country of his former habitual residence as a result of such events, is unable or, owing to such fear, is unwilling to return to it.

The well-founded fear that is the basis of any refugee's claim appears to be a single individual's sentiment, although, as we shall argue below, it may be viewed from several perspectives, even to apply to whole affected groups, and the Jewish people of Nazi Germany were precisely such a group. Thus, the original intent of these definitions is directed at the plight of single individuals, rather than large migrating groups. But, as El Hinnawi argues, environmental disasters, whether wholly natural (such as earthquakes, droughts and tropical cyclones), partly natural, that is such that human activities play a significant role in the severity of resulting disasters (such as floods, tsunamis, hurricanes of particular strength), or even those where human activities play a major role, such as melting ice and permafrost in the Artic, raising sea levels elsewhere, are such that invariably large numbers are affected.

All of these disasters affect disproportionately the poorest people in the world, as they have no infrastructure or social services to protect them, or to mitigate the effects of environmental disasters (Pogge 2008). In addition, land degradation and desertification also render various regions in the South uninhabitable, as does deforestation, and such phenomena generate a mass exodus from the affected region (Goodland 2008: 219–44). Hence it is easy to understand why other countries and their governments, beyond the areas where the disasters occur, are not eager to open their doors, but content themselves with sending aid, at best. This 'aid' is often inappropriate, insufficient and hard to distribute to those most at risk (El Hinnawi 1985: 23–30).

Often environmental refugees simply attempt to migrate to a different area in their own country, perhaps to the cities. But these are both unprepared and unwilling to receive them and to support their many needs:

The End of the Line

> When environmental refugees migrate to urban areas, they expect a 'rosy' quality of life. But soon they find themselves in slums and squatter settlements. In such areas they are usually deprived of access to the basic facilities of drinking water and waste disposal. They are frequently forced to use open water for washing, cleaning and the disposal of waste in unhygienic ways; to break open municipal water mains; to use public places such as open ground to relieve themselves; and to live in makeshift shelters surrounded by accumulating domestic waste (El Hinnawi 1985: 31).

Equally unacceptable are the so-called 'environmental disasters' such as Bhopal, Seveso, 3-Mile Island or Chernobyl (Westra 2007: chs 1–2; El Hinnawi 1985: 35–6). The industrial operations we take for granted everywhere in developed countries and the developing world result in increasingly visible public health hazards that are not limited to the occasional spill, malfunction or other 'accident'. In contrast, they render the conditions of life around their location hazardous for all, but impossible for those who live a traditional lifestyle on the land, as is the case particularly for isolated communities and Indigenous peoples everywhere (Westra 2007: chs 1–2).

Hence in this work we will analyse the impact of these realities exacerbated by globalization and climate change, as well as the proliferation of industrial chemicals. In this regard we will consider the CSR and other regulatory regimes regarding Internally Displaced Persons (IDPs), as well as other international instruments regarding human rights and humanitarian law. Our goal will be to discover whether it is possible to find a legal avenue to mitigate the suffering of these millions of people, starting with the special plight of Aboriginal peoples.

Internally Displaced Persons in International Law

> UNDP, in collaboration with IOM, UNICEF and the World Bank, is preparing a handbook on integrating migration into national development strategies. On behalf of the European Commission with other United Nations agencies and IOM, UNDP is managing a programme on knowledge-sharing related to migration and development (UNGA 2008: 11).

The potentially hopeful presence of the International Organization for Migration (IOM) and Global Forum, devoted to the same issue, lose their relevance when one considers the main focus of the documents referred to: 'development' or, essentially, trade:

> The IOM seeks to engage expatriate communities as partners for development, including through the transfer of knowledge and skills (UNGA 2008: 13).

Clearly, the drafters do not have in mind the starving millions of IDPs and refugees in Sub-Saharan Africa, their deep poverty and the burden of disease; nor do they consider that today's large migrations are, for the most part, the result of trade and 'development', both pursued without any concern for sustainability (Soskolne, Westra et al. 2007) or the connections between environment, human rights and health (Gostin 2008).

The basic difference between 'migration' and 'forced migrations' is clearly recognized in the work of the Refugee Studies Centre at the University of Oxford, together with UNEP, as well researched and analysed in Issue 31 of *Forced Migration Review* (2008). Achim Steiner, the UN Under-Secretary General and Executive Director (UNEP), says,

> Human migration, forced or otherwise will undoubtedly be one of the most significant consequences of environmental degradation and climate change in decades to come (*Forced Migration Review* 2008: 4).

Steiner acknowledges that 'unsustainable human development', together with the rising sea level and the 'loss of coastal wetlands', contributes significantly to the millions who will be fleeing by 2080. Rather than focusing on trade advantages, the challenges to human security policies are grave, and 'environmental migrants' are recognized now as a separate category, whose numbers have not been acknowledged in law yet, but they are constantly increasing because of 'longer term environmental degradation', which aggravates the situation created by the impact of sudden disasters:

> Environmental migrants are understood to be those individuals, communities and societies who choose, or are forced to migrate as a result of damaging environmental and climatic factors (Morton, Bancour and Laczko 2008: 5).

Climate change impacts will follow three separate avenues: (1) 'the effects of warming and drying' will significantly disturb ecosystem services; (2) the increasing presence of catastrophic weather events such as floods or heavy precipitation, will 'generate mass displacement'; and (3) 'sea level rise' will permanently destroy the traditional territories of millions (Morton, Bancour and Laczko 2008: 6). The ongoing development of all these concurrent events, demands 'proactive intervention' (Morton, Bancour and Laczko 2008: 6); it also requires the organizational and institutionalization of several areas of research, with a view to promote readiness for mitigation and assistance.[1] These organizations do not have binding force to impose the conclusions they might reach about the necessity of aid and assistance to migrants, let alone the power to be truly 'proactive', in

1 The Climate Change Environment and Migration Alliance (CCEMA), was established in April 2008 in Munich, by the UNU and the IOM, UNEP and the Munich Re Foundation (MRF) with the goal of ensuring both preparedness and collaboration.

the sense of being able to proscribe the hazardous and negligent human activities that produce 'overwhelming negative' impacts on peoples and environments, and which, in turn, generate mass environmental and climate migrations.

To sum up, the primary responsibility for IDPs rests with their territorial state because of the principles of sovereignty and non-intervention. However, as Goodwin-Gill and McAdam add:

> ... the governing principles of sovereignty and non intervention stand potentially in opposition to often governing principles of international organization, including the commitment to human rights and to international cooperation in the resolution of humanitarian problems (Goodwin-Gill and McAdam 2007: 33).

The major problem is that 'neither the UNHCR nor any other UN agency has any legal authority "to protect" persons within their own country' (Goodwin-Gill and McAdam 2007: 34; UNGA 2005). Hence the protection of IDPs – although a 'broad consensus' exists in principle on the need to protect (Goodwin-Gill and McAdam 2007: 48) – remains unsolved, at least at the international level. The question on the ground remains almost exclusively regional and political, although for certain specific circumstances the internally displaced may be considered in international law, given the ongoing failures of states to provide protection:

> In each case however, there is a clear gap between what may be called *functional* responsibilities and expectations, on the one hand, and the legal obligations of States, on the other hand (Goodwin-Gill and McAdam 2007: 47).

The presence of such 'gaps' does not appear to be purely an oversight, as states have consistently avoided the drafting of a new, binding convention that might solidify and render mandatory the rights of IDPs in relation of their state of origin. Since 1990, however, the legal concept of 'complementary protection', which has had a history dating back to the League of Nations (Marrus 2002), has emerged as the formal 'refugee' definition was found to be increasingly incomplete. Complementary protection was intended as a legal term to be distinguished from the protection 'granted solely on humanitarian grounds', based on humanitarian and human rights law (Goodwin-Gill and McAdam 2007: 286; Executive Committee, Standing Committee 2000: esp. paras 4 and 5). However neither human rights nor humanitarian law apply to all who may need protection: for instance the norms of humanitarian law are applicable only during an armed conflict, and other forms of 'low-intensity conflict' do not qualify (Phuong 2004: 48–9). Human rights law also needs clarification as the protection of life is certainly present within it, as are 'free movement and access to international assistance', as well as 'the right not to be arbitrarily displaced' (Phuong 2004: 51; Stavropoulos 1994: 689).

In addition, the right not to be arbitrarily displaced is not explicitly formulated in any human rights instrument, except the ILO Convention No. 169, but that document refers exclusively to Indigenous and tribal peoples. The Universal

Declaration of Human Rights (UDHR) includes implicitly applicable language, and the Human Rights Committee in 1999 stated,

> … the freedom to choose one's residence (Article 12(1) of the ICCPR) includes protection against all forms of forced internal displacement (Human Rights Committee 'Freedom of Movement' 1999; Phuong 2004: 51).

The only instrument that defines specifically the rights of IDPs and states and others' obligations is the Guiding Principles in Internal Displacement (UN GPID 1998), but these Principles do not represent a binding obligation, and most of the other international instruments from which the protection of IDPs might be inferred include both 'ratification gaps' and 'consensus gaps' (Phuong 2004: 49–50). Hence we can conclude that, at this time, no binding instrument exists for the protection of all IDPs, whereas perhaps Indigenous peoples may fare slightly better.

Nevertheless the problem of IDP protection remains a highly significant one, not only because of the presence of climate change and the pressures of globalization that ensure ever increasing numbers of migrants who are presently unprotected, but also because the problem it represents reflects the culmination of the modern tension between sovereignty and human rights problems (Anghie 2006; Dacyl 1996: 136). For this reason, primarily, refugee law, that is the 1951 CSR, is not only a flawed instrument as such, as we shall see below it cannot properly protect even all its own defined 'clients', but is also less than useful for accommodating the growing new phenomenon, IDPs. This is true even though most of the categories of 'persecution' on which it is founded would lend themselves well to a possible extension to IDPs, at least in principle.

At any rate, solutions for both categories of affected persons, refugees and IDPs, would benefit more from the immediate adoption of preventative measures to protect them 'at source', that is long before the circumstances of their existence deteriorate to the point at which flight is the only option for survival.

Asylum Seekers and Fortified Borders

> What we have come to call a globalized world harbours fundamental tensions between opening and barricading, fusion and partition, erasure and re-inscription. These tensions materialize as increasingly liberalized borders, on the one hand, and the devotion of unprecedented funds, energies, and technologies to border fortification on the other (Brown 2010: 7–8).

The previous two sections emphasized the specificity and the limits of the only international instrument designed for the protection of refugees; an instrument that is both dated in its intent, and totally out of touch with today's situation, as we shall see below. But the first obstacle to a better understanding of the problem lies in the forms of globalization, and the seemingly irreconcilable tensions between national citizens, and the aspirations and interests of 'aliens', fostered and supported by global networks (Sassen 2006). The CSR is based on respect for migrants and openness not only to their plight, but also to their feelings, their subjective understanding of the situation from which they are escaping.

In contrast, while no new instruments have surfaced for the protection of asylum seekers, in contrast, walls and barriers are regularly being erected precisely to fortify many borders, globally. While the opening of the Berlin Wall has been celebrated, as well as the end of apartheid's virtual walls in South Africa, new walls are being erected in many locations, and at least one new apartheid state is functioning and growing with impunity, behind the wall being erected through the West Bank by Israel (Sassen 2006: 8). The latter is being constructed with the support of the US, a country that has also erected its own wall on the Mexican border, using the same builders used by the Israelis (Sassen 2006: 137, n. 1).

South Africa itself has both walls and checkpoints at its borders with Zimbabwe; and India has put land mines in the space between their border and the territory of Kashmir (Brown 2010: 8). There are walls between Egypt and Gaza, China and North Korea, and several other walls in Israel enclose areas in Jerusalem and Bethlehem (Brown 2010: 19). Nor are states the only ones erecting walls: the same motive, generally speaking, that is, protecting the better off from the poor and dispossessed, also motivates the wealthy living in gated communities within the borders of the richer countries.

The connection between economics and migration has also been pointed out by Amartya Sen:

> Increased migration pressure over the decades owes more to the dynamism of international capitalism than just the growing size of the population of third world countries (Sen 1994: 62–71).

As we consider the activities within states themselves, the fortified borders 'without', are not intended to stop 'invading armies, or even [act] as shields against weapons launched in interstate wars' (Brown 2010: 21). In contrast, they are intended as barriers to groups or movements that such states perceive as threatening in various ways.

The walls represent the clearest, most obvious signs of 'border imperialism' (Walia 2013). Walia describes 'border imperialism' as characterized by four main aspect: (1) the concurrent 'securitization' of borders, against migrants, fleeing from 'impoverished and colonized communities'; (2) the ongoing 'criminalization of migration'; (3) the racist approach to citizenship against the presence of aliens; and (4) the concomitant exploitation of migrant labour, on the part of states (Walia 2013: 5). These categories should be remembered as we confront the problem of refugees in all its multiple aspects, in these pages.

It is paradoxical to note that the weak and 'denationalized states' of today (Sassen 1996: xii) still concentrate their power and control at their borders, although they have lost most of their unique strength, their power to elicit loyalty, thus the capacity to truly represent their citizens (Sassen 2006), as their original power has even been replaced by the controlling corporate legal persons that have largely replaced most of the normally expected state functions (Westra 2013).

The starting point of a better understanding of the increasing problem of refugees lies in a better understanding of the state's actions. Wendy Brown argues that the 'absolute' power of sovereignty is in direct conflict with democracy, or the 'rule of the people', because it includes the 'prerogative power' that can 'suspend or set aside legislative power (popular sovereignty)' (Brown 2010: 50). This issue embodies the main paradoxical, self-contradictory characteristic of sovereignty, and the example of that abuse of power can be found easily today: Guantanamo, Abu-Ghraib, extraordinary rendition, Gaza Strip – all immediately evoke multiple crimes, clear illegalities on the part of democratic states.

Brown attempts to define and list the paradoxes of sovereignty and democracy, and some of these 'meanings and operations' are germane to the basic issues of our topic:

> 1. Sovereignty is both a name for absolute power and a name for political freedom.
> 2. Sovereignty generates order through subordination and freedom through autonomy.
> 3. Sovereignty has no internal essence, but rather is completely dependent and relational, even as it stands for autonomy, self-presence and self-sufficiency.
> 4. Sovereignty produces both internal hierarchy (sovereignty is always sovereignty over something) and external anarchy (by definition, there can be nothing governing a sovereign entity ....
> 5. Sovereignty is both a sign of the rule of law and supervenes the law. Or sovereignty is both the source of law and above the law, the origin of juridicism and what resides outside it. It is all law and no law. Its every utterance is law, and it is lawless. (Brown 2010: 52–3)

Brown captures well the two-faced nature of sovereignty, the most important characteristic of which, according to Carl Schmitt, is its 'unlimited authority', which means the suspension of the entire existing order (Schmitt 1985: 12). In such situations, it is clear that 'the state remains, whereas the law recedes' (Schmitt 1985: 12). In fact, it is that 'authority', lawless as it is, that defines who is a friend and who is the enemy (Brown 2010: 54), thus laying the ground for the multiple recent revolts against authority starting with the Occupy movement in the West, and the Arab Spring in Africa (Westra 2014).

If we agree with Sassen's contention that 'citizenship is an incompletely theorized contract between the state and its subjects, based on property-owning citizens on one hand, and "disadvantaged subjects" such as workers which form a clear inequality formalized in the law' (Sassen 2006: 277), then it is obvious that the law itself, *pace* Schmitt, loses its principled base, when it is too close to the interests and the dictates of the sovereign state. As well, the power that is founded on property within the state, has increasingly been transferred to the corporation, singly and collectively, that is to corporate associations such as NAFTA, the WTO or the nascent TPP.

It is these associations that have shown first, and eventually cemented, the weakness of the state, both in its internal and external relations. Internally, in relation to its own citizens, the state is no longer the symbol and essence of a cohesive whole, as the state's constitution is no longer the final arbiter of citizens' protection under national legal regimes. In regard to other states, aggregate corporate decisions now have the final word on issues that might have been decided by bilateral agreements.

For citizens, this series of events represents the 'denationalization of citizenship', as Sassen says:

> The national state is one of the strategic, institutional locations for both the larger contextual changes pertaining to citizenship. Thus I argue that citizenship, even if situated in institutional settings that are 'national', is a possibly changed institution if the meaning of the national itself has changed (Sassen 2006: 280).

The reach of this change has not been fully defined yet. It is certain that the collective identity of today's citizens is no longer circumscribed by what we still think of as our national affiliation. Our cultural background may well be strongly grounded in our history, which is often intimately connected with our national heritage. But it is undeniable that our increasing ties with groups outside our borders (Pogge 1992: 48–75; Sassen 2006: 287), appear to destroy the facile but incomplete identification between nationality and citizenship.

As Sassen acknowledges, speaking of citizenship:

> While many of these distinctions deconstruct the category of citizenship and are helpful for formulating novel conceptions, they do not necessarily cease to be state-based (Sassen 2006: 287).

Yet it seems that the transborder connections formed by the new postnational citizens render them often similar, or at least in many ways easily connected, to the global citizens outside their borders, even when these are asylum seekers seeking entry.

It is surprising that states fortify most strongly their borders for defence against the alien, the other, when the worst enemy of the state is festering and growing, well-established within the state itself. It is the internal corporate power that has arrogated for itself the ability to direct and control state institutions, change and corrupt legal structures (Westra 2013: ch. 4). Even more problematic is the fact that those corporate organizations join with their sisters in other countries to ensure that the uniqueness, the essence of the individual state's decisions, will be superseded by decisions embodying the association's collective goals and interests (Westra 2013: 59–86).

Whatever the reasons driving state actions, singly and collectively, such actions work to deprive asylum seekers of their human rights as well as of their specific rights as refugees, minimal as those are according to the CSR. According to the CSR, their main right is to encounter an open border and a bureaucracy willing and able to hear their case, that is, the reasons for their flight, as well as their subjective assessment of future dangers or harms to be encountered. As we briefly noted (and we will return to this topic below), the fortifications of borders ensures that it is soldiers that repel asylum seekers, rather than functionaries who might be trained to be at least respectful, and more accepting of refugees. For this reason, even the basic rights of potential or actual refugees are regularly denied. So too, their basic right of '*non-refoulement*' is not supported by current practices. Eyal Benvisti remarks that single European governments, for instance, use the EU to decide on issues concerning refugees:

> In the sphere of migration there is clear evidence of European governments preempting their courts by resorting to the apparatus of the EU to regulate migration policies (Benvisti and Downs 2009: 70; European Council Directive 2004/83/EC 2004).

We will discuss European law below, as it represents the defence of a particular 'border', and is the target of countless migrants, as well as the most convenient first country for many.

The Alien at the Border: A Generic Profile

> Anyone who accepts a genuinely democratic theory of political legitimization domestically is thereby committed to rejecting the unilateral domestic right to control and close the state's boundaries, whether boundaries in the civil sense (which regulate membership) or in the territorial sense (which regulate movement) (Abizadeh 2008: 37).

Although the passage above returns once again to the state and its forms of governance, together with the expression of its power, the main question at this time is *who* is the asylum seeker in relation to the rejecting state at whose borders he presents himself. Only after that question has been discussed, can we move on to the basic question: *why* is he at those borders. The answer to the latter question is seldom, if ever, sought, despite the fact that in most cases the answer to the second question should strongly influence the answer to the first one.

For example, if a family who has just lost its house presents itself to you, seeking asylum, surely not only the urgency of its plight, but the possibility of your contribution to the reasons for the loss, ought to influence you response. Your responsibility, even if partial should make a difference both morally and legally to your decision to accept or reject that group. It is worth repeating: the second question is the least debated, although it should be the most important one.

At any rate, the presence of fortified borders, manned by soldiers, not welcoming committees, implies that there is a sharp distinction between citizen and alien. The civil and political rights of the former take precedence over the human rights of the latter. In the previous sections we cast doubts on this sharp distinction between citizen and non-citizen, based on the acknowledgment that the weakened state, no longer a solid, well-defined unit, and its present form of governance serves to undermine that distinction. Further arguments may be adduced in defence of the right of the non-citizen, and the problem of closed borders:

> … I argue that democratic theory either rejects the unilateral right to close borders, or would permit such a right only derivatively and only if it has already been successfully and democratically justified to foreigners (Abizadeh 2008: 37).

As the second option seems to exist, at best, in theory and beyond the sphere of a practical application, the internal justification only remains as a possible option. But before considering the theoretical justification of this democratic option, practical considerations clearly demonstrate the opposition of citizens in almost all countries to the open border option. Hence we must face the 'elephant in the room', that is the status of the asylum seeker in a world of grave divisions between the rich and the poor, the lack of work for too many, even the citizens of a nation. No doubt the unity of all human rights (Weeramantry 1997), as well as Kantian respect for the dignity of all human beings, all militate in favour of the rights of the asylum seekers, whoever they are as they remain autonomous human beings, whose choices ought to be respected (Raz 1986).

Abizadeh argues for the basic importance of freedom of movement based on 'personal autonomy', according to Raz's 'three conditions': the person (1) has the appropriate *mental capacities* to formulate personal projects and pursue them, (2) enjoys an adequate range of valuable *options* and (3) is *independent*, that is, free from subjection to the will of another through coercion or manipulation (Raz 1986: 372–8; Abizadeh 2008: 39–40).

Even in a world ruled in an entirely democratic manner, as Abizadeh proposes, those seeking asylum are, almost by definition, far less in number than the acknowledged citizens of any country to which they present themselves. Hence, their plight would not be resolved even by a fully open, democratic quest for consensus on their admittance. I submit they would fare far better through a return to principled considerations of the authority, perhaps less violent than it presently is, that is presently determined to exclude them.

Raz argues for the use of 'normative power' as he discusses legitimate authority which is precisely the issue, at this point:

> I will define normative power as the ability to change protected reasons. More precisely, a man has normative power if he can by an action of his exercise normative power (Raz 2009: 18).

The normativity here employed is far more than a simple counting of heads to legitimize a decision, or even the adherence to rules and law. Raz adds a comment on the legitimacy of authority (citing Robert Paul Wolff):

> He tacitly and correctly assumes that reason never justifies abandoning one's autonomy, that is, one's right and duty to act on one's judgment of what ought to be done, all things considered. I shall call this the principle of autonomy (Raz, 2009: 27).

Both present laws and democratic decisions should be secondary to the normativity of human rights, based on dignity and autonomy. And if this conclusion seems, at least intuitively, correct, then the consideration of all aspects of the asylum seeker's situation and the issues that forced the migrations should take precedence over both expected authority and procedural considerations.

Hence the vexed question 'who' is the asylum seeker, should be answered simply with the words: she is a human being. David Cole cites Hermann Cohen's words in a commentary on the Bible:

> The alien was to be protected not because he was a member of one's family, clan or religious community but because he was a human being. In the alien, therefore, man discovered the idea of humanity (Cohen 1949: 52).

Nevertheless, these strong words do not resonate in existing legal regimes, they do not even reflect the laws and policies of the state of Israel or any other state, including the US. David Cole compares a 2004 landmark ruling of the House of Lords with the results of similar cases in the US:

> In a landmark ruling in 2004, the Law Lords of Great Britain invalidated a statute authorizing indefinite preventive detention of foreign nationals who were suspected terrorists. The Court found that the statute conflicted with the obligation not to discriminate against foreign nationals, an obligation found in the European Convention on Human Rights … (Cole 2005–6: 627; *A/FC and others v. Secretary of State for the Home Department* 2004, 21).

In this case, international legal standards were incorporated into the UK Human Rights Act, and no conflict was found between a man's nationality and the extent of his human rights, leading Cole to add that 'the Law Lords' decision is the ideal model for the integration of human and Immigrants' rights' (Cole 2005–6: 628). In contrast, Cole notes that 'The United States remains a deeply parochial and nationalist culture', and that attitude permeates that country's legal decisions.

A case in point is that of *Hamdi v. Rumsfeld* (2004). The US Supreme Court eventually ruled that Yaser Hamdi's *constitutional* rights had been violated, by holding him for two years without charges: as a US citizen, he had the right to protection under the Due Process Clause of the Fifth Amendment. According to that clause, the government could not deprive 'any person of life, liberty, or property without due process' (Cole 2005–6: 628). But the Court's repeated insistence on the fact that Hamdi was a US citizen demonstrated clearly that, although the due process clause is intended to protect all persons in the US, regardless of citizenship, that aspect was viewed as most significant by the court (Westra 2012).

Human rights are precisely what they purport to be: they are based on human dignity, and do not change their reach according to the citizenship of the person considered. Hence migrants, asylum seekers and refugees should enjoy the same protection that human rights instruments confer on the citizens of the state at the borders of which they are arriving.

Since 9/11 and the so-called 'war on terror', the US paranoia regarding foreign persons, especially those with an Arab-sounding name, has reached out from the extremes present in the US to much of the Western world. And this despite the fact that terrorism has not been legally defined in international law (Westra 2012). For the US and the countries that follow its lead, that meant that the accepted rules of war no longer applied.

Thus the abominable (and illegal) treatment of suspects as detainees with no trial, no civil liberties and no due process, making use of the 'extraordinary powers of war' (*Rasul v. Bush* 2004; Geneva Convention (III) Relative to the Treatment of Prisoners of War 1949), and the US memos that simply redefined the Convention Against Torture (Memorandum from Jay S. Bybee to Alberto Gonzales 2002), has been spreading like a contagion to other countries intending to curry favour with the US.

The fact that '… American legal culture has long viewed international human rights as "mere surplussage" when it comes to domestic law …' (Cole 2005–6: 632) does not help the position of human rights, when applied to migrants. Even the Alien Tort Statute (1798) has not helped to develop the introduction and application of international human rights instruments, as the US courts have maintained a strict and limited interpretation of the reach of that document (Cole 2005–6: 632). These limitations concur to render the legal position of immigrants and asylum seekers precarious, as they depend primarily on political decisions rather than law.

In the next section, we will turn from the question of 'who' is the asylum seeker, to 'why' she has had to abandon her home, so that the conflict between sovereignty demands and international human rights can be approached from a different perspective.

Why Is the Alien at the Border?

> Asylum claims on non-physical forms of persecution, specifically social and economic deprivation, have received increasing attention in recent years (Ramos 2011: 500).

The increasing number of asylum seekers fleeing from their native countries bears witness to the spread of unlivable conditions almost everywhere in the world, as the United Nations High Commissioner for Refugees has noted (UN High Commissioner of Refugees 2009). A 'status refugee' is escaping persecution. But the term has never been fully defined in international law; as well, persecution is hard to document. The refugee herself (the convention addresses individual persecution) must also express convincingly the 'well-founded fear' she has about the conditions she would meet if she returned to the home country. But the problem remains:

> … the UNHCR *Handbook on Procedures and Criteria for Determining Refugee Status under the 1951 Convention and the 1967 Protocol Relating to the Status of Refugees* (UNHCR Handbook) admits that '[t]here is no universally accepted definition of "persecution" and various attempts to formulate such a definition have met with little success' (Ramos 2011: 504).

Nevertheless, because of a number of reasons unrelated to the common understanding of religious/political persecution that form the basis of the present definition of status refugee, as the number of refugees mounts steadily, the 'public backlash against them has intensified' (Mathew 2009: 309), and the recent events that sum up the so-called 'war on terror' increase public suspicion and resistance. In addition, most courts find the identification of unfavourable economic conditions, or even targeted sanctions, a form of 'persecution' (Anker 1999: 233).

The United States is an egregious example of the divergence between 'paper' commitments and real actions at the border:

> The United States has long been recognized as a country welcoming asylum seekers who are fleeing political oppression, religious persecution, or oppression by the state based on race or ethnicity (Mathew 2009: 311).

The US commitment to human rights includes the commitment to a number of UN instruments, including the UN Charter (1945), the UNDHR (1948) and the Conference on Security and Cooperation in Europe. Thus one would anticipate an ongoing welcoming approach to all strangers seeking refuge. But although in the early 1920s an open door policy was used, after the First and Second World Wars things gradually changed, and

> In 1952 Congress passed the Immigration and Nationality Act (INA) also known as the McCarren-Walter act, providing the basic framework for US immigration policy; however, the INA of 1952 did not expressly contain provisions to handle the resettlement of refugees or displaced persons (Mathew 2009: 312; Tonnas 1993: 302).

When the US recognized the existence of refugees, it also adopted 'stringent requirements', such as the need to have US citizens as sponsors to guarantee them 'housing and employment' (Mathew 2009: 313), thus offering no government assistance or real support. In 1965 the US enacted amendments to the INA, such that the guidelines for the admittance of refugees followed specific ideological guidelines: the asylum seekers had to flee from either communist countries or the Middle East (Mathew 2009: 313). In 1968, the US acceded to the CSR and the 1967 Protocol.

Although there is a strong division between the treatment expected by citizens, and by aliens arriving at the borders of another country, there are not many clearly articulated arguments about the requirements of nationality, beyond the traditional distinction between 'the right of the birthplace (*jus soli*) and the right of descent (*jus sanguinis*), as the two major alternative principles that states use in assigning citizenship at birth' (Carens 1987: 415; Glenn 2013: 191–3).

But are the circumstances of a person's birth the only considerations that are morally and legally relevant to establish citizenship? Some relevant principles are excluded from this view. The main difference in the two traditional approaches, is the ascription of nationality at birth, on the one hand, and the principle of consent, on the other:

> The principle of consent entails the view that the legitimacy of political authority rests upon free consent of those governed … the obligations of citizenship cannot be imposed at birth. Each individual must choose to become a citizen (Carens 1987: 415).

Some, however, believe that all children of citizens and permanent residents should also 'automatically become citizens at birth', thus establishing the connection between citizenship and consent, which might ultimately be favourable to migrants. If an individual's position within a political community requires consent (on the part of the would-be citizen); this position says nothing about the need for consent on the part of the community to which the individual aspires (Carens 1987: 416).

If a political community is a 'voluntary association', then it is – at least in principle – open to all who would join it (Carens 1987: 418). No doubt in some circumstances the political community itself would withdraw its consent, but any approach based on human rights will not accept a sharp distinction between citizens and needy aliens.

Whatever we accept as foundational of citizenship, when we return to the question of asylum seekers, the main point remains unanswered: are 'needy' aliens the same as persecuted refugees? Hence the most important question is how to interpret the former in a way that firmly establishes her position in the latter category.

The previous section answered the question 'who' is the alien in a simple manner: she is a human being, an indisputable member of humanity. We are now attempting to establish why she would need to flee and whether the reasons for the flight may render her position closer to that of a status refugee. The first step is to establish a clear commonality among all asylum seekers, wherever their origins and whatever their eventual destination: what they all share, beyond a doubt, is abject poverty, and the profound hope that they and their children may fare better at their future abode.

In the chapters that follow we will isolate some of the most common causes for their poverty. For now, we need to establish their present status as economic migrants, in law.

The Legal Status of Economic Refugees

> The global world order for the twenty-first century has been constructed upon four centuries of experience under the Westphalian sovereign nation-state concept ... the sovereign nation-state remains the basic organizing actor of international law and order. Human migration can be considered as an exercise of one of the most fundamental human rights – the freedom of movement (Gabor and Rosenquest 2006: 275).

The first common condition of asylum seekers is that they are victims of gross human rights violations: as 'the condition under which an individual lives must be intolerable in order to induce the person to leave his or her country of origin' (Gabor and Rosenquest 2006: 275). All countries have some form of human rights protection guarantee embedded in their Charters or Constitutions.[2] Hence, when a number of citizens suffer hunger, deprivation and grave poverty, conditions extreme enough to force them to flee with their families, the state-sanctioned guarantees of protection and basic rights must have failed completely.

There might have been additional circumstances beyond state failure that contributed to their plight, and we will discuss several of those instances below, but even in the case of additional occurrences, the state maintains at least partial responsibility. Thus the poverty we acknowledged as a basic condition affecting

2 See for instance the Canadian Charter, which guarantees the 'security of persons' to all citizens. Similar provisions can be found in the American Convention on Human Rights, 18 July 1978 OASTS No. 36, 1144 UMTS 123; the European Convention for the Protection of Human Rights and Fundamental Freedoms (1950), Eur. TS No. 5, 213 UNTS 222; the African Charter of Human and Peoples Rights, OAU Doc. (CAB/LEG/67/3) Rev. 5, 21 ILM 58 (1982).

all asylum seekers, also implies that they are, first and foremost, victims before their flight (Westra 2014: ch. 7).

The designation of 'victim' applies to 'economic refugees'; in contrast to 'economic migrants' who are simply seasonal workers who work temporarily in other countries before returning home (Gabor and Rosenquest 2006: 277). This distinction also applies in the International Covenant on Civil and Political Rights (ICCPR 1967):

> Article 12
> 1. Everyone lawfully within the territory of a State shall, within that territory, have the right to liberty of movement and freedom to choose his residence.
> 2. Everyone shall be free to leave any country, including his own.
> 3. The above mentioned rights shall not be subject to any restrictions except those which are provided by law to protect national security, public order (ordre public), public health or morals or the rights and freedoms of others, and are consistent with the other rights recognized in the present Covenant.

There is, however, an important distinction between 'freedom' to leave one's country, and the imposition of such physical conditions that the 'freedom' is transformed into coercion instead. A case in point is that of the Chagos islanders, where the US decided, together with the UK, that Chagos would represent an excellent US base in the Indian Ocean, despite the fact that the island was already inhabited by a peaceful population who lived comfortably with the help of their employer, a company who provided everything they could not grow themselves. When both employment and the expected goods were no longer available, the removal of that population was clearly coerced, not a matter of choice.

Forced Relocation, War Crimes and Genocide: *Bancoult versus McNamara*

> The plaintiffs in this case are persons indigenous to Chagos their survivors or direct descendants, … they bring this action against the United States and various current and former officials of State and the department of Defence ('the individual defendants'), for forced relocation, torture, racial discrimination, cruel, inhuman and degrading treatment, genocide, intentional infliction of emotional distress, negligence and trespass (*Bancoult v. McNamara* 2003).

As the Chagos Archipelago ('Chagos'), 52 islands administered by the British Government, was leased to the US, the US became responsible under the British Indian Ocean Territory Agreement ('BIOT Agreement'). In the late 1960s and early 1970s, the whole Chagos population was moved to Mauritius and Seychelles, to allow a US military facility to settle in their space. The original inhabitants were not allowed to return (*Bancoult v. McNamara* 2003: 22), and were offered no compensation to help ease their transition into a new environment and the loss of their homes.

Those who had not left had to suffer from being forced on 'overcrowded ships for Peros Banhos and Salonen, from whence they eventually were taken to Mauritius and Seychelles' (*Bancoult v. McNamara* 2003: 22c–23). The US Congress went ahead with the construction of a military base on Diego Garcia island, despite hearings where multiple human rights violations were detailed, from the lack of relocation assistance, to harsh removal conditions that caused injuries to the survivors, including miscarriages, and eventual living conditions that still include still poverty, unemployment and other deprivations (*Bancoult v. McNamara* 2003: 31–3).

Before the judgment proper could be decided, the 'individual defendants' all claimed that they had been obeying superior order, based on 'the statutory immunity granted to the Federal Officers under the Federal Employee Liability Reform and Tort Compensation Act' (Federal Employees Liability Reform and Tort Compensation Act 1988).

Even if the individual defendants are eliminated from the action (justly or unjustly), that leaves the United States as the sole defendant. However, all those who perpetrated knowingly the actions involving the Chagos indigenous population violated the tenets of international law:

> Pursuant to the Alien Tort Claims Act, 28 U.S.C. & 1350 ('ATCA'), 'the district courts shall have original jurisdiction of any civil action by an alien for a tort only, committed in violation of the law of nations or Treaty of the United States' (*Bancoult v. McNamara* 2003: 24).

Other issues used to rebut the plaintiff's claims were the fact that 'they had failed to exhaust their administrative remedies', despite the fact that they were not allowed to return to their home base, now a US military basis (in Chagos), nor to the other islands, where the United Kingdom itself was not likely to offer an impartial forum after entering into an agreement with the US that led to the very actions in question.

Another issue was 'the judicial expertise' of the court, as it was required to pass judgment on US policy:

> Neither our federal law nor customary international law provide standards by which the court can measure and balance the foreign policy considerations at play in this case such as the containment of the Soviet Union in the Indian Ocean thirty years ago, and today the support of military operation in the Middle East. The court concludes that it is ill-equipped to review the conduct of the military operation challenged in this case, because they implicate foreign policy and national security concerns … (*Bancoult v. McNamara* 2003: para. 42).

Essentially, if the US Government political branches made a decision 30 years earlier, the court was not prepared to second guess that decision today (*Bancoult v. McNamara* 2003: para. 47). Of course, even if the court was not prepared to question either the decision of the US Government at the time those decisions were made, or the reasons for those decisions, the *way* those decisions were carried out appears to remain untouched by this argument. Even if a country's political or other decisions cannot be judged under ATCA,

> Article 2(3) of the Torture Convention explicitly states that 'An order from a superior official or public authority may not be invoked as a justification for torture' (Steiner and Alston 1996: 1072).

Torture is forbidden by *jus cogens* norms, and so is genocide, so that appealing to this Article appears to be appropriate, and we will address this question below.

This point is also made clearly in the *Filartiga v. Pena Irala* case (1980). In that case, the US Supreme Court recognized that the law of nations

> … may be ascertained by consulting the work of jurists writing professedly on public law; or by the general usage and practice of nations, or by the judicial decisions recognizing and enforcing the law (*United States v. Smith* 1920).

Nevertheless, it must be acknowledged,

> Unlike the criminal remedy, there is no treaty that clearly obliges or even authorizes courts to take jurisdiction over civil actions respecting torture committed abroad with the exception of the US, there is no domestic legislation in any other country that expressly grants courts jurisdiction with respect to these matters (Terry 2002: 110).

Because ATCA permits individual citizens to sue for torture and other such injuries, without the far more complicated requirements of initiating a criminal action for an International Court of Justice or International Criminal Court, this avenue appears to remain the preferred one by claimants in various venues:

> While it is premised on the principle that victims of torture much be compensated, its true role in many cases is admittedly symbolic: the third country tort remedy provides recognition for, and emotional vindication of, the victims of torture and places moral and political pressure on rights abusing governments (Terry 2002: 133).

The End of The Story: *R (on the application of Bancoult) v. Secretary of State for Foreign and Commonwealth Affairs (2008) UKHL 61: an appeal from: [2007] EWCA Civ. 498*

> On 3 November, 2000 the Divisional Court (Laws LJ and Gibbs J) gave judgment in favour of Mr. Bancoult (*R (Bancoult) v Secretary of State for Foreign and Commonwealth Affairs* 2007). They decided that a power to legislate for the 'peace, order and good government' of the territory did not include a power to expel all the inhabitants.

Beyond the ATCA trials, Bancoult and other Chagossians also attempted to find justice from the other super power involved in their case: the British Government. Lord Hoffman describes the original lifestyle of the inhabitants of Chagos, working for the 'Company' (Chagos Agalegal Company Ltd.), tending coconut trees and producing copra, working their gardens and keeping chickens and pigs to add to the provisions the Company provided for its workers. Yet, despite their lack of education and their simple lifestyles, they had 'a rich community life, the Roman Catholic religion and their own dialect, derived from the French' (*R (Bancoult) v. Secretary of State for Foreign and Commonwealth Affairs* 2007: para. 5).

For this case, their main points of contention were based on the history of their interaction with the UK Government:

1. The British Indian Ocean Territories Order (BIOT) (British Indian Ocean Territories Order 1865 SI No. 1920), had made the Chagos Archipelago a separate colony. The Order also appointed a Commissioner of BIOT, with the power to 'make laws for the peace, order and good government of the territory'; hence the inhabitants retained British citizenship (British Indian Ocean Territories Order 1865 SI No. 1920: para. 6).
2. In 1966, Her Majesty's Government corresponded with the government of the US: the result was to grant a lease of at least 50 years to the latter, to establish a base on Diego Garcia, and to occupy other islands as required. In 1967 the UK Government bought out the Company which was only allowed to run the coconut plantations until July 1971 when the US required vacant possession. This prompted the commissioner to make the Immigration Ordinance 1971 (section 4(1)) providing that only a special permit would allow the former inhabitants to re-enter the territory.
3. From 1968 to 1971 the UK Government removed the whole population, primarily to Mauritius and the Seychelles, without the use of force, but stating that the Company was ceasing its operations, and no more supplies would be available to them (*Chagos Islanders v. Attorney General* 2003).
4. The whole operation established a 'callous disregard for their interests', and the members of the community were left to fend for themselves in the slums of 'Port Louis'. The ordinance denying them the right to return had been prompted by US concerns about 'non-aligned countries' objecting to

the construction of a military base in the Indian Ocean (*Chagos Islanders v. Attorney General* 2003: para. 10). In more recent times other objections could be raised about the alleged renditions flying into that base, or taking place, with concomitant torture episodes, in ships anchored just beyond Chagos. The miserable conditions of the Chagossians in Mauritius, their poverty and unemployment prompted negotiations between Mauritius and the UK, eventually culminating until 1977 ('depleted by inflation') to 595 Chagossian families. The Chagossians sought legal advice, and with the support of Michael Vencatessen, issued a writ in the High Court in London, on behalf of all Chagossians, and eventually a trust fund of £4 million was set up in Mauritius in exchange for abandoning all claims, and this was signed by most Chagossians.

5. After the judgment (Divisional Court, Laws LJ and Gibbs J) in favour of Mr Bancoult on 3 November 2000 effectively quashed Section 4(1) of the Immigration Ordinance as *ultra vires*, Mr Robin Cook (Foreign Secretary) announced a feasibility study to attempt to resettle the Chagossians in their former territory. He concluded his press release saying,

> This government has not defended what was done or said thirty years ago. As Lord Justice Laws recognized, we made no attempt to conceal the gravity of what happened. I am pleased that he has commended the wholly admirable conduct in disclosing material to the court, and praised the openness of today's foreign office (para. 17).

The points that remained in contention were the Chagossians' right to return and the very legality of the official Constitution Order and the Immigration Order, as well as their 'irrationality', as

> The Orders were not made in the interest of the Chagossians, but in the interest of the United Kingdom and the United States (para. 28).

Further, the authority to remove persons of British citizenship from their chosen residence, without – at any time – any compensation was also questioned. Lord Hoffman and the other Lords recognized the impact of the law made for a colony, citing Blackstone (1809: 137):

> But no power on earth except the authority of Parliament can send any subject of England out of the land against his will; no, not even a criminal.

The Crown, therefore, and its appointed Commissioner, has no authority to transport anyone, against their will (para. 44), by what constituted, essentially, threats of starvation to them and their families. But even the acknowledged wrong that had been done at the time did not result in a favourable judgment at this time: the main problem was the costs and logistics of total resettlement, although the

Chagossians were now permitted to return for a time, to visit family graves and the like.

The Chagossians' migration was indeed forced like many other by lack of resources and economic pressures from outside, although the main causative factors at the time were clearly political. Their case is worth studying in detail, because of the different treatment they received at the hand of US first, then UK courts. The former appealed to procedural flaws in the case. The UK Court instead tackled the factual elements of the case head-on, and admitted its own fault in regard to the series of events outlined above.

The Asylum Seeker in Law: The Flight from Poverty and Deprivations

> The United States has traditionally been and remains a magnet for economic migrations. Opportunities for a Better life and the 'American Dream' attract both legal and illegal migrants. However, current American immigration procedures do not include any avenue for immigrants who risk to enter the United States as economic refugees (Gabor and Rosenquest 2006: 278; 8 USC §§ 1101 (a)(15) (H)(ii) (temporary agricultural laborers), (a)(42) (refugee) (2000)).

To some extent this passage emphasizes a 'dream' that no longer exists. Rifkin believes that the 'American dream' is tied to an old system and an old dream (Rifkin 2004: 85), whereas the European Union's 'transformational governing model, is a beacon of change in the global era' (Rifkin 2004: 96). As we shall see below, the treatment of asylum seekers is also more favourable in Europe than it is in North America or Australia, for instance.

The fact remains that the 'American dream' itself was intended to be specific to the US so that neither universalism nor multiculturalism were ever part of its characteristics (Rifkin 2004: 17; Westra 2013: 129–30). We have reviewed some aspects of the US regimes in the previous sections, hence, before turning to the European approach (European Council Directive 2004), we should consider whether international law offers any better guidance than that embodied in the CSR, which might be specific to economic migrants.

The starting point may well be the United Nations Charter, especially Article 55:

> Article 55 of the United Nations Charter provides the following:
> With a view to the creation of conditions of stability and well-being which are necessary for peaceful and friendly relations among nations based on respect for the principle of equal rights and self-determination of peoples, the United Nations shall promote;
> a. higher standards of living, full employment and conditions of economic and social progress and development;
> b. solutions of international economic, social, and health and related problems; and international cultural and educational cooperations and

> c. universal respect for, and observance of, human rights and fundamental freedoms for all without distinction as to race, sex, language or religion.

The main principle promoted by this Article is that of equality, and Articles 6 and 7 of the International Covenant on Economic, Social and Cultural Rights support explicitly the right to work and for everyone 'the opportunity to gain his living by work which he freely chooses or accepts' (Gabor and Rosenquest 2006: 283; International Covenant on Economic, Social and Cultural Rights 1966). The Chagos Island case was an instance of deliberate, intended deprivation of both work and livelihood, surprisingly involving the UK, complicit with the US in those illegal actions.

But Article 55 itself states that individuals are entitled to employment, to conditions of economic and social progress under universal respect for human rights. Hence states should ensure that such conditions are met, although 'It is difficult to determine when a state has committed a gross violation of its international obligation by depriving an individual citizen of the fundamental human right to productive employment' (Gabor and Rosenquest 2006: 283). Even if that right is hard to enforce, the undeniable right of people to their own resources is both clear and entrenched in law:

> Indigenous peoples possess collective rights which are indispensable for their existence, well-being and integral development as peoples (ECOSOC, Commission on Human Rights 2006, prepared by the Chairperson-Rapporteur, Luis-Enrique Chavez).

Hence it is perhaps best to view the problem as one of 'economic persecution' rather than one of denial of the right to employment, as the latter would not fit large numbers of asylum seekers. The UNHCR Handbook explains:

> … the distinction between economic hardship and persecution is 'sometimes blurred' when improper racial and political motivations underlie economic deprivation (Ramos 2011: 512; UNHCR, 2011, §63).

This approach – that is, of 'economic persecution' – would be particularly appropriate to the situation of Indigenous peoples and local communities, affected by unwanted and most often hazardous forms of 'development', such that 'plunder' appears to be a better description (Mattei and Nader 2008) rather than any situation intended to advance their economic interests.

For the most part, development activities are planned to take place where (1) the resources can easily be found and (2) local communities do not have the political power to fight back, to resist and say 'no' to unwanted intrusions into their territories. However, courts have tended to apply literal standards when dealing with refugees, consistent with the 'five grounds' of persecution listed in the CSR.

More recently, some changes have occurred:

> … the court found that limiting persecution to physical abuse was an incorrect formulation of the standard. The UK Immigration Appeal Tribunal (IAT) also stated in another case that if a state does not protect against discrimination, that causes 'an inability to earn a living or to find anywhere to live', the Refugee Convention can be engaged (Ramos 2011: 513; *Sec'y of State for the Home Dept. v. Sijakovic* 2001).

The main point that emerges is that courts tend often to take the position that the main issue should be the reasons for the hardships a refugee encounters and the deprivations that affect him, instead of limiting the focus to the resulting hardships, be they 'economic or physical' (Ramos 2011: 513; *Sec'y of State for the Home Dept. v. Sijakovic* 2001). Yet even this hopeful advance fails to acknowledge that there is no sharp distinction between 'economic' and 'physical' hardships: the lack of means to support oneself or one's family, the lack of food, safe water or shelter is – no doubt – as 'physical' as any other kind of persecution.

James Hathaway has been advocating that international human rights should be fundamental to refugee law (Hathaway 2005: 4–6). Hathaway's position emphasizes the basic intended purpose of the drafters of the CSR regarding the overarching importance of human rights law. At any rate, the connection between persecution and economic disadvantage is supported by the prohibition of the use of force in Article 2(4) of the UN Charter, although that Article is highly controversial to this day; but its provisions do not need to be limited to hostile relations between states:

> The prohibition of the use of force led to fundamental divisions as to whether the prohibition of the 'use of force' included *economic coercion*, the scope of the right to self-defense, the right to use force to further self-determination and to intervene in civil wars (Gray 2008: 7).

'Economic coercion' therefore can be understood as the imposition of an impermissible use of force, thus an illegal action of states, whether directly imposed by the state itself, or indirectly imposed, as when states are complicit with the legal persons whose 'development' plans result in 'economic coercion', imposed on impoverished local communities.

The next chapters will explore the specific situations that render people desperate enough to flee their homes and countries, and discuss some of the principal causes of their abject conditions. The end results are not in question – several situations that affect persons in different areas of the world can be listed under three main headings, which produce the conditions that precede the flight of asylum seekers: (1) climate change, (2) globalized neoliberal forms of 'development' and (3) wars and other conflict situations.

All of these combinations of circumstances result in grave deprivations, multiple breaches of human rights, as the result of all these clusters of events, fitting under these three headings, all produce extreme poverty and major deprivations.

The following chapters will explore these basic causes that give rise to the flights that characterize asylum seekers. In all cases, as we shall see, the situations engendered are such that no other solution presents itself to the victimized people, who wish to survive and protect their families, perhaps even attempt to give them a more secure future.

References

8 USC §§ 1101 (a)(15)(H)(ii) (temporary agricultural laborers), (a) (42) (refugee) (2000).

A/FC and others v. Secretary of State for the Home Department [2004] UKHL 56.

Abizadeh, Arash, 2008, 'Democratic Theory and Border Coercion (No Right to Unilaterally Control Your Own Borders)', *Political Theory*, 36.1, 37–65.

Anghie, Thomas, 2006, *Imperialism, Sovereignty and International Law*, Cambridge University Press, Cambridge.

Anker, Debora E., 1999, *Law of Asylum in the United States*, 3rd edition, Refugee Law Center, Boston, MA.

Bancoult v. McNamara, 217 FRD 280, 2003.

Benvisti, Eyal and Downs, George W., 2009, 'National Courts, Domestic Democracy and the Evolution of International Law', *European Journal of International Law*, 20.1, 59–72.

Blackstone, W., 1809, *Commentaries on the Laws of England*, 15th edition, vol. 1.

British Indian Ocean Territories Order, 1865, SI No. 1920.

Brown, Wendy, 2010, *Walled States, Waning Sovereignty*, Zone Books, NY; 2nd printing 2012.

Carens, Joseph, H., 1987, 'Who Belongs? Theoretical and Legal Questions about Birthright Citizenship in the United States', *University of Toronto Law Journal*, 37, 413–43.

Chagos Islanders v. Attorney General (2003) EWCH 2222 (QB), (2003) All ER (D) 166.

Christian Aid Report, May 2007, 'Human Tide: The Real Migration Crisis'.

Cohen, Hermann, 1949, *Jeremiah, Hebrew Text and English Translation, with an Introduction and Commentary*, ed. H. Freedman, Soncino Press, London.

Cole, David, 2005–6, 'The Idea of Humanity: Human Rights and Immigrants' Rights', *Columbia Human Rights Law Review*, 37, 627–58.

Dacyl, J., 1996, 'Sovereignty Versus Human Rights: From Past Discourses to Contemporary Dilemmas', *Journal of Refugee Studies*, 9.2, 136–65.

ECOSOC, Commission on Human Rights, 2006, 'Human Rights and Indigenous Issues: Report of the Working Group', Annex I, UN Doc.E/CN.4/2006/79 (22 March 2006), prepared by the Chairperson-Rapporteur, Luis-Enrique Chavez.

El Hinnawi, Essam, 1985, *Environmental Refugees*, United Nations Environmental Program (UNEP), Nairobi, Kenya.

European Council Directive 2004/83/EC of 29 April 2004 on minimum standards for the qualification and status of third country nationals and stateless persons as refugees …, OJ(2004)L304/12.

Executive Committee, Standing Committee, 18th Meeting, 'Complementary Forms of Protection: Their Nature and Relationship to the International Refugee Protection Regime', UN Doc.EC/50/SC/CRP.18 (9 June 2000).

Federal Employees Liability Reform and Tort Compensation Act of 1988, Fub.L.No.100–694, 102 Stat.4563 (1988) (codified at 28 USC §§ 2671–80).

Filartiga v. Pena-Irala, US Court of Appeals, 2d ct, 1980 630 F 2d 876.

Forced Migration Review, Issue 31, October 2008, ed. Marion Couldrey and Maurice Herson, University of Oxford.

Gabor, F. and Rosenquest, John B. IV, 2006, 'The Unsettled Status of Economic Refugees from the Americana and International Legal Perspective: A Proposal for Recognition Under Existing International Law', *Texas International Law Journal*, 41, 275–94.

Geneva Convention (III) Relative to the Treatment of Prisoners of War, 12 August 1949, Art. 1, 6 UST, 3316, 3318, 75 UNTS 135, 138.

Glenn, H. Patrick, 2013, *The Cosmopolitan State*, Oxford University Press, Oxford.

Goodland, Robert, 2008, 'The World Bank's Financing of Climate Change Damages Integrity', in Westra, L., Bosselmann, K. and Westra, R., eds, *Reconciling Human Existence with Ecological Integrity*, Earthscan, London, 219–44.

Goodwin-Gill, Guy S. and McAdam, Jane, 2007, *The Refugee in International Law*, 3rd edition, Oxford University Press, Oxford.

Gostin, Lawrence, 2008, 'Meeting Basic Survival Needs of the World's Least Healthy People: Toward a Framework Convention of Global Health', *Georgetown Law Journal*, 9632, 331–92.

Gray, Christine, 2008, *International Law and the Use of Force*, 3rd edition, Oxford University Press, Oxford.

Guiding Principles on Internal Displacement (UN GPID) UN Doc. E/CN.4/1998/53/Add.2 (1998), noted in Comm. Hum. Rts. res. 1998/50, www1.umn.edu/humanrts/instree/GuidingPrinciplesonInternalDisplacement.htm (accessed 24 May 2014).

Hamdi v Rumsfeld, 542 US 507 (2004).

Hathaway, James C., 2005, *The Rights of Refugees Under International Law*, Cambridge University Press, Cambridge.

Human Rights Committee 'Freedom of Movement' (Article 12) CCPR/C/21/Rev.1/Add.9, CCPR General Comment 27, 2 November 1999.

International Covenant on Civil and Political Rights (ICCPR), GA, Res. 2200A (XXI), Art. 12, 6ILM 368–83, 999 UNTS 171: into force 23 March 1967.

International Covenant on Economic, Social and Cultural Rights (ICESCR), GA Re. 2200A (XXI) 21 UN GAOR, Supp. (No. 16), at 49, UN Doc.A/6316 (1966).

International Symposium on Desertification and Migration, 'The Almeria Statement', Almeria, Spain, 9–11 February 1994.
Marrus, M.R., 2002, *The Unwanted: European Refugees from the First World War through the Cold War*, 2nd edition, Temple University Press, Philadelphia, PA.
Mathew, Dessi, 2009, 'Claims of Political Asylum Based on Non-Physical Forms of Harm, such as Economic sanctions and Deprivations', *Pave International Review*, 21, 309–34.
Mattei, U. and Nader, L., 2008, *Plunder: When the Rule of Law Is Illegal*, Blackwell Publishers, Oxford.
McAdam, Jane, 2007, 'Climate Change Refugees and International Law', Paper for the NSW Bar Association, 24 October 2007.
Memorandum from Jay S. Bybee to Alberto Gonzales, Regarding Standards for Conduct for Interrogation under 18 USC §§ 2340–2340A (1 August 2002).
Morton, Andrew, Bancour, Philippe and Laczko, Frank, 2008, 'Human Security Policy Challenges', *Forced Migration Review*, 31, 5–7.
Myers, N., 1993, 'Environmental Refugees in a Globally Warmed World', *Bioscience*, 43, 752–61.
——, 2005, 'Environmental Refugees: An Emergent Security Issue', 13th Economic Forum, Prague, 23–27 May 2005.
Phuong, Catherine, 2004, *The International Protection of Internally Displaced Persons*, Cambridge University Press, Cambridge.
Pimentel, D., Westra, L. and Noss, R.F., 2000, *Ecological Integrity: Integrating Environment, Conservation and Health*, Island Press, Washington, DC.
Pogge, Thomas, 1992, 'Cosmopolitanism and Sovereignty', *Ethics*, 103.1, 48–75.
——, 2008, 'Aligned: Global Justice and Ecology', in Westra, L., Bosselmann, K. and Westra, R., eds, *Reconciling Human Existence and Ecological Integrity*, Earthscan, London, 147–58.
R (Bancoult) v Secretary of State for foreign and Commonwealth Affairs [2007] QB 1067 (Bancoult 1).
R (on the application of Bancoult) v. Secretary of State for Foreign and Commonwealth Affairs (2008) UKHL 61: an appeal from: [2007] EWCA Civ. 498.
Ramos, Lauren Michelle, 2011, 'A New Standard for Evaluating Claims of Economic Persecution Under the 1951 Convention Relating to the Status of Refugees', *Vanderbilt Journal of Transnational Law*, 44, 499–525.
Rasul v. Bush, 542 US 466, 2004.
Raz, Joseph, 1986, *The Morality of Freedom*, Clarendon Press, Oxford.
——, 2009, *The Authority of Law*, 2nd edition, Oxford University Press, Oxford.
Rifkin, Jeremy, 2004, *The European Dream*, Arches/Penguin, New York.
Sassen, Saskia, 1996, *Losing Control?: Sovereignty in an Age of Globalization*, Columbia University Press, New York.
——, 2006, *Territory Authority Rights: From Medieval to Global Assemblages*, Princeton University Press, Princeton, NJ.

Schmitt, Carl, 1985, *Political Theology: Four Chapters on the Concept of Sovereignty*, trans. George Schwab, MIT Press, Cambridge, MA.
Sec'y of State for the Home Dept. v. Sijakovic [2001] UKIAT Appeal No. HX-58113–2000.
Sen, Amartya, 1994, 'Population, Delusion and Reality', *New York Review of Books*, 41.15, 62–71.
Soskolne, Colin L., Westra, Laura, Kotzé, Louis J., Mackey, Brendan and Rees, William E., 2007, *Sustaining Life on Earth*, Lexington Books, Lanham, MD.
Stavropoulos, M., 1994, 'The Right Not to Be Displaced', *American University Journal of International Law and Policy*, 9, 689–749.
Steiner, Henry and Alston, Philip, 1996, *International Human Rights in Context: Law, Politics and Morals*, Oxford University Press, Oxford.
Stern, Nicholas, 2007, *The Economics of Climate Change: The Stern Review*, Cambridge University Press, Cambridge.
Stockholm Declaration of the United Nations Conference for the Human Environment, 16 June 1972, ILM 11 141.
Terry, J., 2002, 'Taking *Filartiga* on the Road', in Craig Scott, *Torture as Tort*, Hart Publishing, Oxford, pp. 109–34.
Tonnas, Katherine, 1993, 'Out of a Far Country: The Sojourns of Cubans, Vietnamese, Haitians and Chinese to America', *Southern University Law Review*, 20, 295–406.
UNGA, res. 60/168, 'Protection and Assistance to Internally Displaces Persons', 16 December 2005 (adopted without a vote).
——, 2008, *International Migration and Development, Report of the Secretary-General*, 11 August 2008, A/63/265.
United Nations High Commissioner for Refugees (UNHCR), 2009, 'Iraqis, Afghans, and Somalis Top List of Asylum Seekers in Industrialized World', 21 October 2009, available at http://www.unhcr.org/4adf24079.html (accessed 3 February 2015).
——, 2011, *Handbook and Guidelines on Procedures and Criteria for Determining Refugee Status*, Geneva.
United States v. Smith, 18 US, 153, 160–161, 5 L. Ed. 57 (1920).
Walia, Harsha, 2013, *Undoing Border Imperialism*, AK Press and the Institute for Anarchist Studies, Oakland, CA.
Weeramantry, Christian J., 1997, Separate Opinion, Gabcikovo-Nagymaros case, ICJ (1997), Rep. 7.
Westra, Laura, 1997, 'Terrorism at Oka', in Wellington, A., Greenbaum, A.J. and Cragg, W., eds, *Canadian Issues in Environmental Ethics*, Broadview Press, Peterborough, ON, pp. 247–91.
——, 1998, *Living in Integrity*, Rowman Littlefield, Lanham, MD.
——, 2006, *Environmental Justice and the Rights of Unborn and Future Generations*, Earthscan, London.
——, 2007, *Environmental Justice and the Rights of Indigenous Peoples*, Earthscan, London.

——, 2012, *Faces of State Terrorism*, Brill, Leiden.
——, 2013, *The Supranational Corporation*, Brill, Leiden.
——, 2014, *Revolt against Authority*, Brill, Leiden.

Chapter 2

Climate Change Refugees: Law, Human Rights and Ethics

Donald A. Brown

Introduction: The Enormous Challenge of Climate Refugees

This chapter examines the legal, human rights and ethical dimensions of the fact that human-induced climate change is already displacing people from their communities while threatening to create millions of climate refugees, that is people who are forced to leave their homes, communities and often their nations because of the adverse effects of global warming. Although as a matter of international law, the word refugee is often limited to individuals who are displaced from their country, this chapter will use the term refugee to include all people who are forced to leave their communities because of climate change without regard to whether they leave their nation and cross national boundaries.

In addition to the immense personal human suffering that people experience when they are forced to leave their communities because the ecological systems on which their life depends no longer will support life as usual due to climatic change, the problem of climate refugees is also expected to create enormous challenges for the international community. This is so particularly for those parts of the world in which millions of people may need to relocate due to increased droughts, flooding, rising seas, soil and coastal erosion, loss of water supplies, agricultural incompatibility with higher temperatures, and desertification. As we will see, waves of refugees may also be created when climate change degrades ecological systems to levels that trigger violent conflict and war.

The exact number of climate refugees that are expected in this century is somewhat contentious because some of the climate events that will force people to abandon their communities are difficult to predict with accuracy. In fact, there are at least four scientific problems with predicting the number of refugees that will be caused by climate change at any one time.

First, although the number of climate refugees that will be caused by a changing climate between now and 2100, for instance, will depend on the magnitude of warming experienced in this century, the amount of warming experienced will depend upon atmospheric concentrations of greenhouse gases (ghg) in the next 85 years. Yet it is impossible to know accurately future ghg atmospheric concentrations because these levels will depend upon the energy policies enacted, technologies installed and population levels in this century, as well as whether global temperatures increase to levels that begin to release carbon that is stored in the biosphere. Because there is considerable scientific uncertainty about when carbon stored in oceans, soils and forests will be released by specific temperature increases, predicting atmospheric ghg concentrations in this century can only be accomplished by making assumptions about what temperatures will create positive feedbacks from stored carbon as well as how parts of the biosphere that are now absorbing some of the carbon being released by human activities will become saturated and thereby, because of their inability to store additional carbon, cause more rapid elevated atmospheric carbon concentrations.

Second, even if future ghg atmospheric concentrations could be determined, there is still some scientific uncertainty with what temperatures will be experienced by different atmospheric ghg concentrations, an issue referred to as the problem of 'climate sensitivity'. The scientific community deals with the uncertainty about climate sensitivity the way it deals with other climate issues about which there is some uncertainty, namely making predictions about what temperatures will be at different atmospheric concentrations that are accompanied by probability bounds.

Third, even if it were possible to predict with confidence temperatures that will prevail during this century, it is very difficult to predict climatic change impacts at any one place on the earth because of the limitations of global climate models to predict with accuracy climate conditions at the local scale. It is also very difficult to predict climate impacts at the local scale due to the fact that the climate system is somewhat chaotic, meaning small changes in one part of the system can trigger big changes in other parts of the system. Yet how many climate refugees will be created in this century will depend on, among many other things, where specifically harsh climate impacts are experienced at the local scale including where intense storms and droughts precisely arise that cause floods or diminish agricultural productivity or drinking water supplies.

Fourth, the number of climate refugees that are actually caused by climate change will depend on whether adaptation responses are taken in anticipation of a changing global climate. If, for instance, people move from small island states which are vulnerable to rising seas before the rising oceans force them to move, people on these islands may not be strictly classified as climate refugees because people who are moved peacefully and consensually from places of declining natural resources are not usually counted as refugees.

For these and other reasons it is difficult to predict with high levels of confidence how many people will become climate refugees in this century and where the greatest needs of climate refugees will arise. However it is still very likely that human induced climate change will produce tens of millions of climate refugees by 2100. Recent estimates of the number of climate refugees that will be created in this century range from 50 million predicted by the Intergovernmental Panel on Climate Change (IPCC) in 2007 (Vidal 2009) and 150 million by 2050 predicted by the Climate Justice Foundation (Pearce 2014).

The most recent 5th Assessment Report of the IPCC concluded that adverse climate change impacts 'are already occurring on all continents and across the oceans and the world, in many cases, is ill-prepared for risks from a changing climate' (IPCC 2014a). IPCC also found that millions of climate change refugees may flood into Europe as they flee extreme weather and food shortages (Spencer 2014). And so, the problem of climate refugees is not only of great concern due to the suffering and hardships experienced by the refugees themselves, climate refugees are also a huge potential threat to parts of the world which may be inundated by tens of thousands of refugees seeking relief from degraded ecological conditions.

Until recently, most of the refugee problems that received the greatest attention of the international community were created by people fleeing war and violence. The concept of climate refugees has arisen as a source of great international concern only in the last decade, an idea that initially conjures up a vision of rising seas, storms or droughts forcing people to flee inhabitable conditions Yet, recent analyses of links between climate change and national security have concluded that climate change is leading to growing military tensions around the world and armed conflict which may create large numbers of additional refugees. For instance a report prepared for the United States found that climate change-induced drought in the Middle East and Africa is leading to conflicts over food and water and escalating longstanding regional and ethnic tensions into violent clashes (Davenport 2014). This report also concluded that climate change effects are 'threat multipliers that will aggravate stressors abroad, such as poverty, environmental degradation, political instability and social tensions – conditions that can enable terrorist activity and other forms of violence' (Davenport 2014).

Another recent study found that changes in climate, such as increased drought and above-average annual temperatures, have caused a rise in human violence across the world from domestic violence to riots, civil wars and the break-up of governing institutions (Freccia 2014). This paper also warned that rising ghg emissions could result in greater amounts of violence around the world, a development that will almost certainly lead to more refugees.

The threat of increasing numbers of climate refugees is not simply a potential future nightmare for the refugees themselves, there is strong evidence that several recent very destructive conflicts around the world in Darfur, Rwanda, Somalia and Burundi have been at least exacerbated by droughts caused by climate change (Edwards 2012: 59). In addition, the great human tragedy of the ongoing conflict in Syria has been linked to drought, water shortages, crop-failure and displacement likely caused by or exacerbated by climate change (Femia and Werrell 2014). These conditions led to a massive exodus of farmers, herders and agriculturally-dependent rural families from the countryside to Syrian cities thus triggering internal political unrest. Although the causes of the Syrian conflict include factors other than climate-caused ecological degradation such as poor land management practices and simmering ethnic tensions, Syria is a clear example of a conflict in waiting that could be triggered by deteriorating ecological conditions caused by climate change. For this reason, given marginal food and water supplies with which billions of people around the world are already currently struggling, there is reason to be very concerned about increased violence in a warming world and the growing number of climate refugees that could be generated by this conflict.

Nevertheless, the inability to predict accurately the exact number of climate refugees that will be arise in this century is no justification for concluding that the problem of climate refugees is not likely to be an immense challenge for the international community in the coming decades. In fact, climate change's most devastating impacts may be those caused by huge conflicts over scarce resources.

Legal Challenges for Climate Refugees

This section examines whether international refugee law, a body of law that creates duties for nations to protect refugees, adequately deals with climate refugees and, given the limitations of this body of law, whether there are potential legal remedies under civil and human rights law for people who are forced to abandon their communities due to deteriorating ecological conditions caused by climate change.

International Refugee Law

The term 'refugee law' usually refers to a body of international law created at the international and regional levels to protect the rights of people forcibly displaced by conflict, persecution, natural disasters and development projects. This body of law does not include a category for climate refugees because it was drafted before the problem of climate refugees was recognized. As we shall see, this body of law does contain some provisions that might be relevant to a few of the problems faced by climate refugees, although overall international refugee law falls very short of adequately dealing with the most serious problems of climate refugees.

Fundamental international refugee laws include the 1951 Convention on the Status of Refugees (Convention 1951) and its 1967 Protocol (Protocol 1967). Under the 1951 Convention Section Article 1, Section i(A)2 the term 'refugee' shall apply to any person who:

> … owing to well-founded fear of being persecuted for reasons of race, religion, nationality, membership of a particular social group or political opinion, is outside the country of his nationality and is unable or, owing to such fear, is unwilling to avail himself of the protection of that country; or who, not having a nationality and being outside the country of his former habitual residence as a result of such events, is unable or, owing to such fear, is unwilling to return to it (Convention 1951: Article 1(A)2).

Thus, according to this provision, refugees are defined by three basic characteristics:

- they are outside their country of origin or outside the country of their former habitual residence;

- they are unable or unwilling to avail themselves of the protection of that country owing to a well-founded fear of being persecuted; and
- the persecution feared is based on at least one of five grounds: race, religion, nationality, membership of a particular social group, or political opinion (RULAC 2014).

The 1967 Protocol makes no changes to the definition of 'refugee' in the 1951 Convention (Protocol 1967).

It is generally accepted that climate refugees do not meet this definition of the 1951 Convention. However, if a government consciously withholds assistance from victims of climate change in order to punish them for reasons of race, religion, nationality, member of a particular social group or political opinion, then they may qualify for refugee status under the 1951 Convention (Edwards 2012).

The main benefit of being classified as a refugee under the 1951 Convention is that the refugee is protected against *refoulement*, that is being forcefully returned to the country in which that refugee has a reasonable fear of being persecuted. Classification as a refugee under the 1951 Convention and its Protocol also gives a refugee certain rights including but not limited to rights to identity papers and travel documents, free exercise of religion and religious education, free access to the courts, including legal assistance, access to elementary education, access to public relief and assistance, protection provided by social security, protection of intellectual property, such as inventions and trade names, protection of literary, artistic and scientific work, equal treatment by taxing authorities and the rights to: belong to trade unions, belong to other non-political nonprofit organizations, engage in wage-earning employment, own property, practise a profession, self-employment, access housing, access higher education, choose a place of residence, and move freely within the country (HREA 2003).

Yet under international refugee law there are no conventions or protocols that expressly provide protection and assistance for people crossing international borders because of climate change. As a result there are several important climate refugee issues that are unresolved in international law. One is which nations have responsibility to accept climate refugees that are forced to flee their nations of origin because of deteriorating ecological systems. And another, which nations, if any, are responsible for compensating climate refugees for the harms, damages or reasonable adaptation costs that the climate refugees must endure.

Thus far we have considered issues that arise under international law for refugees that cross national borders. What international legal protections exist for persons displaced by climate change within a county? In this respect, the United Nations General Assembly adopted in 1998 the Guiding Principles on Internal Displacement (UN GPID 1998).

These principles define internally displaced persons as:

> [p]ersons or groups of persons who have been forced or obliged to flee or to leave their homes or places of habitual residence, in particular as a result of or

> in order to avoid the effects of armed conflict, situations of generalized violence, violations of human rights or natural or human-made disasters, and who have not crossed an internationally recognized State border (UN GPID 1998: Scope and Purpose).

Thus, because the guidance on internally displaced persons specifically includes natural or human-made disasters that cause migration as the basis for classifying people as displaced persons, these principles are more applicable to climate refugees than to those who cross national borders under the 1951 Covenant. Yet the responsibility of protecting internally displaced persons under the GPID resides with the nations in which the displaced persons reside (UN GPID 1998: Principle 3). However, the nations in which most persons reside that are displaced internally by climate change are rarely among those nations that are most responsible for climate change. In addition these nations are often very poor without sufficient financial resources to adequately protect internally displaced people.

The GPID provides when property or possessions of the internally displaced persons are not recoverable, the nation has a duty to provide assistance to these persons and to obtain for them appropriate compensation or other form of reparation (UN GPID 1998: Principle 29). Yet the nations who bear this responsibility are not the nations that are usually responsible for climate change, nor do they usually have the financial resources to provide compensation or reparations. Thus, GPID is not the solution to some of the climate refugee's most vexing problems.

In addition to these above identified international and intra-national legal instruments, that are relevant to how displaced persons are protected under law, are a number of regional agreements which deal with refugee rights. These include the Organization of African Unity Convention Governing the Specific Aspects of Refugee Problems in Africa, adopted in 1969 (OAU Convention 1969), and the Cartagena Declaration on Refugees, adopted in 1984 (Cartagena Declaration 1984). Both of these documents provide a somewhat expanded definition of 'refugee' compared to the 1951 Convention in ways that provide more flexibility to include victims of ecological degradation while continuing to limit protection to refugees that cross national borders. Yet as in the other legal instruments on refugees examined above, these regional refugee instruments do not provide means for making those actually responsible for climate change liable for compensation or reparations to those who suffer from the need to be relocated.

Civil Liability for Harms Suffered by Climate Refugees

What theories of legal liability exist for climate refugees to recover damages for the harms that they suffer? Such questions are a matter of tort law in common law jurisdictions.

A tort is a violation of civil duties. That is a tort, in common law, is a civil wrong. Tort law deals with situations where a person's or entity's behaviour has unfairly caused someone else to suffer loss or harm. A tort is not necessarily an illegal act but an act that causes harm. Tort law allows anyone who is harmed to recover their losses. Thus tort law is intuitively a good place to look for potential remedies for climate refugees.

Although climate change is clearly harming millions of people without their consent, matters which are within the province of tort law, the few cases that have mostly been filed in the United States so far by citizens to establish specific financial liability for those who cause climate change have been unsuccessful. US courts have usually dismissed these actions on the grounds that climate change is a political rather than a legal issue. One observer of litigation in the United States that has attempted to establish financial responsibility for climate change damages on the basis of tort theory summarizes a number of unsuccessful attempts as follows:

> Finally, there is one other barrier to justiciability which may be the most difficult to overcome. The 'political question doctrine' permits judges to defer climate change questions for political consideration reasons. The doctrine highlights the fact that climate change concerns are more appropriate for the legislative branch of the government than for the judiciary (Butti 2011: 33).

One case is particularly representative of the trend of courts to dismiss civil litigation seeking to establish financial responsibility for climate change-caused harms. In *Kivalina v. ExxonMobil Corporation, et al.* the plaintiffs sought to prove that the actions of the defendants, the majority of which were fossil fuel companies, caused financial damages to them from flooding the Alaskan village of Kivalina (Kivalina 2012).

The allegations made by the plaintiff, an Alaskan village, asserted that some of the defendants including ExxonMobil Corporation, BP America, Inc., Chevron Corporation, ConocoPhillips Company, Peabody Energy Corporation, American Electric Power Company, Inc., Duke Energy Corporation and The Southern Company, conspired to misinform the public on the science of climate change either individually or through their various front groups or industry trade associations. The complaint in this case further asserted that the object of the conspiracy was to create unwarranted doubts about the existence of global warming and its causes among the public and that the defendants did this to protect their economic interests.

The plaintiffs also claimed that some of the defendants have conspired to mislead the public about the science of global warming, actions which led to the failure of the US to reduce its ghg emissions, thereby creating flood damage to the village of Kivalina.

The plaintiffs further alleged that the defendants also funded 'front groups', including phony citizens' organizations and bogus scientific bodies, who regularly published views expressing doubts about global warming in mainstream publications such as the *Wall Street Journal*. The plaintiffs also claimed that the defendants funded and circulated misleading advertising which questioned the 'science' of global warming and human causation, and continued to fund projects which sought to undermine the science while defendants were being told by the scientists that were advising them that climate change was a serious threat.

Despite the allegations that if true would clearly establish tortious behaviour, the case was subsequently dismissed by the US Court of Appeals for the Ninth Circuit in October 2012 on the basis that climate change raises political issues that need to be decided by legislative action rather than by a court (Kivalina 2012).

Kivalina was just one of several recent cases seeking to recover damages from those who caused climate change under tort theories of liability that have been dismissed on the grounds that climate change liability is a matter that must be resolved by legislatures not courts.

Many observers of these attempts by civil litigants to use tort law to establish financial liability for causing climate change have concluded that the real reason why courts are dismissing these cases is because they do not know what to do about how to allocate responsibility for climate change damages given that greenhouse gases are being emitted by every country in the world and huge numbers of high-emitting entities and individuals in both rich and poor countries. There are just too many governments, entities and individuals who are responsible for climate change, along with competing unresolved theories about what considerations should be followed in proportioning responsibility for climate change damages, for courts to feel comfortable about determining a specific level of damages to one nation, entity or individual. Unresolved criteria for apportioning responsibility include, for instance, claims that historical and per capita emissions levels and the ability of nations to pay have been advanced as frameworks for allocating national responsibility for climate change. For this reason, it is not likely the courts will award climate change-caused damages in the absence of some international agreement on how to allocate responsibility for climate change, a matter that will be revisited in the last section of this chapter, on ethics.

Although tort law is not likely to provide protection and compensation to climate refugees because of the challenges in allocating responsibility, it is not clear that civil liability for climate change damages will not eventually be adjudicated in courts on other legal theories. As we will see in the next sections on human rights and ethics there are numerous well-settled legal principles that could form the basis of establishing legal responsibility. Only time will tell whether a court that has the jurisdiction to do so will begin to determine the damage obligations of the nations and entities that are most responsible for climate change.

Human Rights and Climate Refugees

Climate change is increasingly understood as a serious human rights problem. In fact, climate change deeply threatens the least contentious human rights including the right to life, food and subsistence along with many other widely recognized human rights (Caney 2010).

In addition, the worst effects of climate change are likely to be felt by those individuals and groups whose rights protections are already precarious, including millions of people in the world's poorest countries (Bonano et al. 2008). Thus climate change will very likely displace people whose ability to sustain themselves was already under threat, an outcome which has human rights implications.

Climate change violates the right to life because a changing climate will and is killing people through more intense storms, floods, droughts and heat waves. It is often because climate change threatens human lives that people are forced to move.

Climate change will violate the right to subsistence by increasing: (a) droughts which will undermine food security, (b) water shortages, (c) sea level rise, which will put under water some agricultural areas and some small island developing states, and (d) flooding which will lead to crop failure. It is because climate change threatens basic subsistence that many people become displaced. Because of this there is a large and rapidly growing literature linking climate change to existing internationally protected human rights (see, for example, the report of the International Council on Human Rights Policy on links between climate change and human rights, ICHRP 2008).

Thus there is little question that most climate refugees may claim that their human rights have been violated by climate change. Because of this, climate refugees can appeal to a rapidly growing body of international human rights law to establish responsibility among those who have caused climate change and achieve just treatment as refugees. In addition, because some climate refugees must contend with armed conflict, climate refugees can appeal to humanitarian law for protection against warring factions. Yet, as we shall see, despite unquestionable violations of human rights caused by climate change and the numerous advantages in approaching climate change as a human rights problem, there are still some significant limitations in using a human rights approach to resolve the problems of climate refugees.

Advantages of a Human Rights Approach to Protecting Climate Refugees

Because climate change clearly violates human rights, certain policy consequences follow, which include:

- The costs to those causing climate change entailed by policies to reduce the threat of climate change are not relevant for policy. That is if a person is violating human rights, he or she should desist even if it is costly. The abolition of slavery, for instance, was immensely costly for slave owners, yet because basic human rights were violated, the costs to the slave owner of abolishing slavery were not relevant. This is so because human rights are understood to establish duties and responsibilities that are not diminished by economic self-interest.
- If climate change is a human rights problem, compensation is due to those whose rights have been violated (Caney 2010). Therefore, the human

rights approach imposes on nations a duty to prevent climate refugees and a responsibility to help people adapt to climate impacts and pay costs of relocation and compensation for harms experienced. (See the section on ethics below for a discussion of ethical and legal concepts that makes nations responsible for adaptation to climate change and compensation for climate change-induced harms.)

- Human rights apply to each and every human being because they are based on the idea that all human beings are born free and are entitled to certain rights. For this reason, human beings are entitled to be protected from being relocated without consent even within their own country if human-induced climate change makes continued subsistence in areas where people live impossible. Thus a human rights approach to climate change creates legal obligations for nations to prevent climate change that will force people to relocate not only to other nations but domestically when climate change makes human subsistence impossible.
- If it is a human right not to suffer a particular harm, it is still wrong to violate that right just because one can pay compensation. It is, for instance, wrong for a nation to refuse to lessen a climate change threat that will violate people's human rights even if those harmed can be paid compensation.
- Human rights usually take priority over other human values such as efficiency and promoting happiness. This is so because rights are usually understood to trump consequences; in philosophical terms they are deontological not consequentialist-based obligations.
- Governments have a duty to protect all citizens' human rights by law. This duty is understood to impose a responsibility on nations to adopt laws to protect human rights. If, then, climate change is violating human rights, nations have a duty to pass laws to prevent harms cause by climate change.
- According to human rights law all rights have: (a) a right-holder, usually all the citizens of a nation, that is the party who has the right, (b) an object, or what the right is, and (c) an addressee, the party who must make the right available (Moecki et al. 2010). For human rights violated by climate change, the rights-holder is all the citizens of the nation that promised to protect human rights, the addressee is the nation or other government entity, courts or legislatures in the nation in which the right holder lives, and the object is the rights to life, health and sustainable food among many other human rights infringed by climate change. For this reason, people threatened with the need to leave their community to protect themselves against climate change impacts have a right to petition their governments to protect them from climate change impacts.
- Human rights law creates obligations for nations to protect, provide and fulfil the human rights of their citizens that the nations have agreed to in ratifying human rights treaties.
- The duty to protect the human rights of its citizens requires governments to protect citizens not only from the acts of the government that would

deprive citizens of human rights but also to protect citizens from the climate change-causing activities of entities within the nation's jurisdiction that contribute to their harm. Thus, under a human rights approach to climate change, nations have a duty to take action to prevent entities within their jurisdiction with high ghg emission to reduce such emissions.

- A human rights approach to climate refugee problems has the advantage of providing the opportunity for potential climate refugees to participate in an expanding existing international human rights legal structure which allows individuals to make complaints against nations who are failing to provide the human rights protections it agreed to when it ratified any one of many international or regional human rights treaties. Thus a complaining party whose human rights are violated may appeal to human rights committees and tribunals that have been established by human rights treaties to assure that the human rights protected under the treaties are complied with. (For a list of existing human rights legal treaties and committees see, Office of High Commissioner for Human Rights 2015.) By filing complaints with appropriate human rights committees and tribunals, climate refugees can usually have their human rights violations investigated and adjudicated. Furthermore, in the case of human rights protected by the European, Africa, an Inter-American regional human rights regimes, the merits of individual complaints can be adjudicated in human rights courts that have been agreed to by nations that have acceded to the jurisdiction of these courts. Under existing human rights regimes, nations must respond to complaints from those citizens who allege that a nation is failing to protect their human rights. After reviewing the complete record established by a complaint, either a human rights committee or a human rights court will adjudicate the merits of the complaint.

Limitations of a Human Rights Approach to Climate Refugee Problems

Some of the limitations of a human rights approach to the problems of climate refugees include:

- Because nations usually have duties only to their citizens under human rights law, it is often not clear what the duties of nations are to citizens living outside their jurisdiction. This is known as the problem of 'extraterritoriality'. Therefore, if a person is forced to leave his or her community or nation because of climate change caused by other nations, that citizen has no clear right to use existing human rights law as a remedy against foreign national governments. The citizen, however, can always petition his or her own government to do what it can to reduce the threat of climate change.
- International treaties which create human rights obligations for nations have weak enforcement capability. Although a citizen of a nation that has

ratified any of the international human rights treaties has a right to file a complaint against his or her nation for failing to protect the citizen against human rights violations, if the nation refuses to provide the human rights protection there is usually no way of forcing the nation to do so unless the human rights violations are so extraordinarily destructive that the UN Security Council can be convinced to act. Thus, if nations ultimately fail to provide the human rights protections they have agreed to under human rights treaties, the only remaining remedy is to attempt to shame the nation publically for its unwillingness to provide the promised human rights protections. However, because all nations that have ratified one of the major human rights treaties must report periodically to the committees established by the treaties, there is some hope that nations not currently providing the human rights protections they have agreed to will improve performance over time.

- Because climate change is a problem to which all nations contribute, courts and international rights tribunals will have difficulty in determining the appropriate allocation of responsibility among nations. This is the problem of allocating responsibility discussed above. Although various equity frameworks that could serve as a basis for allocating responsibility among nations for climate change are under discussion in international climate negotiations, no such framework has yet been agreed to by the international community that could be used by courts or human rights tribunals to guide them on how to allocate responsibility for climate change-caused damages or the costs of reasonable adaptation to a changing climate. For this reason, a human right's approach to the problem of climate refugees is not likely to determine specific financial remedies to cover relocation costs or pay compensation for damages until an equity framework for allocating national responsibility for climate change is agreed to by the international community or determined by a court.
- The existing human rights regimes are not well suited to deal with the hundreds of thousands of complaints that could be filed by individual climate refugees. If too many climate refugees file complaints with a human rights tribunal, climate refugee issues will completely overwhelm the human rights legal regimes that now exist around the world.
- Human rights complaints often take many years to wind their way through existing human rights tribunals. The existing human rights legal regimes are not likely therefore to provide relief for climate refugees fast enough to prevent the suffering that climate refugees often experience.

Conclusions about a Human Rights Approach to Climate Refugee Problems

As we have seen there are significant limitations in using a human rights approach to resolve climate refugee problems including territorial limitations on national human rights obligations, weak enforcement capability among human rights tribunals and challenges entailed by the problem of allocating responsibility. Despite these limitations, citizens around the world seeking to make nations responsible for the problems of human suffering caused by the creation of climate refugees can nevertheless use a human rights approach as a weapon to pressure governments for failing to reduce the threat of climate change or to provide funding for damages experienced by climate refugees on normative and ethical grounds (to be discussed in the next section). Because the nations that have ratified human rights treaties have agreed to have their performance on their implementation of human rights promises reviewed on a periodic basis, usually either every two or four years, citizens and NGOs have a regular opportunity to pressure nations and shame them for their failure to provide promised human rights protections for climate refugees.

Because human rights law imposes legal duties on nations to ensure that human rights protections are enjoyed by their citizens, if courts eventually adjudicate climate change obligations, human rights law is likely to be considered in determining elements of national responsibility for climate change. For instance, because the cost to polluters is not a legitimate excuse under human rights law for failing to ensure that human rights protections are achieved, litigation to protect the human rights of potential climate refugees based upon human rights law could limit the force of arguments made by nations based upon costs to them. Thus, human rights law may be relevant to future litigation on climate change responsibilities.

Ethical and Legal Obligations of High-Emitting Nations to Climate Refugees

Thus far we have described the limitations under current law to provide justice and adequate remedies for the enormous hardships that climate change refugees face. Under existing law, climate refugees will likely continue to suffer from two problems in particular for which current law provides no adequate resolution.

The first is finding an acceptable place to move to when conditions in the refugees' nation of origin become intolerable because of climate change. In fact, some small island developing states that will be soon inundated by rising seas are already beginning to face this problem. A huge question for them is which nations have a duty to accept them. Under current law there is no clear duty on nations to accommodate climate refugees.

The second major problem under existing law relevant to climate refugees is the lack of clear duty on those who are most responsible for climate change to compensate refugees for the climate change-caused harms they have or will suffer. Given that climate change is an existential threat to some people and places where millions of poor people now live, there is a huge need to develop new international law to provide adequate remedies for climate refugees. This section examines some of the ethical principles which should serve as a basis for expanded law on climate refugees. The section describes ethical principles for concluding that nations that have been emitting ghgs at levels above their fair share of safe global emissions have a duty to enact laws that provide adequate remedies for climate refugees. The section also identifies legal principles that have been adopted by the international community that are consistent with these ethical principles.

Without doubt, those nations that have been consistently emitting ghgs above their fair share of safe global emissions have clear ethical duties to amend existing law to provide adequate remedies for these two problems. As the recent 2014 IPCC, Working Group III, report concluded, after reviewing the extensive ethical and legal literature on responsibility for climate change damages:

> Common sense ethics (and legal practice) hold persons responsible for harms or risks they knowingly impose or could have reasonably foreseen, and in certain cases, regardless of whether they could have been foreseen (IPCC 2014b: AR5, WG III, ch. 4, p. 49).

Thus those who cause climate change have an ethical responsibility to protect those who could be seriously harmed by human-induced warming, by funding responsible adaptation measures and compensating those who are harmed. This is a conclusion that follows from numerous ethical theories and several international law principles.

Almost all the world's religions, basic human rights theories and numerous other ethical arguments hold that no person has a right to greatly harm someone else without their consent. In fact, as we have seen, the right to life and security is considered a core human rights principle that has been accepted by almost all nations in the world. Thus, all nations that are responsible for the violation of human rights caused by climate change have clear duties to assure that human rights are enjoyed and that harms caused by climate change are compensated for.

Some nations have denied responsibility for compensation and adaptation costs in climate change negotiations. Yet norms about responsibility for damages from human-induced climate change are well established not only by most ethical theories but also in a variety of international agreements, including the Rio Declaration on Environment and Development (UN 1992b) and the United Nations Framework Convention on Climate Change (UN 1992a).

The Rio Declaration on Environment and Development states in relevant part:

- States have, in accordance with the Charter of the United Nations and the principles of international law, the sovereign right to exploit their own resources pursuant to their own environmental and developmental policies, and the responsibility *to ensure that activities within their jurisdiction or control do not cause damage to the environment of other States or of areas beyond the limits of national jurisdiction* (UN 1992b: Principle 2, emphasis added).
- National authorities should endeavor to promote the internalization of environmental costs and the use of economic instruments, taking into account the approach that *the polluter should, in principle, bear*

the cost of pollution, with due regard to the public interest and without distorting international trade and investment (UN 1992b: Principle 16, emphasis added).
- States shall develop national law regarding liability and compensation for the victims of pollution and other environmental damage. States shall also cooperate in an expeditious and more determined manner to develop further international law *regarding liability and compensation for adverse effects of environmental damage caused by activities within their jurisdiction or control to areas beyond their jurisdiction* (UN 1992b: Principle 13, emphasis added).

Additional norms relevant to national responsibility for damages caused by one nation to another are contained in the United Nations Framework Convention on Climate Change, including:

- Recalling also that States have, in accordance with the Charter of the United Nations and the principles of international law, the sovereign right to exploit their own resources pursuant to their own environmental and developmental policies, *and the responsibility to ensure that activities within their jurisdiction or control do not cause damage to the environment of other States or of areas beyond the limits of national jurisdiction* (UN 1992a: Preface, emphasis added).
- The Parties should protect the climate system for the benefit of present and future generations of humankind, *on the basis of equity and in accordance with their common but differentiated responsibilities and respective capabilities*. Accordingly, *the developed country Parties should take the lead in combating climate change and the adverse effects thereof* (UN 1992a: Art. 3, emphasis added).
- The Parties should take precautionary measures to anticipate, prevent, or minimize the causes of climate change and mitigate its adverse effects. Where there are threats of serious or irreversible damage, lack of full scientific certainty should not be used as a reason for postponing such measures, taking into account that policies and measures to deal with climate change should be cost-effective so as to ensure global benefits at the lowest possible cost (UN 1992a: Art 3).
- *The developed country Parties* and other developed Parties included in Annex II *shall also assist the developing country Parties that are particularly vulnerable to the adverse effects of climate change in meeting costs of adaptation to those adverse effects* (UN 1992a: Art 4, para. 4, emphasis added).

These provisions of international law have been agreed to by almost all nations and establish clear national responsibilities to: (a) not harm others beyond their jurisdiction by activities that cause climate change, (b) pay for the damages to those beyond their borders who are harmed by excessive domestic ghg emissions, (c) pay for the adaptation costs of persons who need to respond to impending climate change harms, and (d) not use scientific uncertainty as an excuse for failing to take protective action.

We have also seen above that the duty to protect and compensate refugees can also be derived from well settled human rights law.

Thus far we have explained why high-emitting nations have clear ethical and legal duties to fund both refugees' reasonable adaptation costs needed to protect them from climate change and to compensate climate refugees for climate change damages they have sustained. Yet, there are a number of issues that make it difficult to say precisely what levels of compensation or funding high emitting nations should contribute to these financial obligations. Looking at these issues in detail is beyond the scope of this chapter. (For more detailed analysis of these difficulties see Brown 2013: ch. 7; and Grasso 2009.)

These issues include: (a) the need to determine when the obligation of any nation is triggered by historical ghg emissions, (b) difficulties in determining which adaptation and compensation needs are attributable to human-induced warming versus natural variability, (c) challenges in allocating responsibilities among all nations that have emitted ghg above their fair share of safe global emissions, (e) challenges in prioritizing limited funds among all adaptation and compensation needs, and (f) the need to set funding priorities in consultation with those who are vulnerable to climate change impacts as a matter of procedural justice.

Thus although there are many challenges to determining the precise obligations on nations for refugees' adaptation and compensation needs, these difficulties do not justify nations ignoring their obligations to climate refugees. The fact that there are challenges in working through what precisely are any nation's obligations for climate change is not justification for that nation failing to fund reasonable adaptation needs or compensation for losses and damages experienced by climate refugees.

Conclusion

We have demonstrated that international refugee law, civil tort law and human rights law have significant limitations in their ability to protect climate refugees. This is true despite strong ethical and international principles that would make those responsible for causing climate change responsible for the harms experienced by climate change refugees.

Therefore both the precise responsibility for any nation's funding obligations to climate refugees for adaptation and damages and which nations should accept climate refugees should be determined by a new Protocol wherein specific national obligations are proportioned on the basis of national ghg emissions levels, taking per capita and historical emissions levels into account, in developing allocation formulas both for accepting climate refugees and for funding the reasonable adaptation and compensation costs of climate refugees.

As we have seen, a strong argument can be made that new laws accomplishing these objectives are already required by clear ethical and legal international law principles.

References

Bonano. C., Zetter, R. and Morris, T., 2008, *Environmentally Displaced People: Understanding the Linkages Between Environmental Change, Likelihoods and Forced Migration*, Policy Briefing Series, Refugee Studies Centre, University of Oxford, Oxford.

Brown, Donald, 2013, *Climate Change Ethics: Navigating the Perfect Moral Storm*, Routledge and Earthscan, London and New York.

Butti, L., 2011, 'The Tortuous Road to Liability: A Critical Survey on Climate Change Litigation', *Sustainable Development Law and Policy*, 11.2, 32–6 and 82–4 (Climate Law Reporter), http://digitalcommons.wcl.american.edu/cgi/viewcontent.cgi?article=1467&context=sdlp (accessed 22 May 2014).

Caney, Simon, 2010, 'Climate Change, Human Rights and Moral Thresholds', in Gardiner, S., Caney, S., Jamieson, D., and Shue, H., eds, *Climate Ethics: Essential Readings*, Oxford University Press, New York, pp. 163–80.

Cartagena Declaration on Refugees, 1984, Annual Report of the Inter-American Commission on Human Rights, OAS Doc. OEA/Ser.L/V/II.66/doc.10, rev. 1 (1984–85), www1.umn.edu/humanrts/instree/cartagena1984.htm (accessed 25 May 2014).

Convention on the Status of Refugees, 1951 (Convention, 1951), 189 UN 137, adopted 28 July 1951, entered into force 22 April 1954.

Davenport, C., 2014, 'Climate Change Deemed Growing Security Threat by Military Researchers', *New York Times*, www.nytimes.com/2014/05/14/us/politics/climate-change-deemed-growing-security-threat-by-military-researchers.html (accessed 22 May 2014).

Edwards, A., 2012, 'Climate Change and International Refugee Law', in Rayfuse, R. and Scott, S., eds, *International Law in the Era of Climate Change*, Edward Elgar, Cheltenham, UK and Northampton, MA, pp. 58–83.

Femia, F. and Werrell, C., 2014, 'Syria: Climate Change, Drought and Social Unrest', *Climate and Security*, http://climateandsecurity.org/2012/02/29/syria-climate-change-drought-and-social-unrest/ (accessed 24 May 2014).

Freccia, Tim, 2014, 'Climate Change Causes Violence', *SciDev*, www.scidev.net/global/conflict/news/climate-change-causes-rise-in-violence.html (accessed 21 May 2014).

Grasso, M., 2009, 'An Ethical Approach to Adaptation Funding', *Global Environmental Change*, www.yumpu.com/en/document/view/9873146/

an-ethical-approach-to-climate-adaptation-finance-marco-grasso#sthash.ZWunx03Y.dpuf (accessed 21 May 2014).

Guiding Principles on Internal Displacement (UN GPID) UN Doc. E/CN.4/1998/53/Add.2 (1998), noted in Comm. Hum. Rts. res. 1998/50, www1.umn.edu/humanrts/instree/GuidingPrinciplesonInternalDisplacement.htm (accessed 24 May 2014).

Human Rights Education Association (HREA), 2003, 'Study Guide: The Rights of Refugees', www1.umn.edu/humanrts/edumat/studyguides/refugees.htm (accessed 23 May 2014).

Intergovernmental Panel on Climate Change (IPCC), 2014a, 'IPCC Report: A Changing Climate Creates Pervasive Risks but Opportunities Exist for Effective Responses', www.ipcc.ch/pdf/ar5/pr_wg2/140330_pr_wgII_spm_en.pdf (accessed 19 May 2014).

——, 2014b, *Working Group III, Mitigation of Climate Change*, http://www.ipcc.ch/report/ar5/wg3/ (accessed 1 February 2015).

International Council on Human Rights Policy (ICHRP), 2008, *Climate Change and Human Rights: A Rough Guide*, www.ichrp.org/files/reports/45/136_report.pdf (accessed 24 May 2014).

Kivalina v. ExxonMobil Corporation, et al. 696 F.3d 849 (9th Cir., 2012).

Moeckli, D., Shah, S., Sivakumaran, S. and Harris, D., 2010, *Human Rights Law*, Oxford University Press, Oxford, New York.

Office of the High Commissioner for Human Rights (OHCHR), 2015, http://www.ohchr.org/EN/HRBodies/Pages/TreatyBodies.aspx (accessed 14 May 2014).

Organization of African Unity (OAU), 1969, Convention Governing the Specific Aspects of Refugee Problems in Africa (OAU Convention), 1001 UNTS 45, www/refworld.org/docid/3ae6b36018.html (accessed 25 May 2014).

Pearce, Fred, 2014, 'UN Climate Report Is Cautious on Making Specific Predictions', *Yale Environment 360*, http://e360.yale.edu/feature/un_climate_report_is_cautious_on_making_specific_predictions/2750/ (accessed 21 May 2014).

Protocol Relating to the Status of Refugees, 1967 (Protocol, 1967), 606 UNTS 267, entered into force 4 October 1967, www1.umn.edu/humanrts/instree/v2prsr.htm (accessed 25 May 2014).

Rule of Law in Armed Conflicts Project (RULAC), 2014, *International Refugee Law*, www.geneva-academy.ch/RULAC/international_refugee_law.php (accessed 21 May 2014).

Spencer, B., 2014, 'UK Warned of "Climate Change Flood of Refugees": Droughts and Heatwaves Could Force Millions to Flee Their Country', *Daily Mail*, www.dailymail.co.uk/news/article-2593851/UK-warned-climate-change-flood-refugees-Droughts-heatwaves-force-millions-flee-country.html (accessed 21 May 2014).

United Nations (UN), 1992a, United Nations Framework Convention on Climate Change, UN Doc. A/AC237/18.

——, 1992b, The Rio Declaration on Environment and Development, UN Doc. A/CONF.151/26.

Vidal, John, 2009, 'Global Warming Could Create 150 Million "Climate Refugees" by 2050', *The Guardian*, www.theguardian.com/environment/2009/nov/03/global-warming-climate-refugees (accessed 21 May 2014).

Chapter 3

Escape from Development and the Plunder of Resources: Causality and Responsibility

Laura Westra

Introduction

> A number of domestic political issues take shape at the nexus of what Sassen terms 'denationalized economic life and renationalized political life', including those concerned with labor, agriculture, manufacturing, energy, and the environment. Each of these generates calls for national preferences that chafe against free-market contexts. However, nothing rivals the image of immigrant hordes as an incitement to xenophobic nationalism and to demands for fierce state protectionism, amid globalization (Brown 2010: 68–9; Sassen 1996: xii).

The same citizen who concurs loudly with all those who protest against immigrants – largely seen as attacking the few available jobs in an era of austerity and depressed economics – most often fails to revolt against, or even notice the take-over of her government by the powers of legalized economics that cause both the need for austerity measures and economic depressions (Westra, L. 2012: 80–81). The ongoing take-over by corporate power of government institutions is in direct conflict with institutional 'cosmopolitanism', which reigned in Europe at the time of the formation of states in medieval times (Glenn 2013: 86–92).

The historical development of states, could not be more different than what is present in state governance today. The papal teachings coexisted with a juridical 'corpus Christianum', as empire and church 'were associated with the notion of unity' (Glenn 2013: 38). Yet that 'unity' did not ensure that the King's authority would be beyond critique, in fact in the thirteenth century the law and its fundamental norms 'provides explicitly for rejection of unlawful acts by those in authority', as natural law was seen 'to limit the sovereignty of the prince' (Glenn 2013: 45).

At any rate, the early formal states developed boundaries, imprecise though these were: they were 'soft border zones', administered by appointed noblemen ('marquises'). At that time, the borders were not viewed as impenetrable limits of secular authority; this is confirmed in the writings of Marsilius of Padua, who defended 'the emperor' against the Pope (Glenn 2013: 66; Ullman 1988). Important written legal codes contribute to the definition of borders, except in the case of Indigenous peoples whose unwritten laws lead to the presence of 'aboriginal rights' and 'aboriginal title', based in part on unwritten law, but also on treaty rights: both are admitted and recognized in Canada (Fluker 2014; Morse 2002; Westra 2007).

Further, in many states, specific religions offer a 'powerful normative background', based on such religions as Confucianism or Buddhism, for instance, in contrast with written laws, all of which influences strongly the composition of the state (Glenn 2013: 68). But the state only achieves closure, when it has achieved a written constitution:

> A written constitution is essential for a successful revolution since it is the marker of a 'revolutionary zero hour', a rupture with an ancient regime. As an element of closure, the written constitution also nationalizes the constitutional order, at least for a time, and in some measure, and depending on its success (Glenn 2013: 70).

However, even this 'closure' does not eliminate the presence of natural law, after the formation of states, as it was still being taught at universities in the seventeenth and eighteenth centuries, and was viewed as a 'dominant form of moral and political thought' as it emerged, for instance, in the work of Grotius in the sixteenth century, and continues to exist. Today it is embodied in *jus cogens* norms, and the resulting *erga omnes* obligations, albeit with very limited practical reach.

At any rate, a unified state is necessary in order to have borders, and in order 'to institutionalize the connection between people and the territorial state through the nation of citizenship' (Glenn 2013: 187):

> This modern notion of citizenship was appropriate for a state territorially defined, but it presents two major deficiencies: The first is that it has no inherent, historically justified, content. Content had to be provided by legislation, so we see clearly in relation to citizenship, the fundamental information base of all forms of human identity. The citizens of a state are perhaps most clearly of all an epistemic community, there is no inherent citizenship; it is stipulated by national legislators for each state (Glenn 2013: 187).

What emerges from Glenn's analysis is the weakness, the vagueness, of the notion of citizenship, so that its entitlements remain equally vague, and the reasons for the sharp distinction between citizens and non-citizens far less sharply defined than expected. Hence we can raise the question of what is the difference between the concept of a cosmopolitan citizen, and that of a citizen, as communally construed and territorially bound.

By some standards, the citizens of many democratic countries cannot be called true 'citizens', for instance, for Aristotle, citizens were people who were actively involved in the running of their citystate, and that was their defining characteristic (Westra 2010: 8–25). For Aristotle, the involved, active citizen has a clear goal: to promote the 'good life' for his city-state:

> The good life is the chief end for both the community as a whole and for each of us individually. But men also come together and form and maintain political associations merely for the sake of life … (Aristotle, *The Politics*).

Today's democratic states are organized and run in direct conflict with Aristotelian doctrine; the 'common good', happiness itself viewed as a moral ideal, no longer exists as the goal of any state, as this has been replaced by the right to individual choices and preferences, with no specific connection to morality. Thus we can isolate two basic components of citizenship for Aristotle, the commitment to and involvement in civic life, and the goal of helping to achieve the good life for the 'state' as a whole.

The modern citizen has no such lofty ideals and for the most part does not participate in the running of the government, beyond voting at regular intervals. Thus protesters, those who participate in social movements, from Civil Rights to Occupy, the Arab Spring participants, and in Canada, the Idle No More movement, together with many others around the world, appear to be the only groups of citizens who are deliberately active in attempting to reach positive change in their governing institutions, and are inspired by an ideal (Westra 2014b).

In those cases, whether or not they are territorially based, they might be defined as the only true 'cosmopolitan citizens' beyond their respective national origins. Thus it seems clear that territorial locations cannot be the only distinguishing characteristics of citizens. This was also noted in Chapter 1, as today's existence of 'post-national citizens', appears to have a lot more in common with cosmopolitan beliefs and interests, at least in principle.

Citizenship, Nationality and Migration

> The foreign-born population in contemporary states is now systematically increasing. It now represents one-third of the entire population of Luxembourg, one-quarter of the population of Switzerland, one-fifth that of Canada (Glenn 2013: 193).

It is hard to find the rights or respect due to transnational citizens, when it seems obvious that even the very personhood of migrants seems to be on hold for, in fact in question by, many governments. In February 2014, even Switzerland, a model of a peaceful, civilized state, decided to defy Europe's open-borders regulations, by deciding to refuse migrants, with the approval of most of their own citizenry. The question is how serious is the concept of personhood in law, when it can simply disappear when territoriality is no longer present?

This raises the further question of the true reach of UN human rights instruments, which do not match the disjunct of human rights personhood, on the one hand, and the diminished personhood of aliens and migrants, on the other (Bosniak 2010). Thus the presence and the treatment of migrants brings into question the very notion of equality before the law (Glenn 2013: 194), for all that – in theory – it is a cherished tenet of most so-called democratic states.

The basic common denominator of all asylum seekers, I have argued, is their poverty, which makes them despair of ever being able to better their situation and that of their families. Hence, what they all share is either the lack of remunerated employment in developed countries and urban settings, or a complete lack of resources, in underdeveloped areas where Indigenous and other land-based communities exist. Globalization touches each person in the globe, in various ways, all of which purports to bring 'advancement', 'progress' or 'development' to those affected by corporate activities.

The results of these impacts on urban workers can be considered first, not because they are more worthy of consideration, but because they are thought of less as poverty-stricken than those whose subsistence is based on direct access to land and water on their lands.

It is an accepted fact that while corporations' incomes are growing beyond those of several countries, their 'adjustments' have not trickled down to the workers they employ (Rifkin 1995: 166–7):

> The mounting statistics reveal a workforce in retreat in almost every sector. Forced to compete with automation on the one hand, and a global labor pool on the other, American workers find themselves squeezed even closer to the margins of economic survival (Rifkin 1995: 168).

This dated analysis does not eventually show improvement in the next 20 years or so. In fact, the same author, later, speaks of the 'slow death of the American dream':

> The first thing to understand about the American Dream is that from the very beginning it was meant to be exclusive to America. It was never meant to be a dream shared with or exported to the rest of the world. Its power rested in its particularism, not its universalism … Its exclusivity is now what makes it increasingly suspect and inappropriate in a world that is beginning to forge a global consciousness (Rifkin 2004: 17).

Relentlessly, the American Dream of hard work and almost instant rewards has given way to an increasingly unjustified optimism on the part of American workers, whose poverty can be contrasted to the glaring unfairness of the economic inequality that persists and increases, and which owes nothing to 'hard work' or other basic virtues:

> What is striking about the United States is that while the level of inequality generated by the market – a market shaped and distorted by politics and rent seeking – is higher than in other advanced industrial countries, it does less to temper this inequality through tax and expenditure programs. And as the

> market-generated inequality has increased, our government has done less and less (Stiglitz 2012: 74).

In the face of these mounting inequalities, workers' wages have certainly not kept pace with the riches at the top. Unions have lost a lot of the hard-won gains achieved in the 1970s and 1980s, while 'the threat of capital outflow, should workers get too demanding about rights and wages, keeps workers wages low' (Stiglitz 2012: 60). Now if the situation is so dire in a country generally believed to be rich, powerful and the very home of opportunity for the poor, we can easily extrapolate from this situation to the conditions of workers in the offshore corporations around the globe.

And what is indeed the final result of the richest country's race to the bottom is the presence of atrocious conditions for workers in offshore industrial developments, and the corresponding poverty of those not lucky enough to secure any employment at all: that is, poverty that is deep and all pervasive enough to force migration. As well, although US citizens are not among asylum seekers, their situation strongly influences their own reactions, thus that of their asylum seekers from Mexico and elsewhere, attempting to be accepted by the US to gain opportunity for a better life.

Globalization and Workers' Rights

> ... the UN Secretary Generally, in establishing in 1999 the UN's Global Compact Program (a Joint project of the UN and the world's business leaders), noted two distinct sets of duties of corporations: to respect human rights 'within their sphere of influence', and to avoid 'being complicit in human rights abuses' – the latter term referring to corporate involvement in governmental action (Ratner 2001–2002: 510).

Much of what was discussed thus far contains lack of respect for human rights, within its 'sphere of influence' (broadly understood), and 'complicity in human rights abuses' (Ratner 2001–2002: 510), and we will return to some of those issues and the litigation that reflects them below. But there is a class of individuals, that is, those employed by the corporation, whose rights have been considered far longer than the less obvious rights we have discussed in this chapter:

> ... the ILO suggests that governments, labour unions and business leaders view the sphere of employer-employee relations as an appropriate target for detailed international regulation (Ratner 2001–2002: 509).

The International Labour Organization (ILO 1989) has defended worker's rights, starting from the Treaty of Versailles of 1919, and established the principle 'to abolish the injustice, hardship and privation' suffered by workers and 'to guarantee fair and humane conditions of labour' (Steiner and Alton 2000: 242).

Many of the standards proposed by the ILO are now covered under economic and social rights, and other conventions that deal with freedom of association and the right to organize trade unions, forced labour, minimum working age, hours of work, weekly rest, sickness protection, accident insurance, invalidity and old age insurance and freedom from discrimination in employment (Steiner and Alston 2000: 242).

In 1941, US President Roosevelt nominated 'freedom from want' as one of the four freedoms he supported. He said:

> We have come to a clear realization of the fact that the individual freedom cannot exist without economic security and independence. Necessitous men are not free men. In our day these economic truths have become accepted as self-evident. We have accepted, so to speak, a second bill of rights, under which a new basis of security and prosperity can be established for all – regardless of station, race, or creed (Eleventh Annual Message to Congress, 11 January 1949: 2881).

After outlining details of his vision, Roosevelt adds 'All of these rights spell security' (Eleventh Annual Message to Congress, 11 January 1949: 2881). The rights outlined by Roosevelt and those named in the work of the UN preparatory committee, were foundational for the drafting of the Universal Declaration of Human Rights (1948), and many were further spelled out in the wording of the two Covenants of 1966 (Steiner and Alston 2000: 244–5).

Hence it is clear that, although the right to be free from toxic exposures and other chemical substances noxious to our health and development are not established in international law, workers' rights come a lot closer to a level of security not enjoyed by others within the corporate 'sphere of influence'. Of course codification of a right is by no means the same as its implementation. Additionally, there are now a host of situations that even Roosevelt at his best and most idealistic could not have anticipated.

Regarding workers' rights, the most significant difference between today and Roosevelt's times may be found in the phenomenon of globalization, coupled with the increasing emergence of offshore production, which effectively moved the requirements of worker's rights to no-man's land. indeed, the US discovered the advantages of contracting out some of its most dubious operations. A recent example of that phenomenon can be found in the section on 'Toxic Trespass' in my work on 'State Terrorism', and the use of Dyn-Corp to perform illegal services for the CIA. In fact extraordinary renditions are only a small portion of the work of such 'contractors': the gaolers of Abu-Ghraib were also not regulated by any military code or other national regulation; and the torturers themselves were located in those parts of the world where torture was legally practised (Westra, L. 2012: ch. 4).

In a similar vein, multi-national companies (MNCs) can and do routinely contract parts of their manufacturing offshore, regardless of the absence of enforceable or enforced human/workers' rights at those locations:

> Marxists bemoan how workers are treated simply as cogs in this wheel of capitalist efficiency, compelled by the labour market to produce any good when demand for it increases and opportunity for capitalist profit making arises. Marxists argue this 'alienates' workers from a social activity central to their lives, and will eventually foment resistance (Westra, R. 2012: 116).

The 'demand' and 'opportunity' converge offshore, as resource and labour-rich third world countries provide more favourable conditions than those present in the West, where all costs of production, including labour, are higher.

For instance, China's regime now provides the sort of workforce that no longer exists in the West, with worker's conditions amounting to real slavery: workers are compelled to work, mobility is non-existent, migrants have no protection and no guaranteed remuneration, and 15-hour workdays are routine, as is child labour (Westra, R. 2012: 162–5; see also pp. 230–31, nn. 80–89).

Essentially, all MNCs have initiated a system of relocation for both their manufacturing and assembly operations, in the quest for even less regulated regimes than those they face in the home country (Westra, R. 2012: 75). A banner example of offshore relocation of corporate operations, beyond a partial manufacturing and assembly, is of course the infamous Bhopal situation, where thousands of workers perished in a disaster that laid bare a total lack of public health and environmental regulations in India, culminating in the effect of Union Carbide's disinformation campaign, which convinced workers that they were producing 'good medicine for plants' (Baxi 2010).

That blatant lie convinced the workers it would be safe to move into a 'shantytown' adjacent to the toxic effluents from the plant itself. The night of the final explosion should qualify as an example of 'toxic terrorism', and spur citizens around the world to demand urgently a different 'war on terror', far more justifiable than the ongoing one, given the numbers of victims that exist from various forms of toxic exposure.

There is no need to elaborate further the effects on the health and safety of workers, present not only by chemical and pesticide operations, but also by unregulated third world offshore havens. The lack of regulatory infrastructure in India and in China and other so-called 'developing countries' is well known. The beneficiaries from this general retreat from laws and regulations are, of course, the corporations themselves, the power of which has grown exponentially. A prime example is the wealth and power of Wal-Mart:

> Wal-Mart has indeed become emblematic of a transformation in organization of value-claims themselves … Logistics, a term co-opted from the military, is the term encompassing the state-of-the-art way goods are moved across such networks and supply chains. Wal-Mart, for example, handles 85 per cent of supply chain management in house (Westra, R. 2012: 89).

The working conditions and health of workers is not Wal-Mart's concern, and the point is hardly worthy of elaboration. But there are also many operations in North America, where the racial background or ethnicity of the workers ensures that no serious effort is made to ensure not only their health, but even their survival.

It seems that the 'development' brought by globalization is for the sole and exclusive benefit of the corporations and the governments that support them both in North America and beyond. In the third world, the working conditions offered by industry are joined by the elimination of the resources of local communities, either through pollution or appropriation, as we shall see below. The question that must be answered is, who is at fault? Who is responsible for this ongoing story of irresponsibility and harms, perpetrated with impunity? Hence, before looking at the third world jurisprudence and conditions, it is necessary that we pause and raise the question of responsibility and accountability of those whose power originates the first victimization of impoverished people, which leads to migrations and the further victimization of asylum seekers.

The Question of Responsibility for Asylum Seekers: Before the Flight

> 1. Responsibility as a *cause*. 'Responsible for' can in a number of contexts be replaced by 'caused' or 'to have as a consequence' or some such expression that indicates a causal connection (Bovens 1998: 24).

This paragraph describes only one of the five aspects of responsibility listed by Mark Bovens, as an adaptation of H.L. Hart's analysis of that topic (Hart 1968: 211–30). The others are (2) responsibility as *accountability*, or 'liability-responsibility' (Hart 1968: 215), which captures the moral and political sense of the term, as well as its important legal aspect; (3) responsibility as *capacity*, that is the ability to exercise responsibility; (4) responsibility as a *task*, or "role-responsibility" (Hart 1968: 212), which is particularly significant given that those who reach a decision that will result in eventual extreme conditions that produce flight can only do so in their role or function within an organization (or institution), as no individual acting as such can possibly produce the circumstances that affect great numbers of migrants.

Finally, there is responsibility as a *virtue*, which is not part of Hart's legal discussion but, according to Bovens, should be considered as part of Hart's 'role responsibility', which defines how that role is played (Bovens 1998: 26). Hence we could and should raise several questions about how the 'task' or the 'role' is played by authorities. For instance, who is responsible for the policies that result in harm and, eventually, in migrations? Bovens raises the question in his discussion of 'passive responsibility', which he views as particularly relevant as we consider the 'behaviour of complex organizations':

> It is impossible to produce an unambiguous and universally acceptable list of criteria for responsibility in the sense of accountability. Classic forms are after all the subject of classic debates … Political, legal, and moral responsibility, for example, do not always coincide (Bovens 1998: 28).

Yet the question of when does a government official or a corporate executive officer (CEO) behave responsibly is basic to an analysis of the causal connection existing between the roles/tasks assigned to both, and the ensuing results. The question of the human right's of asylum seekers is so grave that it is absolutely necessary to start by analysing that causal nexus. Their plight is not initiated when they arrive on foreign soil as they try to land when arriving from the sea. Yet that is where the best known jurists and legal scholars who specialize on regimes regarding asylum seekers focus their work. That is, of course, necessary, but it is not sufficient, if we intend to deal properly with the issue, and if we intend to understand fully both the legal and the moral implications of their plight.

In fact, the victimization of such people has a long development, a history that cannot be ignored, as boatload follows boatload of desperate migrants (Raveendram 2012: 1277–312). As well, we cannot limit our quest for that nexus by limiting our research only to proximate causes. We need to reach much further instead, to discover the seeds, the origin s of their situation (Westra 2014b: chs 7, 8). I have argued about the great number of existing victims of legal activities, everywhere in the world: I discuss both the victims of legal persons, and of government activities in conflicts. At this time, Chapter 4 will address the latter while this chapter discusses the former.

However, it is not only legal corporate persons who are responsible for the various ills that prompt migrations, but, as noted in the previous chapter regarding climate refugees, the victimization also arises from complicit governments. We can start with Bovens' analysis of what he terms 'passive responsibility' which, he argues, includes 'four categories according to which the diverse criteria for responsibility as accountability can be classified':

1. transgression of a norm
2. causal connection
3. blameworthiness
4. relationship with the agent (Bovens 1998: 28–30).

As we consider each of these aspects of responsibility, we will see how many aspects of corporate/bureaucratic behaviour are (or should be) accountable/ responsible for the development of situations that foster grave human rights breaches, that eventually result in migrations.

Asylum seekers do not spring up automatically like mushrooms after the rain: they are the product of failed responsible actions that originate from complex organizations, wholly or in part. We can follow Bovens' analysis considering each criterion in turn. Given the undeniable need for an established norm before someone may be responsible for its transgression, *nulla poena sine lege* appears to be our required starting point.

But it is here that the strongest difficulties arise: many of the 'norms' transgressed, as we shall see, are not codified as specific articles in a constitution or in a UN regime of international law. Some may exist in preambular texts, others may have been part of ongoing debates, others may exist clearly, but the categories to which they apply may be debated. For example, in another context, the conflict between the right to life, generally accepted as a basic norm of law, and the emerging debates regarding the starting point of human life, leave even that clear norm in doubt (WHO 2013; Grandjean 2013; Landrigan and Etzel 2013; Westra 2014a). Bovens writes:

> If someone is to be held responsible for the conduct of a complex organisation, it must be at some point established that that person has by his conduct contravened some norms. That norm need not explicitly exist; in many cases it is explicitly formulated only in the closure of the process of calling to account by the forum (Bovens 1998: 29).

There has to be a clear causal connection, at least, even if the norm has not been stated explicitly at the time when some damage has occurred, and the conduct of the organization and/or institution we believe should be held responsible.

Such responsibility could be based on negligent actions or omissions; in fact the behaviours of those who had a role to play in regard to the protection of a population's rights should represent the *conditio sine qua non*, or the precondition of a certain state of affairs, and therefore can reasonably be viewed as the cause for that population's condition. With the third aspect of 'passive responsibility' we listed following Bovens, we encounter the most serious obstacle to the ascription of responsibility: the question of 'blameworthiness'.

Bovens speaks of 'contributing to a situation', thus rather than a single, undeniable *conditio sine qua non*, we are faced with the problem of multiple causes. The two problems Bovens cites, (a) the mental capacity of someone to engage in a specific behaviour; and (b) the availability or alternative causes of action (Bovens 1998: 30), are both only minimally significant in regard to the ecological and other basic rights breaches that result in migrations.

In Canadian and in general in North American common law, the discharge of poisonous materials into the environment is, most often, viewed as a private nuisance, a tortious act as it is considered to be affecting only the natural environment (Hughes, Lucas and Tilleman 2003: 101; *Hickey v. Electric Reduction Co. of Canada, Ltd.* 1970).

In addition, a 'public nuisance' is a criminal act; where 'a court must balance, in a general manner, the defendant's right to engage in an activity, without undue restriction, against the public right to have its interests protected' (Hughes, Lucas and Tilleman 2003: 101; *Hickey v. Electric Reduction Co. of Canada, Ltd.* 1970). Salmond defines common nuisance:

> A public or common nuisance is a criminal offence. It is an act or omission which materially affects the reasonable comfort or convenience of life of a class of her Majesty's subjects ... (Salmond 1969: 64).

At present, it is far more than 'comfort' or 'convenience' that are at stake, as most often we are facing the deprivation of the means of survival, because corporate (state-sanctioned) activities, such as mining and other extractive industries, severely affect third world local communities. Nevertheless there is usually no 'smoking gun', no immediately perceivable wound or other observable harm to a specific individual, as we confront instead the challenge of the 'indeterminate plaintiff' (Hughes, Lucas and Tilleman 2003: 115; *Jones v. Mobil Oil Canada Ltd.* 1999; *Hoffman v. Monsanto Canada Inc.* 2002).

The ideal approach in all these cases would be the application of *Rylands v. Fletcher* (*Rylands v. Fletcher* 1868; *Cambridge Water Company v. Eastern Counties Leather* 1994), which added the requirement of 'foreseeability of damage to Rylands' 'non-natural use' condition; but strict liability is no longer an option, despite the presence of thousands of untested harmful substances in use.

Further, there is yet another challenge to be met in the case of ecologically harmful exposures or deprivations: that of the indeterminate defendant (Hughes, Lucas and Tilleman 2003: 119). That issue emerged in *Snidell v. Abbott Laboratories* (1980). In that case a woman who had used DES (diethylbestserol) during pregnancy had no ill effects, but her daughters, as all the daughters of mothers who took that drug (intended to prevent miscarriage), would eventually suffer cancerous growths.

This case is particularly significant, because one cannot even point to one exclusive manufacturer of the drug, any more than one can isolate *one* chemical substance alone, where multiple, cumulative exposures result in pollution of waters and agricultural resources, following industrial operations or development projects. Such cumulative exposures are (and have been) present in the 'chemical valley' of Sarnia, Ontario, and the Aamjinwaang First Nation which is also located in that area. Health Canada has confirmed multiple health hazards in its ongoing research in the area, but nothing is done to reduce or eliminate emissions from each separate corporate actor in the area, as long as they each meet self-established 'safe' emission standards, with no independent confirmation, and no effort to assess cumulative impacts (Rosenberg-Goldin 2005; Westra 2014a: ch. 2).

It seems that responsibility is fairly easy to establish, although we cannot pinpoint *one* or perhaps even more than one specific 'perpetrator' for any of the complex harms that accumulate, until eventually they render a specific area unlivable. In fact, for the most part the problem is not only that of establishing responsibility, but also, and this is far more taxing, to hold those responsible accountable for their actions, most of which are presently viewed as perfectly legal.

From Responsibility to Accountability

> Though it was noted that role responsibility might take either legal or moral form, it was not found necessary to treat these separately. But in the case of the present topic of liability-responsibility separate treatment seems advisable. For responsibility seems to have a wider extension in relation to the law than it does in relation to morals … (Hart 1968: 215).

The step from moral to legal responsibility is the one that should be pursued at this time, if those who have the 'capacity' to harm (Hart 1968: 227, 230), can be held accountable for their actions. The first question that arises, as we consider legal accountability for the conditions that prompt the flight, is which decisions have the power, the capacity to destroy livelihoods by altering the conditions that support the life of communities and have done so for centuries? Do they originate from bureaucracies or from the plans of corporate headquarters? Finally, what are the specific crimes for which we demand accountability?

We must seek these answers in present agricultural practices, and the decisions of those responsible for those practices, as the current topic is deprivation and lack of food as the reason for seeking asylum elsewhere. There are several problems that contribute to the situations that prompt flight, as multiple complex factors contribute to the scarcity or unavailability of food today. These include, for instance, the need for soil stewardship, especially at a time when climate change renders the situation more complex yet (2009 Statement on Soil Stewardship Draft).

In 2005 Jared Diamond wrote a bestseller (Diamond 2005) in which he explains how several old civilizations disappeared because of neglecting environmental threats to their soil and allowing its degradation, based on erosion, loss of fertility and land salinization. Thomas Sauer and Michael Nelson document a 'litany of reports cataloging human destruction of natural resources in general, and soils in particular' (Sauer and Nelson 2011: 3–16). The authors add that two 'key' decisions have not been made, that might have helped the situation if adopted: '(1) long-term planning and (2) willingness to reconsider core values' (Sauer and Nelson 2011: 3–16).

More general has been the appeal to a return to ecological integrity, starting with the landmark work of Aldo Leopold (Leopold 1949; Westra 1994; Pimentel, Westra and Noss 2000). As early as 1994 I argued that the present mind-set dictates practices, policies and regulations that are divisive and inefficient; and economics with a profit orientation that is limited to the promotion of corporate interests. A commitment to ecological integrity would not permit the indiscriminate use of pesticides and other chemicals in and on food, and the conflict between that use and safe agriculture are many and have been acknowledged for decades now (Draper 1991; Pimentel et al. 1992; Pimentel, Kirby and Shroff 1993; Goodland and Pimentel 2000; Flader 2011).

Related to the general quest for ecological integrity is the critique of the increasing spread of GMOs (Westra 2011). At first sight, we can agree with the work of numerous scholars who have worked on the issue through the years: practices that contribute to the disintegrity of the land, or that combine with climate change to cause or exacerbate soil depletion, are a significant part of the plight of those who suffer famine and deprivation and are forced into the quest for asylum. Similarly, the take-over by industrial agriculture, through the forced use of GMOs in many areas in both developed and developing countries, together with the prevalence of industrially raised livestock combine to render the conditions of the world's poor increasingly unacceptable.

Those who make the decisions to promote the problems listed above, are fully cognizant of the effects and impacts of what they produce/promote. Hence the causal responsibility that is undeniable should lead to accountability: those who make the decisions to manufacture, distribute and promote are also those who know best the composition and the effects of their products. Hence, the 'role' they play, the power they exercise, renders them similar to the ship's captain, who directs the route a vessel must follow (Hart 1968: 212). A similar role is played by a superior officer commanding a soldier to take a certain action (Hart 1968: 213): both the captain and the officer exercise the responsibility demanded by their role.

However, in both cases, but especially in the latter, those who execute those orders also bear some amount of responsibility for the consequences that ensue, both morally and, after Nuremburg, legally (Nuremberg Charter 1945). Of course the principles of Nuremberg expand significantly, rather than restrict, the presence of responsibility for actions for which some persons should be held responsible, and accountable.

However, as we consider those whose responsibility sets in motion the circumstances that cause famines and other grave deprivations, there is one missing aspect, that is the intent to harm, or *mens rea*. In fact, as Hart remarks:

> When a person is said to be not responsible for a particular act or crime, or when (as in the formulation of the M'Naughten Rules and s.2 of the Homicide Act, 1957) he is said not to be responsible for his acts and omissions in doing some action on a particular occasion; the reason for saying this is usually some mental abnormality or disorder (Hart 1968: 219).

Thus, missing the 'mental abnormality', an impossible condition for an institution, a complex organization or even a government bureaucracy, it should be easy to connect the harm to the perpetrators.

Nevertheless, a number of common problems intervene: first the question of unhealthy and hazardous environmental exposures from industrial operation from Bhopal to Seveso. The corporations that produce the damage are permitted to test their products and procedures *in house* (both in Canada and the US), without further impartial confirmation of the safety of their assessment (Landrigan and Etzel 2013: 20). Second, the same lack of impartial supervision affects pesticides and other agricultural products intended to enhance productivity following other market imperatives. Third, the increasing preference for cheap meat almost guarantees the pursuit of unhealthy practices, as grains are grown for feeding cattle rather than humans. Finally, the generally acknowledged problem of the primacy of particular economic interests over any other consideration works against the human right to food:

> The right to food is the right of every individual, alone or in community with others, to have physical and economic access to sufficient, adequate and culturally acceptable food that is produced and consumed sustainably, preserving access to food for future generations (Committee on World Food Security 2013: para. 81; UNHRC 2014).

This right, established and clearly connected with the very right to life, established beyond a doubt the responsibility of those whose role is related to the production, growth and distribution of food. Hence, given that deep poverty and the inability to provide the bare minimum required for their survival and that of their families is the main root of refugee exodus, this recent UN document (UNHRC 2014) establishes the need to hold accountable all those who participate in what the UN itself terms a 'broken' system, incapable of delivering what is needed, especially to the world's poor.

Rights, Entitlement and Accountability

> Thus, the normative content of the right to food can be summarized by reference to the requirements of availability, accessibility, adequacy and sustainability, all of which must be built into legal entitlements and secured through accountability mechanisms (UNHRC 2014: 3).

On March 11 2014, Friends of the Earth International praised this UN Report:

> This report is the only recipe for the eradication of hunger. Its recommendations are bold and simple: our current food systems must be reversed, not only reformed (martin.drago@redes.org.uv).

The Report emphasizes the interface between (1) the right to work, (2) the right to social security and (3) the right to food. Thus the first aspect that is urgently in need of radical re-orientation is the way current agricultural production and distribution are managed. The first problem that emerges is that 'boosting agricultural production' (UNHRC 2014: 4) is totally insufficient, as the present practices increase the profits of large industrial conglomerates without, however, increasing nutrition, especially for children. Even the FAO *State of Food Insecurity in the World 2013* (FAO 2013: 8) provides limited and even misleading information regarding the 'advances' in hunger reduction it reports (Lappe et al. 2013).

Current practices not only foster inadequate nutrition as well as poor health for children, but they also contribute significantly to the elimination of local farming communities, decimated by large agroconglomerates. These corporations only consider the quantity, rather than the quality of their production while, at the same time, they ignore both the health and the environmental 'collateral' effects of their operations, due to the overuse of pesticides and other 'industrial modes of agricultural production', which contribute significantly to climate change (UNHRC 2014: 5):

> Globally over 165 million children are stunted – so malnourished that they do not reach their full physical and cognitive potential, and 2 billion people globally lack vitamins and minerals essential for good health (UNHRC 2014: 4).

But perhaps the worst harms inflicted on large numbers of people are inflicted through climate change, because the projected proliferation of meat production (FAO 2009) indicates that the expected demand for meat production in 2050 will 'reach 470 million tons', which the UN document describes as an entirely unsustainable situation (UNHRC 2014: 5).

Industrial meat production requires feeding animals cereals and grains diverted from feeding poor people who cannot afford anything else; thus, much of the desperate poverty and hunger that motivate flights from third world countries originates from the practices that enrich agribusiness, while depriving the poor of the basic necessities. Nor is meat production and availability at the current levels beneficial to those who can afford to consume it:

> … in high income countries, the net health impacts of meat consumption are turning negative: at current levels, it is contributing to chronic diseases, including obesity, type 2 diabetes, cardiovascular diseases and cancer (UNHRC 2014: 6).

In addition, the various chemicals used for both animal fodder, other industrial crops and industrially grown meat use extreme amounts of water, increasingly scarce today (Barlow 1999). Finally, the chemical substances used contribute significantly to a number of developmental problems and diseases for children, adults and older persons, when prebirth exposures occur (Landrigan and Etzel 2013). The effects of these early exposures also include irreversible diminished brain capacity in children and young adults, autism and other forms of neurotoxicity, including long-term effects and emergence of Parkinson's and Alzheimer's diseases (Grandjean 2013; Westra 2014a).

Finally, we cannot forget that 'livestock is found to be responsible for 51 per cent of anthropogenic greenhouse gas emissions'; as well 'livestock production accounted for 70 per cent of the land surface of the planet' (UNHRC 2014: 6; Tukker et al. 2011: 1776). When agricultural development was essentially led by states (as in the 1960s and 1970s), the initial mistakes were made that eventually precipitated the present situation. At that time, farmers were not paid fair prices, and the largest producers, able to compete globally, were subsidized. The rural migrations and urban sprawls that resulted were the prelude to both hunger and poverty in many countries, in South America, Asia and Africa.

The present situation is now based on the preferences and choices of large industrial agriculture and livestock production, supported by the governments of the countries where production occurs, but also by those that are the home bases of those operations on the one hand, and of the poor countries that provide the raw material, and the necessary resources, on the other.

Once those whose given 'roles' enable them to make the decisions that create and support these interconnected problems, it is easy to see who is responsible, thus who should be held accountable for the entrenchment and continuation of the complex practices that harm the health of the rich, while victimizing the poor:

> Foresight studies have suggested that, if current mandates are implemented, the price of cereals and other crops could be 35 per cent higher by 2030 than under a reference scenario where biofuel consumption remained constant at 2008 levels, putting an estimated 136 million more people at risk of hunger (UNHRC 2014: 10).

Hence justice, distributive fairness, human beings' right to normal development, and poverty reduction all require the urgent radical reform of global food systems. From the standpoint of the topic of this work, the issue of poverty reduction is perhaps the most compelling reason for seeking accountability.

An international network of peasant organizations, Via Campesina, was eventually attached to the Human Rights Council Advisory Committee in 2012 (UNHRC 2012). In July 2013, an intergovernmental working group received a mandate from the Human Rights Council (Re.21/19) to work on a United Nations declaration on 'the rights of peasants and other people working in rural areas' (UNHRC 2014: 12).

As far as wealthy countries are concerned, through constant media pressure, agribusiness corporations have created the ideal conditions to ensure profit and control, through the de facto 'veto powers' they have acquired in the 'political system', as

> Finally, the habits of consumers themselves have changed: in high income countries, the consumption of highly processed, high energy (though nutrient poor) foods has increased year on year, becoming an accepted unquestioned part of modern life (UNHRC 2014: 14).

It is ironic that the same rich states that are now controlled by corporations that benefit immensely from the *status quo* are also those that fortify themselves against asylum seekers, erect walls and barriers both material and legal against the asylum seekers, the poor and desperate millions *they* have helped to create in the process of acquiring the power and influence they now enjoy.

A particularly despicable aspect of states' refusal to accept asylum seekers, or the responsibility for several factors leading to their plight, is the fact that – most often – children are involved, not only in the eventual flight, but also in the starvation that precedes it. Nor are these circumstances only affecting children in the third world, as the richest countries of the world refuse to accept their responsibility as well.

An Aside on the Rights of the Child Economic Migrant Seeking Refuge

> Nearly 50% of the world's refugees are children under 18 years of age. In 2005, the latest year for which numbers are available, the total number of juveniles apprehended by the organization tasked with border security within the Department of Homeland Security (DHS), the US Custom and Border Protection (USCBP), was 114,569 (Morales-Singh 2008: 514; United Nations High Commissioner for Refugees 2006).

The abject poverty experienced by children in Central and South America forces them to seek some kind of work to help with an often impossible family situation. Children who attempt to find some work in the United States start by leaving their country by riding freight trains on an incredibly hazardous journey, which, at best, culminates in their arrival in a country where 'unaccompanied children' are routinely detained although their only crime is to flee poverty and lack of opportunity:

> [The children] are cold, hungry and helpless. They are hunted like animals by corrupt police bandits and gang members … A University of Houston Study found that most are robbed, beaten, or raped, usually several times. Some are killed … to evade authorities, the children jump on and off the moving train cars. Sometimes they fall, and the wheels tear them apart (Morales-Singh 2008: 514; Nazario 2006: 5).

The problem of asylum seekers is becoming increasingly acute, especially in the case of claims of 'economic persecution', which, at this time, are not technically part of the five grounds of persecution listed in the 1951 Convention on the Status of Refugees (Convention on the Status of Refugees (CSR) 1951; 1967 Protocol to the Status of Refugees 1979; Protocol Relating to the Status of Refugees 1967; Ramos 2011). The terrible situation of adult refugees, most often subjected to conditions that are contrary to both established law and morality, become unbearable when the vulnerability of children is added:

> Because their claims for relief from removal implicate a type of human rights violation that U.S. refugee and immigration law does not protect – i.e. violations of economic rights – these children are routinely returned to deplorable living conditions in their country of origin (Morales-Singh 2008: 516).

Thus the obligation of '*non-refoulement*' does not apply to US law in their case (Morales-Singh 2008). The harm of persecution based on one of the five grounds established by the 1951 Convention is based on subjective appreciation on the part of the refugee, of the past treatment they endured, and of the anticipated future circumstances they might expect, together with the fear these considerations elicit. Additionally the convention refugee's fear must also be validated by objective general knowledge of the circumstances that prompted their flight. However, not only do children have a special need for protection because of their vulnerability compared to that of adults, but, in addition, US law does not recognize the denial of economic rights as persecution (Morales-Singh 2008: 523; Westra 2014a: ch. 4).

When this callous disregard for the most vulnerable is added to the specific deprivations that affect children disproportionately, both the gravity of the situation facing the poor families and the severity of the responsibility that accrues to those who are responsible are increased.

Deprived and Dispossessed Populations: Who Should Be Held Accountable?

> Collective and hierarchical models of accountability are in a sense constructions. For one does not look at who 'really' did it, but in order to get round the problem of many hands, constructs a form of accountability (Bovens 1998: 106).

The 'collective model of responsibility', according to Bovens, is based on several basic conditions, one of which is especially relevant: '(a) the collective must be characterised by a high degree of *de facto* solidarity', a condition that seems basic to group responsibility. In contrast, the fact that '(d) those who are held responsible should have the chance to exercise a certain degree of influence on the eventual outcome', appears to be off the mark. Even silence, coupled with ongoing participation in some measure in the activities and goals of a specific complex collectivity, is sufficient to ensure that a certain amount of responsibility is retained.

No doubt that is implied by Peter French's emphasis on the Corporate Internal Decision-making Structure of the corporation (CID Structure) (French 1984), which apportions responsibility according to the degree of input into corporate decisions. But it is his contention that *all* who participate in the corporate decisions or operations are – in various measure – accomplices in the crimes that are being committed by a specific corporate collectivity.

States have the responsibility to empower corporations to operate, but they also have the obligation to protect citizens, especially now that corporations are no longer created for a single limited purpose as they initially were (Westra 2013: ch. 2). Thus, enabling corporate bodies to perpetrate wholesale starvation of whole populations while pursuing their economic objectives, as we saw in the work of the Special Rapporteur de Shutter, should be viewed as a crime against humanity.

> The ILC identified as *jus cogens* the prohibition of aggression and the illegal use of force, the prohibitions against slavery and the slave trade, genocide and racial discrimination and apartheid, the prohibition against torture, the basic rules of international humanitarian law and the right to self-determination (Report of the International Law Commission 2001: 283–4, paras 4–5; Talmon 2006: 99).

To those norms, others were added, such as the prohibition of cruel, inhuman and degrading treatment (German Federal Constitutional Court 2003), 'crimes against humanity', the prohibition of piracy and the principle of 'permanent sovereignty over natural resources' (Talmon 2006: 100). As well, the 'basic rules for the protection of the environment' was viewed as part of *jus cogens* by the German Constitutional Court (Order of the German Federal Constitutional Court 2004: 178). This expanding list appears to cover both acts that can only originate from a state, and others that describe many harmful activities we have discussed as part of industry.

It is important to note that not only does the obligation apply to the states involved, or perhaps to 'quasi-states' or corporations, if that position can be accepted, but that the same obligation *not* to accept an illegal situation is the duty of all 'third states' and the global community itself.

When US state/corporate interests are viewed essentially as one, as for instance in the 2006 Terrorism Act which identifies acts hostile to corporate/industrial operations with acts against the state (Clements 2012), and when this identification, like the one covering so-called 'counter-terrorist' measures, views as totally permissible all sorts of murderous, aggressive acts, then the impunity with which both are treated should not occasion any surprise. If you can kill, even using drones which, by definition, cannot distinguish between combatant and non-combatant, in the advancement of US economic interests, then surely simply depriving people of their livelihood should be viewed as a far lesser crime (Westra 2014b).

> The inequitable distribution of resources driven by the strong at the expense of the weak which constitutes the broad definition of plunder, finds in the rule of law the rhetoric of legitimization. This rhetoric constricts the very meaning of the word plunder, to the point of naturalizing, legalizing and ultimately denying the outrageous disparity in resource allocation, following many social processes in contexts of power imbalance (Mattei and Nader 2008: 137).

The enrichment of corporate 'criminals' proceeds apace with the impoverishment of the rest (or the 99 per cent, according to the Occupy Movement). The impunity of corporate harmful actions is supported and defended through that enrichment. The present situation is the continuation of 'colonial domination', now hiding behind the mask of neoliberal 'development' (Mattei and Nader 2008: 137; Westra, L. 2012: 87–92). Mattei and Nader dub the situation, which combines elements of criminality with the legal infrastructure of impunity, the 'imperial rule of law' (Mattei and Nader 2008: 137).

Nor is the obligation of 'leaders' of all kinds to provide for the satisfaction of the basic needs of all those for whom they are responsible a recent development, although it is now entrenched in many UN instruments, especially the ICESCR and the ICCPR. Even in Ancient times, in the Bible, we find that God actually responds to the people's needs, when these are related by Moses:

> The whole congregation of the children of Israel complained against Moses and Aaron in the wilderness. The children of Israel said to them, 'If we only had died by the hand of the Lord in the Land of Egypt, when we sat by the fleshpots and ate our fill of bread. For you have brought us into the wilderness to kill the whole assembly with hunger' (Exodus 16.2–4).

Aside from what Moses and God himself thought of the requests of the 'Children of Israel', this passage seems to express, in a nutshell, the argument of this work in simple words. The statement can be divided into three separate but connected arguments. First, that hunger is the first human consideration, the most basic need of all people; second, that ensuring the survival of the people they command and lead is the first responsibility of such leaders; third, these basic rights and responsibilities *precede* for all people the civil and political rights to which they might be entitled.

The Hebrews even professed to prefer slavery itself to suffering the hunger that appeared to accompany the liberation they had enjoyed with Moses. Nor was their request for food judged to be unacceptable: God himself, through Moses, informed the people that their (just) request was to be met, and food was to be given to them, enough to satisfy their hunger. It is therefore worthy of note that those responsible for the welfare of the Hebrews, a responsibility arising from their status as leaders, accepted that the very boon they had bestowed upon these peoples, that of freedom from slavery, was not sufficient to remove their *primary* obligation to provide for their survival.

In Biblical times, the situation was much simpler than it is today: whoever was the 'leader', the 'chief' of a city, region or group, was responsible for the welfare of the citizens of his community. Today, responsibility for the citizens of a given area or nation has given way to a diffuse responsibility for the human rights of all those affected by the decisions of all countries' leaders, in fact, as *erga omnes* obligations entail, every leader can be held responsible for any and all human rights breaches anywhere, both to those of their own citizens, and to those of other nations (at least in principle), provided that the harmful practices that produce harms to human rights originate with the state held responsible.

Hence, leaders' responsibility has increased exponentially, as has the potential for harm of numerous human activities (Jonas 1984). In contrast, the ability of a community to object democratically to a ruler's decision at the time of Moses brought almost immediate results and redress for their plight; whereas those who are deprived of necessities or are otherwise oppressed in democratic countries, and those who readily and noisily defend and proclaim their rights through marches and protests, only succeed in bringing some of the worst issues to the attention of the media, at best.

But thus far, we have not seen any ruler's or government's immediate response to redress the human rights violations so clearly and so quickly shown on television or reported in other media outlets. We know about the outrageous situation in the occupied Palestinian territories, through the UN Rapporteur's reports (UNHRC 2008; Amnesty International 2009; Westra 2007: ch. 6); we are regularly informed about the effects of climate change on island communities, Indigenous and local communities, and the people of the Arctic regions; we see the hundreds of thousands of refugees in the democratic Republic of Congo, in Sudan and elsewhere, we see their abysmal living conditions, their hunger, their lack of water, of medicines and of their very human dignity (Westra 2007).

Yet our international legal institutions appear to be unable or unwilling to respond to the many human rights crises that develop almost daily, and show no sign of decreasing, let alone of disappearing.

The State's Role: Beyond 'Gatekeeping'

> Therefore the paradigmatic shift in our understanding of the state must involve a move away from the concept of the state as a medieval gatekeeper towards a more modern concept. In this concept, the state is still the ultimate authority in the regulation of migration, but the legitimacy of its regulatory power should be based not on its ability to control immigration. Just as is the case in the area of free movement of goods and capital, the legitimacy of its regulatory policies should be determined by whether its actions are welfare-improving (Mehmet 2009: 85).

States' actions, like corporate activities, are carried out by employees and functionaries, all of whom are part of the internal operation of a complex organization. For corporate participants, any conflict that might arise with their own conscience and moral principles might lead, at worst, to dismissal. That is a far lesser personal harm than that incurred by army personnel who might find themselves in a similar situation and refuse to obey superior orders. The best known example of the latter situation, clearly demonstrating the problem of 'many hands' regarding personal responsibility, is that of the My Lai massacre Lt Calley was ordered to carry out, a so-called 'search-and-destroy mission' during the Vietnam war. Calley was the commander of a platoon whose action resulted in the death of 107 civilians in 1968. He was eventually condemned to four years' detention, served for the most part at home (Bovens 1999: 48).

Even in this extreme case, like in many other cases, the rules of Nuremberg prevail. In contrast, almost like examples taken from army situations, within a corporate milieu, there exists a strong pressure to conform,

> … to engage in loyal 'teamwork', often strengthened by 'groupthink' mechanisms, and social pressure that make it particularly difficult to back out of reprehensible activities (Bovens 1998: 124).

The presence of these pressures has also been recognized and critiqued in Canadian criminal law (Bill C-45) according to which actors within an organization may be viewed as responsible for an offence, 'whether by act or omission'.

Bill C-45, and the Canadian Criminal Code

The main changes effected to the Criminal Code are:

> S 1(1) extends the definition of 'every one', 'person' and 'owner' to include 'an organization'. In turn, 'organization' means,
> (2)(a) a public body, body corporate, society, company, firm, partnership, trade union or municipality, or
> (b) an association of persons that
> (i) is created for a common purpose,
> (ii) has an operational structure, and
> (iii) holds itself out to the public as an association of persons ….

Here and in the amendments to Section 22.1, Bill C-45 ensures that a wide array of actors within an organization may be viewed as responsible for an offence, 'whether by act or omission' (Section 22.1(ii)); it also ensures that, if the prosecution is required 'to prove fault – other than negligence' (Section 22.2), then senior officers or representatives may manifest the requisite 'mental state' also by '(c) knowing that a representative of the organization is or is about to be a party to the offence, or does not take all reasonable measures to stop them from being a party to the offence'. The Bill also adds a Section (217.1) to define 'the legal duty to take reasonable steps to prevent bodily harm', on the part of anyone who is in the position to direct and order how work is to be done.

In addition, several sections deal with making or causing to be made false statements with respect to the financial conditions of the organization (Section 362(1)(c)),or in general, committing fraud or causing it to be committed. For the sake of the present purposes, I will limit my observation and my discussion to the aspects of Bill C-45 that are directly relevant to this work, thus to ecocrime rather than white collar crime in general.

However, to my knowledge, this section of the Canadian Criminal Code has existed since 2003 but has never been appealed to in the jurisprudence since then.

These aspects of the Canadian Criminal Code reflect the problematic side of a corporate culture that shares much of its unquestioning silence in the face of unspeakable horror with the silence and lack of critiques that prevailed in Nazi Germany during the Second World War:

> As Eichmann told it, the most potent factor in the soothing of his own conscience, was the simple fact that he could see no one, no one at all, who actually was against the Final Solution (Arendt 1965: 116).

Hence, the compliance of the followers of corporate culture is comparable to the activities of the perpetrators of genocide, and the differences that exist between these two sets of actions, substantive though they are, are not sufficient to establish a difference *in kind* between government and corporate crimes. Bovens cites Nagel, stating, 'the great modern crimes are public crimes' (Nagel 1978: 75), but himself adds that 'the great modern crimes are corporate crimes' (Bovens 1998: 131).

Responsibility, in the sense of 'being a responsible person', no matter what one's role in an organization, is and remains extremely difficult, as it may impose a grave burden on individuals who might want to adhere to a personal morality and still retain their ability to provide for themselves and their families. Nevertheless, as in the decision-making structure of a corporate organization, which includes all those involved in the carrying out of corporate operations, when we seek to establish the accountability of corporate criminals we must include both those involved in the bureaucracies of the states that permit/enable their operations, and all those who work within the corporations, albeit with different degrees of responsibility.

As we saw, the roots of the poverty and the hunger that cause the need to flee, both the impoverishment of people in large cities in advanced Western countries and the deprivations caused by the elimination of the resources needed by third world people, can be found in the corporations who are the main beneficiaries of the situation, and, within the corporations, primarily the CEOs in each organization, although their operations are based on and supported by government approval in all cases.

Thus, as we trace the aetiology of the flight from those particular conditions, we find the clear causal link between the specific *chosen* activities of those involved in the food industry, including those who facilitate and promote their operations. The latter, it bears repeating, are state bureaucracies, legally bound to protect their citizens, and legally obliged to follow the mandates of conventions, charters and other UN documents related to their interactions with both natural and legal persons.

In contrast, corporate bodies only have non-binding directives, and lists of 'ethical commitments', most of which are simply ignored. Hence, the effects of their negligence and non-compliance continue unabated, and unpunished. Perhaps we can view the situation described in the UN Report (UNHRC 2014) as a symptom of an even graver, deeper structural problem, as both gross inequality and hunger/

malnutrition are the products of the same wrong-headed system, moving steadily forward in the wrong direction, as recent OECD Reports indicate (Richardson and Ali 2014; OECD 2014):

> In fact the OECD report once more demonstrates that the capitalist system, organized on the basis of the private ownership of production, is obsolete, irrational and incompatible with further social progress. The only way to ensure the right of all people to a decent job, housing, healthcare, and education is through the socialist reorganization world society on the basis of social need, not private profit (Damon 2014).

As UN Special Rapporteur Oliver de Schutter affirmed, a radical reorganization of the food supply systems is absolutely necessary. But, while that radical change appears to be necessary, it seems it is not sufficient, as long as the general system of neoliberal globalization is still in place. The treatment of asylum seekers and the presence of fortified borders is only one aspect of the conflict between the present instantiations of state sovereignty, with its emphasis on economic interests and its total neglect of the rights of humanity.

Cosmopolitanism and Sovereign Rights in Conflict

> … sovereignty is only a legitimate claim insofar as it seeks to guarantee the basic rights, and satisfy the basic needs of humanity, in line with universally agreed principles and standards (Salomon 2007: 28).

Cosmopolitanism, and true universality, were discussed in the first chapter of this book. Its history is far longer than the existence of sovereign states. Yet today the very existence of international law and the international community of states impose upon states responsibilities well beyond their own borders (Cassese 2007: 245–77). Aside from the possibility of the ordinary responsibility of inconsistent state conduct regarding an international obligation or imposing some specific damage on another state (Cassese 2007: 252), both of which require the objective element of a 'material or moral damage' (Cassese 2007: 253), both of which represent violations of bilateral treaties or multilateral conventions, there is the question of 'aggravated state responsibility' (Cassese 2007: 262).

This sort of moral/legal obligation incurred by states is of a different kind, as 'aggravated state responsibility'

> … arises when a State violates a rule laying down a community obligation, that is, either a customary obligation *erga omnes* protecting such fundamental values as peace, human rights or self-determination of peoples, or an obligation *erga omnes contractantes* laid down in a multilateral treaty safeguarding those fundamental values (Cassese 2007: 262).

Both human rights and humanitarian law, following upon the provisions of the UN Charter and the adoption of the 1966 Conventions, cover aspects of the basic collective human rights under discussion. The emergence of certain values such as the prohibition of the use of force, support for the self-determination of peoples, and the acknowledgement of large-scale violations of human rights, takes on a 'collective dimension' that clearly separates these forms of state responsibility from other ordinary wrongs.

Hence the emergence of the concept 'cooperation' of states, which indicates the collective aspects of their responsibility; beyond the limits of their sovereignty, the recognition of the 'interdependence' of states emerges as a foundational aspect of the development of international law. In fact,

> In 1923, the Permanent Court of International Justice affirmed what Judge Weeramantry felt was necessary to reaffirm in 1996, and that is that 'the sovereignty of states would be proportionally diminished and restricted as international law developed' (Salomon 2007: 26; Judge Weeramanty, Advisory Opinion, 8 July 1996, as cited in 'Legality of the Threat or Use of Nuclear Weapons', dissenting opinion 226, at 495).

Therefore, the defence of basic collective human rights is not a position that stands against present legal regimes, but one which indicates and details the parameters of the eventual goal to be reached by the long-anticipated 'development' of international law. This development is already in evidence as the global community speaks openly in their critique of any state that does not practise 'democracy' for instance, while it stops short of expressing a forceful condemnation of those who do but still promote and practise immoral and illegal policies (such as the state of Israel).

It is as though the moral vigilance of the international community ends – at best – at the ballot box – so that whatever decisions the new democratically elected government takes are *ipso facto* rendered 'right' (in the sense of justifiable and morally correct) because they emerge from an elected government, despite the fact that many such governments pursue the most indefensible practices (even Hitler's leadership was preceded by an election!). In conclusion then, although

> … under the Charter, UN Member States relinquish a degree of their sovereignty, and in its stead accept international cooperation in the respect for, and observance of, human rights as a common purpose of their contemporary, collective activities, the international community does not seem at this time to extend its obligation to recognize the emerging *erga omnes* responsibility to force states to implement *jus cogens* norms as their gravest moral and legal obligations (Salomon 2007: 21).

Sovereignty at the Border

> Inside, sovereignty expresses power beyond accountability. Outside, sovereignty expresses the capacity for autonomous agency, including aggression or defense against other sovereign entities (Brown 2010: 52).

The first thing to note, in regard to collective human rights, is the porousness of the fortified borders that restrain them. The same arms and tanks that are used today to hold refugees at bay have been used in earlier times to increase the reach of the very same borders to include other citizens, who are perhaps temporarily, incorporated within the colonizing state, with some conditions, but without serious efforts to limit their admission.

Since the Second World War, outright colonizing is no longer acceptable for most countries, as the UN proscribes aggression on the part of most states, aside from those protected by American exceptionalism (primarily the US and Israel) (Lipset 1996). But the observation regarding the flexibility and porousness of most borders remains true: neoliberal imperialism conquers markets, whole resource-rich regions and nations even, which are now controlled through loans, trade alliances and other deals.

The ultimate result is still that a state has control over people beyond its borders, and the Western states' efforts aim at including these aliens in various manners, from controlling their ideologies, to controlling their resources, to political alliances, or all three. The walls themselves may serve a double purpose, a continuation of sorts of the kind of border labour used long ago by west-bound railroads:

> In the last two decades, globalization has dramatically increased both the quantity of this migration and the value of keeping it illegal. Northern capital today requires labour that is maximally cheap and exploitable, hirable at subminimum wage, without benefits or regard for regulations on overtime, health, environment or safety, and easily dispatched when not needed (Brown 2010: 111).

Within this structural framework, based on globalization as a modification and outgrowth of capitalist systems, food cultivation and distribution promotes the interests of some, at the expense of famine for millions (UNHRC 2014).

But that is not our main topic at this time, although the awareness of causal chains and circumstances serves to demonstrate the inappropriateness of current responses by major states at their borders, and the denial of human rights that it implies, but it further confirms the conditions that generate flight. It is within this capitalist system, as the colonization of old was transformed into the current forms of imperialism, that the victimization of people can continue to thrive.

This is an extremely uncomfortable conclusion to reach. It is not one or another specific problem that causes or contributes to the poverty and the pervasive deprivation that causes the flight: it is the presence of a structural framework that requires a radical re-structuring, that appears to be beyond the ability of even people of good will and strong conviction to repair.

Although most of this chapter deals with famine and the lack of resources as a form of persecution giving rise to refugee situations, to my knowledge, no such case has been tried in a court of law to date. In contrast, the obvious urgency surrounding climate refugees has already produced one case in New Zealand, where the causal link between Western nations' consumer habits are in direct conflict with the rights of people to their own lands and resources:

> … the right Tuvaluans have to go on living on their islands in the future, puts the international community under an obligation to avoid a future mass displacement of this island people. The primary imperative, one second to none, is to drastically cut green-house gas emissions, on a global scale; next comes the funding of considerable measures in support of effective adaptation on the local level (Kempf 2009: 200).

However, this reasonable proposal has not been accepted in the Western world thus far, any more than the OECD Rapporteur's request for radical changes to food systems has. The latter is much more recent, so that it is possible (although not probable) that some powerful countries' organizations and institutions may decide to move in the right direction. Yet it is difficult to put much hope in such a development when one considers that the victims of climate change, or climate refugees, do not fare much better, despite the current global acceptance of the reality of their plight. Diane Saxe describes the first climate refugee case going to appeal in New Zealand:

> On 1st May 2014, the New Zealand Court of Appeal will hear Ione Teitiota's claim to become the world's first climate refugee. Mr. Teitiota is from a remote atoll in the Pacific nation of Kiribati, one of the lowest-lying nations on Earth. He is trying to convince New Zealand judges that he's a refugee – suffering not from persecution but form climate change (Saxe 2014).

Teitiota was frustrated in his bid to become the world's first 'climate refugee', despite the fact that his 'low lying homeland is likely to be engulfed by waves by the end of the century and to become unlivable before long' (Marks 2014: 1). The Court found that his claim was an attempt to turn the CSR 'on its head' (Marks 2014: 1), but his plight is emblematic of that of millions who face extreme climate change risks, increasing economic deprivations, as their food supply is disappearing. The environmental degradation engendered by storm surges and flooding means increasing soil contamination, as traditional crops no longer grow, and water sources are inquinated by salination.

The island that is home to Teitiota, his wife Angua Erika, and his three children, Yolisa (5), Tebukaiti (3) and Riango (16 months), lies only three metres above sea level, and the relentless effects of climate change events link this case to the topic of this chapter, that is to the form of persecution that arises as traditional resources disappear, together with safe water and the very homes of the islanders (Marks 2014: 2). The rigidity exhibited by the New Zealand Court shows clearly the precarious position of millions of victims of the negligent practices of affluent nations, whose crimes were not acknowledged at the time of the drafting of the CSR, any more than they are now, when the science that confirms them is increasingly indisputable.

It is worth noting that although these causal links were discussed separately in different chapters, the causes that produce the flights are as linked as are their effects. Climate change ensures that resources are depleted, and that water becomes scarce, which leads to conflicts that arise regarding all these issues, engendered by globalization.

Galtung addresses the question of 'structural/cultural violence', and it seems that the present instantiations of capitalism fit that description, as they retain (1) the primacy of economic interests and (2) emphasis on unlimited growth:

> One way cultural violence works is by changing the moral colour of an act from red/wrong to green/right or at least yellow/acceptable; an example being murder on behalf of oneself, wrong, murder on behalf of the country, right. Another way is by making reality opaque so that we do not see the violent act or fact, at least not as violent (Galtung 1996: 126).

This chapter discussed the circumstances that prompt the flight of asylum seekers. The next chapter considers yet another reason for flight, before the book turns, in Part II, to a consideration of how asylum seekers are received after their flight, on their arrival, as well as the legal arguments and instruments that might help to redress to some extent the injustices that are perpetrated upon them from the start. Finally, Part III proposes some possible ways to mitigate the problems faced by refugees.

References

1967 Protocol to the Status of Refugees, 1979, UN Doc. HCR/IP/4/Eng.Rev.l.

2009 Statement on Soil Stewardship Draft, 2011, from the 2009 Bouyoucos Conference on Soil Stewardship in an Era of Climate Change, 'An Urgent Appeal for Soil Stewardship', in Sauer, T.J., Norman, J.M., and Sivakumar, Mannawa V.S., eds, *Sustaining Soil Productivity in Response to Global Climate Change*, WileyBlackwell, Ames, IA, pp. 6–7.

Amnesty International, 2009, 'Israel/Gaza, Operation "Cast Lead": 22 Days of Death and Destruction', London, UK.

Arendt, Hannah, 1965, *Eichmann in Jerusalem: A Report on the Banality of Evil*, Viking Press, New York.

Aristotle, 1973, *The Politics*, edited and translated by Ernest Barker, Oxford University Press, Oxford.

Barlow, Maude, 1999, *Blue Gold*, A Special Report Issued by the International Forum of Globalization (IFG).

Baxi, Upendra, 2010, 'Writing About Impunity and Environment: The Silver Jubilee' of the Bhopal Catstrophe', *Journal of Human Rights and the Environment*, 1, 23–44.

Bosniak, L., 2010, 'Persons and Citizens in Constitutional Thought', *International Journal of Constitutional Law*, 8.1, 9–29.

Bovens, Mark, 1998, *The Quest for Responsibility*, Cambridge University Press, Cambridge.

Brown, Wendy, 2010, *Walled States, Waning Sovereignty*, 2nd edition, Zone Books, New York.

Cambridge Water Company v. Eastern Counties Leather [1994] 1 All ER 53 (HL).

Cassese, Antonio, 2007, *International Law*, Oxford University Press, Oxford.

Clements, Jeffrey, D., 2012, *Corporations Are Not People*, Berrett-Koehler Publishers, San Francisco, CA.

Committee on World Food Security, 2013, rep. 40th sess. Rome 7–11 October (CFS 2013/40 REPORT).

Convention on the Status of Refugees (CSR), 1951, 189 UNTS 150, into force 22 April 1954.

Damon, Andre, 2014, 'The OECD's "Society at a Glance" Report: A Portrait of a Failed System', World Socialist Web Site, 24 March, http://www.wsws.org/en/articles/2014/03/24/pers-m24.html (accessed 25 January 2015).

Diamond, Jared, M., 2005, *Collapse: How Societies Choose to Fail or Succeed*, Viking Press, New York.

Draper, Elaine, 1991, *Risky Business*, Cambridge University Press, New York.

Eleventh Annual Message to Congress (11 January 1949), in Israel, J., ed., *The State of the Union Messages of the Presidents*, 1906, Vol. 3, p. 2881.

Food and Agriculture Organization (FAO), 2009, 'How to Feed the World in 2050', at www.fao.org/fileadmin/templates/wsfs/docs/expert_paper/How_to_Feed_the_World_in_2050.pdf (accessed 3 February 2015).

——, 2013, *The State of Food Insecurity in the World 2013: The Multiple Dimensions of Food Security*, Rome.

Flader, Susan L., 2011, 'Aldo Leopold and the Land Ethic: An Argument for Sustaining Soils', in Sauer, T.J., Norman, J.M., and Sivakumar, Mannawa V.S., eds, *Sustaining Soil Productivity in Response to Global Climate Change*, WileyBlackwell, Ames, IA, pp. 43–66.

Fluker, Shaun, 2014, 'Environmental Norms in the Courtroom: The Case of Ecological Integrity in Canadian Parks', in Westra, L., Taylor, P. and Michelot, A., eds, *Confronting Ecological and Economic Collapse: Ecological Integrity for Law, Policy and Human Rights*, Routledge, Abingdon, pp. 21–31.

French, Peter, 1984, *Collective and Corporate Responsibility*, Columbia University Press, New York.

Galtung, Johan, 1996, *Peace by Peaceful Means: Conflict, Development and Civilization*, Sage, London.
German Federal Constitutional Court, 2nd Chamber, Order of June 245 2003, 2 BvR 685/03,B Verf GE 108, p. 129, at para. 67.
Glenn, H. Patrick, 2013, *The Cosmopolitan State*, Oxford University Press, Oxford.
Goodland, Robert and Pimentel, David, 2000, 'Environmental Sustainability and Integrity in the Agriculture Sector', in Pimentel, D., Westra, L., and Noss, R., eds, *Ecological Integrity: Integrating Environment, Conservation and Health*, Island Press, Washington, DC, pp. 121–38.
Grandjean, Philippe, 2013, *Only One Chance (to Develop a Brain)*, Oxford University Press, New York.
Hart, H.L.A., 1968, *Punishment and Responsibility: Essays in the Philosophy of Law*, Oxford, New York.
Hickey v. Electric Reduction Co. of Canada, Ltd. (1970) 21 DLR (3d) 368 (Nfld. TD).
Hoffman v. Monsanto Canada Inc. 2002 SKQB, 190.
Hughes, E., Lucas, A.R., and Tilleman, W.A., eds, 2003, *Environmental Law and Policy*, Edmond Montgomery, Toronto.
International Labour Organization (ILO), 1989, Convention No. 169, 28 ILM 138.
Jonas, H., 1984, *The Imperative of Responsibility*, University of Chicago Press, Chicago, IL.
Jones v. Mobil Oil Canada Ltd. (1999) 248 RI (QB).
Kempf, Wolfgang, 2009, 'A Sea of Environmental Refugees? Oceania in an Age of Climate Change', in Hermann, E., Klenke, K., and Dickhardt, M., eds, *Form, Macht, Differenz: Motive und Felder ethnologischen Forschens*, Univeritätsverlag Göttingen, Göttingen, pp. 191–205.
Landrigan, P. and Etzel, R., 2013, *Children's Environmental Health*, Oxford University Press, New York.
Lappe, F.M., Clapp, J., Anderson, M., Broad, R., Messer, E., Pogge, T., and Wise, T., 2013, 'How We Count Hunger Matters', *Ethics and International Affairs*, 27.3, 251–9.
Leopold, Aldo, 1949, *A Sand County Almanac and Sketches Here and There*, Oxford, New York.
Lipset, Seymour Martin, 1996, *American Exceptionalism*, W.W. Norton, New York.
Marks, Kathy, 2014, 'World's First "Climate Change Refugee" Has Appeal Rejected: "When Kiribati Disappears, We're Going to Die with Our Kids"', 12 May 2014, http://beforeitsnews.com/environment/2014/05/worlds-first-climate-change-refugee-has-appeal-rejected-when-kiribati-disappears-were-going-to-die-with-our-kids-2501012.html (accessed 28 January 2015).
Mattei, Ugo, and Nader, Laura, 2008, *Plunder: When the Rule of Law Is Illegal*, Blackwell Publishing, Malden, MA.
Mehmet, Ugur, 2009, 'The Ethics Economics and Governance of Free Movement', in Antoine Pécoud and Paul de Gucheteneire, eds, *Migration Without Borders*, UNESCO Publishing, Paris, pp. 65–96.

Morales-Singh, M. Beth, 2008, 'To Rescue, Not Return: An International Human Rights Approach to Protecting Child Economic Migrants Seeking Refuge in the United States', *Columbia Journal of Law and Social Problems*, 41, 511–45.

Morse, B., 2002, *Comparative Assessment of the Position of Indigenous Peoples in Quebec, Canada, and Abroad*, vol. 3, book l, Executive Council, Quebec.

Nagel, Thomas, 1978, 'Ruthlessness in Public Life', in Hamshire, Stuart, ed., *Public and Private Morality*, Cambridge University Press, Cambridge, pp. 75–94.

Nazario, Sonia, 2006, *Enrique's Journey: The Story of a Boy's Dangerous Odyssey to Reunite with His Mother*, Random House, New York.

Nuremberg Charter, 1945, Charter of the International Military Tribunal, 82 UNTS 279.

OECD, 2014, *Society at a Glance 2014: OECD Social Indicators*, OECD Publishing, http://www.oecd.org/els/societyataglance.htm (accessed 1 February 2015).

Order of the German Federal Constitutional Court of 26 October 2004, 2BvR 955/00 Deutsches Verwaltugsblatt 2005, pp. 175–83.

Pimentel, D., Kirby, C. and Shroff, A., 1993, 'The Relationship Between "Cosmetic Standards" for Food and Pesticide Use', in Pimentel, D. and Lehman, H., eds, *The Pesticide Question: Environmental Economics and Ethics*, Chapman and Hall, New York, pp. 85–105.

Pimentel, D., Stachow, U., Takacs, D.A., Brubaker, H.W., Dumas, A.R., Meaney, J.J., O'Neil, J.A.S., Onsi, D.E., and Corzilius, D.B., 1992, 'Conserving Biological Diversity in Agricultural/Forestry Systems', *Bioscience*, 42.5, 354–62.

Pimentel D., Westra, L. and Noss, R., 2000, *Ecological Integrity: Integrating Environmental Conservation and Health*, Island Press, Washington, DC.

Protocol Relating to the Status of Refugees, 606 UNTS 267, in force 4 October 1967.

Ramos, Lauren Michelle, 2011, 'New Standard for Evaluating Claims of Economic Persecution Under the 1951 Convention Relating to the Status of Refugees', *Vanderbilt Journal of Transnational Law*, 44, 499–525.

Ratner, Steven, 2001–2002, 'Corporations and Human Rights: A Theory of Legal Responsibility', *Yale Law Journal*, 111, 443–545.

Raveendram, Manasi, 2012, 'Plight of the Boat People: How to Determine State Obligations to Asylum Seekers', *Notre Dame Law Review*, 87.3, 1277–312.

Report of the International Law Commission, 2001, 53rd Sess., GAOR, 56th Sess., Supp. No. 10 (A/56/10).

Richardson, Dominic, and Ali, Nabil, 2014, *An Evaluation of International Surveys of Children*, OECD Social, Employment and Migration Working Papers No. 146, DELSA/ELSA/WD/SEM(2013)2, 17 February 2014.

Rifkin, Jeremy, 1995, *The End of Work*, Tarcher/Putnam, New York.

——, 2004, *The European Dream*, Tarcher/Penguin, New York.

Rosenberg-Goldin, Dorothy, 2005, *Toxic Trespass*, Video, Master's Thesis, O.I.S.E., Toronto.

Rylands v. Fletcher (1868) LR 3 HL 330.

Salmond, John, 1969, *The Law of Torts*, 15th edition, Sweet & Maxwell, London.

Salomon, Margot, 2007, *Global Responsibility for Human Rights*, Oxford University Press, Oxford.

Sassen, Saskia, 1996, *Losing Control?: Sovereignty in an Age of Globalization*, Columbia University Press, New York.

Sauer, T. and Nelson, M., 2011, 'Science, Ethics and the Historical Roots of Our Ecological Crisis', in Sauer, T.J., Norman, J.M., and Sivakumar, Mannawa V.S., eds, *Sustaining Soil Productivity in Response to Global Climate Change*, WileyBlackwell, Ames, IA, pp. 3–16.

Saxe, Diane, 2014, 'First "Climate Refugee" Case Going to Appeal in New Zealand', 8 April, available at http://envirolaw.com/climate-refugee-court-case/ (accessed 3 February 2015).

Snidell v. Abbott Laboratories, 607 P.2d, 924 (Cal. 1980).

Steiner, Henry J. and Alton, Philip, 2000, *International Human Rights in Context*, 2nd edition, Oxford University Press, Oxford.

Stiglitz, Joseph E., 2012, *The Price of Inequality*, Norton, New York.

Talmon, Stefan, 2006, 'The Duty Not to "Recognize as Lawful" a Situation Created by the Illegal Use of Force and Other Serious Breaches of a *Jus Cogens* Obligation: An Obligation without Substance?', in Tomuschat, C. and Thouvenin, J.-M., eds, *The Fundamental Rules of the International Legal Order: Jus Cogens and Obligations Erga Omnes*, Martinus Nijhoff, Leiden, pp. 99–126.

Tukker, A., Goldbohm, R.A., de Koning, A., Verheijden, M., Kleijn, R., Wolf, O., Pérez-Domínguez, I., and Rueda-Cantuche, J.M., 2011, 'Environmental Impacts or Changes to Healthier Diets in Europe', *Ecological Economics*, 70.10, 1776–88.

Ullman, W., 1988, *Law and Jurisdiction in the Middle Ages*, ed. George Garnett, Variorum, London.

United Nations Human Rights Council (UNHRC), 2008, *Human Rights Situation in Palestine and other Occupied Territories: Report of the Special Rapporteur on the Situation of Human Rights in the Palestinian Territories Occupied Since 1967, John Dugard*, 21 January 2008, UN doc. A/HRC/7/17.

——, 2012, *Final Study of the Human Rights Council Advisory Committee on the Advancement of the Rights of Peasants and Other People Working in Rural Areas*, 24 February 2012, UN doc. A/HRC/19/75.

——, 2014, *Report of the Special Rapporteur of the Right to Food, Oliver De Schutter, Final Report: The Transformative Potential of the Right to Food*, 25th sess., Agenda Item 3, 24 January 2014.

United Nations High Commissioner for Refugees (UNHCR), 2006, 'The State of the World's Refugees 2006', http://www.unhcr.org/4a4dc1a89.html (accessed 24 January 2015).

Weeramanty, S., 1996, as cited in 'Legality of the Threat or Use of Nuclear Weapons', in *Summaries of Judgments, Advisory Opinions and Orders of the International Court of Justice*, United Nations.

Westra, Laura, 1994, *The Principle of Integrity*, Rowman Littlefield, Lanham, MD.
——, 2007, *Environmental Justice and the Rights of Indigenous Peoples*, Earthscan, London.
——, 2010, 'Ecology and the Law Democracy, Globalization and the Greek Roots of Ecological Problems', in Engel, J.R., Westra, L., and Bosselmann, K., eds, *Democracy, Ecological Integrity and International Law*, Cambridge Scholars Press, Camridge, pp. 8–25.
——, 2011, 'Ecological Integrity and Biological Integrity: The Right to Food', in Sauer, T.J., Norman, J.M., and Sivakumar, Mannawa V.S., eds, *Sustaining Soil Productivity in Response to Global Climate Change*, WileyBlackwell, Ames, IA, pp. 103–16.
——, 2012, *Faces of State Terrorism*, Brill, Leiden.
——, 2013, *The Supranational Corporation*, Brill, Leiden.
——, 2014a, *Child Law: Children's Rights and Collective Obligations*, Springer, Berlin.
——, 2014b, *Revolt Against Authority*, Brill, Leiden.
Westra, Richard, 2012, *The Evil Axis of Finance*, Clarity Press, Atlanta, GA.
WHO, 2013, *State of the Science of Endocrine Disrupting Chemicals 2012*, http://apps.who.int/iris/bitstream/10665/78102/1/WHO_HSE_PHE_IHE_2013.1_eng.pdf?ua=1 (accessed 3 February 2015).

Chapter 4
Exodus after Conflict

Satvinder Juss

Introduction

A decade ago world leaders at the 2005 UN World Summit endorsed the idea of 'Responsibility to Protect' as a restraint on state sovereignty. This was intended to curb a country's tendency to mistreat its citizens. A state's sovereignty was thus declared to be inseparable from its 'responsibility to protect' those on its territory. Sovereignty was not merely a form of control. There was a duty to protect those over whom sovereignty was exercised. But what about a state's responsibility to others? What about its responsibility towards those, who although not on its territory, look to that state for protection? At first blush, a state would not have 'responsibility' for such people. They have no jurisdiction on them. But is this necessarily correct? If sovereignty can be exercised to exclude individuals, in need of protection, does it necessarily follow that such sovereignty can be exercised irresponsibly with all due disregard for human suffering? Surely not. And, if a state has contributed to a particular calamity (regional or international), such as by waging war, or by destabilizing another state such that the other state's citizens were then forced to leave, what then? Surely, the principle of 'responsibility to protect' falls to be applied even more forcefully on the offending state. Further, if the international community has been culpably involved in such action then its 'responsibility to protect' is even more pronounced in such a situation.

To suggest otherwise is to suggest that they are rogue nations, not prepared to live in a community of nations, where each may act irresponsibly towards the other. The idea that a state cannot escape responsibility in these circumstances has recently been propounded by James Souter.[1] Two objectives of refugee law are already particularly well-known, namely, 'as a response to a fundamental humanitarian imperative' and 'as an expression of moral condemnation of the persecutory or otherwise illegitimate actions of refugee-producing states', which enjoyed its heyday during the Cold War. He argues for a third objective which also has an 'important moral function: as a form of reparation for past injustice'. In his view, this 'stems from a special obligation on the part of states to provide asylum to refugees for whose lack of state protection they are responsible, whether through their military interventions, support for oppressive regimes or imposition

1 Souter, James, 2013, 'Towards a Theory of Asylum as Reparation for Past Injustice', *Political Studies*, 62.2, 326–42.

of damaging economic policies'. In this way, the institution of asylum can be used 'as potentially providing a means by which states can rectify the harm they caused to individuals by turning them into refugees'.[2]

It is accordingly a paradox that while we are yet again readily prepared to go to war in Syria and Iraq, we are not prepared to admit refugees from those areas. Our pretext in Britain is that we are facing a battle of Britain,[3] It is a truism, all too often overlooked, that wars produce refugees. We may watch dictatorships tumble, revolutions simmer, and the unfortunate 'Arab Spring' cruelly morph[4] into something altogether more sinister as the rise of ISIS marches on unabated.[5] Yet our refugee law is helplessly trapped, unable in this morass to provide any effective protection to those who most need it. Powerless to make sense of what unfolds before it, the Canadian government even more helplessly announces a closed door policy for Syrian refugees, so that 'after three and a half years of bloody civil war in Syria, Canadian reaction to the conflict's refugee crisis remains virtually

2 Ibid. at p. 326.

3 Forsyth, James, 2014, 'Michael Fallon Says UK Should Reconsider Military Action in Syria to Combat ISIS', *The Spectator*, 23 September, http://blogs.spectator.co.uk/coffeehouse/2014/09/the-new-battle-of-britain-michael-fallon-secretary-of-state-for-defence/ (accessed 25 February 2015), where Forsyth writes of the Secretary of State for Defence that, 'he seems morally offended at the suggestion that we should leave it to other countries to deal with Islamic State and irritated at the failure of some to grasp that the struggle against Islamic extremism is "Britain's business"', and inquiring as a result of attacks on the streets of London: 'how much more evidence do you need that this is a very clear and dangerous threat to our way of life and to all the democracies of the west. This is a new Battle of Britain'. On this basis, 'Fallon ... outlines the case for extending British participation to Syria, "The government of Iraq is also entitled to argue that it is under attack from ISIL forces in Syria or coming from Syria. ... Iraq is under attack not just from terrorists inside its own borders but it is under attack from terrorists in the north of Syria and if Syria continues to be unwilling or unable to deal with ISIL then at least the question arises as to whether we shouldn't assist Iraq in doing so". With the US-led coalition already striking sites in Syria, it seems that this will be the British justification for joining these bombing raids'.

4 See Juss, Satvinder and Harvey, Colin, 2013, *Contemporary Issues in Refugee Law*, Edward Elgar, Cheltenham, which refers to this theme.

5 It seems the USA underestimated the size of ISIS which is seven times what has previously been thought by US intelligence agencies: see, Cockburn, Patrick, 2014, 'War with Isis: Islamic Militants Have Army of 200,000, Claims Senior Kurdish Leader', *The Independent*, 16 November, http://www.independent.co.uk/news/world/middle-east/war-with-isis-islamic-militants-have-army-of-200000-claims-kurdish-leader-9863418.html (accessed 25 February 2015).

inaudible, despite increasingly desperate pleas for help and a growing sense of urgency'.[6] This is a denial of the humanitarian foundations of refugee law.[7]

The Preamble of the 1951 Refugee Convention is a sobering reminder of this reality when it states that the United Nations High Commissioner for Refugees (UNHCR) 'is charged with the task of supervising international conventions providing for the protection of refugees'.[8] That gives the Refugee Convention a clear 'protection' basis. It is significant too that the evident desire at the time, of preventing human rights violations, included also the objective of protecting the rights of refugees.[9] The person who feared persecution based on one of the listed grounds in the Refugee Convention had the right to leave her country and find safety elsewhere under the adopted definitions.[10] Yet, in the twenty-first century today there must be clear concerns about the extent to which the 'protection' basis of the Refugee Convention can be properly met. The situation in the Middle East today is a telling case in point.

In mid-2014, the United Nations Refugee Agency, the UNHCR, announced how 'Syrians are now the world's largest refugee population under UNHCR care, second only in number to the decades-long Palestinian crisis'. Indeed, 'the Syria operation is now the largest in UNHCR's 64-year history'. It is a catastrophe on an epic scale. According to the UN High Commissioner for Refugees, António Guterres, the Syrian crisis 'has become the biggest humanitarian emergency of our era, yet the world is failing to meet the needs of refugees and the countries hosting them'. Whilst there was some international response, 'the bitter truth is that it falls far short of what's needed'. Why is this? One would have thought that recent developments in twentieth-century refugee law which recognize the persecution of those fleeing the barbarism of FGM,[11] the pursuit of gay and lesbian communities,[12]

6 Goodspeed, Peter, 2014, 'Canada's Closed Door Policy for Syrian Refugees', *Aljazeera*, 2 November, http://www.aljazeera.com/indepth/opinion/2014/11/canada-closed-door-policy-syria-201411164759117409.html (accessed 25 February 2015).

7 This was accepted in the seminal case of *Horvath v. Secretary of State for the Home Department* [2000] UKHL 37, [2000] 3 WLR 379, [2001] 1AC 489, http://www.bailii.org/uk/cases/UKHL/2000/37.html (accessed 25 February 2015).

8 See Preamble at http://www.unhcr.org/4ca34be29.pdf (accessed 25 February 2015).

9 The preamble to the Refugee Convention of 1951 expressly notes and relies on the dedication to fundamental rights and freedoms contained in the Universal Declaration of Human Rights adopted in December 1948.

10 Rosensaft, Menachem Z. and Rosensaft, Joana D., 2001, 'The Early History of German-Jewish Reparations', *Fordham International Law Journal*, 25.6, S1–S45, pp. S1, S8.

11 *Secretary of State for the Home Department v. K* [2006] UKHL 46, [2006] 3 WLR 733, [2007] 1 AC 412, http://www.bailii.org/uk/cases/UKHL/2006/46.html (accessed 25 February 2015).

12 *HJ (Iran) v Secretary of State for the Home Department (Rev 1)* [2010] UKSC 31, [2011] AC 596, [2010] 3 WLR 386, http://www.bailii.org/uk/cases/UKSC/2010/31.html (accessed 25 February 2015).

and the discrimination of women in societies world-wide,[13] heralded the advent of a new age for refugee law. Such eye-catching forays, encapsulating as they do a fragment of the world's refugee population, conveniently leave the vast swathe of oppressed humanity untouched. Real progress is delusional and refugee law today is an exercise in crisis management. Those fleeing war, famine, population control polices and environmental disasters, remain lost in the weft and warp of refugee law. Twentieth-century refugee law is very firmly grounded on self-interest pure and simple.

In his article, 'Millions Uprooted: Saving Refugees and the Displaced' the UN High Commissioner for Refugees, Antonio Guterres, had some years earlier argued for the establishment of a 'co-operative legal and policy framework based on humanitarian principles that will ensure that people who have fled serious economic, social, or environmental crises in their own countries are not subsequently deported from the countries to which they have fled'.[14] He had advocated, 'temporary forms of protection and material assistance, at the least, should be provided to the most vulnerable among them' and that '[p]eople who need international protection must have access to the territory of other states and be allowed to make their cases in fair and effective asylum procedures'. In his view, '[b]order controls should be designed to be sensitive to the rights and safety of refugees'. Antonio Guterres, when he wrote, was all too aware himself that '[t]he twenty-first century will be characterized by the mass movement of people being pushed and pulled within and beyond their borders by conflict, calamity, or opportunity'. He was aware that '[w]ar and human rights violations are already scattering millions across the world in search of safety'. He could see that 'unresolved poverty, and enduring insecurity, is prompting many people to leave their homes' and that '[a]t few times in history have so many people been on the move'.

In Syria, an already desperate situation was by mid-2014 progressively getting worse following recent upsurges in fighting. The front lines were shifting. New areas were emptying out. But refugee law was silent. One example was the recent arrivals to Jordan, who were running from attacks in the areas of Raqaa and Aleppo. It is in this context that the UNHCR reported how Syria's intensifying refugee crisis had passed a record 3 million people. Conditions inside that country had reached horrifying levels. So, why shouldn't any sane rational person seek to flee from such mayhem? And, why shouldn't international law provide a mechanism for them to be able to do so legitimately? After all, the evidence showed that

13 *Islam v. Secretary of State for the Home Department Immigration Appeal Tribunal and Another, Ex Parte Shah, R v.* [1999] UKHL 20; [1999] 2 AC 629; [1999] UKHL 20, [1999] 2 WLR 1015, http://www.bailii.org/uk/cases/UKHL/1999/20.html (accessed 25 February 2015).

14 Guterres, Antonio, 2008, 'Millions Uprooted: Saving Refugees and the Displaced', *Foreign Affairs*, 87.5, 90–99, p. 90. Available at http://www.foreignaffairs.com/articles/63572/antÃ³nio-guterres/millions-uprooted (accessed 25 February 2015).

there were cities where populations had been surrounded. The people were going hungry. Civilians were being indiscriminately killed. In the words of the UNHCR,

> Almost half of all Syrians have now been forced to abandon their homes and flee for their lives. One in every eight Syrians has fled across the border, fully a million more than a year ago. A further 6.5 million are displaced within Syria. Over half of those uprooted are children.[15]

Aid agencies were remarking on how increasing numbers of families were arriving in a shocking state, exhausted, scared and with their savings depleted. Most of them had been on the run for a year or more. This is a fact that most observers also forget, that when refugees flee they have been on the move for months, and sometimes even years. Only a couple years earlier in 2012,[16] the UK reported on the plight of Afghan children and young males who had trekked bare foot through ice and snow – from Kabul through to Iran, Turkey, Greece, Macedonia, Serbia, Croatia, Slovenia and Italy – before arriving in France, before making their desperate claims for asylum.[17] Many went onto the United Kingdom from there.[18] These were, 'among the world's most vulnerable migrants. … in flight from violence or the aftershocks of violence that affect children in particularly harsh ways' and it was noted how 'those who turn up in Paris have spent up to a year on the road, on the same clandestine routes as adults, but at far greater risk', and that 'no one quite knows how many unaccompanied Afghan children have made it to Europe' although in Paris they were the biggest nationality among the 1700 lone foreign minors in the care of the authorities.

In the Syrian case, refugees had been fleeing from village to village before taking the final decision to leave. Yet, precisely because of this, there were, according to the UNHCR, 'worrying signs … that the journey out of Syria is becoming tougher, with many people forced to pay bribes at armed checkpoints proliferating

---

15 'Needs Soar as Number of Syrian Refugees Tops 3 million', UNHCR, News Stories, 29 August 2014, http://www.unhcr.org.uk/news-and-views/news-list/news-detail/article/needs-soar-as-number-of-syrian-refugees-tops-3-million.html (accessed 25 February 2015).

16 See Brothers, C., 2012, 'Out of Afghanistan: Incredible Stories of the Boys Who Walked to Europe', *The Observer*, 29 January, recording that the country is so dangerous it's no wonder so many leave, travelling alone across the Middle East in search of a new life. Available at http://www.theguardian.com/world/2012/jan/29/out-afghanistan-boys-stories-europe (accessed 25 February 2015).

17 As recounted in, Juss, Satvinder Singh, 2013, 'Refugee Law and the Protection of Children Fleeing Conflict and Violence in Afghanistan', *Journal of Conflict and Security Law*, 18.2, 289–330, at pp. 294–5, available at http://jcsl.oxfordjournals.org/cgi/reprint/krt001?ijkey=diD2Q63tZ3HvuZ4&keytype=ref (accessed 25 February 2015).

18 As observed in the UK Tribunal case of *Master Tariq Niazi v SSHD* (AA/12931/2011).

along the borders'.[19] Human smugglers were getting involved because 'refugees crossing the desert into eastern Jordan are being forced to pay smugglers' hefty sums (US$100/£60 a head or more) to take them to safety'.[20] Yet, the majority did not manage to venture far so that 'most of the refugees remain in countries neighbouring Syria, with the highest concentrations in Lebanon (1.14 million), Jordan (608,000) and Turkey (815,000)'. The inevitable effect of this 'led to an enormous strain on their economies, infrastructure and resources'. The victims of this scourge themselves did not fare any better because, 'more than four in five refugees are struggling to make a living in urban areas, with 38 per cent living in sub-standard shelter'. It is unsurprising then that, 'many newly arriving refugees say they only left Syria as a last resort' and that 'a growing number, including more than half of those coming to Lebanon, have moved at least once before fleeing, and one in 10 have moved more than three times'. In fact, from 19 September 2014, the Syrian refugee crisis worsened, with an unprecedented influx of more than 144,000 refugees[21] crossing into Turkey,[22] mainly ethnic Kurds fleeing militant threats to towns and villages in northern Syria. The UN Secretary-General called for a swift election of a new Lebanese president, underlining the urgent need to support Lebanon to cope with the overwhelming number of Syrian refugees.[23]

What explains the lack of action by Western states to the unfolding refugee crisis in our midst? The answer lies in the very words used to justify the latest thrust to war in the Middle East in the words of Secretary of State for Defence, Michael Fallon, namely, that we are facing 'a new Battle of Britain'. The conventional wisdom today is that we face decades of terror from an obscure,

---

19 'Needs Soar as Number of Syrian Refugees Tops 3 Million' UNHCR, News Stories, 29 August 2014.

20 For an account of the relationship between 'human smuggling' and 'human trafficking' see Juss, S., 2012, 'Human Trafficking, Asylum, and the Problem of Protection' in Juss, S., ed., *The Ashgate Research Companion to Migration Law, Theory and Policy*, Ashgate, Farnham. In the Afghan cases also there was evidence of human smuggling which was fuelled by '[t]he rising fear among some Afghans for the future of their country and the existence of a class of well-off professionals' especially among the country's elite in Kabul, which has resulted in 'a growing and lucrative business in smuggling a tide of mostly young, unaccompanied Afghan males overseas': see, Boone, Jon and Bakshi, Nooruddin, 2012, 'Boom Time for Afghanistan's People Smugglers', *The Guardian*, 18 January, http://www.guardian.co.uk/world/2012/jan/18/afghanistan-people-smugglers-taliban-europe (accessed 25 February 2015).

21 'UN: Turkey Received as Many Syrian Refugees in Three Days as Europe Did in Three Years', *Middle East Monitor*, 24 September 2014, available at https://www.middleeastmonitor.com/news/europe/14335-un-turkey-received-as-many-syrian-refugees-in-three-days-as-europe-did-in-three-years (accessed 25 February 2015).

22 'UNHCR Airlifts Urgent Aid into Turkey to Help Refugees Fleeing ISIS', UNHCR, News Stories, 25 September 2014.

23 'Ban: Lebanon Underfunded over Refugee Crisis', *The Daily Star*, 27 September 2014.

shapeless, omnipresent and fiendish force. There is no doubt, as Karen Armstrong has explained, that 'IS [Islamic State] uses violence to achieve a single, limited and clearly defined objective that would be impossible without such slaughter' so that given that 'mass killing is a thoroughly modern phenomenon' what we are witnessing 'is another expression of the dark side of modernity'.[24] Yet, to view this carnage as a simple act of terrorism is reductionist. What is really happening in the Middle East is battle for the soul of Islam. Various warring Islamic groups are involved. This is the narrative of all normal historical conflicts in the world. Insurrections, political assassinations and civil wars all add up to make a new historical epoch.

For Secretary of State Michael Fallon to suggest that simply to wage war in a 'new battle of Britain' will eliminate the evil of IS is delusional. Yet, its implications are far-ranging for such policy sentiments impact on the true interpretation of international refugee law today: who should Western governments admit, and who should they exclude from sanctuary, as they continue their 'war on terror'? Since Syria is a source of perceived terrorism, in much the same way as Afghanistan has been, refugee law is used as a tool of counter-insurgency to exclude as many people from that region as possible – not to admit them – on the assumption that their admission is a security risk to the receiving states. If this is so, it brings into question the principle of 'Responsibility to Protect' as a restraint on the sovereign state right to exclude refugees.

War Refugees in Conflict Situations

Wars create refugees. In 2012, two years before the UNHCR report on Syria in 2014, when the war in Afghanistan was at its high-point, it was Afghanistan which was 'the largest producer of refugees in the world, both in absolute numbers and as a proportion of the national population' largely because of 'the general lack of security' in that country'.[25] This was a situation exacerbated after 9/11, by the invasion of that country by NATO forces in a US-led alliance to preserve the USA as a hegemon state. When in the first major case regarding Afghan refugees in the UK, *GS (Afghanistan)*,[26] the Upper Tribunal of the Immigration and Asylum Chamber, an administrative appellate tribunal determining immigration appeals,

---

24 Armstrong, Karen, 2014, 'The Deep Roots of Islamic State', *New Statesman*, 21–27 November 2014, pp. 24–31, p. 31.

25 *AK (Article 15(c)) Afghanistan CG* [2012] UKUT 00163(IAC), at para. 46. This report is by Theo Farrell and Olivier Schmitt in their March 2012 study published by the Division of International Protection, UNHCR, 'The Causes, Character and Conduct of Armed Conflict, and the Effects on Civilian Populations, 1990–2010'.

26 *GS (Article 15(c): indiscriminate violence) Afghanistan CG* [2009] UKAIT 00044.

set out 'to put this determination into context',[27] it did so by its blunt assessment of how '[t]he current conflict was triggered by the US led invasion of Afghanistan in late 2001' such that the present 'phase of internal armed conflict has been ongoing since 2002', wherein 'Afghanistan has endured almost constant warfare since the Soviet invasion in 1979'. Another decision of the Upper Tribunal in 2012, *AK (Afghanistan)*,[28] explained how,[29] 'Afghanistan is not only war-stricken; it is riven by ethnic frictions, political factionalism, high levels of poverty, impunity, serious abuses of human rights by both state and non-state actors …' and that it was trapped in a morass of, 'ineffective governance, high levels of corruption, weak rule of law, an anaemic legal system, and a high risk of infiltration, corruption or subversion by insurgents, warlords and criminal groups'.[30] The same, as it now appears, is becoming the situation in Syria. Yet, under the Refugee Convention 1951, a person seeking to escape from this state of affairs is generally unable to claim refugee status. This is because he or she may not be able to show that they are individually at risk on account of what is a condition of generalized violence that is not specifically directed at him or her.

The United Nations High Commissioner for Refugees (UNHCR) officially refers to them as 'war refugees'. Yet, despite the direct and unmistakable link between wars and refugees, the UNHCR itself recognizes that there is an uphill struggle in their recognition as 'refugees' in these circumstances. The UNHCR Handbook deals with such 'War Refugees' under the heading of 'Special Cases',[31] thus indicating their inherent conceptual difficulty for refugee lawyers. The general position is confirmed in paragraph 164, which explains that, 'Persons compelled to leave their country of origin as a result of international or national armed conflicts are not normally considered refugees under the 1951 Convention or 1967 Protocol'.[32] This is immediately then qualified by paragraph 165 of the Handbook which follows on to say:

> However, *foreign invasion or occupation* of all or part of a country can result – and occasionally *has resulted – in persecution* for one or more of the reasons

27 Ibid., at para. 13, where the tribunal adopted the Skeleton Argument of Counsel for the appellant, Mr. Mark Symes (at para. 37) .

28 *AK (Article 15(c)) Afghanistan CG* [2012] UKUT 00163(IAC).

29 Ibid.

30 These were the opening remarks of the Tribunal's judgment in May 2012, on the plight of unaccompanied children and vulnerable young adults (at para. 1).

31 See UNHCR, 1979, *Handbook on Procedures and Criteria for Determining Refugee Status* (reissued 2011), Geneva., at ch. V.

32 This provision goes on to add that, 'They do, however, have the protection provided for in other international instruments, for example the Geneva Conventions of 1949 on the Protection of War Victims and the 1977 Protocol additional to the Geneva Conventions of 1949 relating to the protection of Victims on International Armed Conflicts'. Nevertheless, the general position is clear that the 1951 Refugee Convention does afford immediate protection.

> enumerated in the 1951 Convention. In such cases, refugee status will depend upon *whether the applicant is able to show that he has a 'well-founded fear of being persecuted'* in the occupied territory and, in addition upon *whether or not he is able to avail himself of the protection of his government, or of a protecting power whose duty it is to safeguard the interests of his country* during armed conflict, and whether such protection can be considered to be effective. (Emphases added.)

The Handbook concludes this section at paragraph 166 with the words that, '… every case has to be judged on its merits, both in respect of well-founded fear of persecution and the availability of effective protection on the part of the government of the country of origin'. There is, therefore, in this section on 'War Refugees' a powerfully explosive mixture of the potentially opposing interests of the individual on the one side, and the occupying foreign power on the other. Protection, especially where it is to come on account of the insecurity and instability caused by an invading foreign power, is not something which is ever going to be easy to provide in these circumstances. And so it has been. It was for this reason why it eventually fell to European Union law, over half a century later, to provide a form of alternative protection.

This came in the form of 'subsidiary' protection pursuant to Article 2 of Directive 2004/83/EC (the Qualification Directive),[33] which acts as a surrogate to refugee status. To be eligible for 'subsidiary' protection, such a person will have to demonstrate a plausible risk of 'serious harm' to him or her in a certain particularized context. Article 15 defines the context of the serious harm in a way that is particularly relevant to the plight of 'war refugees' as, 'Serious and individual threat to a civilian life or person by reason of indiscriminate violence in situations of international or internal armed conflict'.[34] In *QD (Iraq)*, Sedley LJ explained the importance of such a law in that, 'the Directive brings together classical Geneva refugee status with what it calls subsidiary protection status'. Both the '*non-refoulement*' obligations with respect to those who cannot establish an affirmative right to asylum, 'assumed by all EU member states as part of the Council of Europe' as well as 'the humanitarian practices adopted by many EU states, towards individuals who manifestly need protection' would be safeguarded, because they are 'imperilled by endemic violence'.[35] The result is

33 Council Directive 2004/83/EC of 29 April 2004 on minimum standards for the qualification and status of third country nationals or stateless persons as refugees or as persons who otherwise need international protection and the content of the protection granted. Available at http://eur-lex.europa.eu/LexUriServ/LexUriServ.do?uri=CELEX:32004L0083:EN:HTML (accessed 14 August 2012).

34 Ibid.

35 *QD (Iraq) v. SSHD* [2009] EWCA Civ. 620, at para. 9.

that such persons are required to be granted subsidiary protection status,[36] unless an internal relocation alternative is open to them,[37] or until the risk in the country of origin ceases.[38]

The reality is that the application of Article 15(c) has proved quite challenging. The powerful interests of states – especially those that have waged war – are not easy to reconcile with the meagre interests of an individual, who may count for little or nothing in the grand order of things. So, to qualify for protection an applicant has to show a risk that was 'individual' to him or her. Ironically, however, the 'risk' has to be from an 'indiscriminate' source that is not individuated. In the words of Jean-Francois Durieux, 'the nonsensical wording of Article 15(c)'[39] makes it hard to conceive of 'any rational way of resolving the contradictions inherent in the wording of Article 15(c)' thereby making it practicably impossible to make sense of 'this bizarre provision'.[40] Eminent judges have echoed these sentiments. In the rueful remarks of Sedley LJ in *QD (Iraq)*, Article 15(c): 'both on its own and even more so when married with article 2(e), is highly problematical – in large part, … because of poor drafting'. There are three immediate reasons for this, namely, '(1) the ostensibly cumulative but logically intractable test of "real risk" of a "threat"; (2) the contradictory postulation of an "individual threat" to life or safety from "indiscriminate violence"; (3) the requirement of "armed conflict" when there may well be only one source of indiscriminate violence'.[41] Durieux said

---

36 Article 18 of the Qualification Directive, which deals with the 'Granting of subsidiary protection status' stipulates: 'Member States shall grant subsidiary protection status to a third country national or a stateless person eligible for subsidiary protection in accordance with Chapters II and V'.

37 Article 8 of the Qualification Directive, which deals with, 'Internal protection' stipulates the following provisions: '1. As part of the assessment of the application for international protection, Member States may determine that an applicant is not in need of international protection if in a part of the country of origin there is no well-founded fear of being persecuted or no real risk of suffering serious harm and the applicant can reasonably be expected to stay in that part of the country. 2. In examining whether a part of the country of origin is in accordance with paragraph 1, Member States shall at the time of taking the decision on the application have regard to the general circumstances prevailing in that part of the country and to the personal circumstances of the applicant. 3. Paragraph 1 may apply notwithstanding technical obstacles to return to the country of origin'.

38 Article 16 of the Qualification Directive, which deals with 'Cessation' stipulates: '1. A third country national or a stateless person shall cease to be eligible for subsidiary protection when the circumstances which led to the granting of subsidiary protection status have ceased to exist or have changed to such a degree that protection is no longer required. 2. In applying paragraph 1, Member States shall have regard to whether the change of circumstances is of such a significant and non-temporary nature that the person eligible for subsidiary protection no longer faces a real risk of serious harm'.

39 Durieux, Jean-Francois, 2012, 'Of War Flows, Laws and Flaws: A Reply to Hugo Storey', *Refugee Survey Quarterly*, 31.3, 161–76, at p. 172.

40 Ibid., p. 173.

41 *QD (Iraq)*, at para. 19.

of Article 15(c), that the way around this conundrum is to focus on: 'the reality of contemporary refugee flows – civilians fleeing the indiscriminate effects of generalised violence'. This should make it clear to us precisely 'which threatened rights and interests participants in the regime feel duty-bound to protect in the face of such situations and which threats are serious enough to warrant, at a minimum, non-refoulement',[42] This author argued that the terminology of Article 15(c) with respect to the concept of 'armed conflict' should be considered *sui generis* with its own meaning.[43] This has fortunately recently been confirmed by the European Court of Justice when it observed:

> the answer to the question referred is that, on a proper construction of Article 15(c) of Directive 2004/83, it must be acknowledged that an internal armed conflict exists, for the purposes of applying that provision, if a State's armed forces confront one or more armed groups or if two or more armed groups confront each other. It is not necessary for that conflict to be categorised as 'armed conflict not of an international character' under international humanitarian law; nor is it necessary to carry out, in addition to an appraisal of the level of violence present in the territory concerned, a separate assessment of the intensity of the armed confrontations, the level of organisation of the armed forces involved or the duration of the conflict.[44]

It remains to be seen how effectively this will be applied in future cases. But it is surely helpful that for the time being the court has explained that, 'it is not necessary, when considering an application for subsidiary protection, to carry out a specific assessment of the intensity of such confrontations in order to determine, separately from the appraisal of the resulting level of violence, whether the condition relating to armed conflict has been met'.[45] In fact, 'the finding that there is an armed conflict must not be made conditional upon the armed forces involved having a certain level of organisation or upon the conflict lasting for a

---

42 Durieux, 2012, 'Of War Flows, Laws and Flaws: A Reply to Hugo Storey', p. 175.

43 Juss, S.S., 2013, 'Problematizing the Protection of "War Refugees": A Rejoinder to Hugo Storey and Jean-François Durieux', *Refugee Survey Quarterly*, 32, 122–47. Also see other commentaries: Chetail, V., 2014, 'Armed Conflict and Forced Migration: A Systemic Approach to International Humanitarian Law, Refugee Law and Human Rights Law', in Clapham, A. and Gaeta, P., eds, *Oxford Handbook of International Law in Armed Conflict*, Oxford University Press, Oxford, pp. 700–734; Cantor, D. and Durieux, J-F., 2014, *Refuge from Inhumanity? War Refugees and International Humanitarian Law*, Brill, Leiden; Rikhoff, Joseph, 2015, 'International Criminal Law and Refugee Law: Lessons Learned?', in Jalloh, C. and Marong, A., eds, *Promoting Accountability for Gross Human Rights Violations in Africa under International Law: Essays in Honour of Prosecutor Hassan Bubacar Jallow*, Leiden: Martinus Nijhoff Brill, forthcoming.

44 *Aboubacar Diakité v. Commissaire général aux réfugiés et aux apatrides*, C285/12, 30 January 2014, at para. 35.

45 Ibid., at para. 32.

specific length of time'.[46] What the court has done is to explain how those fleeing indiscriminate violence may find sanctuary. It has not set out to provide a legal definition of 'armed conflict'. That concept remains *sui generis* to the framework that provides for it.

So, what threatened rights should the international community protect under Article 15(c)? The answer to this question has been provided by the *UNHCR Eligibility Guidelines for Assessing the International Protection Needs of Asylum Seekers from Afghanistan*, 17 December 2010.[47] One recent case on Afghanistan said of the Guidelines that, '[t]hey include references to a considerable body of empirical data about conditions in Afghanistan, as well as UNHCR's evaluation of it in the form of guidelines',[48] which a court or a tribunal of inquiry will not ordinarily have access to. The kinds of risks that emanate in Afghanistan, according to the Guidelines, are of two types. The first deals with persons who have a specific risk profile. The position of the UNHCR here is that they 'require a particularly careful examination of possible risks'. It is not difficult to see why. They include all the usual suspect classes of women, ethnic groups and people suspected of supporting the wrong side.[49] A more recent UNHCR report, *Safe at Last: Law and Practice in Selected EU Member States with respect to Asylum Seekers Fleeing Indiscriminate Violence* (UNHCR, July 2011),[50] is also one where the authors note in relation to Afghanistan, that, '… it was UNHCR's view at the time of the research in 2010 that there was a worsening security situation in certain parts of the country' so that, '[t]he violence continued to cause significant population displacement and high numbers of civilian casualties, in particular due to suicide attacks and the use of improvised explosive devises'.[51]

In fact, the tribunal in *AK (Afghanistan)*,[52] in 2012 described that country as 'war stricken'.[53] Indeed, the situation there had so escalated that, 'by virtue of the involvement since November 2001 of U.S. and other international forces, what is

46 Ibid., at para. 34.

47 HCR/E.G./AFG/10/04. Available at http://www.unhcr.org/refworld/docid/4d0b55c92.html (accessed 25 February 2015).

48 *AK (Article 15(c)) Afghanistan CG* [2012] UKUT 00163(IAC), at para. 86.

49 More specifically, they include '(i) individuals associated with, or perceived as supportive of, the Afghan Government and the international community …; (ii) humanitarian workers and human rights activists; (iii) journalists and other media professionals; (iv) civilians suspected of supporting armed anti-Government groups; (v) members of minority religious groups …; (vi) women with specific profiles; (vii) children with specific profiles; (viii) victims of trafficking; (ix) lesbian, gay, bisexual, transgender and intersex (LGBTI) individuals; (x) members of (minority) ethnic groups; and (xi) persons at risk of becoming victims of blood feuds'.

50 Available at http://www.unhcr.org/refworld/docid/4e2ee0022.html (accessed 25 February 2015).

51 Ibid., p. 22.

52 *AK (Article 15(c)) Afghanistan CG* [2012] UKUT 00163(IAC).

53 Ibid., at para. 1.

now known as "the Long War" also has an international dimension'.[54] The Upper Tribunal recognized now 'the global resonance of this conflict'. Yet, despite this, it declined to take these clear findings of fact to their logical conclusion and to hold that anyone having to flee from the conditions of 'indiscriminate violence' now appertaining in Afghanistan can plausibly be regarded as falling within the protection mechanisms of Article 15(c). Instead, the Upper Tribunal held that, 'it is as well that we emphasise at the outset that our task as judges in this case is a limited one'.[55] It focused on the fact that, 'there are return and reintegration packages available' to Kabul, and whereas, '[i]t would be unwise to exaggerate the importance of such packages: they are chiefly designed to cushion against immediate travails on return' so that, 'by assisting with skills training and inquiries related to employment opportunities, they clearly do help position returnees advantageously …'.[56]

This was despite the fact that the appellant was, 'considered as a single young male returning on his own without any family support', and yet it was held that 'he would be able to live in Kabul in safety and without undue hardship'.[57] Once again, the interests of hegemonic states was being preserved. Yet, the Guidelines here specifically set out to endorse and elaborate upon the difficult concept of 'War Refugees' as specially set out in the UNHCR Handbook at paragraphs 164 and 165. In fact, in another decision by the Upper Tribunal, *HM and Others*[58] it was even said that, '[t]hough very considerable weight is almost always to be attached to UNHCR guidelines on risk categories in particular countries, it is not accepted that departure from the guidelines should only take place for a cogent and identified reason'. This is remarkable given that the Guidelines very often alone help to put flesh on the bare-bones of the hapless and ill-drafted provisions of Article 15 of the Qualification Directive.

Burden-Sharing and Dublin II

We often forget that everyone has the right to claim asylum, wherever that may be, and this principle which was first enshrined in the United Nations Convention Relating to the Status of Refugees 1951,[59] created to guarantee people in Europe those rights after the atrocities of the Second World War, and extended thereafter

54 Ibid., at para. 2.

55 Ibid., at para. 3.

56 Ibid., at para. 224.

57 Ibid., at para. 253.

58 *HM and others (Article 15(c)) Iraq CG* [2012] UKUT 00409 (IAC) (13 November 2012), http://www.bailii.org/uk/cases/UKUT/IAC/2012/00409_ukut_iac_2012_hm_ors_iraq_cg.html (accessed 25 February 2015).

59 United Nations Convention Relating to the Status of Refugees 1951. Available at http://www.unhcr.org/3b66c2aa10.html (accessed 25 February 2015).

by the 1967 Protocol to people in other countries around the world, has been replicated in one international instrument after another since then. Until conflict and persecution no longer exist, those rights must be upheld. Those fleeing to the borders of Europe from war-torn and strife-ridden countries of Afghanistan, Iraq, Syria and the regions of the Middle East and Africa are often fleeing conditions of real persecution and ill-treatment. They are in search of a 'safe country'. Not all the countries of Europe are safe for all purposes and for all people. Burdens between the states of Europe have to be shared because potential asylum-seekers cannot all go to one region or one country so as to impose a disproportionate burden there. So what they are required to do through international arrangements between European states is to apply for asylum at the first 'safe country' they come to, and all countries of Europe are deemed to be safe, whether or not they are. Yet the 'safe country' notion is a legal fiction. It is nothing more than a legal *mantra* adopted in the Common European Asylum System. The effect is often to deny sanctuary to those who are clearly in need of it. So, how does the system work?

We may begin by recognizing that international cooperation has long been recognized as a necessary prerequisite for the satisfactory solution to the plight of refugees. This is clear from the Preamble to the 1951 Refugee Convention.[60] Yet, its actual implementation remains one of the most controversial issues in refugee protection. The difficulties in implementation arise from managing 'burden-sharing' in a fair and sensitive way. The Dublin II system attempts to do this. This was explained by Mr Justice Cranston in *Saeedi*, in terms that, '[t]he Dublin Regulation (EC) No 343/2003 is the cornerstone of the Common European Asylum System. It establishes a system of determining responsibility, according to specific criteria, for examining an asylum claim lodged in a Member State or in Iceland, Norway or Switzerland, which all participate in the Dublin system'. As he explained,

> [t]he Regulation aims at ensuring that each claim is examined by one Member State as 'on the one hand, to guarantee effective access to the procedures for determining refugee status and not to compromise the objective of the rapid processing of asylum application and, on the other, to prevent abuse of asylum procedure in the form of multiple applications for asylum submitted by the same person in several Member States with the sole aim of extending his/her stay in the Member States'.[61]

---

60 The Refugee Convention 1951 states in its Preamble: 'Considering that the grant of asylum may place unduly heavy burdens on certain countries, and that a satisfactory solution of a problem of which the United Nations has recognized the international scope and nature cannot therefore be achieved without international co-operation', Available at http://www.unhcr.org/4ca34be29.pdf (accessed 25 February 2015).

61 *Saeedi, R (on the application of) v. Secretary of State for the Home Department & Ors* [2010] EWHC 705 (Admin) (31 March 2010), at para. 59, http://www.bailii.org/ew/cases/EWHC/Admin/2010/705.html (accessed 25 February 2015).

It remains the case nevertheless that the most sophisticated mechanism developed by states to embody this principle is currently contained in the so-called Dublin II Regulation and remains the same under Dublin III which came into force on 19 July 2013,[62] though the cases discussed in this chapter naturally are all concerned with the Dublin II Regulation.[63] However, from its inception this system has been subject to scrutiny by domestic as well as international courts. Nadine El-Nany[64] has offered a powerful critique of Dublin II. She has explained how the central, binding EU instrument for the implementation of the 'safe country' concept is the Dublin Regulation,[65] incorporating the Dublin Convention,[66] agreed at Schengen, into EU legislation, and it is the pivotal binding EU instrument. The Dublin Convention states that responsibility lies with the first Member State with which the asylum applicant establishes contact. This may be by the issue of a transit visa, the legal presence of a close family member, or in the absence of these, the first physical contact with the territory.[67] States Parties are required to readmit individuals transferred on the basis of the Dublin regime, whilst respecting the principle of mutual recognition with regard to the application of its rules. But as Lavenex has concluded, European cooperation is founded on 'the assumption of common standards of refugee protection'[68] and Costello has referred to 'the most worrying' element of the application of the 'safe country of origin' concept being

62 'Dublin III Regulation Enters into Force Today', Electronic Immigration Network, 19 July 2013, http://www.ein.org.uk/news/dublin-iii-regulation-enters-force-today (accessed 25 February 2015).

63 This section draws from Juss, Satvinder, 2013, 'The Post-Colonial Refugee, Dublin II, and the End of Non-Refoulement', *International Journal of Minority and Group Rights*, Special Issue, 20.2, 307–35.

64 El-Nany, Nadine, 2013, 'The "New Europe" and the "European Refugee": The Subversion of the European Union's Refugee Law by Its Migration Policy', in Juss, Satvinder S., ed., *The Ashgate Research Companion on Migration Law, Theory, and Policy*, Ashgate, Farnham, pp. 3–24, p. 14.

65 Commission Regulation (EC) No 1560/2003 of 2 September 2003 laying detailed rules for the application of Council Regulation (EC) No 343/2003 establishing the criteria and mechanisms for determining the Member State responsible for examining an asylum application lodged in one of the Member States by a third-country national [2003] OJ L 222.

66 Convention determining the State responsible for examining applications for asylum lodged in one of the Member States of the European Communities 15 June 1990 [1997] OJ C254/1.

67 Articles 4–8, Dublin Convention, and Articles 28–38, Convention implementing the Schengen Agreement of 14 June 1985 between the Governments of the States of the Benelux Economic Union, the Federal Republic of Germany and the French Republic on the gradual abolition of checks at their common borders 14 June 1985 [1985] OJ L 176. See Lavenex, S., 1998, '"Passing the Buck": European Union Refugee Policies towards Central and Eastern Europe', *Journal of Refugee Studies*, 11.2, 126–45, p. 130.

68 Ibid.

the ensuing decline in procedural safeguards.[69] As we have seen confirmed in the cases discussed above, claims originating from countries designated as 'safe' are treated as 'manifestly unfounded' or inadmissible.[70] The only consensus among all actors involved seems to be its unsatisfactory performance and its continuous need for reform.

There is recognition of the failure of the 'safe country' notion in that the EU has now successfully negotiated a recast Dublin II Regulation that needs to provide an appropriate response to Member States' obligations of protection in the context of international cooperation, as interpreted by the European Court of Human Rights in the *M.S.S. v. Belgium and Greece* case (judgment of 21 January 2011) and by the Court of Justice of the European Union in the *N.S. v Secretary of State for the Home Department* (C-411/10) case (judgment of 21 December 2011), which are discussed below.

Nevertheless, problems have arisen in relation to *refoulement* of refugees from Italy, Greece and Hungary. The treatment of Dublin returnees in Hungary gives rise to serious concerns (the *non-refoulement* principle is not duly observed, returnees are immediately issued an expulsion order and routinely detained without considering their individual circumstances and so on). The Hungarian Helsinki Committee has prepared a short information note in order to raise awareness about the seriousness of the situation and to urge national Dublin units and courts to examine carefully the conditions returnees would face in Hungary before actually deciding on the return.[71] The current situation leads to an improper application of the Dublin Regulation and to the serious violation of asylum-seekers' human rights.

It is of course right that in an ideal world, people would be able to access protection in any country of their choosing. But the reality, as enshrined in Dublin II, is far removed from this (and remains the same under Dublin III which came into force on 19 July 2013[72]). What is needed therefore is a common European asylum system, which (i) does not define adequate protection by reference to those countries that have managed no more than reach minimum standards, but (ii) ensure that adequate protection is defined in terms of where people can access fair, humane and effective asylum systems, and (iii) are able to do so in whichever European country they choose to access protection. Until such time, however, what the courts should do is ensure that the relatively few that do manage to get

69 Costello, C., 2005, '*The Asylum Procedures Directive and the Proliferation of Safe Country Practices: Deterrence, Deflection and the Dismantling of International Protection?' European Journal of Migration Law*, 7.1, 35–70.

70 Ibid.

71 See, Hungarian Helsinki Committee, 2011, 'Access to Protection Jeopardized: Information Note on the Treatment of Dublin Returnees in Hungary', December 2011, http://www.refworld.org/docid/4f3e10ab2.html (accessed 31 January 2015).

72 'Dublin III Regulation Enters into Force Today', Electronic Immigration Network, 19 July 2013, http://www.ein.org.uk/news/dublin-iii-regulation-enters-force-today (accessed 25 February 2015).

to a country in Europe, where they can secure safety and security, are given an impartial and fair hearing on the merits of their claim, so that those who need protection are allowed to stay and are not subject to *refoulement*. The need for this principle is clear from the cases arising before the courts.

Nasseri,[73] concerned an Afghan national who crossed into Greece in December 2004 and claimed asylum, but when that application was rejected on 1 April 2005, he entered the UK on 5 September 2005 concealed under a lorry. When detected he again claimed asylum.[74] Greece agreed to take him back, following a request from the UK government, for his asylum claim to be determined there. The applicant resisted on grounds that there was a real risk that, if sent to Greece, he would be returned to Afghanistan to face inhuman or degrading treatment, contrary to Article 3 ECHR.[75] Lord Hoffmann highlighted that the duty to investigate possible claims of human rights infringements is part and parcel of the protection of a person's rights and that the Court will conduct an investigation which amounts to 'a rigorous scrutiny of the claim' such that 'unless a Member State has done so, it runs the risk of being held in breach'.[76] Despite that there is, however, no guidance at the moment as to when or if the duty arises, and the nature of the duty, where the subject is the potential breach of fundamental EU law rights; this is a matter in issue between the parties. This is the main question that will be discussed in this chapter.

In *EM* the Court of Appeal was faced with a formidable argument on behalf of all four Eritrean applicants. It was argued that the 'presumption of state compliance' can be rebutted by adequate 'evidence of personal risk', predicated typically but not necessarily on that 'person's own experience'. Evidence such as a UNHCR report is simply part of a body of evidence, which may legitimately go beyond what the High Commissioner reports. Given the apparent prevalence of the inhuman and degrading conditions described by the four applicants here, it is perfectly reasonable to infer that the Italian system, like the Greek, is not merely functioning erratically but is truly dysfunctional.[77] Sir Stephen Sedley strained to disagree. His Lordship held that there was in the objective evidence, 'a great deal of support to the accounts given by three of the claimants of their own experiences of seeking asylum in Italy'. However, the question under the law as it now stood was not whether each of the four claimants faces a real risk of inhuman or degrading treatment if returned to Italy. If this was the question 'their claims would plainly be arguable and unable to be certified. But we are

---

73 *Nasseri* [2009] UKHL 23 (6 May 2009), http://www.bailii.org/uk/cases/UKHL/2009/23.html (accessed 25 February 2015).

74 Ibid., at para. 2.

75 Ibid., at para. 4.

76 Ibid., at para, 15. Reliance was placed by Lord Hoffman on *Chahal v. United Kingdom* (1996) 23 EHRR 413, at para. 96 and on *Vilvarajah v. United Kingdom* (1991) 14 EHRR 248, at para. 108.

77 Ibid., at para. 49.

unable to accept that this is now the law' because '[t]he decision of the CJEU in *NS v United Kingdom* has set a threshold in Dublin II and cognate return cases which exists nowhere else in refugee law. It requires the claimant to establish that there are in the country of first arrival 'systemic deficiencies in the asylum procedure and in the reception conditions of asylum seekers … [which] amount to substantial grounds for believing that the asylum seeker would face a real risk of being subjected to inhuman or degrading treatment …'.[78]

As Sir Stephen Sedley explained, 'the sole ground on which a second state is required to exercise its power under article 3(2) Regulation 343/2003 … is that the source of risk to the applicant is a systemic deficiency, known to the former, in the latter's asylum or reception procedures. Short of this, even powerful evidence of individual risk is of no avail'. One is bound to say that this is most troubling. The suggestion that 'even powerful evidence' of fundamental human rights violations cannot prevent removal is a denial of refugee law and violation of the *jus cogens* of *non-refoulement*. It is nothing short of a travesty. This is because, as His Lordship went onto explain, '[t]he totality of the evidence about Italy' is such that it is 'extremely troubling'. The reason why the applicants could not succeed in their claims in this case, however, was that '[w]hile undoubtedly at a number of points it either overtly alleges or powerfully suggests systemic failure, it is neither unanimously nor compellingly directed to such a conclusion'. This was despite the fact that, 'what amounts to a systemic deficiency must to a considerable degree be a matter of judgment, perhaps even of vocabulary' because on the whole, 'the evidence does not demonstrate that Italy's system for the reception of asylum seekers and refugees, despite its many shortcomings and casualties, is itself dysfunctional or deficient'.[79]

When the matter went to the Supreme Court in early 2014[80] the decision was reversed in the most spectacular fashion thereby laying bare the fallacy of the system of burden-sharing under Dublin II, but also raising a question mark over the efficacy of the Common European Asylum System ('CEAS'). The Court held that:

> Violation of article 3 does not require (or, at least, does not necessarily require) that the complained of conditions said to constitute inhuman or degrading conditions are the product of systemic shortcomings. It is self-evident that a violation of article 3 rights is not intrinsically dependent on the failure of a system. If this requirement is grafted on to the presumption it will unquestionably make its rebuttal more difficult. And it means that those who would suffer breach of their

78 Ibid., at para. 61.

79 Ibid., at para. 63.

80 *EM (Eritrea), R (on the application of) v. Secretary of State for the Home Department* [2014] UKSC 12 (19 February 2014), http://www.bailii.org/uk/cases/UKSC/2014/12.html (accessed 25 February 2015), overruling *EM (Eritrea) & Ors v. Secretary of State for the Home Department* [2012] EWCA Civ 1336 (17 October 2012), http://www.bailii.org/ew/cases/EWCA/Civ/2012/1336.html (accessed 25 February 2015).

article 3 rights other than as a result of a systemic deficiency in the procedure and reception conditions provided for the asylum seeker will be unable to avail of those rights in order to prevent their enforced return to a listed country where such violation would occur.[81]

Under the heading, 'Should Refugees Be Treated Differently from Asylum Seekers?' Lord Kerr, delivering the judgment of the Court, explained that there was no distinction to be made between asylum-seekers and recognized refugees complaining about Article 3 violations for the purposes of Dublin II, and stated:

Should Refugees Be Treated Differently from Asylum Seekers?

75. Of the four appellants, two are asylum seekers (EH and EM), and two are refugees (AE and MA). AE and MA submit that their transfer to Italy is not governed by Dublin II and is not within the scope of EU law because they are refugees. …

76. The respondent, … [argued] that asylum seekers are an 'underprivileged and vulnerable population group requiring special protection in the form of basic reception facilities' whereas refugees are 'on a par, as regards rights and obligations … with the general population' – see *Hassan and others v Netherlands and Italy* 40524/10 (27 August 2013) para 179.

77. The Court of Appeal noted that questions had been raised in the course of argument as to whether the return to Italy of a claimant *already granted refugee status there* would fall under Dublin II but decided that the reasoning of the CJEU in *NS* required them to adopt a 'uniform approach' to all of the present appeals – see para 48.

78. It seems to me that the relevant matter is not whether Dublin II treats refugees and asylum seekers differently or the same, *but that it relates to anyone who has applied for asylum in the country from which he might be transferred*, whether or not he has previously been recognised as a refugee in the country to which it is proposed he be transferred. This reflects the nature of Dublin II as a chiefly procedural instrument. 'Refugee' is defined, but referred to only once, obliquely, in article 7: 'Where the asylum seeker has a family member, regardless of whether the family was previously formed in the country of origin, who has been allowed to reside as a refugee in a Member State, that Member State shall be responsible for examining the application for asylum, provided that the persons concerned so desire'.

---

81 Ibid., at para. 42.

> 79. An applicant or asylum seeker is defined in article 2(d) of Dublin II as 'a third country national who has made an application for asylum in respect of which a final decision has not yet been taken'. A third country national is defined in para (a) of the same article as 'anyone who is not a citizen of the Union within the meaning of article 17(1) of the Treaty establishing the European Community'. *The appellants meet these criteria and all are subject, therefore, to the provisions of Dublin II.* Whether their respective positions as asylum seekers who have previously been granted refugee status and asylum seekers who have not been granted that status will make it more or less likely that they will be at risk of violation of their article 3 rights if returned to a listed country will *depend on an examination of the particular circumstances of their individual cases.* One can anticipate an argument that those who have refugee status in Italy are less likely to suffer such a violation because they can assert their rights under the Qualification Directive but whether such an argument would prevail must depend on the evaluation of the evidence which is presented on that issue'. (Emphases added.)

In so stating, the Supreme Court has surely erred in suggesting that the return of recognized refugees to their country of asylum can be dealt with as a 'Dublin matter'. If this is so, it must seriously be questioned whether anything at all is actually now left of the CEAS. In conclusion the following may be said. In *Saeedi* Cranston J told us that the Dublin Regulation was the cornerstone of the CEAS. It established a system of determining responsibility for an application lodged in a Member State which alone has examined the claim. The purpose is so that a failed asylum-seeker cannot make multiple applications from one country to the next. This raised the question of, what if it is unsafe, as Greece is according to EUECJ in *Nasseri* or in *MSS*, or as is Italy,[82] or as is Hungary?[83] The orthodoxy view was that

82 In *Tarakhel v. Switzerland* (App no. 29217/12), the ECtHR on 4 November 2014 ruled that individual guarantees were needed from Italian authorities for asylum seeker returns to that country, so that sending a family of asylum seekers back to Italy without first obtaining individual guarantees concerning their care would be a violation of Article 3 of the European Convention on Human Rights. See 'European Court of Human Rights Rules Returns to Italy under Dublin Regulation May Violate Convention', Electronic Immigration Network, 4 November 2014, http://www.ein.org.uk/news/european-court-human-rights-rules-returns-italy-under-dublin-regulation-may-violate-convention (accessed 25 February 2015).

83 See Toth, Csaba, 2014, 'German Court: Hungary Does Not Meet Minimum EU Asylum Standards', *Budapest Beacon*, 18 July 2014, http://budapestbeacon.com/public-policy/german-court-hungary-does-not-meet-minimum-eu-asylum-standards/ (accessed 25 February 2015), where it is reported that an appeals court in Stuttgart granted an Iranian refugee's request that he not be deported back to Hungary, citing its 'inhuman and degrading behaviour' towards asylum-seekers. The German judiciary body granted the right to an Iranian refugee coming from Hungary to seek asylum in Germany, based on the argument, that 'Hungary does not meet minimum standards of asylum required by the EU'.

there had to be a systematic breach by the state, and not individual failings by the state in particular cases. So sovereignty was deployed to put at even further risk people already vulnerable (see CJEU in *NS (Afghanistan)*). It has now taken a UK court in *EM (Eritrea)* to say that what was said there was that a 'systemic breach would be enough' and *not* that there *had* to be a systemic breach. However, if one looks at paragraphs 75–9 of that judgment of the Supreme Court, it is doubtful whether anything now remains of the concept of safe procedures and of reliable reception conditions in any of the EU Member States. Yet, this underpins Dublin II and the entire CEAS. What this surely now suggests is that the return of someone, for example from Italy, is to be determined on exactly the same grounds as return to any other foreign country.

At the end of 2014, the Grand Chamber of the European Court of Human Rights in *Tarakhel*[84] held as well that a removing state retains responsibility for a refugee's Article 3 violations such that he/she cannot be subjected to inhuman and degrading treatment by virtue of the removal. This case concerned applicants who had applied for asylum in Switzerland, and were resisting return to Italy under Dublin II. They maintained that the reception arrangements for asylum seekers in Italy were beset by systemic deficiencies, relating to: difficulties in gaining access to the reception facilities owing to the slowness of the identification procedure; the accommodation capacity of those facilities, which they regarded in any case as insufficient; and the inadequate living conditions in the available facilities. In support of their arguments, the applicants referred *inter alia* to the findings of the Swiss Refugee Council.[85]

The European Court held that, 'the Swiss authorities could, under the Dublin Regulation, refrain from transferring the applicants to Italy if they considered that the receiving country was not fulfilling its obligations under the Convention'[86] and that 'it considers that the decision to return the applicants to Italy does not strictly fall within Switzerland's international legal obligations in the context of the system established by the Dublin Regulation'[87] so that, 'the presumption of equivalent protection does not apply in this case' with the result that, 'Switzerland must therefore be considered to bear responsibility under Article 3 of the Convention in the present case'.[88] Were it not for the brave and principled efforts of the courts in some cases those seeking safety from conflict and calamity would have little to fall back on in the vindication of their rights.

84 *Tarakhel v. Switzerland*, 29217/12, Grand Chamber Judgment [2014] ECHR 1185 (4 November 2014), http://www.bailii.org/eu/cases/ECHR/2014/1185.html (accessed 25 February 2015).

85 Ibid., at para. 57.

86 Ibid., at para. 90.

87 Ibid., at para. 90.

88 Ibid., at para. 91.

Refugee Law, National Security and Exclusion[89]

And so we come to 'terrorism' itself – the very impulse that is infecting the debates around refugee policy in the developed world today. Enlightened jurisprudence of the West once accepted that nothing much was to be gained in refugee law by the use of the emotive phrase 'terrorist'. After all, the 1951 Refugee Convention did not use the phrase in Article 1(F) when describing the so-called 'Exclusion Clauses'. The jurisprudence moreover openly recognized that refugees will often come from countries where political struggles are raging so that in *Singh* the Federal Court of Australia observed that,

> [i]f there is a political struggle in which agents of the government, including police, have a policy of torturing and killing those who oppose the government, we see no reason why crimes directed at those agents, or police officers, may not be regarded as political (that is, as satisfying the 'incidence' test) even though they may be characterised as crimes of revenge.[90]

Political violence is not an exception. It is a mundane fact of life in such conflicts. For this reason, political violence cannot be eliminated from such conflicts. Terror cannot end. There may be suicide bombs in Syria, Iraq or Afghanistan. But they are not all an expression of a religious culture. As Karen Armstrong has highlighted, '[i]n 2008, MI5's behavioural science unit noted that "far from being religious zealots, a large number of those involved in terrorism do not practice their faith regularly … many lack religious literacy"'.[91] Accordingly, as she explains, '[i]t would be a mistake to see IS as a throwback' because it is 'a thoroughly modern movement that has become an efficient, self-financing business with assets estimated at $2bn'.[92] This is a good example of how political organizations transform themselves in the process of a struggle and there is no better example of this today than the splintering into various groups of Al Qaeda over the last decade, one of which is IS. Thus has modern terror today come to be waged by small, decentralized, highly mobile groups disassociated from any recognized state or government we know.

Where a person has committed an international crime, and then seeks surrogate international protection as a refugee fearing for his or her life, the starting point for the courts are the provisions of Article 1F of the Refugee Convention itself, which are deliberately in terms that they, 'shall not apply to any person' against

89 This section draws heavily from the author's 2012 paper 'Terrorism and the Exclusion of Refugee Status in the UK', *Journal of Conflict and Security Law*, 17.3, 465–500.

90 Mr. Justice Kirby in *MIMA v. Singh* (2002) 186 ALR 393, at paras 64–7, esp. para. 67.

91 Ibid.

92 Ibid.

whom it can be said that there are 'serious reasons for considering' him to be guilty of three particular kinds of actions. First, that he has 'committed a crime against peace, a war crime, or a crime against humanity'. Second, that he has 'committed a serious non-political crime outside the country of refuge'. Third, that he has 'been guilty of acts contrary to the purposes and principles of the United Nations'. The meaning of these terms is not specifically explicated. Instead, they are to be understood, 'as defined in the international instruments drawn up to make provision in respect of such crimes'.[93] The meaning is clearly an evolving one but the important question here is what is meant by 'international instruments'. There is an expanding list which governments can rely upon as an important cog in the rapidly turning wheel of counter-insurgency state measures designed to neuter at source the claims of undesirable refugees. First, there is the Qualification Directive (2004/83/EC) which provides a common standard for the application of the Refugee Convention's requirements across the 27 Member States of the EU.[94] In this instrument Article 12(2)(a) precisely mirrors article 1F(a) itself.[95] Article 12(3), however, then provides in addition that article 12(2) 'applies to persons who instigate or otherwise participate in the commission of the crimes or acts mentioned therein'.[96] Second, there is the Statute of the International Criminal Tribunal for the former Yugoslavia[97] (ICTY), which defines, in Articles 2 to 7, comparatively succinctly the war crimes which it governs.[98] Article 7 then sets out

93 Article 1(F)(a) of the Refugee Convention.

94 It states at the outset (at para. 1) that, 'A common policy on asylum, including a Common European Asylum System, is a constituent part of the European Union's objective of progressively establishing an area of freedom, security and justice open to those who, forced by circumstances, legitimately seek protection in the Community'. Available at http://www.refworld.org/pdfid/4157e75e4.pdf (accessed 25 February 2015).

95 Article 12(2) states: 'A third country national or a stateless person is excluded from being a refugee where there are serious reasons for considering that: (a) he or she has committed a crime against peace, a war crime, or a crime against humanity, as defined in the international instruments drawn up to make provision in respect of such crimes; (b) he or she has committed a serious non-political crime outside the country of refuge prior to his or her admission as a refugee; which means the time of issuing a residence permit based on the granting of refugee status; particularly cruel actions, even if committed with an allegedly political objective, may be classified as serious non-political crimes; (c) he or she has been guilty of acts contrary to the purposes and principles of the United Nations as set out in the Preamble and Articles 1 and 2 of the Charter of the United Nations.' See http://www.asylumlawdatabase.eu/en/content/en-qualification-directive-directive-200483ec-29-april-2004#Art%2012%20QD.

96 Ibid.

97 Available at http://www.icty.org/x/file/Legal%20Library/Statute/statute_sept08_en.pdf (accessed 25 February 2015).

98 Articles 2–5 cover the following issues:

Article 2 – This states that the International Tribunal shall have the power to prosecute persons committing or ordering to be committed grave breaches of the Geneva Conventions of 12 August 1949.

the principles for determining individual criminal responsibility.[99] These include a variety of criminal offences all of which militate against the grant of asylum to a person guilty of such crimes.[100] Whereas these instruments may readily meet the definition of 'the international instruments drawn up to make provision in respect of such crimes' there have also been three major post-9/11 resolutions of the UN Security Council the use of which is questionable in the context of exclusion. Yet, each of these have implications for those around the world, and not least now in the former 'Arab Spring' countries which involved insurrections, political assassinations and civil wars.

First, there was United Nations Security Council Resolution 1373 (28 September 2001)[101] which expressly provided that, '... acts, methods and practices of terrorism are *contrary to the purposes and principles of the United Nations* and that knowingly financing, planning and inciting terrorist acts are also contrary to the purposes and principles of the United Nations'.[102] This is further demonstrated by United Nations Security Council Resolution 1377 (12 November 2001),[103] which is the second major development, following hot on the heels of the first, and it recalled the earlier resolution and reaffirmed: '... its unequivocal condemnation of all acts, methods and practices of terrorism as criminal and unjustifiable, regardless of their motivation, in all their forms and manifestations, wherever and by whomever committed'.[104] It is significant that the 'motive' of a person involved in any 'methods and practices of terrorism'

Article 3 – This states that the International Tribunal shall have the power to prosecute persons violating the laws or customs of war, which includes employment of poisonous weapons, wanton destruction of cities, towns or villages, attacks on undefended towns and dwellings, or buildings; the damage of institutions of religion, charity, education, arts and sciences, and historic monuments, and the plunder of public or private property.

Article 4 – This states that the International Tribunal shall have the power to prosecute persons committing genocide, defined to include an intent to destroy, in whole or in part, a national, ethnical, racial or religious group.

Article 5 – This states that the International Tribunal shall have the power to prosecute persons responsible for crimes when committed in armed conflict, whether international or internal in character, and directed against any civilian population, such as murder, extermination, enslavement, deportation, imprisonment, torture, rape, persecutions on political, racial and religious grounds, and other inhumane acts.

99 Article 7 makes it clear that a person who planned, instigated, ordered, committed or otherwise aided and abetted in the planning, preparation or execution of a crime referred to in Articles 2 to 5 of the present statute, shall be individually responsible for the crime.

100 They include, for example, 'determines that justice so requires'.

101 Available at http://www.un.org/News/Press/docs/2001/sc7158.doc.htm (accessed 25 February 2015).

102 Ibid., at p. 1.

103 Available at http://www.unhcr.org/refworld/docid/3c4e9456e.html (accessed 25 February 2015).

104 Ibid., at p. 2.

is deemed irrelevant. So one can be what used to be called a 'freedom-fighter', but still be caught by these provisions as a terrorist – a name unknown to the Refugee Convention. All states are called on 'to take urgent steps to implement fully resolution 1373'[105] and to 'intensify their efforts to eliminate the scourge of international terrorism'.[106] Indeed, in what is universally considered to be the most dangerous part of the world today, the International Special Assistance Force was early in Afghanistan authorized and mandated by United Nations Security Council Resolution 1386 (20 December 2001)[107] 'to assist the Afghan Interim Authority in the maintenance of security in Kabul and its surrounding areas, so that the Afghan Interim Authority as well as the personnel of the United Nations can operate in a secure environment' for a period of six months.[108] A third development from the UN Security Council required the promulgation of new stricter domestic laws because, United Nations Security Council Resolution 1624 (September 2005)[109] called upon states to 'adopt measures, consistent with international obligations, to prohibit, by law, incitement to commit a terrorist act or acts and to deny safe haven to those guilty of such conduct'. The recognition that states have to act 'consistent with international obligations' is significant, because it does mean that given the international obligation to admit refugees,[110] states cannot act in a slap-dash unprincipled manner. Moreover, there are also General Assembly resolutions, such as 49/60 of 9 December 2004,[111] on 'measures to eliminate international terrorism' which set out to declare that 'acts, methods and practices of terrorism constitute a grave violation of the purposes and principles of the United Nations'[112] as well as 'including those which jeopardize the friendly relations among States' and 'hinder

105 Ibid., at p. 2.

106 Ibid., at p. 2.

107 Available at http://www.nato.int/isaf/topics/mandate/unscr/resolution_1386.pdf (accessed 25 February 2015).

108 Ibid., at Article 1.

109 Available at http://www.un.org/News/Press/docs/2005/sc8496.doc.htm (accessed 25 February 2015).

110 Article 33 imposes a duty of '*non-refoulment*' on states when considering applications for refugee status: Article 33. Prohibition of expulsion or return ('*refoulement*'). 1. No Contracting State shall expel or return ('*refouler*') a refugee in any manner whatsoever to the frontiers of territories where his life or freedom would be threatened on account of his race, religion, nationality, membership of a particular social group or political opinion. 2. The benefit of the present provision may not, however, be claimed by a refugee whom there are reasonable grounds for regarding as a danger to the security of the country in which he is, or who, having been convicted by a final judgement of a particularly serious crime, constitutes a danger to the community of that country. Available at http://www.unhcr.org/3b66c2aa10.pdf (accessed 25 February 2015).

111 A/RES/49/60, 84th plenary meeting, 9 December 1994. Available at http://www.un.org/documents/ga/res/49/a49r060.htm (accessed 25 February 2015).

112 Ibid., at Article 2.

international cooperation'.[113] If the suggestion here is that states impose a blanket ban on genuine refugees because of an obligation to adopt 'measures to eliminate international terrorism' the suggestion is wrong in terms of international law.

In September 2014 a fourth binding resolution was passed that would compel all countries to put in place domestic laws to prosecute those who travel abroad to join terrorist organizations and those who help them, including by raising funds. This was UN Security Council Resolution 2178 of 24th September 2014[114] on threats to international peace and security caused by terrorist acts. This resolution,[115] proposed by the United States, for the first time establishes international standards for nations to prevent and suppress the recruiting of their citizens by terrorist organizations, and bar the entry and transit across their territory of suspected foreign terrorists. It requires member states to 'prevent and suppress the recruiting, organizing, transporting or equipping of individuals who travel to a state other than their states of residence or nationality for the purpose of the perpetration, planning, or preparation of, or participation in, terrorist acts or the providing or receiving of terrorist training, and the financing of their travel and of their activities'. There is a requirement that domestic laws 'prosecute' and 'penalize' them. The resolution calls on countries to make concerted efforts to prevent radicalization. They have to put in place 'rehabilitation and reintegration strategies for returning foreign fighters'. The impact of the resolution has been such that already several European countries and other nations are putting new laws and administrative rules in place. Indeed,

> Counterterrorism officials say the weight of a Security Council resolution could strengthen and unify the legal and political framework to help stem the flow of fighters to conflicts like those in Syria and Iraq, and help address the longer-term threat of battle-hardened Westerners, including Americans, returning to carry out attacks in their home countries.[116]

The implications are wide-ranging because 'American intelligence officials say 15,000 foreign fighters are now in Iraq and Syria; they are from 80 countries and include more than 2,000 Europeans and 100 Americans' but the effect of the resolution would now mean that states criminalize attempts to travel abroad to join

113 Ibid., at Article 1.

114 http://www.un.org/en/ga/search/view_doc.asp?symbol=S/RES/2178%20(2014)&referer=http://www.un.org/en/sc/documents/resolutions/2014.shtml&Lang=E (accessed 25 February 2015).

115 Schmitt, Eric and Sengupta, Somni, 2014, 'Obama to Lead U.N. Effort to Halt Movement of Terror Recruits', *New York Times*, 21 September, http://www.nytimes.com/2014/09/22/world/obama-to-lead-un-effort-to-halt-movement-of-terror-recruits.html?_r=1 (accessed 25 February 2015).

116 Ibid.

a terrorist organization and prevent suspected foreign terrorists from entering or traveling through their territory. Three problems are immediately evident.

First, although the resolution is passed under Chapter VII of the United Nations Charter, implying that it is legally binding, it would be difficult to enforce. Second, the text calls on a United Nations panel responsible for monitoring compliance with sanctions against Al Qaeda to investigate where Member States fall short in responding to foreign fighters. Yet, simply traveling to Syria or Iraq to join an extremist group is not a crime in many countries. It is therefore not clear what the guidelines are for individual countries and how implementation is to be monitored. This is important because the resolution puts pressure on some of the United States' most vital allies in the region, such as Turkey, which has to monitor its 800 miles of borders with Syria and Iraq, that has been freely used by militants joining a variety of rebel groups fighting the governments of both countries, including Islamic State (IS), otherwise known as ISIS. But perhaps most importantly, it is unclear from the resolution what is a terrorist organization. Is each state to decide this question for itself? It would appear so. But if this is the case, there will be anomalies. The United States considers Hamas to be a terrorist organization. An increasing number of countries, especially in Europe, do not.

The tendency to vague and imprecise standards can have troubling consequences for genuine refugees. In *JS (Sri Lanka)*[117] the UK Supreme Court determined that more exacting standards of precision and individual responsibility had to be applied if genuine refugees were to be excluded from international protection. In inquiring into '[w]ho are to be regarded' as 'war criminals' within the meaning of Article 1F(a), it answered by asking that 'assuming that there are those within an organisation who clearly *are* committing war crimes, what more than membership of such an organisation must be established before an individual is himself personally to be regarded as a war criminal?' This was an important consideration because 'there can only be one true interpretation of article 1F(a)' and that is 'an autonomous meaning to be found in international rather than domestic law'. Whilst it was accepted that these must be those international instruments 'existing when disqualification is being considered, not merely those extant at the date of the Convention',[118] nevertheless 'because of the serious consequences of exclusion for the person concerned' the fundamental position was that 'the article must be interpreted restrictively and used cautiously'.[119] Accordingly, as Lord Hope explained, there should be 'a close examination of the facts and the need for a carefully reasoned decision as to precisely why the person concerned is excluded from protection under the Convention'.[120] Lord Kerr stated, 'One needs, I believe, to concentrate on the actual role played by the particular person, taking all material aspects of that role into account so as to decide whether the

117 *JS (Sri Lanka)* [2010] UKSC 15.
118 *JS (Sri Lanka)* [2010] UKSC 15, at para. 2.
119 *JS (Sri Lanka)* [2010] UKSC 15, at para. 2.
120 *JS (Sri Lanka)* [2010] UKSC 15, at para. 44.

required degree of participation is established'.[121] In the words of Lord Brown, 'I would hold an accused disqualified under article 1F if there are serious reasons for considering him voluntarily to have contributed in a significant way to the organisation's ability to pursue its purpose of committing war crimes, aware that his assistance will in fact further that purpose'.[122] The problem with *JS (Sri Lanka)* is that it is difficult to apply. It is difficult to apply in a uniform and principled manner given the spate of UN Security Resolutions on 'terrorism' which are being transposed into refugee law. The distinction may be made in principle but putting it into practice is altogether more difficult.[123]

In *JS (Sri Lanka)*[124] Lord Brown, in referring to the Rome Statute of the International Criminal Court 1998[125] ('the ICC Statute'), went so far as to say that this instrument 'should now be the starting point for considering whether an applicant is disqualified from asylum by virtue of article 1F(a)', underlining the ICC statute's importance by stating, 'ratified as it now is by more than a hundred States and standing as now surely it does as the most comprehensive and authoritative statement of international thinking on the principles that govern liability for the most serious international crimes'. In his view, this 'alone could justify the denial of asylum to those otherwise in need of it'.[126] Yet, it is clear that different approaches can arise in different legal jurisdictions. One noteworthy judgment is that of the German Federal Administrative Court in *BVerwG 10 C 26.12* on 19 November

121 *JS (Sri Lanka)* [2010] UKSC 15, at para. 55.

122 *JS (Sri Lanka)* [2010] UKSC 15, at para. 39.

123 Professor Hathaway has set out to explain, however, how this provision covers three distinct types of crimes. A 'crime against peace' entails the 'planning of or participation in an unlawful war'; a war crime involves, 'the violation of a law of war', which includes the mistreatment of civilians and prisoners of war; and a 'crime against humanity' is one where there has been 'fundamentally inhumane conduct' with examples being 'genocide, slavery, torture and apartheid': see, Hathaway, James, 1991, *The Law of Refugee Status*, Butterworths, London, p. 216. Lord Brown also referred (in *JS (Sri Lanka)* [2010] UKSC 15, at para. 16) to the, 'post World War II war crimes jurisprudence about common criminal purpose three distinct categories of collective criminality. First, the usual sort of joint enterprise case where all the co-defendants have the same criminal intent and each plays a part in executing the crime. Second, the so-called "concentration camp" cases where all those in authority who participate in enforcing the repressive system are to be regarded as co-perpetrators of the war crime of ill-treatment – "really a variant of the first category" as the Chamber itself recognised. Third, cases where the principal offender commits an offence outside the common design but where the defendant foresaw and knowingly took the risk of its occurrence – the standard basis for secondary liability for joint enterprise criminality under domestic law'.

124 *JS (Sri Lanka)* [2010] UKSC 15.

125 Available at http://www.icc-cpi.int/nr/rdonlyres/ea9aeff7-5752-4f84-be94-0a655eb30e16/0/rome_statute_english.pdf (accessed 25 February 2015).

126 *JS (Sri Lanka)* [2010] UKSC 15, per Lord Brown at para. 9.

2013,[127] where the application of Germany's Asylum Procedure Act was also in issue. The British case of *KJ (Sri Lanka)* had previously held that armed campaign against a government is not to be equated with terrorism.[128] In this case, however, a fact finding lower court held that membership of the 'people's liberation forces' was enough to exclude a person from refugee status. The Federal Administrative Court held this was technically correct but proper findings had to be made. The claimant, of Kurdish ethnicity, had joined the militant arm of the PKK, and then headed an art and culture school. He appeared as an artist broadcasting his concerts on Kurdish television station. He was responsible for PKK propaganda. The lower court held[129] that because of the great importance of music, dance and custom as an expression of cultural identity in Kurdish life, the claimant had participated in acts by the PKK that were in violation of the aims and principles of the United Nations. The claimant appealed.[130]

The Federal Administrative Court agreed with the claimant that the court below had to make findings of fact,[131] but did not agree with him that there is a requirement for 'spatial-organisational proximity' within the organization to commit terrorist acts. The correct context was the UN Anti-Terrorism measures.[132] Of relevance was that the, 'acts, methods and practices of terrorism are contrary to the purposes and principles of the United Nations' and that 'knowingly financing, planning and inciting terrorist acts are also contrary to the purposes and principles of the United Nations'.[133] This was evident from UN Resolutions 1373 (2001)[134]

127 *BVerwG 10 C 26.12* (OVG 3L 218/08). This is Germany's supreme administrative court, and was on this occasion presided over by Prof. Dr. Dorig, Prof. Dr. Kraft, Fricke, and Dr. Maidowski.

128 *KJ (Sri Lanka) v. Secretary of State for the Home Department* [2009] EWCA Civ 292, http://www.bailii.org/ew/cases/EWCA/Civ/2009/292.html (accessed 25 February 2015).

129 Ibid., at para. 17.

130 The claimant argued on appeal to the Federal Administrative Court (i) that there had been inadequate findings of fact; (ii) that if exclusion from refugee status was to be founded solely on ideological support for the PKK's armed conflict, then the content of this support must be directed to the use of violent means, and (iii) that this must be situated in both temporal and spatial-organizational proximity to armed conflict; (iv) that on this basis he had never incited criminal acts of terrorism; and (v) that if the Government wanted to argue that propaganda support for violent actions by terrorist organizations can also lead to exclusion from refugee status, then the court below should have clarified his specific actions for the PKK: see, ibid., at para. 3.

131 Ibid., at para. 7.

132 The court observed that the relevant aims and principles for this purpose are set forth in the Preamble and Articles 1 and 2 of the Charter of the United Nations, and are anchored in the resolutions of the UN Security Council on antiterrorism measures.

133 The Federal Administrative Court referred to Recital 22 of Directive 2004/83/EC.

134 See, UN Security Council, Resolution 1373 (28 September 2001): Threats to International Peace and Security Caused by Terrorist Acts, UN Doc. S/RES/1373, which

and 1377 (2001).[135] The Security Council of the United Nations took as its starting point the principle that international terrorist acts are, irrespective of any state participation, contrary to the purposes and principles of the United Nations.[136] Nevertheless, the need for a link[137] or *nexus* to the individual events during the claimant's activity for the PKK[138] was also evident, and it was not enough that the organization of which the individual was a member was on an EU Terror List.[139]

Nevertheless, in two respects, the Court arguably went further than the jurisprudence in *JS (Sri Lanka)*. First, it held that 'even purely logistical acts of support … if they are of sufficient importance' may be enough for individual responsibility.[140] This compares unfavourably with the judgment of the EUECJ in *B and D*[141] that a 'high degree of seriousness' was required of acts and not just 'sufficient importance'.[142] Second, that 'the same applies to serious ideological and propagandistic activities in favour of a terrorist organisation',[143] because 'the importance of the contribution to an act by an accomplice' is one which 'must be

expressly provided (at para. 1) that: '… acts, methods and practices of terrorism are contrary to the purposes and principles of the United Nations and that knowingly financing, planning and inciting terrorist acts are also contrary to the purposes and principles of the United Nations'.

135 See, UN Security Council, Resolution 1377 (12 November 2001): Threats to International Peace and Security Caused by Terrorist Acts, UN Doc. S/RES/1377, which recalled the earlier resolution of 1373 and reaffirmed: '… its unequivocal condemnation of all acts, methods and practices of terrorism as criminal and unjustifiable, regardless of their motivation, in all their forms and manifestations, wherever and by whomever committed'.

136 The Federal Administrative Court referred to ECJ judgment of 9 November 2010 – Cases C-57/09 and C-101/09 – Col. 2010, I-10979 at para. 82 et seqq. = NVwZ 2011, 285.

137 *BVerwG 10 C 26.12* (OVG 3L 218/08), at para. 13.

138 From this, the Court of Justice of the European Union has concluded that this reason for exclusion can also be applied to persons who, in the course of their membership of an organization which is on the list forming the Annex to Common Position 2001/931, have been involved in terrorist acts with an international dimension: see order of 10 October 2013 – *BVerwG 10 B 19.13* – juris at para. 5.

139 *BVerwG 10 C 26.12* (OVG 3L 218/08), at para. 15.

140 The court said that this was so for the purposes of Section 3(2) sentence 1, no. 3 in conjunction with sentence 2 of the Asylum Procedure Act (judgments of 7 July 2011, each at 39, and of 4 September 2012, each at 26).

141 See also *Joined Cases C-57/09 and C-101/09 Bundesrepublik Deutschland v. B and D* [2011] Imm AR 190.

142 As explained by Blake J in *AH (Article 1F(b) – 'serious') Algeria* [2013] UKUT 00382 (IAC), who cites the UNHCR view (at para. 2.2.1) at para. 36 of his judgment.

143 Although the Court accepted that 'merely spouting slogans of the organisation or distributing flyers does not suffice'. The court referred to the Münster Higher Administrative Court, judgment of 9 March 2011 – 11 A 1439/07.A – OVGE MüLü 54, 95 (juris at 61 et seq.); Schleswig Higher Administrative Court, judgment of 1 September 2011 – 4 LB 11/10, AuAS 2011, 262 (juris at 52).

equivalent to that of participation in a serious non-political crime'.[144] The Federal Administrative Court also forged new territory for exclusion when it held[145] that it was not necessary to influence the commission of a terrorist offence for exclusion to operate.[146] The reference to the UN Security Resolutions in this case makes it plain that they will be used to complement the application of the Rome Statute in ways which are bound to be unpredictable and arbitrary. Time will tell how UN Security Council Resolution 2178 of 24 September 2014[147] on threats to international peace and security caused by terrorist acts will be interpreted and applied by the international community.

Conclusion

It is time for a new idea of 'responsibility to protect'. The current idea of such responsibility is rooted in what the state does on its territory. When it is said that prevention requires apportioning responsibility to and promoting collaboration between concerned states and the international community,[148] what this is fundamentally predicated on is that 'the duty to prevent and halt genocide and mass atrocities lies first and foremost with the State, but the international community has a role that cannot be blocked by the invocation of sovereignty'. The focus is on the state and its people because 'Sovereignty no longer exclusively protects States from foreign interference; it is a charge of responsibility where States are accountable for the welfare of their people'. It is said that 'this principle

144 This is so as to comply with the meaning of Section 3(2), sentence 1, no. 2 of the Asylum Procedure Act (judgment of 7 July 2011, each at para. 39).

145 *BVerwG 10 C 26.12* (OVG 3L 218/08), at para. 16.

146 This is because, 'Contrary to the opinion advocated in the appeal to this Court, however, attribution of participation in acts in violation of the aims and principles of the United Nations is not limited to cases in which the applicant for asylum objectively had the possibility of actually influencing the committing of terrorist acts, or publicly approved of or incited such acts. Because there is no need for a specific connection between the act of support and an individual act of terror, … there is no requirement for either spatial-organisational proximity within the organisation to commit terrorist acts, nor for their justification in public. Otherwise, those who are purely desk perpetrators and propagandists would enjoy protection as refugees even though under the required evaluatory approach … which is to keep persons unworthy of asylum from enjoying the status of a "bona fide refugee" … their ideological or propagandistic contribution to terrorist acts appears by no means less important than that of those who participated in the act directly'.

147 http://www.un.org/en/ga/search/view_doc.asp?symbol=S/RES/2178%20(2014)&referer=http://www.un.org/en/sc/documents/resolutions/2014.shtml&Lang=E (accessed 25 February 2015).

148 See 'The Responsibility to Protect', Office of the Special Adviser on the Prevention of Genocide, 16 April 2014, http://www.un.org/en/preventgenocide/adviser/responsibility.shtml (accessed 25 February 2015).

is enshrined in article 1 of the Genocide Convention and embodied in the principle of "sovereignty as responsibility" and in the concept of the Responsibility to Protect'. Yet, there is enough here to suggest that this responsibility attaches just as powerfully to the international community itself. This is because the 'three pillars of the responsibility to protect', as stipulated in the Outcome Document of the 2005 United Nations World Summit[149] and formulated in the Secretary-General's 2009 Report (A/63/677) on Implementing the Responsibility to Protect[150] emphasize the following elements:

> 1. The State carries the primary responsibility for protecting populations from genocide, war crimes, crimes against humanity and ethnic cleansing, and their incitement;
> 2. The international community has a responsibility to encourage and assist States in fulfilling this responsibility;
> 3. The international community has a responsibility to use appropriate diplomatic, humanitarian and other means to protect populations from these crimes. If a State is manifestly failing to protect its populations, the international community must be prepared to take collective action to protect populations, in accordance with the Charter of the United Nations.

There is now mounting evidence that the West's foreign wars have caused many of the refugee flows that the West itself is in turn having to deal with. The development of conceptual, political and operational aspects of the Responsibility to Protect, in a manner that is relevant and meaningful to today's fleeing populations, requires that we place the burden of 'responsibility' on nations that have caused the refugee flows, even if this is in relation to protecting populations which belong to other nations.

---

149 See, A/Res/60/1, paras 138–40, http://www.un.org/en/preventgenocide/adviser/pdf/World%20Summit%20Outcome%20Document.pdf#page=30 (accessed 25 February 2015).

150 See, http://www.un.org/en/ga/search/view_doc.asp?symbol=A/63/677&referer=http://www.un.org/en/preventgenocide/adviser/responsibility.shtml&Lang=E (accessed 25 February 2015).

PART II
Present Challenges, Legal Regimes and Jurisprudence

Chapter 5

After the Flight: International Law and the Rights of Asylum Seekers Today

Laura Westra

Introduction

> Legal theory nevertheless remains imperfect, given the absence of clearly correlative rights in favour of a subject of international law competent to exercise protection, and the uncertain legal consequences which follow where breach of obligations leads to a refugee exodus.
>
> ...
>
> Given the uncertain (and promising) legal situation that follows flight, increasing attention now focuses on the ways and the means *to prevent* refugee outflows (Goodwin-Gill and McAdam 2007: 2–3).

This passage is one of the few that can be found in the scholarly literature that even raises the question of 'breach of obligations' on the part of states that precede an exodus, while – equally rare – the second sentence asks how to 'prevent' refugee outflows. The crux of the issue is the responsibility/accountability of both governing bodies and legal persons, for which I argued in Chapter 3. That responsibility, I believe, changes completely the situation of asylum seekers, from that of somewhat bothersome supplicants, to that of injured parties demanding justice, if not from a specific nation, then from the global community.

We are clearly addressing a question *de lege ferenda*, as, to my knowledge, no presently existing instrument considers the situation from this optic. The complexity of the situation cannot be denied: asylum seekers are demanding justice form a diffuse, complex group of legal individuals who have exercised their rights with no consideration for the 'collateral' damage they have inflicted (Sheldon 2004). Worse yet, it is seldom possible to isolate a specific perpetrator, and the only institutions that actually bear some responsibility to those that have been harmed, that is, the respective state bureaucracies, are and remain, for the most part, complicit in those harms, be they starvation/deprivation of resources or direct or indirect support of the practices that cause extreme weather events. More direct responsibility may be found where a mass exodus originates from a conflict situation often prompted itself by conflicting economic interests, but which is a situation for which states bear a more direct responsibility.

At any rate the key question remains the lack of respect for human rights: the earlier chapters addressed the major clusters of breaches that occur before the occurrence of a mass exodus. At this point, we need to consider what happens after the flight, starting with the legalities that have been in place since 1951, that is, since the existence of the Convention on the Status of Refugees of 1951.

The UNHCR prescribes certain procedures to be followed regarding all applicants for asylum in all countries. But the government of most countries find themselves in an invidious position as their obligation to apply the CSR to refugees at their borders often conflicts with the strong opinions of their constituents regarding these admission (Rousseau, Crepeau, Faxen and Houle 2002):

> In the context of Western host societies in particular, a discourse separating 'deserving' refugees from those deemed to be 'undeserving' or 'false', governs and restricts the acceptance of refugees (Rousseau, Crepeau, Faxen and Houle 2002: 8).

In fact the general public tends to react either with mistrust, because of those seen to be abusing the system, or with strong feelings of rejection, especially in the cases of weaker domestic economies or situations of high unemployment, where all asylum seekers are viewed as usurpers or unfair 'contenders' for the job sought by Western countries' 'real' citizens.

In addition, however, the CSR, as a specific international human rights instrument, has no mechanism it can employ in order to ensure states' compliance, as it relies entirely on the states' good will (Hathaway 2005: 991–1002). Hence, in this chapter, we consider first, how best to trigger state responsibility, against the background of the present reality, before discussing what other instruments could be called upon to establish the gravity of states' obligation to comply. At the same time, the insufficiency of the CSR's purview, starting with its dated definition of refugee, will also be re-examined in the light of today's global changes (Hathaway 2005).

The Responsibility of States

> … whatever the intentions of the drafters, the nature, scope and geopolitical setting of refugee protection today simply differ too fundamentally from the reality of 1951, for the Convention's rights regime to be taken seriously as the baseline of the international response to involuntary migration (Hathaway 2005: 992).

The very need for international intervention in refugee issues depends on the actions of the state involved. There is the state from which the person or group is fleeing, and the responsibility they may bear for allowing, or not mitigating, the conditions that make life unlivable for individuals and groups, in various ways.

Then there is the state where the individuals or groups first arrive on the way to their desired destination. Finally there is the state they are attempting to reach.

Even at their final destination, refugees may be detained, put in special camps, or held in various jail-like receiving areas:

> Most disturbingly, asylum seekers can be detained for failing to arrive with the necessary travel documents, and can remain in detention for the entire length of the asylum process. And while many states have established special holding centres for asylum seekers and irregular migrants, in other countries they are detained in regular jails, alongside common criminals (UNHCR 2006: 43).

Hathaway and Neve's lengthy study of the realities of the refugees' situation clearly demonstrates the urgent need for reform (Hathaway and Neve 1997).

There are at least two major initial problems with the refugee situation today: the first is procedural, that is, connected with the way refugees are treated when they attempt to enter a country; the second is substantive, that is, it refers to the treatment refugees receive once they are admitted.

Non-Refoulement, Interception and Other Difficulties Encountered by Asylum Seekers

> The Executive Committee,
>
> ...
>
> (b) Expressed the opinion that in view of the hardships which it involves, detention should normally be avoided. If necessary, detention may be resorted to only on grounds prescribed by law to verify identity; to determine the elements on which the claim to refugee status or asylum is based; to deal with cases where refugees or asylum seekers have destroyed their travel and/or identity documents or have used fraudulent documents in order to mislead the authorities of the state in which they intend to claim asylum; or to protect national security or public order; ... (UNHCR 1986).

This detailed and explicit declaration of the UNHCR Committee attempts to address the various practices that enable the gatekeepers of many states to detain or restrain asylum seekers, or even to return them to their country of origin, in direct conflict with the requirements of the CSR. The worst problems are faced by large groups of migrants, as their collective rights are seldom respected.

According to natural justice, as well as the CSR itself, they should have the right to be heard (including the right to oral hearing, to call evidence, to counsel and to make submissions); they should also have the right to a fair and impartial tribunal (this includes the right to notice, to full disclosure and to a non-biased assessment of their situation).[1] Of course, the situation is aggravated by the presence of large migrations, due to conflicts, but primarily to man-made and natural disasters.

The refugee crisis to which Hathaway refers is primarily based on numbers: there are, increasingly, large numbers of asylum seekers, as noted in Chapter 1 (Hathaway 1996), and most often their flight is from developing countries to the developed states in the North. The Northern states have a correspondingly decreasing interest in admitting large numbers of impoverished and untrained refugees:

> As the interest convergence between refugees and developed countries has disappeared, Northern states have sought to avoid the arrival of refugees by adopting policies of external deterrence (Hathaway 1996: 49–120; Bell 1980).

At the time of the drafting of the CSR, most of the refugees seeking asylum after the Second World War were Europeans, so that their assimilation was not in question in North America. In contrast, today's refugees are 'different', both racially and socially, and not all desire to be assimilated, or can be easily assimilated should they desire it (Hathaway 1996).

It is worth emphasizing: if the refugees/asylum seekers were part of an indigenous group from any continent, then the whole question would be moot as 'assimilation' in their case, as previously argued, would compound the crime(s) already committed against them in forcing them to leave their territories, by adding the crime of cultural genocide (Westra 2007: ch. 7).

The first problem that faces *all* asylum seekers, without distinction, is the way they are 'greeted' upon their arrival at the border of their country of choice. Their first experience of the new country is, for the most part, not one of welcome, but a harrowing experience of interrogation and detention, even if they are not held back from the country's borders. States want to retain fully their sovereignty over their territories, and that includes strict border controls, such that the first reaction to large influxes of refugees is rejection (Brewer and Kumin 2003).

Perhaps the rejection is neither explicit at the start, nor eventually irrevocable, but the sort of reception that is offered speaks volumes regarding the resistance to invited 'guests'. These feeling and the practices that ensue, are observed by the International Organization for Migration:

> Many States which have the ability to do so, find intercepting migrants before they reach their territories, is one of the most effective measures to enforce their domestic migration laws and policies (UNHCR 2001b: 14).

In fact many states try their best to ensure that migrants never reach their borders in the first place (Brewer and Kumin 2003: 6). Hence interception represents the first of three steps intended to reduce the flux of migrations. In other words, even before refugee seekers arrive at their state of choice, every effort is made by

1 Rocco Galati, in lecture, Osgoode Hall Law School, 20 Nov 2007.

states to prevent them from approaching their borders. The UNHCR Executive Committee has defined interception as 'active intervention' by states to impede migrants, as follows:

> ... one of the measures employed by States to:
> (i) prevent embarkation of persons on an international journey;
> (ii) prevent further onward international travel by persons who have commended their journey; or
> (iii) assert control of vessels where there are reasonable grounds to believe the vessel is transporting persons contrary to international or national maritime law;
> where in relation to the above, the person or persons do not have the required documentation or valid permission to enter (UNHCR 2003).

One of the most egregious examples of the preventive interception is the *Tampa* case (USCR 2002). The *Tampa* was a Norwegian freighter that answered the distress call of a sinking Indonesian ferry. Most of the 430 passengers were Afghans who wanted to seek asylum in Australia, and to be taken to Christmas Island. The government of Australia, however, refused responsibility and responded that either Indonesia or Norway should take responsibility for the refugees; Australia even refused the medical help requested for the affected persons in the group.

Finally, on 1 September, Australia announced its 'solution' to the problem, which was becoming increasingly acute, as the *Tampa* was not equipped for the number of people it was then forced to carry, and even its crew was at risk. Australia paid US$10 million in aid, in exchange for Nauru's agreement (Nauru is a Pacific island state) to accept the asylum seekers, while their claims would be processed with the support of the UNHCR. The authors conclude their narrative by adding, 'Australia's Pacific Solution was born' (USCR 2002).

Essentially, like Australia, most countries would rather not have to face large numbers of refugees at their borders, and thus be bound by the appropriate articles of the convention. Various dilationary tactics are used to practise interception before the actual borders are reached. Some countries require a visa for non-nationals intending to enter their borders: Canada is such a country. In 2001, Canada introduced visa requirements for the citizens of Hungary and Zimbabwe. Visas are not easy to obtain, and represent an impossible requirement for a person who is persecuted in her home country, and hence cannot risk asking her government's officials for a visa.

Other interception practices, are the imposition of sanctions on carriers that attempt to carry refugees who are improperly documented (European Union Council 2001b). This is another manoeuvre often practised in order to avoid 'asylum overload' (Brewer and Kumin 2003: 11). The practice of 'maritime interception', or 'interdiction', is often based on the same rationale. The US intercepts vessels coming from the Caribbean, and Australia, those originating from Indonesia; other countries such as Greece, Italy, Malaysia, Spain and Turkey practise interception both on their contiguous waters and on the high seas. Often interceptions are carried out disguised as 'anti-smuggling' or 'anti-trafficking' operations.

It is often hard to separate intended interceptions from well-intentioned 'rescues at sea', which are required by international law. The US leads the world in interception: according to Brewer and Kumin, from 1982 to 2002, 185,801 people were intercepted at sea (Brewer and Kumin 2003: 11). In addition these migrants are not viewed as asylum seekers, no matter their country of origin, or the location of their interception, that is, this judgment follows even if the interception took place in US waters. Australia has concluded an agreement with Papua-New Guinea, similar to the one with Nauru, but with a significant difference: unlike the Nauru situation, in Papua-New Guinea only Australian authorities process the migrants.

The practice of interception at sea represents a denial of the rights of refugees: the right to seek asylum, and the right to *non-refoulement*. Denial of these rights, in effect, often continues even after refugees manage to reach the borders of their country of choice.

Denial of Refugee Rights: Detention and Other Initial Measures

> Other States viewed detention as *prima facie* a violation of rights; detention for the purpose of deterrence, it was said, went beyond the spirit of the convention, and entry in search of asylum should not be considered an illegal act (Hathaway 1991: 249).

Arriving at a country's borders, for the purpose of seeking asylum is not an illegal act, yet those who do arrive are viewed – to say the least – as a threat to a state's sovereignty, hence several countries, such as the Netherlands, believed that even detention at will would be appropriate for peoples who travelled without the required documents (Hathaway 1991: 250).

As always, in the case of immigrants, it is primarily mass migrations that raise the red flag in the minds of border officials, but even single individuals may create enough uncertainties in the mind of a border examiner in Canada, for instance, to lead him to view detention as a desirable alternative. According to Canadian regulations regarding Refugees, Part 14, 'Detention and Release', lists the factors to be considered:

> 244. For the purposes of Division 6 of Part 1 of the Act, the factors set out in this Part shall be taken into consideration when assessing whether a person
> (a) is unlikely to appear for examination, an admissibility hearing, removal from Canada, or at a proceeding that could lead to the making of a removal order by the Minister, under subsection 44(2) of the act;
> (b) is a danger to the public; or
> (c) is a foreign national whose identity has not been established.

At the outset, the questioning of refugees is, if not hostile, certainly not welcoming. For those who flee a government who may not be willing or able to cooperate with them, securing the appropriate documents requested by the host country's officials may well be an impossible task. Hence the UNHCR itself (UNHCR 1986) explained the need for very serious grounds indeed before detention could be viewed as legal and acceptable.

In the case of *Sahin v. Canada* (*Sahin v. Canada Minister of Citizenship and Immigration* 1985), a Turkish citizen was detained in 1993, upon arrival, and remained in detention to 1994, because he was not in possession of a valid passport or visa (as required by subsection 9(1) of the Immigration Act, and subsection 14(1) of the Immigration Regulations). The applicant argued that his refusal to return to his country of origin was not enough to warrant prolonged detention.

In fact, the right not to return is well-established in international law, and this fact supports the Applicant's position. Goodwin-Gill argues,

> The evidence relating to the meaning and scope of *non-refoulement* in its treaty sense also amply supports the conclusion that today the principle forms part of general international law. There is substantial, if not conclusive authority that the principle is binding on all States, independently of specific assent (Goodwin-Gill 1996: 167).

Yet there was a strong possibility that the applicant would have been forced to return to Turkey, as long as his status as a Convention Refugee was not established. In contrast, an applicant found to be a Convention Refugee is entitled to the protection of section 7 of the Canadian Charter (Goodwin-Gill 1996: 167):

> Section 7 Charter considerations are relevant to the exercise of discretion by an adjudication under section 103 of the Immigration Act which confers on him a necessary but enormous power over individuals.
>
> ...
>
> Fundamentally justice requires that a fair balance be struck between the interests of the person who claims his liberty has been limited and the protection of Society (*Sahin v. Canada* 1985).

Yet, despite the recognition of the gravity of the decision to detain, Rothstein J continues, by adding:

> In many cases, the most satisfactory course of action will be to detain the individual to expedite the immigration proceedings.

In this case, Counsel for the Applicant objected to the treatment the latter had received on the basis of two major challenges to the Canadian Charter of Rights and Freedoms (RSC, 1985, ss. 7, 12):

> 7. Everyone has the right to life, liberty and security of the person and the right not to be deprived thereof except in accordance with the principles of fundamental justice.
> 12. Everyone has the right not to be subjected to any cruel and unusual treatment or punishment.

The prolonged detention of an applicant under section 1032 of the Immigration Act (Immigration Act, RSC 1985), although that Act makes no express reference to the Charter, seems to contravene s. 7, as it is patently unfair to detain someone primarily because an adjudicator is not sure that he will make himself available for possible return to a country to which international law explicitly forbids his return.

A similar problem was encountered by the High Court of Australia (*Al-Kateb v. Goodwin* 2004). In this case the appellant, of Palestinian origins, is presently stateless, and has entered Australia without a visa. The immigration detention provided by the Migration Act 'is not detention for an offence' (*Al-Kateb v. Goodwin* 2004: para. 247), but prolonged detention and 'deprivation of freedom will *after a time* or in some circumstances become punitive' (*Al-Kateb v. Goodwin* 2004: para. 247). The problem is that a non-citizen, who has entered the country unlawfully, now depends upon securing another country that might be willing to harbour him.

Apparently there is an obvious conflict between the principle of *non-refoulement* (Article 33 of the CSR), and the right to, in some sense, force admission into a country unwilling to accept a migrant. The principle applies to all states, even to those that have not ratified the CSR, although,

> … a significant element of contingency attaches to the obligation, particularly in the case of a mass influx that may constitute a threat to the security of the receiving state (Goodwin-Gill 1996: 169).

In the case of the mass exodus of refugees after an ecological disaster, the well-foundedness of the fear that impels the flight is not in question, although its foundation in 'persecution' is a problem and it remains clearly an objectively observable condition as well as a subjective opinion: this renders the situation quite different from that of individual asylum seekers. In contrast, however, the sheer number of migrants may well represent a possible harm to the country to which admission is sought:

> Whenever temporary refuge is sought, the existence of danger caused by civil disorder, domestic conflicts or human rights violations, generates a valid presumption of humanitarian need. This has important consequences for the process of determining the entitlement to protection of individuals or specific groups. In particular, the presumption should shift the burden of proof from the claimant to the state (Goodwin-Gill 1986: 897–918).

The level of obligation of states is not fully specified in any international instrument. The need for protection and assistance is undeniable: *something* must be done to provide aid. What is needed indisputably, is a 'meaningful response to the humanitarian needs of victims of serious disruptions of the public order' (Hathaway 1991). Hathaway proposes four categories of refugees:

> (1) 'refugees defined by the Convention and Protocol'; these are entitled to *non-refoulement* and to all the rights set out in the Convention;
> (2) 'refugees who are protected by regional agreements', who may also be protected against return, and enjoy other specific rights;
> (3) 'refugees who fear harm as a result of serious disturbances of the public order'. These refugees may be entitled to special consideration because of man-made harms to which they have been exposed;
> (4) 'all persons who are involuntary migrants as a result of natural or man-made causes' may claim UNHCR assistance for resettlement and legal protection, but they are not automatically covered by international law (Hathaway 1991).

Although the first chapters of this work have attempted to lay out the legal situation of Convention Refugees and the main problems they encounter, and that has been the main topic of the scholarly work of James Hathaway and Guy Goodwin-Gill, the main topic of this work is the legal status and the conditions of the refugees here listed as the third and fourth categories. These are the persons whose conditions already are and are increasingly becoming intolerable because of climate change and other man-made assaults, but who are not explicitly and clearly protected under international law.

Present Instruments Beyond the CSR (1951) and the Protocol (1967)

> [I]t appears that respect for the peremptory norm of *non-refoulement* in mass influx situations comes at a price: the trade-off for accepting the obligation to admit large numbers is a *de facto* suspension of all but the most immediate and compelling protection provided by the convention. The OAD Convention, the Cartagena Declaration, the Executive Committee Conclusions, the EU Peremptory Protection Directive, and the UNHCR's views, all affirm the applicability of *non-refoulement* to mass influx situations (Goodwin-Gill and McAdam 2007: 336).

The documents listed in the above passage address the problem of mass influx (European Union Council, 2001a: arts. 3(2), 6(2); UNHCR 2001a: paras. 6,13; UNHCR 1980: para. (a); UNHCR 1994: para. (r)). Mass movements from one country to another are based on international cooperation, but the obligation of states to *non-refoulement* is not dependent upon 'burden-sharing arrangements' (Council of Europe Committee of Ministers 2000: preambular passage, para. B).

This fact, together with the reality on the ground wherever the receiving country is located, mean that a mass influx of asylum seekers imposes a grave burden on the country expected even to provide only 'temporary protection', premised on the possibility of an eventual return (Fitzpatrick 2000; Goodwin-Gill and McAdam 2007: 340–41). Temporary protection is intended to apply to both international and EU law, and the receiving state should not confine mass asylum seekers to camps, but should admit them to its territory.

However, according to the temporary protection granted under the Temporary Protection Directive (European Union Council 2001a: see for instance preambular para. 2), cases of mass influx of displaced persons who cannot return to their country of origin have become more substantial in Europe in recent years. In these cases it might be necessary to set up exceptional schemes designed to offer immediate temporary protection: what emerges from such temporary measures is the necessity to consider the fairness and ultimate justice of such arrangements, so that the result is not further victimization of the victims.

No matter how diffuse the responsibility for the conditions that force the mass exodus, it is clear that not only are the asylum seekers victims of harms imposed through negligence and wilful blindness, by systemic, established multi-party practices, but the receiving state may certainly bear only a partial responsibility, and in many cases deserve support from the international community: '... there must also be a greater commitment to preventive approaches and increased readiness to help receiving countries cope' (Goodwin-Gill and McAdam 2007: 339). This collaboration seems to be required, as the international community's response to mass influx is temporary protection:

> Temporary protection has a relatively long history as a concept of international refugee law, yet its meaning and legal basis are far from well-defined. [It is] regularly touted as 'an exceptional measure' and a 'pragmatic tool' to respond to the extraordinary circumstances of mass influx of asylum seekers (Edwards 2012: 2).

The conditions described in Chapters 2, 3 and 4 indicate clearly the limits of the CSR in regard to the mass influx of asylum seekers who originate from situations of collective harms. Minimally, 'temporary protection' is necessary (UNHCR 1981), and additionally, the provision of 'international protection' (UNHCR 1981: 3), and finally, at least one specific instrument was designed for the protection of refugees fleeing from extreme events generated by climate change (UNHCR 2011; see next section for details).

It is remarkable that of the three major causes of mass exodus, only one 'rates' the consideration of the UN High Commissioner for Refugees, while the other two desperate situations – that is (1) deprivation of the means of survival; and (2) the presence of an ongoing conflict situation – do not appear to rise to the level that requires a separate report from the UN High Commissioner for Refugees. In fact,

Erika Feller, Assistant High Commissioner (Protection), UNHCR, described the situations that initiates exodus as follows:

> the classical persecution-driven movement, where refugees, individually or in small groups, flee state or non-state persecution including that comprising deliberately targeted acts of violence;
> the mass-influx situations where large scale displacement is provoked by danger of violence accompanying conflicts or civil disturbance and which overwhelms receiving state apparatuses;
> cross-border displacement provoked by natural disasters or man-made calamities, such as nuclear disasters;
> mixed flows of persons moving as an integral and often indistinguishable part of an asylum/migration movement (Feller 2011: 4).

The remarkable aspects of this list are, primarily: first, describing 'natural disasters', presumably originating from climate change, as 'natural', rather than belonging to the category 'man-made'; second, ignoring the overwhelming number of victims of poverty and starvation (see Chapter 3), as well as the originating cause of their condition. Thus climate issues (although viewed as 'natural'), and mass influx originating from conflicts (see Chapter 4), are apparently viewed as integral components of the problems that render the Convention 'unfit'. With reference to a recent article appearing in the UK *Daily Telegraph*, Feller adds:

> He [Ed West] asserts that the problems are compounded by the reluctance or inability of, in this case, the UK Government, to properly distinguish between economic migration and protection-motivated flight, and he lays at the feet of the convention the responsibility for what he calls 'the people trafficking industry' (Feller 2011: 1; West 2011).

As the 1951 Convention and the 1967 Protocol can be viewed as a 'limiting factor' (Feller 2011: 5) rather than a basis for real protection for today's numbers in mass influx, the first step must be to understand those documents for what they are: at best, simply a 'basic statement' (Feller 2011: 5) which does not lend itself to the complex applications we need today:

> Even article 14 of the Universal Declaration of 1949 went no further than to state that 'Every one has the right to seek: and to enjoy asylum from persecution'. The original formulation, i.e. 'the right to be granted asylum' was dropped (Feller 2011: 5).

In fact the strongest international legal efforts today seem to centre on the criminality of 'human traffickers', in what seems to be a somewhat ill-conceived campaign, if it is not substituted by legal, safer means of escape, given the total lack of alternatives available to asylum seekers. Whether the mass influx attempting to reach Europe, for instance, originates from conditions of abject poverty and starvation (Chapter 3), or from the necessity to escape violence and conflicts in the asylum seekers' native lands (Chapter 4), or even the extreme events arising from climate change (Chapter 2), there are usually no options for refugees other than the dangerous and costly escape offered by illegal 'traffickers'.

Repeatedly we see in the media interviews with new arrivals, say, in Lampedusa, Italy, battered and exhausted, but happy to be alive, as too many perish along the way. Thus, although these asylum seekers no doubt understand both the grave dangers and the illegality of the means of transport chosen, their usual response is that they prefer to accept the risks involved for themselves and their families, rather than continue to face the hopeless situation they left behind. That situation is in some sense parallel to that of young women and children sold into prostitution, in order to facilitate the survival of the rest of their families in the third world:

> Child prostitution, child pornography and the sale and trafficking of children are crimes of violence against children. They must be treated as crimes and attacked as the most serious crimes are attacked, such repellent abuses are so far removed from any notion of work or labour that it seems strange to focus on them in an ILO report. Yet, while they are crimes, they are also a form of economic exploitation akin to forced labour and slavery (International Labour Organization 1998: 31).

Although clearly not to be treated like regular forms of labour, prostitution, the production of pornography and pornographic performances share with all forms of forced labour and slavery the initial impetus that leads children to participate in these criminal enterprises; the desperate poverty in which children most often live in the third world; their suffering is part of the 'structural violence' that is endemic to 'deep poverty' and to 'racism' (Farmer 2005: 26–30). Paul Farmer speaks of the situation that exists in Haiti, one of the poorest countries in the world:

> All the standard measures reveal how tenuous is the peasantry's hold on survival. Life expectancy at birth is less than fifty years, in large part because two of every ten infants die before their first birthday. Tuberculosis and AIDS are the leading causes of death among adults; among children, diarrheal disease, measles, and tetanus ravage the undernourished (Farmer 2005: 31).

Farmer reports the story of Acéphie, a good-looking young girl, still in primary school at 19, but – in all senses of the term – a child, expected 'to help generate income for her family' (Farmer 2005: 33). She was not sold into prostitution, but, as 'hunger was a near-daily occurrence for … [her] family' (Farmer 2005: 33), as she helped to bring produce for sale at the market, she was encouraged when she caught the eye of a soldier. Soldiers were among the few people earning a regular salary in the area, so she became his sexual partner, with her parents agreement, despite the fact that he was married and he entertained other women on occasion.

She was totally unprepared to hear shortly after the end of their relationship that he had died of AIDS. Eventually, through other relations she had while working as a servant in the city at the Embassy, she became pregnant. After a difficult pregnancy, and after contracting a number of infectious diseases, she discovered that she, too, had AIDS, as did the wife of the dead soldier and several of their children (Farmer 2005: 35). Hence, the sexual exploitation of children is not only a direct affront to their human rights, and their dignity, but an indirect attack on their health and survival.

Essentially, when the circumstances that face people are as dire as those facing the families who are so desperately poor that they can resort to selling their children for sexual exploitation, it is understandable that these circumstance might even force the flight with no regard for precautions or any consideration of the illegality involved. This point brings us back to the causality discussed in the previous chapters. The present question goes beyond that, as its focus is the 'legality' of the legal instruments and the actual conditions asylum seekers meet on their arrival.

The question, therefore, is what other instruments or approaches might better fit with the main principles in international law, given the changed circumstances of present refugees, and the changed meaning of 'persecution' that might be applied.

Current Instruments Regarding Mass Influx: Conceptual and Practical Challenges

> 1. Mass displacement poses particular challenges for receiving states, for other states affected in the region and, increasingly, for the international community ....
> 2. The present note attempts: i) to describe and classify the responses to mass influx which have been developed, ii) to identify and analyse the issues at stake which require resolution; and iii) to provide recommendations which could lead to the development of coherent and practical approaches to the problem that, while tailored to the particular context, are in line with globally accepted refugee protection principles based on the 1951 Convention and the 1967 Protocol (UNHCR 2001a: 1).

The first 'device' used by states faced with large numbers of arrivals, is to extend 'temporary protection', without the need for extensive status determination, which would conflict with the immediate requirements for emergency assistance. This approach requires a *prima facie* recognition by a state of the refugee status and of the objective conditions giving rise to the exodus, without, however, a clear definition of these conditions as 'persecution'.

Nevertheless this step is necessary to ensure protection from *refoulement*.[2] The first of a list of 'Areas for Clarification or Reinforcement' in the UNHCR document *Protection of Refugees in Mass Influx Situations* (2001a), is '9. Exclusion of persons not deserving of international protection', although no specific system is suggested to distinguish 'deserving' from 'non-deserving' refugees. Other listed areas include the quest for appropriate solutions for protracted situations, and a reconsideration of resettlement criteria (UNHCR 2001a: 2–3). Clearly 'temporary protection' in cases of mass influx requires 'a need for resettlement countries to reconsider their resettlement criteria' (UNHCR 2001a: 3). At any rate, the first step is the need for

> 14. Defining the trigger for temporary protection:
> Agreeing on what constitutes mass or large-scale displacement is an essential first step in order to define the triggering factor for activating temporary protection. Mass displacement is prompted by a significant event or situation in a country of origin, which is easily recognizable as the trigger for an exodus. In numerical terms, what counts as 'large-scale' or 'mass' influx will necessarily differ from country to country and/or from region to region, and must be decided on a case-by-case basis (UNHCR 2001a: 3).

Clearly, the question of the duration of 'temporary protection' is and will remain a bone of contention. More important, though, remains the effort to fit seamlessly mass influx into the framework of the 1951 Convention and the 1967 Protocol. Given the limitations it imposes, that approach might not the most fruitful, although some of the major scholars working on the topic maintain its support (Foster 2007: 58–65). The question of 'fear' needs to be reconsidered: the required element of 'fear' is viewed as 'self-evident from the event or situation which obviously precipitated the flight' (Foster 2007: 4).

This document seems to consider that the fear has been generated by an indisputable 'act of God', as no questions are raised about the possibility of a responsible actor or actors, at least as contributors to the 'event' that generates the fear. As well, the description of the origin of the exodus as an 'event' is problematic in itself: the model appears to be that of a sudden natural disaster, such as an earthquake or a tsunami. What this assessment excludes is the possibility of an indictable person or persons whose activities might have precipitated the event. It also excludes the existence of a slowly developing crisis, one which develops incrementally over time, until it becomes unbearable.

2 Both the General Assembly Resolution 428(V) Annex, para. 2t and the 1969 OAU Convention, Governing the Specific Aspects of Refugee Problems in Africa, Addis Ababa, 10 September 1969, in force 20 June 1974, 1001 UNTS 14691, as well as the Cartagena Declaration on Refugees (OAS), 19–22 November 1984 emphasize the primacy of *non-refoulement*.

Both economic deprivation and diminishing resources fit this pattern, a case similar to the case of the proverbial frog in the warming pot of water, staying in it until, slowly, the water reaches a boil. What is missing from this unquestioning approach to the causes of mass exodus is what is explicitly noted in the ILC Report of 2013, which highlights this neglected aspect of the mass influx of refugees:

> The commission had before it the sixth report of the special rapporteur (A/CN.4/662) dealing with aspects of prevention in the context of persons in the event of disaster risk reduction, *prevention as a principle of international law and international cooperation on prevention* (ILC 2013: ch. VI, paras 50–62).

However, the reference to prevention, which entails some form of human agency as operational before the situation becomes extreme enough to force the flight, is not elaborated further, nor does it occur with more details. We noted in Chapters 2, 3 and 4 that the most extreme situations tend to develop with increasing frequency today. In all cases, it seems necessary not to lose sight of the question of causality, which remains the basis of any proposed preventive action.

In contrast, the UNHCR's 'Summary of Deliberations on Climate Change and Displacement' (UNHCR 2011), starts by stating as one of its main messages:

> Responses to climate-related displacement need to be guided by the fundamental principles of humanity, human dignity, human rights and international cooperation (UNHCR 2011: 1).

Yet, below, it adds: 'the terms "climate refugee" and "environmental refugee" should be avoided as they are inaccurate and misleading' (UNHCR 2011: 1), without further clarification or explanation, other than a further comment in the section titled 'Setting the Scene'. Here the Summary lists all the severe results, both short- and long-term of climate change's impacts on all aspects of people's life, health and livelihood, increasing the concern for human displacement and migration (UNHCR 2011: 2). Still, there is no indication of why the terms to be avoided are 'inaccurate and misleading'.

A further puzzle is that the report even states that, with reference to small island states, the 'language that such states will "disappear" (i.e. the loss of their international legal personality), or "sink" ought to be avoided' (UNHCR 2011: 2). Once again, no explanation is given as to the advocated permanence of the 'international legal personality' of an island which has disappeared. This approach brings to mind Isola Ferdinandea, a small island of volcanic origin, which rose from the sea in early 1831 near Sicily, Italy, close to the present harbour town of Sciacca. While the Spanish, French and English were debating its 'nationality', and whose banner should fly on it, the island quietly disappeared. To my knowledge, no one asserted that its 'international legal personality' had persisted, although this example does not refer to a state, as in the case of Nauru for instance.

At any rate, the report emphasizes 'the impact and not solely the causes of displacement' (UNHCR 2011: 3):

> Future climate-related displacement whether internal or external is likely to be characterised by multiple causality, such as conflict and loss of livelihoods. The 'tipping point' for a disaster is not just a physical one; in fact the social tipping point often occurs much earlier and can trigger the decision to leave one's community (UNHCR 2011: 2–3).

Yet, in the face of the acknowledgment of such 'tipping points', the report simply harks back to the 1951 Convention, expressing a concern that, where circumstances dictate legal approaches too distant from the language and the sense of the Convention, present regimes would represent further hazards as 'only a few rights are currently recognized as giving rise to the obligation of non-refoulement' (UNHCR 2011: 4), adding:

> It remains to be seen whether flight from the impacts of climate change could meet the threshold set in existing human rights jurisprudence (UNHCR 2011: 4).

In addition, the Summary acknowledges that 'Climate change may further have particular impacts for indigenous peoples as well as nomadic and other mobile communities', another situation of extreme need that is routinely ignored. Entire populations of land-based Indigenous communities may be turned into persons desperately needing assistance and asylum, although they may not be able to leave their normal place of residence (UNHCR 2011: 5). This may happen because of existing legal boundaries that limit Indigenous lands, such as that of First Nations in Canada, as according to the treaties under which they occupy a certain territory, they cannot simply relocate elsewhere (Westra 2007). Similarly in the case of extreme weather events such as the mud slide of May 2014 in Afghanistan, which left a whole population without shelter, water or food (Massoud and Fayez 2014: A6). Neither of these two groups can become 'asylum seekers', but the question is, should such populations be simply considered 'victims' of extreme climate or environmental events, with no recourse, or rights, because, despite their obvious plights, and their desire to flee their circumstances, they cannot effectively leave their land? We shall return to this issue below. For now, we might take comfort by including in our discussion Point 24 in the 'Institutional Responses' of the document we have been reviewing:

> A range of actors will need to be engaged to address various issues, including *the prevention of the causes of displacement*, as well as the needs of those affected in post-emergency and/or return or relocation phases (UNHCR 2011: 6).

At any rate, it is clear that the recent instruments intended to deal with asylum seekers try to maintain the primacy of the 1951 Convention, while struggling with questions of interpretation of its language, and the seemingly necessary next step, that is, to ensure the coherence between all possible interpretations and existing human rights and humanitarian law. These challenges and difficulties regarding the interpretation and understanding of the meaning of the 1951 Convention are the topic of the next section.

The Challenges of Interpretation, and the Status of the 1951 Convention Today

> One of the most significant developments in refugee law jurisprudence in recent years has been the well-documented move towards an understanding of 'being persecuted', as well as other elements of the definition, that is informed and understood in the context of international human rights standards (Foster 2007: 27).

The main elements of the definition of 'refugee' (see Chapter 1) is the basic category of 'persecution'; equally important is the notion of a specific 'social or political group', as the target of that persecution. The first question is whether these concepts should be discussed/analysed in isolation, each separately. Foster argues that the analysis of a single concept at a time is not the best approach:

> In other words, priority is given neither to a purely textual or literal approach, nor to one that focuses only on context or purpose. Rather, 'the determination of the ordinary meaning cannot be done in the abstract, only in the *context* of the treaty and in the light of its *object and purpose*' (Foster 2007: 41; Aust 2000: 188).

If we accept the holistic interpretation of the convention, then both the language and the context lead directly to human rights law, as the appropriate focal point. This focal point is particularly evident when we consider the phenomenon of mass influx and the recent response to it in the form of temporary protection. The meaning of 'temporary protection' is not based on a specific definition, but varies according to the numbers and the locations of the asylum seeking groups in mass influx situations (Edwards 2012: 5; UNHCR 2012).

Foster's discussion on the interface between persecution and socio-economic rights, is based on Hathaway's analysis (Hathaway 1991: 106–7), as it includes the support of the UDHR, the ICCPR and the ICESCR. His definition of persecution then becomes:

> ... the sustained or systemic failure of state protection in relation to one of the core entitlements (Hathaway 1991: 106–7).

Hathaway then proposes 'four distinct types of *obligation*' (Hathaway 1991: 109; Foster 2007: 114–19). The first category includes the 'main' rights, binding according to the ICCPR, which are non-derogable, as they include 'arbitrary deprivation of life, protection against torture or cruel, inhuman or degrading punishment or treatment' (Hathaway 1991: 109–10), and as such, he argues, the 'serious possibility of a violation of a first category right *will always* constitute a risk of persecution' (Hathaway 1991: 112).

These violations represent examples of the first category of obligations on the part of states, as he adds, 'the threat of execution, assault, torture, slavery, or enforced conformity of belief exemplifies failure by the state to protect *core* values' (Hathaway 1991: 112). The second category proposed, includes rights that are no longer judged to be absolutely non-derogable, but they are such that they could be superseded in specific circumstances, such as a public emergency. They include freedom from arbitrary arrest, the right to equal protection for minorities, the right to the presumption of innocence, the protection of privacy, and the freedom of movement, among others.

Hathaway considers the failure to ensure these rights to 'generally constitute a violation of a state's basic duty of protection' (Hathaway 1991: 110), unless the derogation on the part of the state can be proven to be due to a grave emergency. The third category includes 'the right to work, including just and favourable conditions of employment, remuneration and rest; entitlement to food, clothing, housing, medical care, social security and basic education …' (Hathaway 1991: 111). However, these rights, while non-binding in a non-derogable form, arise from the ICESCR, and require all states to progressively realize their implementation to their utmost ability.

Finally the fourth category includes two rights not presently codified in the ICCPR or the ICESCR: 'the right to own, and to be free from arbitrary deprivation of property, and the right to be protected from unemployment …' (Foster 2007: 116). If this list is accepted, based as it is on generally accepted international legal instruments, then the conditions of groups described as asylum seekers fleeing from extreme climate change events, as well as those whose exodus is prompted by conflicts, should be placed in a special category as witnesses to the culpability of the states who permitted (or are in some way complicit in) the development of such extreme situations.

Equally the development of grave conditions of poverty and hunger as noted in Chapter 3 are primarily the result of activities and practices not only allowed by a state, but such that the state's active collaboration in the pursuance of their interests is and has been the basis of the conditions leading to a mass exodus. Hathaway notes the requirements of the ICESCR, which include a gradual increase of optimal conditions, achieved gradually according to their capabilities, in the case of developing countries. No such condition is posed on industrialized, 'developed' countries instead. Yet the relationship between rich and impoverished countries, given the conditions of so-called 'free trade' and debt imposition on the latter, renders the same developed countries clearly responsible for the dire results that eventually cause the flight.

While it might be difficult to isolate a 'social group' that would define the asylum seekers victimized by the deprivation of basic rights (Shue 1996), as well as the civil and political rights which follow, without falling into too broad and general terms, the concept of persecution, understood as unwarranted deprivation of basic rights, appears to fit well.

In contrast, in the case of climate change events and effects (see Chapter 2), for instance, even the 2014 declaration by Barack Obama[3] points to the fact that the affected, persecuted 'group', at this time, includes all of the human collectivity in various degrees: the victimization includes rich and poor, although the poor are clearly the 'social group' that bears the heaviest burden.

On the question of starvation and poverty itself (see Chapter 3), we are all at risk, again in varying ways: unnatural, unhealthy and often dangerous food in the affluent West, real starvation in the global South. As far as conflict situations are concerned, however, different regions pose different levels of risk (see Chapter 4). Thus, while the concept of 'social groups' appears hard to adapt to current situations, the concept of persecution appears much more flexible. But a move in that direction – *pace* Hathaway – adds another level to the issue of the treatment of Convention Refugees, now asylum seekers. The 1951 Convention is based on the acknowledgment of the refugee's subjective fear of persecution, confirmed by the common knowledge of the objective conditions present in the country of origin.

But after we acknowledge that the states of origin of asylum seekers have perpetrated human rights breaches, even if their 'crime' is simply one of collaborating with and supporting other institutions and organizations that have initiated the proscribed acts, after Nuremberg, we are obliged to go beyond assistance to the victims of persecution – especially in the case of non-derogable obligations (Hathaway's first category), but also in the case of the defence of minorities and other clear breaches of human rights according to the ICESCR, the CRC, CEDAW and other such international instruments – to states' *erga omnes* obligation to act singly and collectively against the state in which the persecution originates.

Thus the question that arises is whether a more nuanced interpretation of the language of the 1951 Convention, even when understood in a holistic way, does not add a dimension that, while desirable, adds a dimension that is totally foreign to the Convention as it stands. In fact, accepting Hathaway's interpretation and, in general, emphasizing the primacy of human rights and humanitarian law adds a second, more demanding layer to the already present obligatory state responsibility.

Respect for life and the basic subsistence rights of all human beings, regardless of race, creed, gender and location, are indeed fundamental human values internationally (Shue 1996). These rights are codified in all manner of International Charters, Commissions, rules and regulations. If our democratically elected governments do not have the duty to protect us and our subsistence

---

3 Wednesday, 7 May 2014, 'Foretelling Devastating Impact, Will White House Climate Report Spark Action on Global Warming?' available at: http://www.democracynow.org/2014/5/7/foretelling_devastating_impact_will_white_house (accessed 3 February 2015); see also IPCC (2013).

rights, including the right to a healthy, livable habitat, then our most basic and fundamental values are at stake.

For instance, in Canada today, after the Charter came into force, but also traditionally in the Anglo-Saxon world, civil liberties are placed very high on the hierarchy of fundamental values. I have argued that life and subsistence conditions, in any society, ought to be prior and primary, and therefore that both stigma and even imprisonment in varying degrees ought to be appropriate punishment in principle for those who commit assaults, but also for those who fail in their duty of care for others, whether or not death was foreseen or foreseeable (Westra 2000: 279–300). For the latter, their assaults or negligence are not focused in time, place, or even on one victim, but they affect whole communities through their actions. The causative link may not be a single one, let alone 'the' cause, but that does not stop the prosecution of more 'diffuse' crimes, such as the selling or importing of a prohibited substance.

An even clearer example of what I would term responsibility for diffuse harm can be found in the aggravated assault case of *R. v. Cuerrier* (1998). The case concerned a man, advised by a public health nurse in 1992 that, because he was HIV positive, he was to use condoms when engaging in sexual intercourse, and that he was to inform all prospective sexual partners of his condition. Cory J, in his factual background exposition, adds, 'the respondent angrily rejected this advice. He complained he would never be able to have a sex life if he told anyone he was HIV positive'.

Eventually Cuerrier formed a relationship with KM, who, in February 1993, was informed by another public health nurse that, while her tests were negative, Cuerrier was indeed HIV positive. After their breakup, Cuerrier formed another sexual relationship with BH, again not disclosing his condition. Subsequently, when the second woman also found out, Cuerrier was charged with two counts of aggravated assault. In addition, a question was raised about whether uninformed consent was still truly consent, given the dishonesty of the accused, who, Cory J added, engaged in 'fraudulent misrepresentation'. Cory J stated:

> The possible consequences of engaging in unprotected intercourse with an HIV positive partner is death. In these circumstances there can be no basis for distinguishing between lies and a deliberate failure to disclose. Without disclosure of his HIV status, there cannot be true consent.

When Cuerrier was advised of his duties with respect to all future sexual partners, there was no specific person named or intended, nor was any question raised about his intent to do harm, or to cause death. But the possible death of any partner in his case could be viewed reasonably as a 'consequence within the risk' (Hart and Honoré 1985: 94). Like the environmental harms we have described, the lack of openness and transparency on the part of this risk imposer was termed 'fraudulent misrepresentation', and his actions described as 'aggravated assaults', although it would have been hard to prove *mens rea* in his case.

Lack of transparency on the part of risk imposers, misrepresentations about the possible gravity of the risks and unconcern about the negligence with respect to the duty of care are all typical in environmental crimes. When one engages in intercourse, especially with a stranger, there is also, even in the best of cases, some element of risk, but so is an element of choice or preference gratification.

Clearly, neither choice, nor preference gratification is involved in any of the forms of grievous harm imposed on groups, communities and populations. The risks and the harms involved do not indicate an element of choice on the part of those harmed. However, when we consider the 'diffuse harm' involved in the Cuerrier case, we face a proximate, direct causality, and a single, identifiable perpetrator.

Neither the immediacy nor the proximity of the causes(s) is readily visible in the crimes that force the exodus, but this difficulty ought to be noted, but not used to reduce or even avoid the responsibility for the final consequences and effects of these crimes. However, just as the harm is 'diffuse' and nonspecific for the most part, so is the responsibility.

Glanville Williams states:

> It may also happen in a particular case that the consequence is produced by the simultaneous operation of two conditions), i.e. by two independent causes such that either of them would have been adequate to produce (the consequence) (in Hart and Honoré 1985: 235).

Hence, we might want to look at these and other circumstances as 'concurrent causes' and 'contributory negligence', rather than hope to find 'the' cause, hence, more easily discover a perpetrator. Hart and Honoré provide a suggestion: 'When joint or several tortfeasors have contributed to the same harm, the obvious rule is that each should be liable for the whole harm' (Hart and Honoré 1985: 235).

This appears to be a better principle for both torts and crimes, because we can immediately start tracing back decisions, and the application of regulations for months, maybe even years, and still find additional causes in a long series of contributory causes.

At any rate, what emerges is the responsibility and obligation of states, which includes a non-derogable obligation not only to support, welcome and assist asylum seekers, but also to dismantle walls and fences, and to be prepared to be accountable to the international community for contributions to the harms that motivate the flights. In the next section we return to the accountability of states.

State Responsibility and Accountability for Persecution, and the Pursuit of Open Borders

> But when accommodations were made for non-white, non-Christian groups people started complaining about the 'tribalization' of society and the loss of a common identity – even though those newer polyethnic rights are in fact

> primarily intended to promote integration. It is difficult to avoid the conclusion that much of the backlash against multiculturalism arises from a racist or xenophobic fear of these new immigrant groups (Kymlicka 1995: 179).

The argument of the first chapters reaches the inescapable conclusion of the responsibility of states for the resulting extreme situations that result in the need for flight. In this chapter we tried to establish what legal regimes and institutions exist today to redress the grave harms suffered by third world citizens for the most part. The next two chapters will discuss present instruments and the related case law in more detail. But there is no document that speaks of accepting responsibility for the harms faced by the poor and those needing refuge in general, despite the brief references to 'prevention' and to the quest for causality.

That responsibility should be emphasized and the corresponding accountability should be acknowledged. In that case, there is no need for the limited, specific wording of the CSR: other's rights to be free from harm at our hands, the very limits of our freedom to act, singly and collectively, are clearly specified in law: even the lack of a specific intent to harm may, at most, influence the court at the sentencing stage, but does not clear a perpetrator from all blame, just reduces the penalty imposed (*R. v. Desouza* 1992).[4]

It may seem inappropriate to introduce criminal law categories, and yet what we have noted in Chapters 2, 3 and 4 are the consequences of attacks of various sorts, by various means, not simply actions that result in torts, as compensation is not sufficient to alleviate all the problems listed. Furthermore, given the complexities involved in legally redressing the situations that cause persons to flee, as well as the poor fit between recent and current situations and existing legal instruments, an appeal to criminal law appears to be illuminating.

Our focus will remain on the negligent activities and the risks imposed by most of the current industrial operations as they take place in the global South. Thus it might be easier to understand and treat those multiple attacks, noted in Chapters 2–4, when we consider the appropriate laws, regulatory regimes and jurisprudence in criminal law. It is well known that environmental hazards as well as health risks are far easier to avoid than to remedy after the harms have occurred: that is the principle behind vaccination requirements, for health, and any number of environmental regulations.

4 This case is particularly appropriate in order to clarify the role of *mens rea* in assault cases, as the facts indicate. At a New Year's party, in a crowded room where Mr Desouza had not met all the celebrants invited, he had imbibed too much, and when he decided to throw a beer bottle at a wall, he had no specific intent or purpose. The bottle shattered, and one of the glass shards severely injured a woman in the room. Desouza correctly argued that he did not know her, and had no reason to intend to harm her. Still the court found him guilty for the physical damage he had inflicted, even without a specific intent to harm.

I proposed a review of criminal law when I proposed that very approach to argue for the existence of 'ecocrimes' (Westra 2004).[5]

In many ways, not only are the laws themselves outdated (such as the CSR), but the present multitude of asylum seekers and refugees represent a *sui generis* phenomenon in many cases, not simply the expansion of an earlier occurrence. Therefore, we should reach beyond the attempted re-interpretation of existing rules and legal responses, and perhaps consider different ways of approaching the problem. It might be helpful to start by outlining just why these refugees often represent a *sui generis* phenomenon. These are some of the novel or more nuanced categories we are encountering today:

1. Today's asylum seekers are not the product of some illegal act of state or the illegal actions of others, they are the result of immoral, negligent practices on the part of enterprises that are supported by their home states and, for the most part, are judged to be legal.
2. In the case of climate change, many of the refugees are not even able to flee, as the floods, earthquakes, mud slides or snow avalanches which are part of extreme weather events, may well trap them in schools, churches and other public buildings, away from their homes and unable to continue their normal life: the US hurricane Katrina is an example of this kind of extreme event.
3. Others attempt to escape from extreme poverty, trapped right where they used to live, but unable to move, such as the people of Ogoniland, in Nigeria, suffering the effects of Royal Dutch Shell Oil's version of 'development' (Westra 2007: Appendix 1).
4. Others are the children, the aged and the unborn, who cannot escape the terrible effects of conflicts, where spent uranium or depleted uranium (DU) have been used: they are unable to flee the results of US bombing in Fallujah, for instance, or that of Israel, in Gaza (Westra 2014a).
5. The same impotent inability to flee ongoing harms by industrial chemical substances, including mining and other extractive operations, are inflicted upon Indigenous peoples who live in reservations, limited by borders negotiated by treaties and other agreements. Canadian First Nations are often under attack from industry and are unable to move or sell legally (Grandjean 2013: ch. 9).[6]

5 I will reprise some of that argument with the supporting jurisprudence in the next two sections, although I have not followed any possible more recent dispositions of some of the cases I will cite. As we are speaking, at best, of *lex ferenda*, what follows is intended primarily in support of an aspirational proposal, rather than proposing the application of *lex lata* already in existence, thus this *lacuna* should not be too grave an obstacle.

6 Chapter 9 of Grandjean's *Only One Chance* (2013), titled 'Inconvenient Truths: Vested Interests Can Endanger Brain Development', discusses the problems of mercury

Essentially, all these categories are better defined as IDPs, that is as people who do not even have the protection of an outdated Convention to defend their rights. They are not able to flee, yet they are all desperately in need of asylum and assistance, but they fit no present mould or category. They are simply 'victims' of activities that are presently legal, although they can be defined as unjust and immoral (Westra 2014b: chs 7 and 8). They are not technically 'asylum seekers', but their plights are extreme, and no instrument is available for their protection.

We need to accept that for all forms of victimization, it is necessary to emphasize the victims' humanity and their rights, primarily by ensuring the prevention of the situations that are the cause of the ongoing 'attacks' to which they are subjected, and the enforcement of accountability for those responsible, even through a novel approach, such as that of criminal law or other legal regimes. The next section reviews some Canadian criminal case law regarding the imposition of risk, negligence and public safety.

Negligence, Risk and Public Safety

From a common-sense point of view, 'negligence' appears a good category to use in our effort to characterize ecoviolence and related crimes without a clear, specific focus. By specific focus, I mean something like the latest oil spill next to the Galapagos Islands: one disabled vessel with an environmentally hazardous cargo; no specific intent to kill wildlife and despoil wild ecosystems; yet clearly a shipping operation and negligent or careless monitoring of traffic, much too close to a unique, ecologically sensitive area.

It is relatively easy to trace responsibility in such a case, and even to ascribe liability. But what are we to say in the numerous cases where we discover multiple causes, numerous players with varying degrees of power and responsibility and no simple, one-to-one relations to one another, but the crime is engendered by a series of cumulative and synergistic effects instead? It is clear that, distasteful as this might be to those who are committed to subjective awareness of consequences and clear intentionality for a crime, the only thing that *can* be done to trace the sequence of events back to its many causes, and to understand its history, is to start by observing the consequences, the facts or the material elements of the crime. We must also keep in mind that 'symmetry' is an established principle in law (McLachlin J in *R v. Creighton* 1993).

This pragmatic approach corresponds to the 'objective' understanding of negligence that is found in common law, in contrast with that 'subjective standard of responsibility' that represents the perception of negligence found in European countries, such as Germany or Russia (Fletcher 1971: 407). For Canadian as for British law, 'because negligence is "objective" or "external", it is not a form of *mens rea*' (Fletcher 1971: 407). Yet the continental understanding may import 'an

pollution from a paper and pulp operation near the White Dog and Grassy Narrows First Nation in Ontario, Canada.

element of will' into the negligent act, in a way akin to our 'wilful blindness' (Fletcher 1971: 409).

In British law, the category of 'Homicide by Excessive Risk-Taking' (Fletcher 1978: 259) comes very close to what happens in general, in all (or too many) cases of ecoviolence, although some demonstrate clearly the resulting harm within a reasonable length of time, while other cases do not. The Bhopal case provides an almost instant and clearly visible causal connection between the perpetrator of ecoviolence and the homicides and other harms that followed. Floods, famines and cholera pandemics (Colwell 1996), fostered, and to some extent engendered by global climate change through anthropogenic stress do not provide a clear causal link sufficient to establish specific culpability. Recently, Nicola Lacey and Celia Wells have argued:

> Not only are there more man-made events as technology grows, but technology also affects the previously 'natural', flooding is the best example here. What looks like a natural disaster is often attributable to some human industrial or agricultural activity, further upstream (Lacey and Wells 1998: 574).

However, although there are many early cases where corporations were charged and prosecuted, rulings were handed down confirming that a 'corporation could not be indicted for an offence against the person' (Lacey and Wells 1998: 575).

Fletcher argues that there are 'three important factors' to be considered before assessing the culpability for the risk incurred: first, 'the likelihood of causing death under these circumstances', second, the dimension termed 'the gravity of the risk'; third, 'the benefits of the risk', or the presence of 'countervailing benefits' (Fletcher 1978: 260). Fletcher also points out:

> … the profound difference between being mistaken about whether there is a risk at all and being mistaken about whether the benefits of the risk outweigh its costs (Fletcher 1978: 261).

These points should be considered in order. First, we have noted that ecoviolence consists of various harms and even death inflicted through environmental means. For the most part negligence is understood according to an objective standard (interpreted according to the 'conduct of a reasonable person'). Yet some US decisions (*Commonwealth v. Welansky* 1944), hold 'that the actor must at least know of the facts that constitute the risk', and that 'inadvertence – merely being inattentive to a grave and unjustified risk – cannot properly be regarded as culpable' (Fletcher 1971: 401–37).

Perhaps a common citizen could claim 'inadvertence', or 'being inattentive to the possibility of grave risks', but this excuse could not be adduced convincingly by those elected to be responsible to the general public, or by those whose business it was to run the farm operations, as it was their specific area of expertise. This pattern is not unique as it is repeated with variations in most Northwest affluent countries wherever economic interests of any group supersede the health of citizens and of their habitat. Both those who lobby for deregulation and 'free markets', and those who push for 'workers' interests', when either of these conflict with environmental protection or a precautionary approach (Brown 1995: 64–76; Raffensperger and Tickner 1999) in regard to public health, must be aware of the risks and the potential harm they are promoting.

Another important question, is that of the possibility of 'countervailing benefits'. What are the examples Fletcher uses to elucidate this point? He speaks of a doctor performing a very hazardous operation in order to attempt to save a life, or a police officer being forced to shoot at an armed and dangerous felon in a crowd (Fletcher 1971: 261). For both cases, two conditions obtain:

1. the 'risk-taking' is related to a life-saving activity;
2. the life that is at risk is the one the risk imposer is trying to save/protect.

In other words, this is the best possible reason, in both cases, for undertaking a risky activity. In both cases, one could actually (in the case of the operation) or potentially (in the case of a citizen in the crowd harbouring the escaping criminal) either receive or reasonably expect consent. For the first case, in most democratic countries, a surgeon needs the patient's consent for any operation, let alone a particularly risky one, and that consent must be informed and uncoerced. For the crowd situation, one could visualize a parallel response: it would be reasonable to expect that anyone in a crowd, upon discovering that an armed and dangerous felon was present, would not only permit, but request armed police presence for her protection.

From the moral point of view, the most damning argument against speaking of 'benefits' to be weighed in the balance is the question of justice and fairness, particularly appropriate in our context. In Fletcher's examples, the risks are imposed to those who are already at risk, and the 'benefits' sought are to remove the risk of death. Not only is it disingenuous to compare economic advantage with lifesaving, but the comparison is fallacious in another important sense: the benefits that may accrue are not intended solely for those at risk through ecoviolence, and in fact harms and benefits may be apportioned to totally different groups.

In fact, Fletcher's insightful analysis of negligence, supports the argument that criminal negligence is a good way to approach ecoviolence, which is primarily corporate/institutional crime, resulting in assaults to the person on a grand scale. For instance, Fletcher states:

> Analyzing negligent and intentional acts in terms of objectivity, subjectivity, justification and excuse demonstrates the underlying structural unity of both forms of criminal responsibility (Fletcher 1971: 430).

Constructive Liability, Recklessness, Wilful Blindness and Objective Dangerousness

> 'Constructive Liability' exists where responsibility is attributable to an actor for a result without requiring proof that it was foreseen or foreseeable (Healy 1993: 265).

The previous section concluded by arguing for an objective standard for negligence, rather than a mental one. To continue the argument in support of attributing criminal liability for regulatory offences regarding the environment, we need also to examine recklessness, omissions and other related forms of fault. It is useful to start by considering *Leblanc v. The Queen* (1975). The accused, a bush pilot, 'was charged with criminal negligence causing death contrary to s. 203 of the Criminal Code'. What is important from our point of view is not the sort of episode that gave rise to specific charges in this case, but what was said in several places, as the courts rejected Leblanc's appeal. The wording is quite instructive. At one point, for instance, the editorial to the actual appeal states:

> The requisite *mens rea* for criminal negligence is 'advertent negligence' and although the act itself will, in most cases, prove the *mens rea*, it is open to the Crown to prove it by affirmative evidence.

Although this editorial has no legal weight, it indicates the general thrust of the judgment in the case. More to the point, Dickson J (Laskin CJ and Beetz J concurring) stated:

> On a charge of criminal negligence the requisite *mens rea* is determined by an objective standard, so that similar fact evidence cannot be admissible to prove any subjective intent (at 244).

In a discussion of *R v. Creighton* and other cases purporting to pose a constitutional challenge, Patrick Healy observes:

> Parliament can impose criminal liability and punishment as it sees fit, provided that it acts within legislative jurisdiction and observes the fundamental principle of proportionality between elements of liability and the proposed punishment. This principle excludes imprisonment as punishment for offences of absolute liability. In rare circumstances the gravity of the offence and the punishment will require proof of an element of recklessness in the proscribed act. Otherwise the principle of proportionality does not exclude liability for some form of negligence or for constructive liability (Healy 1993).

This passage affirms the traditional standards, while clearly indicating the recent shift to objective standards for faults of negligence. Healy views the last 20 years of 'Canadian jurisprudence' as moving away from strict *mens rea* requirements in many cases. He adds:

> There is abundant evidence in recent decisions and legislation of a growing shift toward the sanction and punishment of what people do and the effects of their conduct (Healy 1993: 267).

This conclusion is particularly encouraging from our point of view, as the cases he cites in support of this claim are certainly not all regulatory offences, in fact they are *both* assaults and regulatory offences, thus providing additional support for the claims advanced here and in the previous chapter about the similarity between assaultive and environmental regulatory offences crimes (*R. v. Wholesale Travel Group, Inc.* 1991, at 216; *R v. Desouza* 1992).

It is this progression from Charter mandated emphasis on intentional mental states for criminal liability, to a combination of objective, 'reasonable person' standards, and the material elements of fault (the 'act' more than the actor), that supports my argument and may allow it to move forward, from a philosophical, normative argument about what ought to be (critical morality) to what will be as a final goal of substantive justice.

Healy also addresses the question of what constitutes 'constructive liability':

> … constructive liability exists where responsibility is attributed to an actor for a result without requiring proof that it was foreseen or foreseeable … (Healy 1993: 269).

The 'constructive' aspect here described exceeds the reality of the *Walkerton* case, chosen as an example of ecoviolence for our discussion. Both industry and government institutions had enough knowledge and expertise, or at least access to those with such expertise, that the harms that ensued were at least foreseeable, minimally, as contradicting EPA (RSO, 1990, E. 19; Pt. II, 6(1) and 5.14(1)). There is an exception envisioned in s. 13(2), in regard to farm wastes, and that 'exception' recurs in all acts. Given present technologies, used in all farming, and also given the magnitude of the waste produced by factory farming, many 'exceptions' appear to be inappropriate.

Returning briefly to *R. v. Creighton*, McLachlin, J emphasizes several points that are applicable to our present problem. First, she cites Lord Ellenborough, CJ:

> He who deals in a perilous article must be wary how he deals, otherwise, if he observes not proper caution … he will be responsible … (It is) a universal principle that when a man is charged with doing an act of which the probable consequences may be highly injurious, the intention is an inference of law resulting from doing the act …

and also,

> … when a person began doing wicked acts for his own base purposes, he risked his own life as well as that of others. That kind of crime does not differ in any significant degree from one committed by using a deadly weapon, such as a bludgeon, a pistol or a knife. If a man once begins attacking the human body in such a way, he must take the consequences if he goes further that he intended when he began … (*R. v. Creighton* 1993).

Hence, both the 'thin skull' rule and an objective standard are sufficient to ensure that what started as a dangerous negligence in regard to emissions, or negligent omissions in regard to monitoring and controls, represents, minimally, the foreseeable risk of bodily harm. When infants and the aged are disproportionately affected, proportionality needs to be considered very seriously. McLachlin J adds:

> I turn first to the distinction between appreciation of the risk of bodily harm and the risk of death in the context of manslaughter. In my view, when the risk of bodily harm is combined with the established rule that a wrongdoer must take his victim as he finds him and the fact that death did in fact occur, the distinction disappears (*R. v. Creighton* 1993).

If certain groups (children and the aged) were disproportionately affected, one must also consider the equality rights (Charter s. 15(1)) of those harmed, and a constitutional challenge ought to be instituted on the part of the citizens. What is happening now, instead, is that the citizens are asked to acquiesce to a government 'payoff'. To paraphrase Mark Sagoff, 'they ask for justice, for answers about why this terrible thing happened to them', and they are offered economic redress instead (Sagoff 1988).

It is true that the facts as they presently stand do not appear to manifest the desire to do bodily harm or to kill on anyone's part. More uncertain is the question of 'recklessness', whereas 'wilful blindness' appears far more plausible. McIntyre defines 'recklessness' in *Sansregret*:

> Recklessness involves knowledge of a danger or a risk and persistence in a course of conduct which creates a risk that the prohibited results will occur (*R. v. Sansregret* 1985).

Colvin proposes returning to *Caldwell* (1982) for some illuminating passages that set the stage for subsequent debates between those favouring a 'subjectivist' versus those preferring an 'objectivist' understanding of recklessness (Colvin 1991). Caldwell had apparently been engaged to do some work by the proprietor of a hotel, with whom he eventually had a disagreement. One evening, when drunk, he set fire to the hotel. Although no serious damage was done, he was tried 'on two counts of arson, under the Criminal Damage Act, 1971 (UK) c. 48. He pleaded not guilty to a serious count under s. 1(2), which reads:

> A person who without lawful excuse destroys or damages any property whether belonging to himself or another -
> (a) intending to destroy or damage any property or being reckless as to whether any property would be destroyed or damaged; and
> (b) intending by the destruction or damage to endanger the life of another or being reckless as to whether the life of another would thereby be endangered;
> shall be guilty of an offense (Colvin 1991: 141).

In this case, Lord Diplock's analysis of 'recklessness' appears to reject the requirement for a subjective awareness of the risk, and – in addition – concludes that the defence of intoxication is irrelevant when 'recklessness' is alleged. He says:

> 'Reckless' as used in the new statutory definition of the *mens rea* of these offences is an ordinary English word. It had not by 1971 become a term of legal art with some more limited esoteric meaning than that which it bore in ordinary speech, a meaning which surely includes not only deciding to ignore a risk of harmful consequences resulting from one's acts that one has recognized as existing, but also failing to give any thought to whether or not there is any such risk in circumstances where if any thought were given to the matter it would be obvious that there was (Colvin 1991: 142; *Commissioner of Police of Metropolis v. Caldwell* 1982).

The last sentence of this judgment imports the 'objective' element of *mens rea* to which Canadian Courts have often objected within the context of recklessness (*R. v. Tutton and Tutton*). The objective interpretation of 'recklessness' is, clearly, the preferable one for environmental offences where, paradigmatically, there is no connection or even acquaintance between many perpetrators working together to bring about hazardous circumstances, through the institutional or corporate CID Structure (French 1984), and the public at risk.

In *Sansregret*, at p. 233, McIntyre J states:

> Negligence, the failure to take reasonable care, is a creature of the civil law and not generally a concept having a place in determining criminal liability. Nevertheless it is frequently confused with recklessness in the criminal sense and care should be taken to separate the two concepts. Negligence is tested by the objective standard of the reasonable man … In accordance with well-established principles for the determination of criminal liability, recklessness, to form a part of the criminal *mens rea* must have an element of the subjective.

He concludes:

> It is, in other words, the conduct of one who sees the risk and who takes the chance. It is in this sense that the term recklessness is used in the criminal law and it is clearly distinct from the concept of civil negligence.

This may well be the case, but it ought to be questioned from a moral point of view, as Stribopoulos has argued (Stribopoulos 1999). The clearest example is that of war crimes where a 'subjective' element, that is a form of intent directed at a specific person or group, is often absent, and those who actually commit the crimes (not order, command or direct them) are often less than fully aware of what the result of their actions might be.

Beyond Domestic Criminal Law: Existing Remedies in International Law

> There may be no easier way for the international community to meet its responsibility to protect *than by providing asylum and other international protection on adequate terms* (Barbour and Gorlick 2008).

The previous section emphasized the various categories of causal responsibility available to convict those whose activities result in circumstances that inflict harm on others, in national Canadian law. From negligence to recklessness, to wilful blindness, what is common to all aspects of the origins of environmental, health or other harms, or culpable deprivations of human rights, is that there are multiple avenues that can be pursued to protect victims of harms and secure a conviction for those responsible within domestic law.

In addition, it is worthy of note that all the categories reviewed did not include the intent to harm the victims, although that lack did not eliminate the responsibility for the harms inflicted. But when we consider refugees and asylum seekers, we confront global harms and international law instruments and categories, not national criminal and tort laws. Hence the important question is what is available in international law that corresponds, even loosely, to the torts and crimes discussed above.

We quickly discover that there are many difficulties in this enterprise. The first obstacle to this quest is the main problem we have identified right from the first chapter of this work: the unacknowledged causal link between the conditions that cause the flight and the presence of negligent, reckless imposition of harms on the part of legal persons, primarily large economic enterprises, and the governments that are complicit. That complicity manifests itself in permitting and – in fact – encouraging the industrial activities that cause harm, or in being responsible for the conflicts that support the governments' interests, and extends their influence, while engendering unlivable conditions for whole populations.

Nevertheless, in 2004 the UN's *A More Secure World: Our Shared Responsibility* (United Nations 2004) addressed the international community's responsibility to protect (R2P) populations from 'genocide, war crimes, ethnic cleansing, and crimes against humanity' (Barbour and Gorlick 2008: 6). Furthermore, the *2005 World Summit Outcome* (United Nations 2005) 'established a four-part approach to R2P':

> Each individual state has the primary responsibility to protect its population from genocide, war crimes, ethnic cleansing and crimes against humanity; and this responsibility includes prevention.
> The international community should assist states to exercise this responsibility, and ensure early warning capabilities are established and maintained.
> The international community has a complementary responsibility to protect populations from genocide, war crimes, ethnic cleansing and crimes against humanity. The responsibility is met through appropriate diplomatic, humanitarian, and other peaceful means through the UN and in accordance with Chapters VI and VII of the *UN Charter*.
> On a case-by-case basis, where the above means are inadequate and national authorities manifestly fail to protect their populations, the international community is prepared to take Chapter VII action through the Security Council (Barbour and Gorlick 2008: 6–7).

Here we encounter the main obstacles to the wholehearted acceptance of the role R2P could play in the protection of asylum seekers; first, the crimes listed are clear violations of *jus cogens* norms, and hence impose *erga omnes* obligations upon states (Vienna Convention on the Law of Treaties 1969), but only one of the major causes of unlivable conditions we have discussed – that is, the presence of conflict situations – is named explicitly, whereas the deprivation of resources or the presence of extreme climate change conditions are not acknowledged. The second problem, is the requirement of approval from the Security Council in order to initiate Chapter VII action, and to redress the clear instantiations of the proscribed crimes.

In fact this clause renders the very possibility of protective action subject to the interests and the preferences of the states possessing veto powers, mainly the US. The next section discusses this major issue in the context of the global condemnation of the exceptionalism practised by Israel with the support of the US as the clearest ongoing example of the difficulties involved in the reliance on R2P as it presently stands.

A clear example of the ambiguity of the R2P initiative also lies in the escalating conflict in Syria, in early 2012, between US-backed Syrian 'rebel' forces and the regime of President Bashar al-Assad. One would need an in depth analysis of the political background of Middle East states, from an expert in Middle East politics and history, to attempt anything but a superficial opinion on the situation.

In contrast, 'The provisions of the World Summit Outcome Document have received recognition by the Security Council, as Resolution 1674 (UNSC Resolution 1674 (POC) S/RES/1674) has reaffirmed paragraph 138 and 149 of the Outcome Document regarding the responsibility to protect populations from genocide, war crimes, ethnic cleansing, and crimes against humanity' (Avellino 2014). The Security Council did not respond in a timely manner to the reports of chemical weapons being used in Syria and the mounting numbers of civilian deaths.

Part of the problem was the presence of vetoes from Russia and China, both of whom did not approve of the NATO intervention in Libya, which they judged to have been ineffective (Avellino 2014: 7). Thus political advantage and other state-centred considerations most often supersede global concern about grave situations involving breaches of human rights and humanitarian laws. The latter had been acknowledged by both China and Russia, as they had voted for Resolution 1970 (2011), that had proposed that Libya's situation should have been referred to the International Criminal Court for the crimes committed after February 2011 (Focarelli 2011).

The responsibility to protect must be understood together with the increasingly stronger presence of human rights and humanitarian international laws on the one hand, and the well-established traditional doctrines of state sovereignty and the rights of the state to their territorial integrity on the other:

> [T]he impetuous development and propagation in the international community of human rights doctrines, particularly after the adoption of the Universal Declaration of Human Rights in 1948, has brought about significant changes in international law, notably in the approach to problems besetting the world community. A state-sovereignty-oriented approach has been gradually supplanted by a human-being-oriented approach (*Prosecutor v. Tadic* 1995).

Against this background, the International Commission on Intervention and State Sovereignty (ICISS) (ICISS 2001) proposes a broad spectrum obligation on the part of the international community through 'preventive, responsive, and rehabilitative measures' (ICISS 2001: s. 2.29; Barbour and Gorlick 2008: 3). Our question must be, how could this 'new' doctrine be applied to asylum seekers?

First, of the three measures envisioned, the responsibility to prevent is emphasized as the primary responsibility (ICISS 2001: p. XI: 'Prevention is the single most important dimension of the responsibility to protect'). In addition, although the results of the activities described in the first three chapters as causative of the mass influx of asylum seekers are not considered to be equivalent in law to genocide, or ethnic cleansing, the concept of crimes against humanity fits well as a description of the conditions generated by illegal conflicts, and also seems appropriate for describing extreme climate change events and the deprivation of resources, producing famine.

Furthermore, ICISS's focus is on the conditions of victims of state inaction and state actions both:

> R2P puts the focus where it should be on the victims and potential beneficiaries of any action or intervention (Barbour and Gorlick 2008: 22).

Nevertheless, the short-term measures intended to provide protection would benefit from the overlooked potential of R2P to assist asylum seekers and refugees, including IDPs (Barbour and Gorlick 2008: 22). Primarily, but not exclusively, in the case of war zones, it seems that the 'responsibility to protect' should not exclude IDPs and other refugees, as Francis Deng and Roberta Cohen were instrumental in 'conceptualizing sovereignty as responsibility' (Deng and Cohen 1998: 275–80).

Yet most of the literature on R2P deals with 'the use of armed forces for intervention humanitarian' (Barbour and Gorlick 2008: 24), while the protection gaps present for both IDPs and refugees, who would benefit from other strategies, are neglected, as neither has access to any other international legal instruments that is appropriate to their condition. Their plight is routinely confused with issues of international security and even terrorism instead. In contrast:

> The 'Responsibility to Protect' should imply that affected states, donor governments, and partner agencies alike, make all efforts to bring sovereignty, political will, mandates and resources into alignment with better protection (Feller 2006).

Hence, given its mandates and ultimate goals, R2P could be used to initiate new regimes directed at the growing phenomenon of the mass influx of refugees and asylum seekers. It could address prevention at the start, that is deal with the root causes of displacement (Barbour and Gorlick 2008: 25), thus making use of an existing doctrine, if not a legal instrument, to address and especially to redress the existing ongoing violations of human rights, which are the main topic of this work.

The 'Crime of Silence' and the Activities of the Russell Tribunal on Palestine

> 'May this Tribunal prevent the crime of silence' declared Lord Bertrand Russell to define the spirit and objective of the International War Crimes Tribunal constituted in 1966 to investigate crimes committed in Vietnam and judge them according to international law.[7]

The Russell Tribunal on Palestine (RToP) unfortunately has no legal status, but its mandate is to uphold and proclaim law and principles: it is a 'tribunal of conscience':

> … faced with injustices and violation of international law, that are dealt with by international jurisdictions, or that are recognized but continue with complete impunity due to a lack of political will of the international community.[8]

The Russell Tribunal has no formal authority, but its real authority derives from its recognition of the principles of international law, and the acknowledgement of the ongoing grave violations of that law. Unlike the Security Council and NATO,

7 Russell Tribunal on Palestine, http://www.russelltribunalonpalestine.com/en/about-rtop (accessed 26 February 2015).

8 Ibid.

the controlling forces of the R2P, this tribunal stands up for the rule of law. We will briefly sum up its activities regarding Israel's occupation of Palestine to demonstrate its position.

In 2010, 'the second international session of the RToP (London, 20–22 November 2010) started its work with a jury intended to examine the following cases':

- corporations providing tangible services and infrastructure that support illegal Israeli settlements and the occupation of Palestinian territory in the West Bank, Gaza and East Jerusalem;
- foreign banks and other financial institutions providing financial services to illegal settlements and Israeli banks and so on trading abroad who provide financial services to illegal settlements;
- foreign companies that manufacture products inside the settlements and industrial zones in the West Bank and Israeli companies that export agricultural and other products from the settlements and industrial zones in the West Bank;
- foreign companies involved in the export of arms and the infrastructure of war, occupation, colonization and repression in the Occupied Palestinian Territories and Israeli companies that export arms and repressive hardware/knowledge abroad.

The Tribunal established the responsibility of corporations under international law, and those obligations were contrasted with the real activities of MNCs. The counterpart of this examination is the Divestment Movement, which urges all those who either hold stocks in any of the complicit corporations to divest, or to ask their banks or pensions to do so.

The third session of the RToP met in Cape Town, 5–7 November 2011:

> The questions submitted to the RToP by the International Organising Committee at the Cape Town session are whether Israel's policy and certain practices affecting the Palestinian population residing in Israeli territory and in the Palestinian territories occupied by Israel:
> 1. amount to a breach of international legal prohibition of apartheid?
> 2. constitute persecution as a crime against humanity?[9]

Unlike the international instruments defining the responsibility of the corporation, which are primarily exhortative and voluntary, the obligations of states are defined by international legal treaties and by *jus cogens* norms leading to *erga omnes* obligations such as the International Convention on the Elimination of All Forms of Racial Discrimination (ICERD 1965), Article 3 of which states:

---

9 Russell Tribunal on Palestine, *Findings of the South African Session, Cape Town, 5–7 November 2011*, http://www.russelltribunalonpalestine.com/en/wp-content/uploads/2011/09/RToP-Cape-Town-full-findings2.pdf, p. 5 (accessed 26 February 2015).

> State Parties particularly condemn racial segregation and apartheid and undertake to prevent, prohibit and eradicate all practices of this nature in territories under their jurisdiction.[10]

In 1973 the Apartheid Convention was adopted, following an earlier UN General Assembly Resolution, declaring apartheid a crime against humanity; 'Israel voted with the majority in favour of that resolution'.[11] Apartheid has been defined as follows:

> 5.3 *Apartheid* is the Afrikaans word for 'separateness' or 'separate development' that was used to designate the official state policy of racial discrimination implemented in South Africa between 1948 and 1994. Indeed, 'apartheid' came to be prohibited by international law because of the experience of apartheid in southern Africa, which had its own unique attributes. However, the legal definition of apartheid applies to any situation anywhere in the world where the following three core elements exist: (i) that two distinct racial groups can be identified; (ii) that 'inhuman acts' are committed against the subordinate group; and (iii) that such acts are committed systematically in the context of an institutionalised *regime* of domination by one group over the other.[12]

In addition, Article 2 of the Apartheid Convention issued the following definition:

> … inhuman acts committed for the purpose of establishing and maintaining domination by one racial group of persons over any other racial groups of persons and systemically oppressing them … [13]

A similar definition can also be found in Article 7(2)(j) of the Rome Statute, but both Israel and the US are not signatories.

In contrast ICERD details a non-derogable state obligation. Even a cursory review of the reality of Israel's treatment of the Palestinians confirms that their practices and policies can and must be defined as 'a systematic and institutionalized regime of racial domination'.[14] Hence these practices and policies demonstrate clearly the presence of a form of structural violence that is strongly proscribed in international law, including in the legal instruments that Israel has ratified, although the *erga omnes* status of that proscription makes their ratification unnecessary to ensure the binding character of the laws at issue.

10 Ibid., p. 9.
11 Ibid., p. 9.
12 Ibid., p. 8.
13 Ibid., p. 10; see also detailed listing of such acts on p. 11.
14 Ibid., p. 20.

Another illegal aspect of the treatment of Palestinians falls under the heading of 'Persecution', according to the ILC Draft Code of Crimes against Peace and Security of Mankind (Art. 18(c)). The constitutive elements of persecution include:

> a material element (*actus reus*): a violation of fundamental rights and freedoms connected to one of the crimes provided for in Art. 7(1) of the ICC Statute; the material element is not limited to violence directed against the victim's body, it also includes damage to property;
> a general mental element (*mens rea* or *dolus generalis*): the perpetrator has intent to engage in a conduct which is in connection with a violation of fundamental rights and freedoms;
> a specific mental element (*dolus specialis*): the conduct is directed against a group on political, racial, national, ethnic, cultural, religious or gender grounds;
> a contextual element: the conduct is committed as part of a widespread or systematic attack directed against a civilian population; the word 'attack' is not limited to a classic military action committed in the context of an armed conflict; it also includes multiple violations of human rights directed against a civilian population.[15]

As well, it includes clearly the 'Siege of the Gaza Strip and Operation Cast Lead' (December 2008 – January 2009).

The fourth session of the Tribunal took place in New York (6–7 October 2012), and it

> ... focused on the complicity of the United States of America (US) and the failings of the United Nations (UN) regarding the Israeli breaches of international law toward Palestine and Palestinians. There is now a situation in which Israel has achieved a status of immunity and impunity, facilitated by the US, despite its complete disregard for the norms and standards of international law.[16]

It is undeniable that Israel could not survive with its regime's extreme exceptionalism, completely isolated from the international community, without the blind support of the US. Starting with the UN's 'Advisory Opinion on the Illegal Consequences of the Construction of a Wall in the Occupied Palestinian Territory' (CJ Decisions on the Wall), the following are some of the violations of international law:

---

15 Ibid., p. 23.

16 Russell Tribunal on Palestine, *Executive Findings of the New York Session, 6–8 October 2012*, http://www.russelltribunalonpalestine.com/en/wp-content/uploads/2010/08/NEW-YORK-SESSION-executive-summary-EN-corr.pdf, para. 2 (accessed 26 February 2015).

Violation of the right of the Palestinian people to self-determination as codified in Res. 1514 (XV) and 2625 (XXV), and recognized by the ICJ in its decision on the Wall;
Violation of customary law, human rights norms (A/RES/194/III, § 11 and customary IHL as codified by the ICRC in 2005, Rule 132, International Covenant on Civil and Political Rights Art. 12(2)) by prohibiting the return of Palestinian refugees to their homes;
Violation of the Security Council (UNSC) Resolutions requiring Israel to withdraw from the Occupied Territory (87 resolutions to this day) and the UN Charter which obliges the Member States to 'carry out the decisions of the Security Council' (Art. 25).
Violation of '[...] the principle of the inadmissibility of the acquisition of territory by war' (UNSC Res. 242), as well as the Security Council Resolutions condemning the annexation of Jerusalem. The Tribunal notes that the Occupied Palestinian Territory refers to the West Bank, including East Jerusalem, as well as the Gaza Strip since Israel's 2005 withdrawal did not end the occupation of the 360 square-mile territory. This appears from the fact that Israel still maintains effective control, per Article 42 of the Hague Regulation, of all air and maritime spaces of the Gaza Strip, as well as control along the land border and inside the Gaza Strip, a 300 m wide buffer zone (600 and 1500 m wide in some places) which is a no-go zone depriving Gaza of 35 % of its cultivable areas;
Violation of the Palestinian people's right to their natural resources and wealth through the Israeli use of Palestinian agricultural land, the exploitation of Palestinian water reserves and preventing Palestinian access to more than 10% of their safe drinking water reserves (A/RES/64/292);
Violation of international humanitarian law prohibiting ....[17]

In addition, 'the establishment of Israel's settlements (4th Geneva C Convention (GC), Art. 49 and 147), the expulsion of Palestinians from their territory', and 'the collective punishment of the Palestinian population of Gaza, where the WHO reports that life will not be sustainable by the year 2020',[18] are only part of the countless illegalities practised by Israel, but only possible with the full support and of the US which, therefore, according to the Nuremberg principles, is complicit in their crimes. Their complicity includes economic aid, diplomatic support and military aid (Israel receives 60 per cent of the US Foreign Military Financing).[19]

---

17 Ibid., para. 3.

18 Article 33 of the Geneva Convention; Russell Tribunal on Palestine, *Executive Findings of the New York Session, 6–8 October 2012*, http://www.russelltribunalonpalestine.com/en/wp-content/uploads/2010/08/NEW-YORK-SESSION-executive-summary-EN-corr.pdf, para. 3 (accessed 26 February 2015).

19 Russell Tribunal on Palestine, ibid., para. 5.

The Russell Tribunal noted clearly that not only the US had and still has the obligation to remedy (rather than support) all the ongoing breaches of international law, but the UN's responsibility is equally as grave. The UN Charter states:

> ... the UN's purpose is 'to maintain international peace and security', 'respect for the principle of equal rights and selfdetermination of peoples', and 'to promote [...] respect for human rights [...] for all' (Art. 1).[20]

The ICJ's Advisory Opinion on the Wall underlines many of the failures of the UN to stand firm on the grave 'violations of international law (including war crimes, the crime of Apartheid, genocide)'. Thus the UN itself violates its own basic principles and international law, and hence,

> Until the United Nations and its member states move seriously to implement their obligations, *it will be left to human rights and other organizations of global civil society to hold Israel so accountable*.[21]

Concluding Thoughts: The New IDPs and Other Asylum Seekers

> The foreigner is the political precondition of the nation-state and the other the ethical precondition of identity. The refugee is the absolute other. She represents in an extreme way the trauma that marks the genesis of the state and self and puts to the test the claims of universalisation of human rights (Douzinas 2000: 358).

The refugee, but also the IDP, poses the ultimate test to the universality of human rights, but also for the real presence of justice in state governments. In the last two sections we have explored risk, negligence and other aspects of environmental and regulatory crimes and the responsibility to protect in international law, proposed as applicable to the causality of the events prior to the flight in Chapters 2 and 3. While, in the case of the asylum seeker, the ultimate responsibility lies with the state and the reception she receives at the border.

For the IDPs remaining within the country, perhaps as victims of an earthquake, a hurricane, a mudslide or other climate-change related event, the responsibility should be shared between the state where the event occurred, and the international community. But this approach represents a very superficial form of justice, unless those who are causally responsible bear the brunt of the burden. Consider the extreme floods in Bosnia in May 2014, or the mud slides in Afghanistan, or the uncontrolled fires in California, all occurring within the same period. These are the results of ecoviolence (Westra 2004) or even of crimes against humanity, which

20 Ibid., para. 9.

21 Ibid., para. 15, emphasis added.

might perhaps be a better label. The classical question therefore needs to be asked: who gains by these activities?

As in all cases of negligence and related categories in domestic criminal law we have reviewed, the intent to harm is, for the most part, absent, although that is not true in the case of conflict refugees. What is present in the other cases is the leitmotif of neoliberal globalization: the single-minded pursuit of economic advancement, power and influence, and the deadly alliance of Western states and multinational corporations, both of which tend to operate with immunity from legal restraint for various reasons (Westra 2013).

We have also shown that the face of the refugee herself has changed, as other categories must be added, including those who suffer the extreme situations that cause asylum seekers to flee, but encounter one further obstacle: they are physically unable to flee.

The obstacle may be the difficulties arising from extreme weather events themselves as the exit route might be blocked; or the problem might be that their legal residence is fixed, thus restraining their freedom of movement. For the latter, primarily Indigenous communities from Central or South America or in the North, the Canadian First Nations or the Inuits of the Arctic, they reside in only one specific location as that is their right of separate governance within the borders of their reserved treaty areas, protected by the agreements signed by their ancestors.

These peoples are in their own area for their own benefit and protection; that geographical location is the source and basis of their cultural and religious traditions guaranteed to them by international law. For those in such communities, a forced relocation would be a double disaster: not only their homes and normal livelihoods would be lost, as they are for all others seeking refuge, but additionally the loss of their cultural identity and land-based religion would entail the loss of their entire identity as a 'people', even while retaining their individual biological existence.

This is an important concluding point, to be reprised in the final chapter of this work. More than the biological existence of refugees is at stake, especially in the case of a mass influx from a specific region: that issue is not even mentioned in the recently available instrument intended to deal with mass influx. The question is what are the rights of asylum seekers, beyond their basic right to subsistence?

In a recent work, Satvinder Juss speaks eloquently of open borders citing the example of the United States, where the openness to migrants helped to forge a strong and rich nation (Juss 2007: 291–7). In contrast, I would emphasize another aspect of the US's original open border policies: that is, their insistence on the 'melting pot' theory of community.

To someone desperate to escape poverty, perhaps that might be a secondary consideration at most, much as it was for the Hebrews led by Moses to the desert, as they blamed Moses for aiding their escape but not providing for their basic necessities (Exodus 17.3–7). They were right, and even God thought so, as he delivered manna, as well as freedom and religious leadership.

However, as we are reaching out and seeking far and wide for ways to protect the rights of people forced to escape, we should also consider that a nation that forces all school children to recite the 'Pledge of Allegiance' each day, who emphasizes relentlessly that they are all Americans, no matter what their cultural roots and traditions, might be viewed as providing a somewhat limited model to emulate, as anyone who has worked and taught in that country can attest.

Perhaps the ideal of multiculturalism present in Canada (Kymlicka 1995) might provide a more respectful ideal for all migrants, including those whose historical roots and cultures have forged their identities over many decades. This conflict is also analysed from a different perspective by Paul Collier (2013), in his plea for respect for cultures, even as we revise current migration rules. We will return to this aspect of migrations in the final chapter of this work.

References

Al-Kateb v. Goodwin [2004] HCA 37, 6 August 2004.

Aust, Anthony, 2000, *Modern Treaty Law and Practice*, Cambridge University Press, Cambridge.

Avellino, Roberta, 2014, 'The Effectiveness of the "Responsibility to Protect" Doctrine in Light of the International Response to the Conflicts in Libya and Syria', *Għ.S.L. Online Journal*.

Barbour, Brian and Gorlick, Brian, 2008, 'Embracing the "Responsibility to Protect": A Repertoire of Measures Including Asylum for Potential Victims', *New Issues in Refugee Research*, research paper no. 159, UNHCR, Geneva.

Bell, Derrick, 1980, 'Brown v. Board of Education and Interest Convergence Dilemma', *Harvard Law Review*, 93, 518–33.

Brewer, Andrew and Kumin, Judith, 2003, *Refugee*, 21.4 (December).

Brown, D., 1995, 'The Role of Law in Sustainable Development and Environmental Decision Making', in *Sustainable Development: Science, Ethics & Public Policy*, Kluwer Academic Press, Dordrecht, pp. 64–76.

Collier, Paul, 2013, *Exodus*, Oxford University Press, Oxford.

Colvin, Eric, 1991, *Principles of Criminal Law*, Thomson Publishing, Carswell Publications, Toronto.

Colwell, Rita, 1996, 'Global Climate and Infectious Disease: The Cholera Paradigm', *Science*, 274, 2025–31.

Commissioner of Police of Metropolis v. Caldwell (1982) AC 3341, (1981) 2 WLR 509, (1981) 73 Cr App R 13, (1981) 1 All ER 961.

Commonwealth v. Welansky, 316 Mass 383, 55 NE 2d 902 (1944).

Council of Europe Committee of Ministers, 2000, Recommendation No. R (2000) 9 on Temporary Protection (3 May 2000).

Deng, Francis and Cohen, Roberta, 1998, *Masses in Flight: The Global Crisis of International Displacement*, Brookings Institution, Washington, DC.

Douzinas, Costas, 2000, *The End of Human Rights*, Hart Publishing, Oxford.

Edwards, Alice, 2012, 'Temporary Protection, Derogation and the 1951 Refugee Convention', *Melbourne Journal of International Law*, 13.2, http://www.law.unimelb.edu.au/files/dmfile/01Edwards1.pdf (accessed 26 January 2015).

European Union Council, 2001a, Council Directive on Temporary Protection, 2001/55/EC, 20 July 2001 (OJ L 212/12, 7 August 2001).

——, 2001b, Council Directive on the Schengen Agreement, 2001/51/EC, 28 June 2001, Supplementing the Provisions of Article 26 of the Convention Implementing the Schengen Agreement of 14 June 1985 (OJ L 187/46, 10 July 2001).

Farmer, Paul, 2005, *Pathologies of Power*, University of California Press, Berkeley, CA.

Feller, Erika, 2006, Statement by the Assistant High Commissioner for Protection, delivered to the 57th Session of the Executive Committee to the United Nations High Commissioner for Refugees, Geneva, 2 October 2006.

——, 2011, 'The Refugee Convention at 60: Still Fit for Its Purpose?' Workshop on Refugees and the Refugee Convention 60 Years On: Protection and Identity, Prato, 2 May 2011.

Fitzpatrick, J., 2000, 'Temporary Protection of Refugees: Elements of a Formalized Regime', *American Journal of International Law,* 94.2, 279–306.

Fletcher, G.P., 1971, 'The Theory of Criminal Negligence: A Comparative Analysis', University of Pennsylvania Law Review, 119.3, 401–37.

——, 1978, *Rethinking Criminal Law*, Little, Brown, Boston, MA.

Focarelli, Carlo, 2011, 'La Crisi Libica: Un Punta disvolta Nella Dottrina Della Responsibilita' di Proteggere?' *Diritti Umani e Diritto Internazionale*, 5.2, 373–7.

Foster, Michelle, 2007, *International Refugee Law and Socio-Economic Rights*, Cambridge University Press, Cambridge.

French, Peter A., 1984, *Collective and Corporate Responsibility*, Columbia University Press, New York.

Goodwin-Gill, G.S., 1986, 'Non-Refoulement and the New Asylum Seekers', *Virginia Journal of International Law*, 26, 897–918.

——, 1996, *The Refugee in International Law*, 2nd edition, Oxford University Press, Oxford.

Goodwin-Gill, Guy S. and McAdam, Jane, 2007, *The Refugee in International Law*, 3rd edition, Oxford University Press, Oxford.

Grandjean, Philippe, 2013, *Only One Chance (to Develop a Brain)*, Oxford University Press, Oxford.

Hart, H.L.R. and Honoré, T., 1985, *Causation in the Law*, 2nd edition, Clarendon Press, Oxford.

Hathaway, J., 1991, *The Law of Refugee Status*, Butterworths, Toronto.

——, 1996, 'Can International Refugee Law Be Made Relevant Again?' in US Committee for Refugees, *World Refugee Survey*, USCR, Washington, DC.

——, 2005, *The Rights of Refugees under International Law*, Cambridge University Press, Cambridge.

Hathaway, James C. and Neve, Alexander, R., 1997, 'Making Refugee Law Relevant Again: A Proposal for Collectivized and Situation-Oriented Protection', *Harvard Human Rights Journal*, 10, 115–211.

Healy, Patrick, 1993, 'The Creighton Quartet: Enigma Variations in a Lower Key', *Criminal Reports* (4th) 23, 265–79.

Intergovernmental Panel on Climate Change (IPCC), 2013, *Climate Change 2013: The Physical Science Basis*, Fifth Assessment Report (AR5) of the Intergovernmental Panel on Climate Change, Cambridge University Press, New York.

International Commission on Intervention and State Sovereignty (ICISS), 2001, *The Responsibility to Protect*, December 2001, International Development Research Centre, Ottawa.

International Labour Organization (ILO), 1998, *Child Labour: Targeting the Intolerable*, International Labour Conference Report VI(1), 86th Session, International Labour Office, Geneva.

International Law Commission (ILC), 2013, Sixty-eighth Session, Supplement No. 10, A/68/10.

Juss, Satvinder, S., 2007, *International Migration and Global Justice*, Ashgate, Aldershot.

Kymlicka, Will, 1995, *Multicultural Citizenship*, Clarendon Press, Oxford.

Lacey, N. and Wells, C., 1998, *Reconstructing Criminal Law*, Butterworths, London.

Leblanc v. The Queen, 68 DLR 3d 243, SCC 26 June 1975.

Massoud, Hussain and Rahim Fayez, 2014, 'Aiding Families Takes Top Priority in the Aftermath of Afghan Landslide', *Toronto Star*, 5 May 2014, A6.

Prosecutor v. Tadic, Case No. IT-94-1, Decision of the Defence Motion for Interlocutory Appeal on Jurisdiction, §97 (Appeals Chamber Decision, 2 October 1995).

R. v. Creighton (1993) 83 CCC 3d 67.

R. v. Cuerrier (1998) 2 SCR 371.

R. v. Desouza (1992) 95 DLR 4th 595.

R. v. Sansregret (1985) 17 DLR 4th 577.

R. v. Tutton and Tutton (1989) 48 CCC 3d 129, 189 CCC LEXIS 2608, SCC.

R. v. Wholesale Travel Group, Inc. [1991] 3 SCR 154.

Raffensperger, Carolyn and Tickner, Joel, 1999, *Protecting Public Health and the Environment*, Island Press, Washington, DC.

Rousseau, C., Crepeau, F., Faxen, P. and Houle, F., 2002, 'The Complexity of Determining Refugeehood: A Multidisciplinary Analysis of the Decision-making Process of the Canadian Immigration and Refugee Board', *Journal of Refugee Studies*, 15.1, 1–28.

Sagoff, Mark, 1988, *The Economy of the Earth: Philosophy, Law and The Environment*, Cambridge University Press, Cambridge.

Sahin v. Canada Minister of Citizenship and Immigration [1985] 1 FC 214.

Sheldon, Leader, 2004, 'Collateralism', in Roger Brownsword, ed., *Global Governance and the Quest for Justice*, vol. 4, Hart Publishing, Oxford, pp. 53–68.
Shue, Henry, 1996, *Basic Rights: Subsistence, Affluence and American Foreign Policy*, Princeton University Press, Princeton, NJ.
Stribopoulos, James 1999, 'The Constitutionalization of "Fault" in Canada: A Normative Critique', *Criminal Law Quarterly*, 42, 227–85.
United Nations, 2004, *A More Secure World: Our Shared Responsibility*, Fifty-ninth session, Agenda item 55, 'Follow-up to the Outcome of the Millennium Summit', UN Doc. A/59/565, 2 December 2004.
——, 2005, *2005 World Summit Outcome*, Sixtieth session, Agenda items 46 and 120, UN Doc. A/Res/60/1, 24 October 2005.
United Nations High Commissioner for Refugees (UNHCR), 1980, *Temporary Refuge*, Executive Committee Conclusions, No. 19 (XXXI), 16 October 1980.
——, 1981, *Report of the Meeting of the Expert Group on Temporary Refuge in Situation of Large Scale Influx*, Geneva, 21–24 April 1981, EC/SCP/16/Ad.1, 17 July 1981.
——, 1986, *Detention of Refugees and Asylum-Seekers*, Executive Committee Conclusions, No. 44 (XXXVII), 13 October 1986.
——, 1994, *General Conclusion on International Protection*, Executive Committee Conclusions, No. 74 (XLV), 7 October 1994.
——, 2001a, *Protection of Refugees in Mass Influx Situations*, Global Consultation on International Protection, EC/GC/01/4, 19 February 2001.
——, 2001b, *Refugee Protection and Migration Control: Perspectives from the UNHCR and IOM*, EC/GC/01/11, 31 May 2001.
——, 2003, *Conclusion on Protection Safeguards in Interception Measures*, Executive Committee Conclusions, No. 97 (LIV), 10 October 2003.
——, 2006, *The State of the World's Refugees 2006: Human Displacement in the New Millennium*, Oxford University Press, Oxford.
——, 2011, 'Summary of Deliberations on Climate Change and Displacement', Expert Roundtable on Climate Change and Displacement, Bellagio, Italy, 22–25 February, 2011.
——, 2012, *Summary Conclusions on Temporary Protection*, Roundtable on Temporary Protection, San Remo, Italy, 19–20 July 2012.
United Nations Security Council (UNSC), 2006, Resolution 1674 (POC), S/RES/1674, 28 April 2006.
US Committee for Refugees (USCR), 2002, *World Refugee Survey 2002*, USCR, Washington, DC.
Vienna Convention on the Law of Treaties, 23 May 1969, 1155 UNTS 331, into force 27 January 1980.
West, Ed, 2011, 'It's Not the Home Office's Fault: The UN Convention on Refugees Is Not Fit for Purpose', *The Telegraph*, 11 January 2011.

Westra, Laura, 2000, 'Institutionalized Violence and Human Rights', in Pimmentel, A., Westra, L. and Noss, R., eds, *Ecological Integrity in the World's Environment and Health*, Island Press, Washington, DC, pp. 279–300.

——, 2004, *Ecoviolence and the Law*, Brill, Leiden.

——, 2007, *Environmental Justice and the Rights of Indigenous Peoples*, Routledge/Earthscan, London.

——, 2013, *The Supranational Corporation*, Brill, Leiden.

——, 2014a, *Child Law*, Springer, Berlin.

——, 2014b, *Revolt Against Authority*, Brill, Leiden.

Chapter 6
The Particular Problems of Migrants and Asylum Seekers Arriving by Sea

Tullio Scovazzi

Introduction

In the last years too many people have put at risk their lives in attempts to cross a border. They are driven by the desire to enter into a country where they will be safe from persecution, poverty, conflicts, natural disasters or other calamities and where they will try to spend a decent life. They are also ready to face social discrimination and vulnerability, after arriving somewhere and living there irregularly.

The hope to migrate is the reason why the waters of some semi-enclosed seas, such as the Mediterranean or the Red Sea, have become the graveyard of thousands of human beings, including children, who are moving from some African countries to reach, respectively, the European Union or Saudi Arabia.[1] Does it really matter if, in many cases, the attempts to migrate are illegal from the point of view of a national legislation?[2] Is the fight against illegal migration the main concern under the perspective of international law where also rules on human rights and refugees' rights should have a role to play? This chapter gives a negative answer to both questions.

The special case of migration by sea is addressed by different, but interlinked, sectors of international law relating to the law of the sea, human rights law and

---

1 Another instance is the border between Mexico and the United States. While, as a result of the 1982 North American Free Trade Agreement, it is increasingly open to the free circulation of goods and capitals, it is very close to a militarized zone, designed to prevent human migration.

2 For a criticism of common views on the need to control and restrict migration see Pécoud, A. and de Guchteneire, P. (eds), *Migration without Borders*, Oxford, 2007. On the subject of this paper see, in general, Ronzitti, N., 'Coastal State Jurisdiction over Refugees and Migrants at Sea', in Ando, N., McWhinney, E. and Wolfrum, R. (eds), *Liber Amicorum Judge Shigeru Oda*, The Hague, 2002, II, p. 1271; Miltner, B., 'Irregular Maritime Migration: Refugee Protection Issues in Rescue and Interception', in *Fordham International Law Journal*, 2006, p. 75; Trevisanut, S., 'Search and Rescue Operations in the Mediterranean: Factor of Cooperation or Conflict?', in *International Journal of Marine and Coastal Law*, 2010, p. 523; Scovazzi, T., 'Human Rights and Immigration at Sea', in Rubio-Marín, R. (ed.), *Human Rights and Immigration*, Oxford, 2014, p. 212.

refugee law.[3] Depending on the specific circumstances, migrants at sea can also be people whose life is threatened, or people who run the risk of being tortured or killed, if deported to certain countries, or people seeking asylum.

The Asymmetrical Right to Emigrate

By definition, a migrant (or immigrant or emigrant, depending on the point of view) is a person who wants to cross one or more borders to leave the territory of a state and to settle in the territory of another state. Immigration is illegal if the crossing of the border occurs without complying with the legislation of the state of destination or the state of transit.

Para. 2, of the 1948 Universal Declaration of Human Rights provides that every individual has the right to leave any country, including his own. The same right is provided for in Art. 12, para. 2, of the International Covenant on Civil and Political Rights (New York, 1966). However, while the human right to emigrate is generally recognized, it remains an asymmetrical right, as it is not complemented by a corresponding right to immigrate.[4] Under customary international law and unless different provisions are applicable because of treaties in force, any state has the sovereign right to allow or not to allow migrant aliens to enter its territory and can adopt legislation governing the entry of aliens.

Today legislation restricting or prohibiting immigration is in force in many states for different reasons. In cases of a massive flows of migrants, some states may be concerned for national security or the welfare of their residents or for the preservation of the cultural identity of the country. It is a matter of fact that the human right to mobility is not fully protected by international law. In the present situation of so-called globalization, goods and capital move freely or almost freely, but not human beings. If they want to escape from persecution, poverty or conflict, humans are often forced to cross borders clandestinely at the cost of great human suffering. Looking at the question from the point of view of the migrant, one may ask what is the meaning of a right to emigrate without a corresponding right to immigrate. Where are migrants entitled to settle if they are rejected by the states of destination? On the high seas? In the unclaimed sector of the Antarctic continent? On the Moon or in outer space?

Immigration and International Law of the Sea

A number of rules of international law of the sea are relevant for migration at sea. They belong to customary international law and are reflected in the United Nations

3 Refugee law could be considered a part of human rights law.

4 For another asymmetrical right, see *infra*, 'The Rights of Refugees'.

Convention on the Law of the Sea (Montego Bay, 1982; UNCLOS)[5] and other treaties. Also as regards migration the typical approach of international law of the sea is based on the question of the so-called jurisdiction, that is the determination of the state that can exercise powers over ships navigating in the different areas into which the sea is divided for legal purposes.

The Territorial Sea

Beyond land, the territory of a state includes a belt of coastal waters, called territorial sea (Art. 2, para. 1), whose breadth cannot exceed 12 nautical miles from the baselines from which the territorial sea is measured (Art. 3).[6] The territorial sea exists *ipso iure*, as a natural prolongation of the land territory of a state. For all matters, including immigration at sea, the territory of a coastal state goes as far as the breadth it has established for its territorial sea.

Within the territorial sea there is a right of innocent passage for ships flying the flag of all states (Art. 17). No violation to the immigration legislation of a coastal state occurs if a foreign ship transporting migrants merely passes through that state's territorial sea, without engaging in any activity that is prejudicial to the peace, good order or security of such state (Art. 19, para. 1). However, passage cannot be considered as innocent if, while in the territorial sea, the foreign ship engages in 'the loading or unloading of any … person contrary to the … immigration … laws and regulations of the coastal State' (Art. 19, para. 2). The coastal state may also take necessary steps in its territorial sea to prevent passage which is not innocent (Art. 25, para. 1). It may also adopt laws and regulations, in conformity with the provisions of UNCLOS and other rules of international law, relating to the prevention of infringements of its immigration laws and regulations during innocent passage through the territorial sea (Art. 21, para. 1, h). Foreign ships exercising the right of innocent passage through the territorial sea must comply with all such laws and regulations (Art. 21, para. 4).[7]

As regards criminal matters, Art. 27, para. 1, provides that 'the criminal jurisdiction of the coastal State should not be exercised on board a foreign ship passing through the territorial sea to arrest any person or to conduct any investigation in connection with any crime committed on board the ship during

5 This treaty entered into force on 16 November 1994 and is today binding on 165 states and one international organization (the European Union). All articles referred to in this paragraph are articles of the UNCLOS.

6 One nautical mile (nm) corresponds to 1852 m. The normal baseline of the territorial sea is to the low-water line (Art. 5). In particular cases, such as deeply indented coastlines or fringes of islands (Art. 7), mouths of rivers (Art. 9), bays (Art. 10) or archipelagic states (Art. 47), straight baselines can be drawn to join appropriate points on land or islands.

7 States bordering international straits may adopt laws and regulations relating to transit passage in respect of, *inter alia*, the loading or unloading of any person in contravention of their immigration laws and regulations (Art. 42, para. 1, d).

its passage'. While the conditional mood ('should not be exercised') does not contribute to the clarity of this provision, there are four exceptional cases where the criminal jurisdiction of the coastal state can be exercised. Two of them ('if the consequences of the crime extend to the coastal State' and 'if the crime is of a kind to disturb the peace of the country or the good order of the territorial sea') can apply to cases where illegal immigrants are disembarked within the territorial sea.

The Contiguous Zone

In a zone that is contiguous to the territorial sea and cannot extend beyond 24 nautical miles from the baseline the coastal state may exercise the control necessary to:

> … (a) prevent infringement of its customs, fiscal, immigration or sanitary laws and regulations within its territory or territorial sea;
> (b) punish infringement of the above laws and regulations committed within its territory or territorial sea (Art. 33, para. 1).[8]

Under the UNCLOS, the control that the state can exercise in the contiguous zone is limited to the purpose of preventing or punishing infringements of its immigration laws and regulations that, respectively, are likely to occur or have already occurred within its territory or territorial sea. For instance, the coastal state can board a foreign ship that is navigating in its contiguous zone if the ship has already committed an infringement to the state's immigration rules by disembarking illegal immigrants into its territory or territorial sea.[9] People on board suspected of smuggling migrants can be arrested and brought to trial. Boarding can also take place if there are clear grounds for believing that the ship is going to infringe the coastal state's immigration rules by disembarking illegal immigrants into its territory or territorial sea. To be sufficiently effective, the term 'to prevent', used in Art. 33, para. 1, b, should imply also the exercise of criminal jurisdiction by the coastal state against those suspected of smuggling migrants, even though they have not yet entered into the territorial sea. But the UNCLOS could have been clearer in this regard,

The Exclusive Economic Zone

Within the exclusive economic zone the UNCLOS does not grant to the coastal state rights relating to immigration. This zone, that cannot extend beyond 200 nautical miles from the baselines, can be established for purposes mostly relating to the

8 Unlike the territorial sea, the contiguous zone must be explicitly proclaimed by the coastal state concerned.

9 The ship can also be pursued and arrested on the high seas in application of Art. 111 (right of hot pursuit).

exploitation of natural resources (see Art. 56). As far as immigration is concerned, the regime applying in the exclusive economic zone is the same that applies on the high seas in general.[10]

The High Seas

The high seas is located beyond national jurisdiction and is open to all ships. On the high seas ships are subject to the exclusive jurisdiction of the flag state, this being the state that has granted them its nationality (Art. 92, para. 1). A ship which sails under the flags of two or more states, using them according to convenience, may not claim any of the nationalities in question and is assimilated to a ship without nationality (Art. 92, para. 2).

Among the freedoms pertaining to all states on the high seas, the main one is freedom of navigation (Art. 87, para. 1, a). The so-called interception at sea[11] to prevent a ship from smuggling migrants can take place on the high seas only with the consent of the flag state.

In exceptional cases, a warship can board a foreign private ship on the high seas (so-called right of visit):

> Except where acts of interference derive from powers conferred by treaty, a warship which encounters on the high seas a foreign ship, other than a ship entitled to complete immunity in accordance with articles 95 and 96, is not justified in boarding it unless there is reasonable ground for suspecting that:
> (a) the ship is engaged in piracy;
> (b) the ship is engaged in the slave trade;
> (c) the ship is engaged in unauthorized broadcasting and the flag State of the warship has jurisdiction under article 109;
> (d) the ship is without nationality; or
> (e) though flying a foreign flag or refusing to show its flag, the ship is, in reality, of the same nationality as the warship (Art. 110, para. 1).

10 Art. 58, para. 2, provides that Arts. 88 to 115, relating to the high seas, and other pertinent rules of international law apply to the exclusive economic zone in so far as they are not incompatible with Part V UNCLOS (exclusive economic zone).

11 See *infra*, 'The Rights of Refugees at Sea'. Interception has been defined 'as encompassing all measures applied by a State, outside its national territory, in order to prevent, interrupt or stop the movement of persons without the required documentation crossing international borders by land, air or sea, and making their way to the country of prospective destination' (United Nations High Commissioner for Refugees, *Interception of Asylum-Seekers and Refugees: the International Framework and Recommendations for a Comprehensive Approach*, UN doc. EC/50/SC/CPR.17, 9 June 2000, para. 10).

As ships engaged in migrant smuggling do not fall into any of the cases listed in Art. 110, they cannot be visited on the high seas.[12] In most cases smugglers of migrants cannot be considered as slave traders, since migrants travel voluntarily and are not deprived of their freedom.

The Smuggling of Migrants at Sea as a Transnational Crime

The Protocol against the Smuggling of Migrants by Land, Sea and Air (Palermo, 2000),[13] supplementing the United Nations Convention against Transnational Organized Crime (Palermo, 2000), provides for a specific international regime against the activities of organized criminal groups engaged in the smuggling of migrants. It entered into force on 28 January 2004 and is today binding on 140 states.

Art. 3, para. a, of the Migrants Protocol, defines 'smuggling of migrants' as follows:

> … the procurement, in order to obtain, directly or indirectly, a financial or other material benefit, of the illegal entry of a person into a State Party of which the person is not a national or a permanent resident.

The definition shows that a clear distinction is made between the smuggler and the migrant. The latter is not the criminal against whom the Migrants Protocol has been adopted. An illegal immigrant is not the smuggler of himself.[14] This explains why the Migrants Protocol also has the purpose of ensuring the protection of the rights of the illegal migrant who is considered the victim of the smugglers.[15]

The Migrants Protocol aims at promoting international cooperation for the prevention, investigation and prosecution of certain offences, provided that they are transnational in nature[16] and involve an organized criminal group. The States

12 However, there are treaties allowing in certain cases a visit and other forms of jurisdiction (see *infra*, 'Some Bilateral Agreements against the Smuggling of Migrants by Sea').

13 Hereinafter: Migrants Protocol.

14 However, an illegal migrant can become a smuggler under the Migrants Protocol if, being involved in 'an organized criminal group', he organizes a trip for himself and for other migrants as well.

15 See *infra*, 'Migration at Sea and Human Rights Law'.

16 Under Art. 3, para. 2, of the United Nations Convention against Transnational Organized Crime, an offence is transnational in nature if '(a) it is committed in more than one State; (b) it is committed in one State but a substantial part of its preparation, planning, direction or control takes place in another State; (c) it is committed in one State but involves an organized criminal group that engages in criminal activities in more than one State; or (d) it is committed in one State but has substantial effects in another State'.

Parties are bound to establish as criminal offences the smuggling of migrants and a number of acts which facilitate smuggling (Art. 6, para. 1).

As regards the smuggling of migrants at sea, the Migrants Protocol follows the same approach taken by UNCLOS, based on the principle of freedom of navigation on the high seas and in the exclusive economic zone and on the jurisdiction of the flag state.[17] In particular, as regards the question of jurisdiction beyond the territorial sea, it provides as follows:

> A State Party that has reasonable grounds to suspect that a vessel exercising freedom of navigation in accordance with international law and flying the flag or displaying the marks of registry of another State Party is engaged in the smuggling of migrants by sea may so notify the flag State, request confirmation of registry and, if confirmed, request authorization from the flag State to take appropriate measures with regard to that vessel. The flag State may authorize the requesting State, inter alia:
> (a) To board the vessel;
> (b) To search the vessel; and
> (c) If evidence is found that the vessel is engaged in the smuggling of migrants by sea, to take appropriate measures with respect to the vessel and persons and cargo on board, as authorized by the flag State (Art. 8, para. 2).

On the basis of freedom of navigation on the high seas, it is only after having received the authorization by the flag state that the boarding and searching of a suspected foreign ship can take place. In this case, Art. 8, para. 2, allows the boarding state also to take 'appropriate measures with respect to the vessel and persons and cargo on board'. Although the Migrants Protocol does not provide precise indications, measures such as the seizure of the ship and the arrest of the smugglers to be subsequently surrendered to the authorities of the flag state for criminal prosecution can be envisaged in this regard.

During the negotiations for the Migrants Protocol, Austria and Italy proposed to include a provision allowing a state to intervene on the high seas if a vessel having no nationality is involved in the trafficking of migrants and 'based on its route, the vessel is undoubtedly bound for its coasts' or if 'the vessel is armed or governed or manned by nationals'.[18] The proposal was not adopted.

Art. 8, para. 4, of the Migrants Protocol enters into the question of the communications between the states concerned, providing for an obligation of the flag state to 'respond expeditiously' to a request for authorization to interfere with a suspected ship:

> A State Party shall respond expeditiously to a request from another State Party to determine whether a vessel that is claiming its registry or flying its flag is

17 *Supra*, 'The High Seas'.

18 See UN Doc A/AC.254/4/Add.1, 15 December 1998, Art. F, para. 1, b.

> entitled to do so and to a request for authorization made in accordance with paragraph 2 of this article.

This means that informal and quick means of communication, such as telephone calls, facsimile letters or electronic mail can be used.

Another practical question of communication addressed by the Migrants Protocol is how to know the name, address (possibly, electronic address) or telephone number of the foreign authority bound to respond expeditiously:

> Each State Party shall designate an authority or, where necessary, authorities to receive and respond to requests for assistance, for confirmation of registry or of the right of a vessel to fly its flag and for authorization to take appropriate measures. Such designation shall be notified through the Secretary-General to all other State Parties within one month of the designation (Art. 8, para. 6).

The Migrants Protocol provides that ships without nationality smuggling migrants can be boarded and searched. However – and this is a major gap – it does not clearly specify what the visiting state can do thereafter:

> A State Party that has reasonable grounds to suspect that a vessel is engaged in the smuggling of migrants by sea and is without nationality or may be assimilated to a vessel without nationality may board and search the vessel. If evidence confirming the suspicion is found, that State Party shall take appropriate measures in accordance with relevant domestic and international law (Art. 8, para. 7).

The reference to the right to 'take appropriate measures in accordance with relevant domestic and international law' is of little help, considering that neither the UNCLOS, nor general international law provide for any specific action and that domestic law can only be in conformity with rules of international law. In the absence of a flag state, does this cryptic wording mean that the boarding state can arrest those who are suspected of migrant smuggling if there are clear grounds for believing that the ship is going to infringe the state's immigration rules by disembarking illegal immigrants into its territory or territorial sea? The answer is far from clear.

The conclusion may be drawn that the drafters of the Migrants Protocol, being too concerned with the preservation of the freedom of the high seas, did not give sufficiently effective tools to states to fight against smuggling of migrants by sea. The emphasis put on communication between the States Parties involved, which seems to be the major innovation of the Protocol, has so far achieved modest results. Despite the already recalled Art. 8, para. 6, only 26 out of all the States Parties have announced the name of the authority bound to respond expeditiously to the requests by other States Parties.[19] It seems that, with or without the Migrants Protocol, the legal framework to tackle illegal migration by sea does not substantively change. The main merit of the Migrants Protocol is to be found elsewhere, that is in the specification of the rights that must be granted to illegal migrants.[20]

Some Bilateral Agreements against the Smuggling of Migrants by Sea

Both the UNCLOS (Art. 311, paras 2 and 3) and the Migrants Protocol (Art. 17) allow for special agreements on a regional or bilateral basis. Such agreements have been concluded, although they are less numerous than those aimed at fighting other crimes at sea, such as drug or weapons trafficking. Due to the fact that the flow of migrants normally goes only in one direction, the agreements in question do not have a reciprocal content but provide for different rights and obligations with respect to either party. Some examples are provided hereunder.

Haiti and the United States

On 23 September 1981, in a period of massive flow of undocumented migrants towards the south-eastern part of the United States, Haiti and the United States of America concluded in Port-au-Prince an Agreement to Stop Clandestine Migration of Residents of Haiti to the United States.[21] It aims at establishing 'a cooperative program of interdiction and selective return to Haiti of certain Haitian migrants and vessels involved in illegal transport of persons coming from Haiti' (preamble). The Agreement derogated to the rules of the international law of the sea on the exercise of jurisdiction by the flag state on the high seas. Haiti consented to boarding on the high seas by the United States authorities of private vessels flying the Haitian flag which may be involved in the irregular carriage of passengers from Haiti. After the boarding, further action, including the detention of people on board, could follow:

> Upon boarding a Haitian flag vessel, in accordance with this agreement, the authorities of the United States Government may address inquiries, examine documents and take such measures as are necessary to establish the registry, condition and destination of the vessel and the status of those on board the vessel. When these measures suggest that an offense against United States

19 Some States Parties (for example, Italy and Panama) have only indicated the name of an authority (the Italian Coast Guard Headquarters and the Maritime Authority of Panama, respectively), without pointing out how to expeditiously contact it. Others (for example, the Netherlands) have only given an ordinary mail address. Is posting a letter in a mail box and waiting for an answer a way to communicate 'expeditiously' nowadays?

20 See *infra*, 'Migration at Sea and Human Rights Law'.

21 Text in *International Legal Materials*, 1981, p. 1198.

> immigration laws or appropriate Haitian laws has been or is being committed, the Government of the Republic of Haiti consents to the detention on the high seas by the United States Coast Guard of the vessels and persons found on board.

The United States had the right to return to Haiti the persons and vessels detained or to surrender them to the Haitian authorities.

> The Government of Haiti agrees to permit upon prior notification the return of detained vessels and persons to a Haitian port, or if circumstances permit, the United States Government will release such vessels and migrants on the high seas to representatives of the Government of the Republic of Haiti.

Haiti was under an obligation to prosecute those who are suspected of illegal trafficking and to confiscate the vessels involved in it:

> The Government of the Republic of Haiti agrees, to the extent permitted by Haitian law, to prosecute illegal traffickers of Haitian migrants who do not have requisite permission to enter the country of the vessel's destination and to confiscate Haitian vessels or stateless vessels involved in such trafficking.[22]

Haiti was entitled to have a representative on board the American vessels engaged in the implementation of the Agreement:

> The Government of the United States agrees to the presence of a representative of the Navy of the Republic of Haiti as liaison aboard any United States vessel engaged in the implementation of this cooperative program.

The Agreement was followed on 29 September 1981 by a Proclamation by the President of the United States on interdiction of illegal aliens[23] and by Executive Order 12324, applying to ships carrying undocumented aliens and flying the flag of the United States, to ships without nationality and to ships flying the flag of a state with which the United States has arrangements authorizing the stopping and boarding.[24]

---

22 It is also provided that 'the United States Government likewise agrees, to the extent permitted by United States law, to prosecute traffickers of United States nationality and to confiscate United States vessels engaged in such trafficking'.

23 According to the Proclamation, 'the continuing illegal migration by sea of large numbers of undocumented aliens into the southeastern United States' has 'severely strained the law enforcement resources of the Immigration and Naturalization Service' and has 'threatened the welfare and safety of communities in that region'.

24 The Executive Order does not prejudice the 'strict observance of our international obligations concerning those who genuinely flee persecution in their homeland' (sect. 3). It

Albania and Italy

By an Exchange of Notes concluded on 25 March 1997,[25] Albania and Italy pointed out that, due to the massive illegal flow of Albanian migrants to other countries, they had agreed 'to strengthen their collaboration in the legal and humanitarian fields'. In particular, Albania agreed that Italy provided 'its collaboration and its assistance in the control and the restraint at sea of illegal expatriations by Albanian nationals'. For an initial and renewable period of 30 days, Albania authorized Italy, through the Italian Navy,

> to stop in international waters and to divert to Albanian ports ships flying the Albanian flag or in any way referable to the Albanian State, as well as to stop in Albanian territorial waters ships of any flag, which are engaged in the transport of Albania nationals who have escaped the controls carried out by the competent authorities in Albanian territory.

However, the 'necessary technical procedures to implement this collaboration in Albanian territorial waters and in international waters' were to be established as soon as possible through an ad hoc protocol. This was done under an Implementation Protocol adopted in Rome on 2 April 1997.

The Exchange of Notes set forth derogations to both the rule of the exclusive jurisdiction of the flag state on the high seas and the rule of the exclusive jurisdiction of the coastal state in its territorial sea, as far as Albania is concerned. Moreover, Albania was granted no control over what Italian ships were doing in the implementation of the Exchange of Notes. In this case, the intercepting party was entitled not to board, but to stop and divert the ships flying the flag of the other party. In fact, a ship can be stopped and diverted even without the need to board it. But this consideration would bring about very sinister consequences in the implementation of the Exchange of Notes, as will later be seen.[26]

Dominican Republic and the United States

On 20 May 2003, the Dominican Republic and the United States concluded an Agreement Concerning Cooperation in Maritime Law Enforcement.[27] As stated in the preamble, it is based on the need for international cooperation in suppressing

---

was revoked and replaced by Executive Order 12807 of 24 May 1992 (see *infra*, 'Sale et al. v. Haitian Centers Council, Inc., et al.').

25 Text, in the Albanian and Italian official versions, in *Gazzetta Ufficiale della Repubblica Italiana*, supplement to No. 163 of 15 July 1997.

26 See *infra*, 'Kater i Rades'.

27 USA, Department of State, *Treaties and Other International Acts Series*, No. 03-520.

the smuggling of migrants, as reflected, *inter alia*, in the Migrants Protocol,[28] in the principles of international law, such as the sovereign equality of states and 'the principle of the right of freedom of navigation'.[29] The parties bound themselves to

> cooperate in combating the unsafe transport of migrants by sea and smuggling of migrants to the fullest extent possible, consistent with international law and available law enforcement resources and priorities related thereto (Art. 2).

As the Agreement is not limited to the smuggling of migrants, but covers also their unsafe transport, it would in principle apply also in the rather unlikely case where the migrants are entitled to legally enter the country of destination, but are transported in unsafe conditions. The Agreement establishes 'a combined law enforcement shiprider program' between the law enforcement authorities of the parties (Art. 4), where

> 'shiprider' means a law enforcement official of one Party authorized to embark on a law enforcement vessel or aircraft of the other Party (Art. 1, para. 14).[30]

The Agreement sets forth derogations to the rule of exclusive jurisdiction of the flag state on the high seas and of exclusive jurisdiction in its territorial sea of the coastal state from which the flow of illegal migrants originates. In addition, it provides for the use of shipriders, who can be embarked on the ships of either party. The shipriders not only ensure the most expeditious means of communication between the parties, but are also in charge of carrying out the enforcement measures. They are given quite broad powers:

> When a shiprider is embarked on the other Party's law enforcement vessel ..., any law enforcement measure, including boardings, search or seizure of property, any detention of a person, and any use of force pursuant to this Agreement, whether or not involving weapons, shall be carried out by the shiprider.
> a. Crew members of the other Party's vessel may assist in any such action if expressly requested to do so by the shiprider, and only within the limits of such request and in the manner requested. Such request, including any request for the use of force, may only be made, agreed to, and acted upon in accordance with the law and policies of both Parties.

---

28 *Supra*, 'The Smuggling of Migrants at Sea as a Transnational Crime'. Even though at the moment of conclusion of the Agreement they were not parties to the Migrants Protocol, both the Dominican Republic and the United States are today parties to it.

29 Is freedom of navigation a right? Is it a principle? Is it a principle of a right? The last terminology, that was used in the Agreement, seems too convoluted.

30 The Agreement between the Bahamas and the United States Concerning Cooperation in Maritime Law Enforcement, concluded in Nassau on 29 June 2004, also provides for a shiprider programme.

> b. Such crew members may use force in self-defense and defense of others in accordance with the applicable laws and policies of their Government (Art. 4, para. 5).

With regard to suspect ships flying the flag of the Dominican Republic, maritime migration law enforcement operations can take place in 'Dominican waters' (Art. 5, para. 1), meaning the internal waters and the territorial sea of the Dominican Republic, as well as 'seaward of any State's territorial sea', meaning the high seas and the exclusive economic zone (Art. 8, para. 1). In the first case, the Dominican Republic allows maritime migration law enforcement operations by the United States if, as provided for in Art. 5, para. 2, there is the authorization by an embarked Dominican shiprider to enter into Dominican waters. In the second case, the Dominican Republic authorizes the United States to board, address enquiries, inspect the documents of and search the suspect vessel and the persons found on board (Art. 8, para. 1). If evidence of unsafe transport of migrants by sea or smuggling of migrants is found, the United States may detain the vessel and the persons on board, pending expeditious disposition of instructions from the Dominican Republic (Art. 8, para. 2).

The right to exercise jurisdiction, which is primarily granted to the Dominican Republic, can be waived in favour of the United States:

> In all cases arising in Dominican waters, or concerning Dominican flag vessels seaward of any State's territorial sea the Government of the Dominican Republic shall have the primary right to exercise jurisdiction over a detained vessel, cargo and/or, subject to Article 10 of this Agreement, persons on board (including repatriation, seizure, forfeiture, arrest, and prosecution), provided, however, that the Government of the Dominican Republic may, subject to its Constitution and laws, waiver its primary right to exercise jurisdiction and authorize the enforcement of United States law against the vessel, cargo and/or persons on board (Art. 9, para. 1).

Italy and Libya

On 29 December 2007 Italy and Libya concluded in Tripoli a Protocol to Face the Phenomenon of Clandestine Immigration.[31] It aims at implementing the Agreement on Collaboration in the Fight against Terrorism, Organized Crime, Illegal

31 The Protocol has not been published in the Italian official journal, in violation of the domestic provisions on the publication of treaties. The Protocol was subsequently recalled in Art. 19, para. 1, of the Treaty of Friendship, Partnership and Cooperation by Italy and Libya, signed in Benghazi on 30 August 2008 (*Gazzetta Ufficiale della Repubblica Italiana*, supplement to No. 40 of 18 February 2009). This treaty was concluded to 'definitively close the sad chapter of the past, for which Italy has already … expressed its regret for the sufferings caused to the Libyan people as a consequence of Italian colonization' (preamble).

Trafficking of Drugs and Psychotropic Substances and Clandestine Immigration, previously concluded by the two countries in Rome on 13 December 2000.[32] The Protocol acknowledges in the preamble that Libya faces great problems because it is a transit country for migrants and it has to control more than 5,000 km of land borders in the desert and more than 2,200 km of borders at sea.

Under the Protocol, Italy and Libya bind themselves to organize maritime patrolling activities using six ships temporarily ceded by Italy to Libya which have on board a mixed crew. However, the Italian police personnel can only engage in the training and formation of the Libyan crews, as well as in the technical assistance and maintenance of the ships. The activities of control, search and rescue allowed by the Protocol can be undertaken in the localities of departure and transit of ships transporting clandestine migrants, as well as within the Libyan territorial sea[33] and on the high seas, in compliance with international treaties in force and according to the operational modalities to be agreed upon.

The Protocol is supplemented by an additional protocol of a technical and operational character, also concluded on 29 December 2007. The additional protocol specifies that the activities to be carried out relate to the 'prevention and countering of illegal migratory flows', something that does not fully correspond to the activities of 'control, search and rescue' mentioned in the main Protocol. The additional protocol also provides that the command of the ships ceded by Italy to Libya is exercised by Libyan personnel, who are responsible for the actions undertaken. A further Protocol has been concluded on 4 February 2009, stating that the two countries will organize maritime patrols with joint crews, to be conducted in Italian, Libyan and international waters. They also undertake to repatriate clandestine immigrants and to conclude agreements with the countries of origin in order to limit clandestine immigration.[34]

Unlike the three bilateral treaties described above, the instruments agreed upon by Italy and Libya do not establish any derogations to the rules of the international law of the sea on the exercise of jurisdiction on the high seas or in the territorial sea. They only provide technical assistance by one party to the activities against illegal migration carried out by the other party.

The Safety of Life at Sea

The duty to render assistance to persons in danger at sea is an expression of the principle of protection of human life which has a longstanding tradition in

32 *Gazzetta Ufficiale della Repubblica Italiana*, supplement to No. 111 of 15 May 2003.

33 Libya claims the Gulf of Sidra as an extent of internal historical waters. It is not clear whether the Protocol applies to the waters of this Gulf.

34 On the operations carried out under the Protocol see *infra*, 'The Italian Push-Back Policy'.

maritime custom. It can be included among the general principles of law, as recalled in Art. 38, para. 1, c, of the Statute of the International Court of Justice. It can be understood as a manifestation of the human right to life set forth in the relevant multilateral treaties, such as Art. 2, para. 1, of the Convention for the Protection of Human Rights and Fundamental Freedoms (Rome, 1950; more commonly known as the European Convention on Human Rights) or Art. 6, para. 1, of the International Covenant on Civil and Political Rights (New York, 1966). It is specifically provided for in several treaties applicable to activities taking place at sea.

The beneficiaries of the right to be assisted at sea are all persons who are in distress, irrespective of the nationality of the ship and of the legality of the activity in which they engage, be they stowaways, migrant smugglers, drugs or weapons or slave traffickers, pirates or terrorists. In the case of migration by sea, the right to be assisted is of paramount importance, as migrants are often transported in inhuman conditions by unseaworthy and overcrowded water craft and are exposed to the dangers caused by bad weather, starvation, dehydration and illness. In too many cases, the illegal migrant is at the same time a person in distress at sea.

Rescue under the UNCLOS Regime

The duty to render assistance to persons in danger at sea, is provided for in the UNCLOS. It is not limited to rescuing and taking on board persons in distress, but has a broader scope and includes the obligation of coastal states to organize a search and rescue service:

> 1. Every State shall require the master of a ship flying its flag, in so far as he can do so without serious danger to the ship, the crew or the passengers:
> (a) to render assistance to any person found at sea in danger of being lost;
> (b) to proceed with all possible speed to the rescue of persons in distress, if informed of their need of assistance, in so far as such action may reasonably be expected of him;
> (c) after a collision, to render assistance to the other ship, its crew and its passengers and, where possible, to inform the other ship of the name of his own ship, its port of registry and the nearest port at which it will call.
> 2. Every coastal State shall promote the establishment, operation and maintenance of an adequate and effective search and rescue service regarding safety on and over the sea and, where circumstances so require, by way of mutual regional arrangements cooperate with neighbouring States for this purpose (Art. 98).

Even though Art. 98 is included in UNCLOS Part VII (high seas), the duty to render assistance at sea has a broader application and covers any kind of marine waters, irrespective of their legal status. This is confirmed by Article 18, para. 2, UNCLOS, which provides that the right of innocent passage through the territorial sea of foreign states is compatible with a stop to render assistance to people in distress.[35]

While every state is bound to assist people in distress at sea, the flag state is bound to ensure that ships having its nationality navigate under appropriate safety conditions. This is also a manifestation of the duty to protect human life at sea. Under Article 94, para. 3, UNCLOS,

> every State shall take such measures for ships flying its flag as are necessary to ensure safety at sea with regard, *inter alia*, to:
> (a) the construction, equipment and seaworthiness of ships;
> (b) the manning of ships, labour conditions and the training of crews, taking into account the applicable international instruments;
> (c) the use of signals, the maintenance of communications and the prevention of collisions.

Art. 94, para. 4, further specifies what kind of measures, relating to surveys of ships and qualification of masters and crews, are required to ensure safety at sea. Under Art. 94, para. 5, the measures in question must comply with generally accepted standards, in particular those resulting from the multilateral treaties adopted within the framework of the competent international organization (that is the International Maritime Organization[36]). In this way the treaties in question indirectly acquire a binding character on all UNCLOS parties.

In fact, too many tragic events show that often ships transporting illegal migrants do not meet the required safety conditions. If migrants travel in conditions that endanger their lives, every state can intervene on the ships in question to rescue and assist the people in peril. Such an action is justified under customary international law as an application of the rule on distress, because there is no other reasonable way to save human life.[37]

35 This is an exception to the rule providing that innocent passage shall be continuous and expeditious (Art. 18, para. 2, UNCLOS).

36 Hereinafter: IMO.

37 The wrongfulness of an act of a state not in conformity with an international obligation of that state is precluded if the author of the act in question had no other reasonable way, in a situation of distress, of saving the author's life or the lives of other persons entrusted to the author's care (Art. 24, para. 1, of the Articles on Responsibility of States for Internationally Wrongful Acts). The life of people in distress at sea can be considered as entrusted to the care of the masters of all ships that are in a position to intervene to rescue them.

Rescue under the IMO Treaties

A number of treaties adopted within the IMO framework aim at ensuring safety at sea.[38] They include the 1972 Convention on the International Regulations for Preventing Collisions at Sea, the 1974 Convention for the Safety of Life at Sea (amended several times),[39] the 1978 International Convention on Standards of Training, Certification and Watchkeeping for Seafarers, the 1979 International Convention on Maritime Search and Rescue (amended in 1998 and 2004)[40] and the 1989 International Convention on Salvage.

Search and rescue activities must be carried out not only by dedicated shore-based rescue units, but also by any ships that navigate in the vicinity of the ship and persons in distress. Under Art. 10, para. 1, of the International Convention on Salvage,

> every master is bound, so far as he can do so without serious danger to his vessel and persons thereof, to render assistance to any person in danger of being lost at sea.

The main obligation established by the SAR Convention is that

> Parties shall ensure that assistance is provided to any person in distress at sea. They shall do so regardless of the nationality or status of such a person or the circumstances in which that person is found (Chap. 2.1.10).

The definition of the term 'search' given by the Annex to the SAR Convention show that the parties are called to establish rescue centres in charge of the co-ordination of search operations:

> 'Search'. An operation, normally co-ordinated by a rescue co-ordination centre or rescue sub-centre, using available personnel and facilities to locate persons in distress (Chap. 1.3.1).

Under the SAR Convention, the Parties are also called to establish by agreement search and rescue regions (Chap. 2.1.4), intended as areas 'of defined dimension associated with a rescue co-ordination centre within which search and rescue

38 In the current terminology 'safety' is different from 'security', as the latter term usually refers to the prevention and suppression of human wilful acts.

39 Hereinafter: SOLAS Convention. See Coppens, J. and Somers, E., 'Towards New Rules on Disembarkation of Persons Rescued at Sea?', in *International Journal of Marine and Coastal Law*, 2010, p. 377.

40 Hereinafter: SAR Convention.

services are provided' (Chap. 1.2.4).[41] The party accepting the responsibility to provide search and rescue services for a specified area is bound to 'use search and rescue units and other available facilities for providing assistance to a person who is, or appears to be, in distress at sea' (Chap. 2.1.9).[42]

The obligations incumbent on parties are not limited to the retrieving of persons in distress, but extend to their delivery to 'a place of safety', as confirmed by the definition of 'rescue' given by the Annex to the SAR Convention:

> 'Rescue'. An operation to retrieve persons in distress, provide for their initial medical or other needs, and deliver them to a place of safety (Chap. 1.3.2).

The thorny question left open by the SAR Convention, and by other treaties providing for assistance at sea as well, is how to determine where the place of safety is located and consequently where the rescued persons are to be delivered. In fact, after being taken on board, the rescued people do not dematerialize, but they continue to exist and should be delivered somewhere. The presence on board of many people may raise problems of overcrowding, lack of food and water or spreading of infectious diseases that make the disembarking of the rescued persons an urgent need. If the operation has been carried out by a private ship, the master may have an interest in not further delaying the voyage, considering that the ship-owner has already incurred the burden of searching and rescuing people in distress.[43] The rescued people may have some good reasons, such as the fear of persecution, to ask not to be disembarked in a certain state. In the absence of precise legal provisions, different views as to the location of the place of safety can be held by the several states that may be involved in the rescue operation, namely the flag state, the state responsible for the search and rescue region, the state in whose exclusive economic zone or territorial sea the search and rescue operations have taken place, the states of nationality of the rescued persons, the state from where the rescued ship has sailed and perhaps also other states.

The SAR Convention, as amended in 2004, does address the question of the location of the place of safety. But it does not provide a clear-cut answer to it:

> Each Party should authorize its rescue co-ordination centres: …

41 The delimitation of search and rescue regions between adjacent or opposed states is not related to, and does not prejudice, the delimitation of any boundary between states (Chap. 2.1.7).

42 However, 'Parties shall co-ordinate their search and rescue organizations and should, whenever necessary, co-ordinate search and rescue operations with those of neighbouring States' (Chap. 3.1.1).

43 It is evident that a situation where the burdens are left on the shoulders of the master and the ship-owner could discourage activities for the search and rescuing of people in distress at sea.

> to make the necessary arrangements in co-operation with other rescue co-ordination centres to identify the most appropriate place(s) for disembarking persons found in distress at sea (Chap. 3.1.6.4).
>
> Parties shall co-ordinate and co-operate to ensure that masters of ships providing assistance by embarking persons in distress at sea are released from their obligations with minimum further deviation from the ships' intended voyage, provided that releasing the ship from these obligations does not further endanger the safety of life at sea. The Party responsible for the search and rescue region in which such assistance is rendered shall exercise primary responsibility for ensuring such co-ordination and co-operation occurs, so that survivors assisted are disembarked from the assisting ship and delivered to a place of safety, taking into account the particular circumstances of the case and guidelines developed by the Organization. In these cases, the relevant Parties shall arrange for such disembarkation to be effected as soon as reasonably possible (Chap. 3.1.9).
>
> The rescue co-ordination centre or rescue sub-centre concerned shall initiate the process of identifying the most appropriate place(s) for disembarking persons found in distress at sea. It shall inform the ship or ships and other relevant parties concerned thereof (Chap. 4.8.5).

From these provisions it appears that all parties to the SAR Convention, depending on the circumstances, are called upon to coordinate themselves and cooperate in order that the rescued persons are disembarked and delivered to a place of safety. However, the party responsible for the search and rescue region is not bound to disembark the persons in its own territory. Nor, at least if the provisions are understood literally, is it bound to find another state where they can be disembarked. It must only exercise a 'primary responsibility' to ensure that the expected coordination and cooperation among parties occur in order to deliver the rescued people to a place of safety, taking into account the interest of minimizing any further deviation from the assisting ships' intended voyage. Such a convoluted wording can only imply that, at the moment of amending the Annex to the SAR Convention, the parties were not able to reach a sufficiently clear and generally agreed solution to the thorny problem of the location of the place of safety.

As stated by the International Court of Justice, an obligation to cooperate implies a duty to act in good faith in order to reach an agreement on matters of common interest or concern.[44] If the states concerned comply with the obligation

44 This was, *inter alia*, stated in the judgment of 20 February 1969 in the *North Sea Continental Shelf* cases (Federal Republic of Germany v. Denmark; Federal Republic of Germany v. Netherlands): 'The parties are under an obligation to enter into negotiations with a view to arriving at an agreement, and not merely to go through a formal process of negotiation ...; they are under an obligation so to conduct themselves that the negotiations are meaningful, which will not be the case when either of them insists upon its own position

to act in good faith, it is likely that an agreement will be reached. However, there cannot be a legal guarantee that such a result will be achieved in any single case.

The SOLAS Convention provides as follows for cases of distress:

> The master of a ship at sea which is in a position to be able to provide assistance, on receiving information from any source that persons are in distress at sea, is bound to proceed with all speed to their assistance, if possible informing them or the search and rescue service that the ship is doing so. This obligation to provide assistance applies regardless of the nationality or status of such persons or the circumstances in which they are found (Regulation 33-1).
>
> Masters of ships who have embarked persons in distress at sea shall treat them with humanity, within the capabilities and limitations of the ship (Regulation 33-6).

A provision has been included in the 2004 SOLAS amendments to relieve the master from the risk of personal liability:

> The owner, the charterer, the company operating the ship … or any other person shall not prevent or restrict the master of the ship from taking or executing any decision which, in the master's professional judgement, is necessary for safety of life at sea and protection of the marine environment (Regulation 34-1).

Again, on the thorny question of the determination of the place of safety, the SOLAS Convention, as amended in 2004, provides for a regime quite close to the regime established under the SAR Convention. The remarks made above can consequently be repeated also for the SOLAS Convention.

Taking into account the amendments to the SAR and SOLAS Conventions, in 2004 the Maritime Safety Committee of IMO adopted under Resolution MSC.167(78) a set of Guidelines on the Treatment of Persons Rescued at Sea. This was done 'realizing the need for clarification of existing procedures to guarantee that persons rescued at sea will be provided a place of safety regardless of their nationality, status or the circumstances in which they are found'. Without having a mandatory character, the Guidelines aim at providing guidance to governments and shipmasters, based on the assumption that the master who rescues people at sea, as he is bound to do, should not be left alone by the states concerned.[45]

According to Guideline 2.5, the intent of the 2004 amendments to the SAR and SOLAS Conventions is to ensure that in every case a place of safety is provided

---

without contemplating any modification of it' (International Court of Justice, *Reports of Judgments, Advisory Opinions and Orders*, 1969, para. 85 of the judgment).

45 'The obligation of the master to render assistance should complement the corresponding obligation of IMO Member Governments to co-ordinate and co-operate in relieving the master of the responsibility to provide follow up care of survivors and to deliver the persons retrieved at sea to a place of safety. …' (Guideline 1.2). For the *Tampa* case, which is relevant in this respect, see *infra*, 'Tampa'.

within a reasonable time'. The responsibility to provide such a place or to ensure that it is provided 'falls on the Government responsible for the search and rescue region in which the survivors were recovered'. As each case involves different circumstances, states should be given enough flexibility to address each situation (Guideline 2.6).

The Guidelines specify the behaviour that is expected from the shipmaster and the states concerned. The former should, *inter alia*,

> understand and heed obligations under international law to assist persons in distress at sea (such assistance should always be carried out without regard to the nationality or status of the persons in distress, or to the circumstances in which they are found);
> do everything possible, within the capabilities and limitations of the ship, to treat the survivors humanely and to meet their immediate needs; ...
> keep the RCC [rescue coordination centre] informed about conditions, assistance needed, and actions taken or planned for the survivors ...;
> seek to ensure that survivors are not disembarked to a place where their safety would be further jeopardized; and
> comply with any relevant requirements of the Government responsible for the SAR [search and rescue] region where the survivors where recovered, or of another responding coastal State, and seek additional guidance from those authorities where difficulties arise in complying with such requirements (Guideline 5.1).

As to the states concerned, the state responsible for the search and rescue region is called upon to exercise a sort of primary responsibility to arrange for a place of safety:

> When the RCC responsible for the SAR region in which assistance is needed is informed about the situation, that RCC should immediately accept responsibility for co-ordinating the rescue efforts, since related responsibilities, including arrangements for a place of safety, fall primarily on the Government responsible for that region (Guideline 6.7).

All States Parties are called upon to co-operate to achieve the objective of promptly disembarking the rescued people:

> Governments and the responsible RCC should make every effort to minimize the time survivors remain on board the assisting ship (Guideline 6.8).

> Responsible State authorities should make every effort to expedite arrangements to disembark survivors from the ship; however, the master should understand that in some cases necessary co-ordination may result in unavoidable delays (Guideline 6.9).

The type of information that should be provided by the master to the rescue and coordination centre shows that the concerns of the assisting ship should also be taken into account, as well as the master's preference about the disembarkation of the survivors. But it is sufficiently clear that it is not for the master of the assisting ship alone to decide where the survivors shall be disembarked:[46]

> The RCC should seek to obtain the following information from the master of the assisting ship:
> information about the survivors, including name, age, gender, apparent health and medical condition and any special medical needs;
> the master's judgment about the continuing safety of the assisting ship;
> actions completed or intended to be taken by the master;
> assisting ship's current endurance with the additional persons on board;
> assisting ship's next intended port of call;
> the master's preferred arrangements for disembarking the survivors;
> any help that assisting ship may need during or after the recovery operation; and
> any special factors (e.g., prevailing weather, time sensitive cargo) (Guideline 6.10).
>
> Potential health and safety concerns aboard a ship that has recovered persons in distress include insufficient lifesaving equipment, water, provisions, medical care, and accommodations for the number of persons on board, and the safety of the crew and passengers if persons on board might become aggressive or violent. … (Guideline 6.11).

The Guidelines explain that the assisting ship cannot be understood as a place of safety[47] and that such a place is to be considered as an intermediate location between the assisting ship and the final destination of the rescued persons:

> A place of safety … is a location where rescue operations are considered to terminate. It is also a place where the survivors' safety of life is no longer

46 To leave the choice to the master would follow a certain logic, considering that he is legally bound to provide assistance to people in distress. The only limit to the master's discretion would be to ensure respect for the human rights of the rescued people (see *infra*, 'Migration at Sea and Human Rights Law' and 'Migration at Sea and Refugee Law'). But it appears that states are not prepared to accept a procedure which would leave them without control of the situation.

47 The Guidelines point out that 'an assisting ship should not be considered a place of safety based solely on the fact that the survivors are no longer in immediate danger once aboard the ship. An assisting ship may not have appropriate facilities and equipment to sustain additional persons on board without endangering its own safety or to properly care for the survivors. Even if the ship is capable of safely accommodating the survivors and may serve as a temporary place of safety, it should be relieved of this responsibility as soon as alternative arrangements can be made' (Guideline 6.13).

> threatened and where their basic human needs (such as food, shelter and medical needs) can be met. Further, it is a place from which transportation arrangements can be made for the survivors' next or final destination (Guideline 6.12).
>
> A place of safety may be on land, or it may be aboard a rescue unit or other suitable vessel or facility at sea that can serve as a place of safety until the survivors are disembarked to their next destination (Guideline 6.14).

However, despite all the efforts to address the question, the Guidelines could not clearly specify what the SAR and SOLAS Conventions were not able to specify, that is which state is under the obligation to provide a place of safety and where such place is located. Hopefully, the problem would be solved through international cooperation, taking into account a number of relevant circumstances:

> Governments should co-operate with each other with regard to providing suitable places of safety for survivors after considering relevant factors and risks (Guideline 6.16).
>
> … These circumstances may include factors such as the situation on board the assisting ship, on scene conditions, medical needs, and availability of transportation or other rescue units. Each case is unique, and selection of a place of safety may need to account for a variety of important factors (Guideline 6.15).

Some of the relevant circumstances are directly related to the particular condition of rescued people who qualify as refugees:

> The need to avoid disembarkation in territories where the lives and freedoms of those alleging a well-founded fear of persecution would be threatened is a consideration in the case of asylum-seekers and refugees recovered at sea (Guideline 6.17).

In conclusion, what can be drawn from present international law of the sea is that there is an obligation on a number of states to cooperate to deliver the rescued people to a place of safety as soon as possible.[48] It is, however, impossible to determine with precision where such a place of safety is located.[49] This does not help to ensure adequate assistance to rescued people.

---

48 See, in general, *The Treatment of Persons Rescued at Sea: Conclusions and Recommendations from Recent Meetings and Expert Round Tables Convened by the Office of the Unites Nations High Commissioner for Refugees*, UN Doc A/AC/259/17, 11 April 2008.

49 The disagreement between Italy and Malta as to where disembarkation should be effected, either in a port of the state of the SAR zone or in the nearest safe port, is an example of the persistent lack of clarity on this essential question.

Rescue under Treaties Relating to Migration by Sea

The obligation to assist people in distress is repeated in some of the already mentioned treaties which specifically address the subject of migration by sea.[50]

The States Parties to the Migrants Protocol declare themselves 'concerned that the smuggling of migrants can endanger the lives or security of the migrants involved' (preamble). They are bound to adopt legislative measures to establish as an aggravating circumstance to the offence of smuggling of migrants the fact that it has taken place in conditions 'that endanger, or are likely to endanger, the lives or safety of the migrants concerned' (Art. 6, para. 3, a). While the authorization by the flag state is required for interventions on ships exercising freedom of navigation, measures taken without authorization are allowed if 'necessary to relieve imminent danger to the lives of persons' (Art. 7, para. 5). Under Art. 9, para. 1, in cases where measures are taken, states parties must

> (a) Ensure the safety and humane treatment of the persons on board;
> (b) Take due account of the need not to endanger the security of the vessel or its cargo.[51]

Under the 1997 Exchange of Notes between Albania and Italy,[52] the parties agree to strengthen their collaboration also to provide 'immediate humanitarian assistance when the life of those who attempt to leave the country [Albania] is endangered'.

The 2003 Agreement between the Dominican Republic and the United States[53] includes the following definition:

> 'Unsafe transport of migrants by sea' means the carriage of migrants on board a vessel that is:
> a. obviously operating in conditions which violate fundamental principles of safety of life at sea, including but not limited to those of the SOLAS Convention, or
> b. not properly manned, equipped or licensed for carrying passengers on international voyages and that thereby constitutes a serious danger for the lives or the health of the persons on board, including the conditions for embarkation and disembarkation (Art. 1, para. 2).

---

50 *Supra*, 'The Smuggling of Migrants at Sea as a Transnational Crime' and 'Some Bilateral Agreements against the Smuggling of Migrants by Sea'.

51 The other conditions listed in Art. 9, para. 1, are the following: '(c) Take due account of the need not to prejudice the commercial or legal interests of the flag State or any other interested State; (d) Ensure, within available means, that any measure taken with regard to the vessel is environmentally sound'.

52 *Supra*, 'Albania and Italy'.

53 *Supra*, 'Dominican Republic and the United States'.

When conducting boarding and search, the law enforcement officials must 'take due account of the need not to endanger the safety of life at sea' (Art. 13, para. 2, d). Moreover,

> when taking action with regard to a vessel found to be engaging in unsafe transport of migrants by sea or smuggling of migrants, the Party concerned shall also ensure the safety and the humanitarian handling of the persons on board and that any actions taken with regard to the vessel are, within available means, environmentally sound (Ar. 13, para. 2, e).[54]

Some Relevant Cases

Some well-known cases show how much the safety of migrants by sea can be in danger. Sadly enough, in certain circumstances, the dangers are posed not only by the behaviour of migrant smugglers, but also by the action taken by states that are bound to protect human life at sea.

Kater i Rades

On 28 March 1997, three days after the entry into force of the already mentioned exchange of notes between Albania and Italy,[55] a collision occurred on the high seas, 35 nm off the Italian Adriatic coast, between the ship *Kater i Rades*,[56] overcrowded with illegal Albanian migrants, and the corvette *Sibilla* of the Italian Navy. *Sibilla*, acting on the basis of the assumed rights granted to Italy by the exchange of notes, enjoined on *Kater* to change her route. As the order was not obeyed, *Sibilla* manoeuvred to divert *Kater*. The result was a collision between a smaller and a much bigger ship (56 against 1285 tons). The smaller sank. Only 34 of the migrants could be rescued by *Sibilla* herself and survived. While 58 corpses were subsequently recovered, the total number of the Albanian migrants who died has not been precisely determined and is estimated at more than 100. Several among them were women and children.

The judgment rendered in Italy on 19 March 2005 by the Tribunal of Brindisi on the criminal aspects of the case put emphasis on appalling elements of fact. First, *Sibilla* tried, without success, to block *Kater*'s propeller by throwing a cable

54 Subject to certain conditions, 'the Government of the Dominican Republic does not object to the U.S. Coast Guard destroying any vessel subject to the jurisdiction of the Dominican Republic and detained pursuant to this Agreement that the U.S. Coast Guard deems to be unseaworthy and/or a hazard to navigation' (Art. 9, para. 4).

55 *Supra*, 'Albania and Italy'.

56 The *Kater I Rades* was a ship cancelled from the registry of the Albanian Navy. It is uncertain whether, at the moment of the accident, she had the Albanian flag or was to be considered a ship without flag.

in the water. Second, as *Kater* made an attempt to escape, *Sibilla* tried to divert her from her route, engaging in 'kinematics and interposition manoeuvres' based on the harassment modalities used within the North Atlantic Treaty Organization (NATO) framework.[57]

Even though there was clearly no intention to cause such a massacre, the behaviour of Italy is an instance of grossly negligent action in violation of the international law obligation to protect human life at sea. A further remark is that on 28 March 1997 Italy had no right to divert Albanian ships on the high seas. The Exchange of Notes was concluded and entered into force on 25 March 1997. But it clearly provided that it was conditional, as regards its implementation, on a further agreement on 'necessary technical procedures'. This agreement was concluded only on 2 April 1997,[58] that is five days after the collision. If on 28 March 1997 *Sibilla* was ever entitled to interfere with *Kater*, it was only to offer assistance to people on an unseaworthy ship and not to further endanger their safety.

The *Kater i Rades* accident should not be seen only from a legal point of view. Looking at the moral aspects of the collision, the most appropriate term in the dictionary to define it is not 'unfortunate', but 'shameful'. It shows to what extent the stronger (a ship of the navy) can disregard the most fundamental rights of the weaker (a ship overcrowded with people hoping for a decent future). Those who want to show their muscles and fight naval battles should choose other enemies.

Tampa

On 26 August 2001, following a request by Australia, the ship *Tampa*, a private ship flying the Norwegian flag en route from Australia to Singapore, rescued on the high seas and within the Indonesian search and rescue region an Indonesian fishing vessel. It carried 433 persons having the nationality of various states (Afghanistan, Pakistan, Iraq, Indonesia and Sri Lanka),[59] who were trying to reach Australia to ask for asylum. They were taken on board the *Tampa*. As the assisted people threatened a mutiny if the ship were to disembark them in Indonesia, the master decided to proceed to the Australian Christmas Island. Having been refused access to the island by Australia, the *Tampa* stopped in the Australian territorial sea and transmitted an emergency signal. She was boarded by Australian troops that took control of the ship. Only on 3 September were the rescued people taken on board an Australian warship to be transported to New Zealand and Nauru. This was

57 The commander of *Sibilla* was convicted to a three-year term of imprisonment and the Albanian pilot of *Kater* to a four-year term. They were reduced by a decision of the Court of Appeal of Lecce of 19 October 2010 to, respectively, two years and four months and three years and four months. The decision was confirmed by the Court of Cassation on 9 May 2014 (17 years after the accident!).

58 *Supra*, Albania and Italy.

59 See Mathew, P., *Australian Refugee Protection in the Wake of the Tampa*, in *American Journal of International Law*, 2002, p. 661.

done after Australia had reached agreements with Nauru and New Zealand which accepted the rescued people on their territory to process their asylum applications.

The *Tampa* case put emphasis on the need not to place an excessive burden on the rescuing ship and promptly provide migrants or asylum seekers with a place of safety. It led states to adopt the already mentioned 2004 amendments to the SAR Convention and the SOLAS Convention.[60]

Cap Anamour

On 20 June 2004, the German private ship *Cap Anamour*, run by a humanitarian non-governmental organization, rescued 37 migrants on the high seas in the Channel of Sicily. The ship subsequently made a short stop for repairs in Malta without informing the local authorities of the presence of the rescued people who stayed on board. Then she sailed for Italy, following the request by the same people to be disembarked there to ask for asylum. However, for over three weeks Italy refused *Cap Anamour* access to its territorial sea. According to Italy, Malta, as country of first arrival, was under an obligation to receive the rescued people and examine their applications for asylum under Article 10 of European Union Regulation 343/2003 of 18 February 2003.[61] It provides that the member state of first arrival is in charge of examining asylum applications by third-country nationals.

Only on 12 July did Italy authorize disembarkation of the migrants on its territory. All the applications for asylum were processed and rejected, with the exception of one. The captain and the first officer of the *Cap Anamour*, as well as the president of the humanitarian organization involved, were accused of breach of the Italian immigration legislation. They were subsequently acquitted (decision of the Tribunal of Agrigento of 7 October 2009).

The *Cap Anamour* case shows the need for better co-ordination among the states concerned, especially at the European Union level. Rescued people cannot be considered hostages waiting for the solution of intra-European legal intricacies.

---

60 *Supra*, 'Rescue under the IMO Treaties'.

61 *Official Journal of the European Union*, No. L 50 of 25 February 2003. See also Regulation 1560/2003 (ibid., No. L 222 of 2 September 2003), laying down detailed rules for the application of Regulation 343/2003. The European Union has established a common policy on asylum. See Moreno Lax, V., 'Current Legal Developments: European Union. The EU Regime on Interdiction, Search and Rescue, and Disembarkation: The Frontex Guidelines for Intervention at Sea', in *International Journal of Marine and Coastal Law*, 2010, p. 621; Rijpma, J., 'The Patrolling of the European Union's External Maritime Border: Preventing the Rule of Law from Getting Lost at Sea', in Del Vecchio, A. (ed.), *International Law of the Sea – Current Trends and Controversial Issues*, The Hague, 2014, p. 77.

Migration at Sea and Human Rights Law

From the place of safety where they are disembarked migrants are expected to proceed to the place of final destination. As a general rule, if illegal migrants are among the rescued people, they should be returned to the state of which they are nationals or permanent residents. Under Article 18, para. 1, of the Migrants Protocol,

> each State Party agrees to facilitate and accept, without undue or unreasonable delay, the return of a person who has been the object of conduct set forth in article 6 of this Protocol and who is its national or who has the right of permanent residence in its territory at the time of return.

However, illegal migrants are entitled to rights granted to them by international human rights law,[62] such as the right not to be returned to certain states. A number of general or specific questions need to be addressed in this regard.

The Human Rights of Migrants to Be Humanely Treated and not to Be Prosecuted

The first human right to be granted to migrants is the right to be humanely treated. The purpose to protect the migrants, who are the victims of smugglers, is clearly stated in the Migrants Protocol.

> The purpose of this Protocol is to prevent and combat the smuggling of migrants as well as to promote cooperation among States Parties to that end, while protecting the rights of the smuggled migrants (Art. 2).

Migrants, in particular the most vulnerable among them, have the right to be treated humanely by immigration officials and to be protected from violence that may be inflicted on them by others:

> States Parties shall provide or strengthen specialized training for immigration and other relevant officials in preventing the conduct set forth in article 6 of this Protocol and in the humane treatment of migrants who have been the object of such conduct, while respecting their rights as set forth in this Protocol (Art. 14, para. 1).

> Each State Party shall take appropriate measures to afford migrants appropriate protection against violence that may be inflicted upon them, whether by individuals or groups, by reason of being the object of conduct set forth in article 6 of this Protocol (Art. 16, para. 2).

---

62 See in general Treves, T., 'Human Rights and the Law of the Sea', in *Berkeley Journal of International Law*, 2010, p. 1.

> In applying the provisions of this article, States Parties shall take into account the special needs of women and children (Art. 16, para. 4).[63]

From a moral point of view, the right to be humanely treated is a sign of the respect due to the dignity of people who try to find the means to earn their bread and to spend a decent life somewhere. This right does not depend on whether migrants are legal or illegal. It is also stated in some of the relevant bilateral treaties:

> … Such officials [law enforcement officials] shall also bear in mind the need to observe norms of courtesy, respect, and consideration for the persons on board the suspect vessel (Art. 13, para. 2, d, of the Agreement between the Dominican Republic and the United States).[64]

> All use of force pursuant to this Agreement shall be in strict accordance with the applicable laws and policies of the respective Party and shall in all cases be the minimum reasonably necessary under the circumstances … (Art. 14, para. 1, of the same agreement).

Another human right that is granted to migrants is that of not being criminalized for an attempt to migrate illegally. Even an asymmetrical right, such as the right to emigrate, has some meaning. If it cannot go so far as to be understood as a right to be admitted into a foreign country, it should at least have the effect of preventing the criminal liability of those who have attempted to migrate. Illegal migrants are very different from migrant smugglers. As clearly declared by Ecuador when ratifying the Migrants Protocol in 2002,

> migrants are the victims of illicit trafficking in persons on the part of criminal organizations whose only goal is unjust and undue enrichment at the expense of persons wishing to perform honest work abroad.

In the relevant treaties the following provisions may be found on the obligation of not prosecuting illegal migrants:

> Migrants shall not be liable to criminal prosecution under this Protocol for the fact of having been the object of conduct set forth in article 6 of this Protocol (Art. 5 of the Migrants Protocol).

---

63 States Parties to the Migrants Protocol are also bound to adopt legislative measures to establish as an aggravating circumstance to the offence of smuggling of migrants the fact that it takes place in conditions 'that entail inhuman or degrading treatment, including for exploitation, of such migrants' (Art. 6, para. 3, b).

64 *Supra*, 'Dominican Republic and the United States'.

> The United States Government appreciates the assurances which it has received from the Government of the Republic of Haiti that Haitians returned to their country and who are not traffickers will not be subject to prosecution for illegal departure (Agreement between Haiti and the United States).[65]
>
> The Government of the Dominican Republic agrees that Dominicans and third country nationals returned to the Dominican Republic and who are not migrant smugglers will not be subject to prosecution for illegal departure (Art. 10, para. 3, of the Agreement between the Dominican Republic and the United States).[66]

The fact that illegal migrants are different from criminals who act at sea, such as pirates, terrorists, drug or weapons traffickers, is not always understood, perhaps due to ignorance and sentiments of xenophobia that are growing in some countries of destination. Two instances may be recalled in this regard.

a. In 2003 a collection of studies on the control of illegal migrant trafficking in the Mediterranean Sea was published in Italy under the sponsorship of two research institutions.[67] One of the papers deals with the subject of non-lethal weapons,[68] starting with the assumption that illegal migrants inevitably mingle with potential terrorists and their flankers.[69] In such a situation, the paper suggests the use of non-lethal weapons to counter craft transporting illegal migrants by sea. The most appropriate among such weapons is an 'intelligent torpedo'. It is launched by ships or aircraft and is devised to block propellers of ships. The paper devotes great attention to the financial aspects of the proposal. It points out that the cost of an intelligent torpedo is about 1 million euros, but that it can be used for about 100 missions, with a regenerating cost of 150,000 euros. It also suggests that spare torpedoes which the Italian Navy keeps in its depots could be transformed into intelligent torpedoes at low cost.
b. Another non-lethal weapon taken in consideration in the paper is the so-called vehicle-mounted active denial system. It produces a radiation beam that causes the skin to overheat. The paper is kind enough to explain to the illegal migrants, including the potential terrorists who are surely on board, how to prevent the main risk determined by such a device, that is 'permanent eye damage' (is this blindness?). It is sufficient for them to

65 *Supra*, 'Haiti and the United States'.

66 *Supra*, 'Dominican Republic and the United States'.

67 Scuola Superiore dell'Economia e delle Finanze and Centro di Studi Geopolitica Economica, *Il controllo dei traffici migratori illeciti nel Mare Mediterraneo*, Rome 2003. The research was coordinated by C. Jean and G.M. Piccinelli and directed by O. Cucuzza.

68 Caglioti and Pierantoni, 'Profili tecnologici – Armi non letali', in ibid., p. 421.

69 Ibid., p. 424.

turn their heads to look in the opposite direction.[70] Such an 'intelligent' paper speaks for itself as a product of raving disregard for legal rules and moral principles.

c. In 1999 the meeting of heads of state and government of NATO Member States adopted a document entitled *The Alliance's Strategic Concept*. It deals with NATO's military capabilities as well as its ability to contribute to conflict prevention and crisis management through response operations. It includes the 'uncontrolled movement of large numbers of people', that is something very close to illegal migration, among the instances of 'armed attack':

> Any armed attack on the territory of the Allies, from whatever direction, would be covered by Articles 5 and 6 of the Washington Treaty [the NATO Treaty]. However, Alliance security must also take account of the global context. Alliance security interests can be affected by other risks of a wider nature, including acts of terrorism, sabotage and organised crime, and by the disruption of the flow of vital resources. The uncontrolled movement of large numbers of people, particularly as a consequence of armed conflicts, can also pose problems for security and stability affecting the Alliance. Arrangements exist within the Alliance for consultation among the Allies under Article 4 of the Washington Treaty and, where appropriate, co-ordination of their efforts including their responses to risks of this kind.[71]

Do these sentences, which are not completely clear, but are clearly threatening, mean that NATO Member States are allowed to use military force to 'defend' themselves against the state from which a movement of illegal migrants comes? Is such a movement a weapon, like a missile, that justifies the use of military force? An affirmative answer to any of the questions would involve a total distortion of the meaning of Art. 51 of the Charter of the United Nations, relating to self-defence (and of Arts 5 and 7 of the NATO Treaty itself).

It should be recalled that in 1993 the United Nations Security Council, in Resolution 841 (1993), noted with concern the occurrence of a humanitarian crisis in Haiti, 'including mass displacement of population, becoming or aggravating threats to international peace and security'. It adopted a trade embargo against Haiti, from where a massive flow of people seeking refuge in neighbouring countries was originating. But it never went as far as considering that situation as an armed attack or an act of aggression by Haiti against other states. This kind of situation has a predominant humanitarian character and should never be assimilated to armed attacks.

---

70 Ibid., p. 437.

71 Para. 24. The passage is implicitly intended to cover the military bombing by NATO Member States of Yugoslavia, from a part of which (Kosovo) a massive flow of people was taking place in 1999.

The Prohibition of Returning a Migrant to a State Where He Risks Being Tortured

Besides the rights granted because of their condition, illegal migrants enjoy all the human rights granted to any individual and arising from customary international law and the treaties in force. Under the Migrants Protocol,

> in implementing this Protocol, each State Party shall take, consistent with its obligations under international law, all appropriate measures, including legislation if necessary, to preserve and protect the rights of persons who have been the object of conduct set forth in article 6 of this Protocol as accorded under applicable international law, in particular the right to life and the right not to be subjected to torture or other cruel, inhuman or degrading treatment or punishment (Art. 16, para. 1).

One of most fundamental human rights is the right not to be subjected to torture or to inhuman or degrading treatment or punishment, provided for, *inter alia*, in Art. 3 of the European Convention on Human Rights, Art. 7 of the 1969 International Covenant on Civil and Political Rights, Art. 5 of the American Convention on Human Rights, Art. 5 of the 1981 African Charter on Human and Peoples Rights and specifically regulated by the 1984 Convention against Torture and Other Cruel, Inhuman or Degrading Treatment or Punishment.[72] All the above-mentioned treaties are consistent in providing that no derogation from this human right can be made.[73] As stated in Art. 2, para. 2, CAT,

> no exceptional circumstances whatsoever, whether a state of war or a threat of war, internal political instability or any other public emergency, may be invoked as a justification of torture.

It is also well-known that the individual is protected against torture also in an indirect way, in so far as international law prevents states from extraditing, expelling or returning a person to a state where there are substantial grounds for believing that the person would be in danger of being subjected to torture. This

72 Hereinafter: CAT.

73 This confirms that to the question of whether a human being can be tortured there is only one simple answer: no, never. According to the International Criminal Tribunal for the Former Yugoslavia, 'the prohibition of torture laid down in human rights treaties enshrines an absolute right, which can never be derogated from, not even in time of emergency (on this ground the prohibition applies to situations of armed conflicts). This is linked to the fact … that the prohibition of torture is a peremptory norm or *jus cogens*' (judgment of 10 December 1998 in the *Furundžija* case, para. 144).

is clearly stated in Art. 3 CAT[74] and is constantly repeated in many decisions of international human rights courts.[75]

Accordingly, also illegal migrants, as any other human beings, cannot be returned to a state where, given the specific circumstances, they run the risk of being tortured or subjected to cruel, inhuman or degrading treatment, even if the state in question is their own state or the state of their permanent residence. For the states which are parties to treaties that ban the death penalty a similar prohibition applies also as regards extradition, expulsion or return to states where the individuals concerned run the risk of being subjected to capital punishment.

Migration at Sea and Refugee Law

The Rights of Refugees

Other human rights relevant for migrants by sea are those linked to the condition of refugee, according to the 1951 Convention Relating to the Status of Refugees (amended by the 1967 Protocol).[76] These rights are explicitly recognized by some bilateral treaties applicable to migration by sea, such as the Agreement between Haiti and the United States[77] and the Agreement between the Dominican Republic and the United States,[78] and, more generally, by the Migrants Protocol:

---

74 'No State Party shall expel, return ("*refouler*") or extradite a person to another State where there are substantial grounds to believe that he would be in danger of being subjected to torture'.

75 For example, the European Court of Human Rights found in the judgment of 7 July 1989 in the case *Soering v. United Kingdom*, that 'it would hardly be compatible with the underlying values of the Convention, that "common heritage of political traditions, ideals, freedom and the rule of law" to which the Preamble refers, were a Contracting State knowingly to surrender a fugitive to another State where there were substantial grounds for believing that he would be in danger of being subjected to torture, however heinous the crime allegedly committed. Extradition in such circumstances, while not explicitly referred to in the brief and general wording of Article 3, would plainly be contrary to the spirit and intendment of the Article'. For the judgment in the case *Saadi v. Italy* see *infra*, note 82.

76 Hereinafter: Refugee Convention. 145 states are parties to the Refugee Convention and 146 to the 1967 Protocol. See Goodwin-Gil, G. and McAdam, J., *The Refugee in International Law*, Oxford, 2007; Kneebone, S. (ed.), *Refugees, Asylum Seekers and the Rule of Law*, Cambridge, 2009; Gammeltoft-Hansen, T., *Access to Asylum*, Cambridge, 2011.

77 *Supra*, 'Haiti and the United States'. 'It is understood that under these arrangements the United States Government does not intend to return to Haiti any Haitian migrants whom the United States authorities determine to qualify for refugee status'.

78 *Supra*, 'Dominican Republic and the United States'. 'Nothing in this Agreement shall … restrict the ability of either Party to take whatever steps it deems appropriate with regard to individuals whom its authorities determine may qualify for refugee status or otherwise merit international protection' (Art. 21).

> Nothing in this Protocol shall affect the other rights, obligations and responsibilities of States and individuals under international law, including international humanitarian law and international human rights law and, in particular, where applicable, the 1951 Convention and the 1967 Protocol relating to the Status of Refugees and the principle of non-refoulement as contained therein (Art. 22, para. 1).

The status of refugee is a matter of fact and does not depend on an official recognition by any authority. A refugee is defined by the Refugee Convention as a person who,

> owing to well-founded fear of being persecuted for reasons of race, religion, nationality, membership of a particular social group or political opinion, is outside the country of his nationality and is unable or, owing to such fear, is unwilling to avail himself of the protection of that country; or who, not having a nationality and being outside the country of his former habitual residence, is unable or, owing to such fear, is unwilling to return to it (Art. 1, para. A.2).

This definition covers people who are persecuted for a number of reasons that are mostly based on political grounds.[79] But it does not include people who are trying to flee conflicts, either international or internal, poverty or natural disasters (so-called war, economic or environmental refugees).[80] Most of the present illegal migrants belong to this kind of people.

Notably, the Refugee Convention does not provide the refugee with a right to receive asylum in any of its States Parties.[81] In this respect, the Refugee Convention does not comply with Article 14, para. 1, of the Universal Declaration of Human Rights ('everyone has the right to seek and to enjoy in other countries asylum from persecution'). Under the Refugee Convention, the refugee is granted only the right not to be returned to a state, including his own, where he would be threatened for a number of specific reasons (right of *non-refoulement*, according to the commonly used French expression):

---

79 See Fishel de Andrade, J., 'On the Development of the Concept of "Persecution" in International Refugee Law', in *Anuário Brasileiro de Direito Internacional*, 2008, p. 114. Arts. 9 and 10 of European Union Council Directive 2004/83 of 29 April 2004 (*Official Journal of the European Union* No. L. 304 of 30 September 2004), provide an interpretation on how the concept of 'persecution' should be understood by Member States.

80 See Westra, L., *Environmental Justice and the Rights of Ecological Refugees*, London, 2009.

81 Such a right might be granted by the domestic legislation of the states concerned. For example, under Article 10, para. 3, of the Constitution of Italy, enacted in 1947, 'an alien who in his country is prevented from effectively exercising the democratic freedoms guaranteed by the Italian Constitution, has the right of asylum in the territory of the Republic according to the conditions established by the law' (unofficial translation).

> No Contracting State shall expel or return ('refouler') a refugee in any manner whatsoever to the frontiers of territories where his life or freedom would be threatened on account of his race, religion, nationality, membership of a particular social group or political opinion (Art. 33, para. 1).[82]

Here is another instance of asymmetrical rights.[83] A refugee, who has a right not to be returned to a country where he is threatened, has no right of entry into a given state. He could be rejected to a state where he is not threatened. But the latter in its turn has no obligation to allow the refugee to enter its territory. If states, one after the other, reject the refugee, where should he be entitled to settle? On the high seas? In the unclaimed sector of the Antarctic continent? On the Moon or in outer space?

It is to be regretted that the Refugee Convention is not clear enough on such a crucial question. However, it seems implied in a treaty recognizing 'the social and humanitarian nature of the problem of refugees' (preamble) that a refugee who is outside his country and presents himself to an official of a state party has a right to submit an application for asylum and to have it processed and screened. States cannot play with 'asymmetrical rights' beyond a certain extent and reach the point where the true objective of a treaty of humanitarian nature is denied. If the refugee cannot decide whether, where and when he will be admitted, he must at least be granted a right to present himself to submit an application to a State Party to the Refugee Convention. This can be called a right to fair and efficient asylum

---

82 The right of not being returned is subject to a condition: 'The benefit of the present provision may not, however, be claimed by a refugee whom there are reasonable grounds for regarding as a danger to the security of the country in which he is or who, having been convicted by a final judgment of a particularly serious crime, constitutes a danger to the community of that country' (Art. 33, para. 2). In the judgment of 28 February 2008 on the case *Saadi v. Italy*, relating to the expulsion from Italy to Tunisia of a Tunisian refugee convicted in his country for crimes related to terrorism, the European Court of Human Rights found that Art. 3 of the European Convention on Human Rights, which prohibits torture or inhumane or degrading treatment, must be given priority over Art. 33, para. 2, of the Refugee Convention: 'Since protection against the treatment prohibited by Article 3 is absolute, that provision imposes an obligation not to extradite or expel any person who, in the receiving country, would run the real risk of being subjected to such treatment. As the Court has repeatedly held, there can be no derogation from that rule. It must therefore reaffirm the principle … that it is not possible to weigh the risk of ill-treatment against the reasons put forward for the expulsion in order to determine whether the responsibility of a State is engaged under Article 3, even where such treatment is inflicted by another State. In that connection, the conduct of the person concerned, however undesirable or dangerous, cannot be taken into account, with the consequence that the protection afforded by Article 3 is broader than that provided for in Articles 32 and 33 of the 1951 United Nations Convention relating to the Status of Refugees' (para. 138).

83 See *supra*, 'The Asymmetrical Right to Emigrate'.

procedures. The right of the refugee to have access to the territory of a State Party to seek asylum is indirectly implied in Art. 31, para. 1, Refugee Convention:

> The Contracting States shall not impose penalties, on account of their illegal entry or presence, on refugees who, coming directly from a territory where their life or freedom was threatened in the sense of article 1, enter or are present in their territory without authorization, provided they present themselves without delay to the authorities and show good cause for their illegal entry or presence.

As consistently remarked by the United Nations High Commissioner for Refugees,[84] who is in charge of supervising the application of the Refugee Convention,

> as a general rule, in order to give effect to their obligations under the 1951 Convention and/or 1967 Protocol, States will be required to grant individuals seeking international protection access to the territory and to fair and efficient asylum procedures.[85]

Accordingly, already in 1979, the UNHCR Executive Committee (*Conclusions No. 15 on Refugees without an Asylum Country*) put emphasis on the need to grant to asylum seekers temporary refuge:

> In cases of large-scale influx, persons seeking asylum should always receive at least temporary refuge. States which because of their geographical situation, or otherwise, are faced with a large-scale influx should as necessary and at the request of the State concerned receive immediate assistance from other States in accordance with the principle of equitable burden-sharing. Such States should consult with the Office of the United Nations High Commissioner for Refugees as soon as possible to ensure that the persons involved are fully protected, are given emergency assistance, and that durable solutions are sought (para. f).

The Rights of Refugees at Sea

Nobody can be a refugee in his own country. Under the already quoted Art. 1, para. A.2, of the Refugee Convention, the status of refugee is attributed to a person who is 'outside the country of his nationality'.[86] This can only be interpreted as referring to someone who is outside the national territory of a given state, including its territorial sea. If the other relevant conditions are met, a person who is on the high

84 Hereinafter: UNHCR.

85 UNHCR, *Advisory Opinion on the Extraterritorial Application of Non-Refoulement Obligations under the 1951 Convention relating to the Status of Refugees and its 1967 Protocol*, 26 January 2007, para. 8.

86 See Goodwin-Gil, G., 'The Right to Seek Asylum: Interception at Sea and the Principle of Non-Refoulement', in *International Journal of Refugee Law*, 2011, p. 443.

seas, that is beyond the territory of his country, or in the territorial sea of a country different from his own, does qualify as a refugee. It follows that the rights of *non-refoulement* and of seeking asylum apply also to refugees found everywhere at sea, provided that they are not within the territorial sea of their state.

As pointed out by the UNHCR, there is today much concern that immigration control measures at sea (so-called interception at sea) do not distinguish between refugees and illegal migrants. In the absence of adequate safeguards, this may result in the rejection of refugees in need of international protection:

> States have a legitimate interest in controlling irregular migration. Unfortunately, existing control tools, such as visa requirements and the imposition of carrier sanctions, as well as interception measures, often do not differentiate between genuine asylum-seekers and economic migrants.[87]

As the identification of asylum-seekers and the processing of their applications are screening activities which normally cannot be carried out on ships, the intercepting state is under an obligation to disembark the potential refugees in a place where they can exercise the right to fair and efficient asylum procedures. Normally this place is located within the intercepting state itself:

> UNHCR's position is that claims for international protection made by intercepted persons are in principle to be processed in procedures within the territory of the intercepting State. This will usually be the most practical means to provide access to reception facilities and to fair and efficient asylum procedures – core components of any protection-sensitive entry system – and to ensure protection of the rights of the individual.[88]

Under certain circumstances, the UNCHR has taken the position that also the processing of asylum claims in a third state (so-called extraterritorial processing) can take place, as an acceptable alternative to processing by the intercepting state:

> However, under certain circumstances, the processing of international protection claims outside the intercepting State could be an alternative to standard 'incountry' procedures. Notably, this could be the case when extraterritorial processing is used as part of a burden-sharing arrangement to more fairly distribute responsibilities and enhance available protection space.[89]

---

87 UNHCR, *Interception of Asylum-Seekers and Refugees: The International Framework and Recommendations for a Comprehensive Approach*, UN Doc EC/50/SC/CPR.17, 9 June 2000, para. 17.

88 UNHCR, Protection Policy Paper, *Maritime Interception Operations and the Processing of International Protection Claims: Legal Standards and Policy Considerations with Respect to Extraterritorial Processing*, November 2010, para. 2.

89 Ibid., para. 3.

According to the UNCHR, arrangements for the temporary reception of refugees for the extraterritorial processing of their asylum claims must address their basic needs 'and provide for a stay consistent with the right to an adequate standard of living'.[90] Prolonged stays in closed reception facilities are not appropriate.[91] People with special needs, such as children, women, trafficked persons or victims of torture or trauma, require special consideration.[92] States with jurisdiction over extraterritorial reception and processing arrangements, such as the intercepting state and all states involved in the processing, are responsible for ensuring a timely outcome for all intercepted persons.[93] This normally consists of settlement or resettlement for persons entitled to refugee status and of return to the country of origin for the others.[94]

The summary conclusions of an expert meeting on 'Refugees and Asylum-seekers in Distress at Sea – How Best to Respond?', held in Djibouti in November 2011 under the sponsorship of UNHCR, include a 'Model framework for cooperation following rescue at sea operations involving refugees and asylum-seekers', which aims at enhancing international cooperation among concerned states and other stakeholders.[95] The document is based on the assumption that

> fundamentally, a core challenge in any particular rescue at sea operation involving asylum-seekers and refugees is often the timely identification of a place of safety for disembarkation, as well as necessary follow-up, including reception arrangements, access to appropriate processes and procedures, and outcomes. If a shipmaster is likely to face delays in disembarking rescued people, he/she may be less ready to come to the assistance of those in distress at sea. Addressing these challenges and developing predictable responses requires strengthened cooperation and coordination among all States and other stakeholders implicated in rescue at sea operations.[96]

---

90 Ibid., para. 23.

91 Ibid., para. 27.

92 Ibid., para. 28.

93 Ibid., para. 30.

94 Ibid., paras 36–59. Four different models of extraterritorial reception and processing have been taken into consideration by the UNHCR, namely: third state processing, carried out in and by a state other than the intercepting state; out of country processing, carried out by the intercepting state in the territory of another state or on part of the territory of the intercepting state that has been declared extraterritorial for migration purposes; regional processing, carried out jointly by several transit or destination states; and processing on board maritime vessels, which however is generally considered as not appropriate.

95 See also the summary conclusions of an expert meeting on 'International Cooperation to Share Burdens and Responsibilities', held in Amman in June 2011 under the sponsorship of UNHCR.

96 Para. 10.

It is envisaged that, in joining the model framework, each concerned state commits to undertake specific responsibilities which may include coordinating search and rescue activities, carrying out such activities, providing a place of disembarkation and initial reception, processing rescued persons, providing solutions for them and providing financial support to affected states. The states concerned are also invited to establish a task force to identify according to relevant factors the most appropriate country for disembarkation,[97] to ensure adequate reception arrangements, to establish mechanisms for profiling and referral to rapidly identify, and differentiate among, rescued persons according to their background and needs, to process asylum claims in accordance with applicable international standards, to provide a range of outcomes to rescued persons and to allow UNHCR to undertake a number of activities.

Regional approaches should also be envisaged, where appropriate. Since a number of years negotiations are being held within the IMO framework for a memorandum of understanding on concerted procedures relating to disembarkation of persons rescued at sea which would apply to the Mediterranean area. No information on the results is available.[98]

The Application at Sea of Human Rights Law and Refugee Law

A tool used by some states to elude international human rights law, including refugee law, is the strange theory that international human rights rules do not apply to persons found outside the national territory of the state. This theory is based on the assumption that human rights provisions apply only within the 'jurisdiction'[99]

97 'Relevant factors in identifying the place of disembarkation include: practical considerations (e.g., maritime safety; geographical proximity; the extent to which the rescuing vessel will be required to deviate from its intended voyage; the needs of rescued persons; facilities at the proposed site of disembarkation, including access to fair and efficient asylum procedures; applicable SAR and SOLAS provisions; the principle of *non-refoulement*)' (para. 4, ii).

98 See IMO circular letters No. 3203 of 18 August 2011, No. 3203/Add/1 of 16 September 2011 and No. 3254 of 12 March 2012. However these documents seem today to have been disabled from access by the public. See also Di Filippo, M., 'Irregular Migration and Safeguard of Life at Sea. International Rules and Recent Developments in the Mediterranean Sea', in Del Vecchio (ed.), 2014, (*supra*, note 61), p. 1.

99 The word 'jurisdiction' is often used to indicate the scope of application of human rights treaties: 'Each State Party to the present Covenant undertakes to respect and to ensure to all individuals within its territory and subject to its jurisdiction the rights recognized in the present Covenant' (Art. 2, para. 1, of the International Covenant on Civil and Political Rights); 'The High Contracting Parties shall secure to everyone within their jurisdiction the rights and freedoms defined in Section I of this Convention' (Art. 1 of the European Convention on Human Rights). 'The States Parties to this Convention undertake to respect the rights and freedoms recognized herein and to ensure to all persons subject to their

of States Parties to the relevant treaties and on a restrictive interpretation of the word 'jurisdiction', that is understood as if it were the word 'territory'.

Apart from cases of illegal migration, this theory has been applied by the United States with regard to the practice of extraordinary renditions. In fact, some non-American nationals suspected of terrorism were secretly kidnapped by American agents in states other than the United States, including several European countries with the complicity of local agents, and were forcibly transported to a third state where torture was carried out to extract information from them. This is an evident and gross violation of a number of fundamental human rights, such as the right not to be subjected to enforced disappearance or torture. However, as stated in 2006 by the United States legal advisor, Mr John Bellinger, Art. 3 CAT (no-return obligation)[100] and other human rights treaties to which the United States is a party as well were deemed not to be binding on the United States' agents when they acted outside the national territory:

> For more than a decade, the position of the US Government, and our courts, has been that all of those terms refer to returns from, or transfers out from the United States. So we think that Article 3 of the CAT is legally binding upon us with respect to transfers of anyone from the United States; but we don't think it is legally binding outside the United States.[101]

As has been rightly remarked, the theory in question leads to a situation of 'legal apartheid' in which, if the United States territory[102] and the American nationals are protected from torture, foreign individuals can be tortured elsewhere under the 'sponsorship' of American agents:

> The rendition, abduction and detention of terrorist suspects have always taken place outside the territory of the United States, where such actions would no doubt have been ruled unlawful and unconstitutional. Obviously, these actions are also unacceptable under the laws of European countries, who nonetheless

jurisdiction the free and full exercise of those rights and freedoms' (Art. 1, para. 1, of the American Convention on Human Rights); 'Each State Party shall take effective legislative, administrative, judicial or other measures to prevent acts of torture in any territory under its jurisdiction' (Art. 2, para. 1, CAT).

100 For the text see *supra*, note 74.

101 Text in Parliamentary Assembly of the Council of Europe, *Alleged Secret Detentions and Unlawful Inter-State Transfers Involving Council of Europe Member States, Draft Report – Part II (Explanatory Memorandum)*, Rapporteur Mr. Dick Marty, Part II, 7 June 2006, para. 272. Whether or not the United States maintains the same position also today is a question that would need further research and goes beyond the scope of the present study.

102 Incidentally, is Guantanamo Bay within the United States' territory? Apparently it is not. But this question also requires further research and goes beyond the scope of the present study.

> tolerated them or colluded actively in carrying them out. This export of illegal activities overseas is all the more shocking in that it shows fundamental contempt for the countries on whose territories it was decided to commit the relevant acts. The fact that the measures only apply to non-American citizens is just as disturbing: it reflects a kind of 'legal apartheid' and an exaggerated sense of superiority. Once again, the blame does not lie solely with the Americans but also, above all, with European political leaders who have knowingly acquiesced in this state of affairs.[103]

The theory that human rights treaties apply only within the territory of States Parties is not only wrong, but is a mockery of the rule of law. Human rights obligations bind states wherever their agents act. In the context of human rights treaties, the term 'jurisdiction' is to be understood as 'power or effective control'. Respect for human rights is due to any individual who is under the power or effective control of any agent of a State Party, wherever he happens to act. The general rule that treaties have to be interpreted in good faith in accordance with the ordinary meaning of the terms of the treaty in their context[104] and in the light of its object and purpose (Art. 31, para. 1, of the Vienna Convention on the Law of Treaties) cannot be undermined and nullified by playing with legal devices on the meaning of the word 'jurisdiction' and on the territorial application of treaties.[105]

As stated in 2004 by the Human Rights Committee in General Comment No. 31 on the nature of the general legal obligation on States Parties to the International Covenant on Civil and Political Rights, such states

> must respect and ensure the rights laid down in the Covenant to anyone within the power or effective control of that State Party, even if not situated within the territory of the State Party.[106]

The Committee Against Torture, established under CAT, held in its decision of 21 November 2008 on the communication *J.H.A. v. Spain*, relating to a case

---

103 Parliamentary Assembly of the Council of Europe, *Alleged Secret Detentions*, quoted *supra*, note 101, para. 4.

104 In any case the ordinary meaning of 'jurisdiction' – a word of which probably nobody knows the precise meaning – is much closer to 'power or effective control' than to 'territory'.

105 Under Art. 29 of the same convention, 'unless a different intention appears from the treaty or is otherwise established, a treaty is binding upon each party in respect of its entire territory'. This provision says that treaties normally do not apply to portions of the territory of a state party. But it does not say anything about the application of treaties beyond national territory.

106 UN Doc CCPR/C/21/Rev.1/Add.13, 26 May 2004, para. 10.

where Spain rescued on the high seas 369 illegal migrants and returned them to Mauritania,[107] that

> jurisdiction must also include situations where a State party exercises, directly or indirectly, in whole or in part, de jure or de facto control, in accordance with international law. ... The State party maintained control over the persons on board the *Marine I* from the time the vessel was rescued and throughout the identification and repatriation process that took place in Nouadhibou.[108]

The present jurisprudence of the European Court of Human Rights confirms that the European Convention on Human Rights binds States Parties beyond their territory[109] and also on the high seas. For instance, in the judgment of 29 March 2010 on the case *Medvedyev and others v. France* the Grand Chamber of the Court held that the interception on the high seas by France of a Cambodian ship engaged in drug trafficking was within the jurisdiction of France for the purposes of the Convention.[110] In the judgment of 23 February 2012 in the case of *Hirsi Jamaa and others v. Italy*,[111] the Grand Chamber of the Court concluded that the Convention applies in cases where a State Party has exercised its jurisdiction outside its national territory. In particular, the Convention applies on the high seas, which cannot be seen as an area outside the law:

> Furthermore, as regards the exercise by a State of its jurisdiction on the high seas, the Court has already stated that the special nature of the maritime environment cannot justify an area outside the law where individuals are covered by no legal system capable of affording them enjoyment of the rights and guarantees protected by the Convention which the States have undertaken to secure to everyone within their jurisdiction.[112]

---

107 See Wouters, K. and Den Heijer, M., 'The Marine I Case: A Comment', in *International Journal of Refugee Law*, 2010, p. 1.

108 Para. 8.2.

109 It seems that the Court is trying to depart from the much criticized decision of 12 December 2001 in *Banković and Others v. Belgium, the Czech Republic, Denmark, France, Germany, Greece, Hungary, Iceland, Italy, Luxembourg, Norway, the Netherlands, Poland, Portugal, Spain, Turkey and United Kingdom*, where it held that 'Article 1 of the Convention must be considered to reflect this ordinary and essentially territorial notion of jurisdiction, other bases of jurisdiction being exceptional and requiring special justification in the particular circumstances of each case' (para. 61). The sad result of this assumption was that the applications by the relatives of Yugoslav civilians killed by bombs dropped by the air forces of States Parties were found inadmissible because Yugoslavia was not a party to the European Convention on Human Rights.

110 The interception took place with the authorization of Cambodia.

111 On the merits of the case see *infra*, 'The Italian Push-Back Policy'.

112 Para. 178.

Accordingly, the Court found that the operations of interception of illegal migrants on the high seas must be carried out in compliance with the obligations arising from the European Convention on Human Rights and its protocols:

> Having regard to the foregoing, the Court considers that the removal of aliens carried out in the context of interceptions on the high seas by the authorities of a State in the exercise of their sovereign authority, the effect of which is to prevent migrants from reaching the borders of the State or even to push them back to another State, constitutes an exercise of jurisdiction within the meaning of Article 1 of the Convention which engages the responsibility of the State in question under Article 4 of Protocol No. 4.[113]

Also the obligation of *non-refoulement* provided for in Art. 33, para. 1, Refugee Convention, which is a human right specifically applying to refugees, binds States Parties wherever their agents act, including the high seas. As pointed out by the UNHCR,

> the principle of *non-refoulement* does not imply any geographical limitation. In UNCHR's understanding, the resulting obligations extend to all governments' agents acting in an official capacity, within or outside national territory. Given the practice of States to intercept persons at great distance from their own territory, the international refugee protection regime would be rendered ineffective if States' agents abroad were free to act at variance with obligations under international refugee law and human rights law.[114]

In international practice a number of instances of dubious compliance with human rights obligations at sea may be found, as the following cases show.

Sale et al. v. Haitian Centers Council, Inc., et al.

Adopted to face a massive flow of refugees from Haiti, Executive Order 12807 of 24 May 1992 (Interdiction of Illegal Aliens), provides that the President of the United States

> has authority to suspend the entry of aliens coming by sea to the United States without necessary documentation, to establish reasonable rules and regulations regarding, and other limitations on, the entry or attempted entry of aliens into

113 Para. 180.

114 UNHCR, *Interception of Asylum-Seekers and Refugees: the International Framework and Recommendations for a Comprehensive Approach*, *supra* note 11, para. 23. See Trevisanut, S., 'The Principle of Non-Refoulement at Sea and the Effectiveness of Asylum Protection', in *Max Planck Yearbook of United Nations Law*, 2008, p. 205.

> the United States, and to repatriate aliens interdicted beyond the territorial sea of the United States (Sect. 1).

The order applies to ships flying the flag of the United States, to ships without nationality and to ships flying the flag of a state with which the United States has arrangements authorizing their stopping and boarding.

By the judgment of 21 June 1993 in the case *Sale et al. v. Haitian Centers Council, Inc., et al.* the United States Supreme Court held that Art. 33, para. 1, Refugee Convention does not prohibit the return to other states of migrant aliens intercepted on the high seas without giving them the possibility to present asylum claims.[115] The general prohibition to 'return' (*refouler*) was understood by the Court in the restricted meaning of a prohibition to exclude someone who already has reached the border. The Court disregarded the fact that a refugee is, by definition, a person who is outside the country of his nationality and not a person who presents himself at the border of another country.[116] The Court relied on the statements made by delegates of a few states during the *travaux préparatoires* for the Refugee Convention, without considering that recourse to the preparatory works, which is a supplementary means of interpretation, cannot change the ordinary meaning of a term used in a treaty (see Arts 31 and 32 of the Vienna Convention on the Law of Treaties). As remarked by the dissenting Justice Blackmun,

> what is extraordinary in this case is that the Executive, in disregard of the law, would take to the seas to intercept fleeing refugees and force them back to their persecutors – and that the Court would strain to sanction that conduct.[117]

> The refugees attempting to escape from Haiti do not claim a right of admission to this country. They do not even argue that the Government has a right to intercept their boats. They demand only that the United States, land of refugees and guardian of freedom, cease forcibly driving them back to detention, abuse, and death. That is a modest plea, vindicated by the Treaty and the statute. We should not close our ears to it. I dissent.[118]

The Australian Excision

In 2001, Australia adopted the Migration Amendment (Excision from Migration Zone) Act. It provides for cutting out (so-called excision) certain portions of Australian territory, such as Christmas, Cocos, Ashmore and Cartier islands, from the 'migration zone', that is the area where applications for protection visas may

---

115 For a comment see Jones, T., *International Decisions: Sale v. Haitian Centers Council, Inc.*, in *American Journal of International Law*, 1994, p. 114.

116 *Supra*, 'The Rights of Refugees at Sea'.

117 *International Legal Materials*, 1993, p. 1059.

118 Ibid., p. 1068.

be made by people having entered Australia without lawful authority, including refugees. Refugees in the excision zone are considered 'offshore entry persons' and are prevented from applying for asylum, unless the Minister for Immigration and Citizenship exercises his discretionary and non-compellable power to allow them to apply. No judicial remedies are available to them. They can be removed to another state (so-called 'declared country'), where their applications for asylum can be processed if the Minister is satisfied that appropriate arrangements are in place to prevent their *refoulement* from the declared country to a state where they can be persecuted.

It is very questionable whether the Australian legislation complies with the obligations arising from the Refugee Convention, to which Australia is a party, and in particular with the obligation to grant to a refugee fair and efficient asylum procedures. There is no reason why this convention should not apply to the entire Australian territory.

The Italian Push-Back Policy

In May 2009, Italy started a policy of intercepting migrants at sea and sending them back to the countries from which their ships sailed, in particular Libya (so-called push-back policy).[119] Most of the intercepted migrants had the nationality of Eritrea, Somalia or other African countries. In the brief period between May and July 2009, a total of 602 migrants were pushed back to Libya and 23 to Algeria, including children and pregnant women.

The report of the visit made in 2009 by a delegation of the European Committee for the Prevention of Torture,[120] established under the 1987 European Convention for the Prevention of Torture and Inhuman or Degrading Treatment or Punishment,[121] cast many doubts on Italy's compliance with its international obligations. First of all, the CPT remarked that cooperation received during the visit by Italy was regrettably unsatisfactory, as documents and information were

119 The already mentioned 2007 Protocol between Italy and Libya (*supra*, 'Italy and Libya') generically provides that the patrolling naval units are bound to act 'in compliance with international conventions in force, according to the operational modalities to be defined by the competent authorities of the two countries'. Nowhere in the Protocol is the Refugees Conv. explicitly mentioned, to which only Italy – but not Libya – is a party.

120 Hereinafter: CPT.

121 Hereinafter: ECPT.

kept confidential in violation of Arts 3[122] and 8, para. 2,[123] of the ECPT.[124] On the substance, the CPT pointed out that the Italian push-back operations were carried out without any concern for the identification of the migrants and their right to present asylum applications:

> The Italian authorities have acknowledged officially that they do not proceed with the formal identification of migrants who are intercepted at sea and pushed back. The CPT has, however, been informed by the UNHCR that among the migrants pushed back there were persons who were registered with the UNHCR and to whom it had previously issued temporary documents. Other migrants, including persons from Somalia and Eritrea, were later interviewed by the UNHCR and found immediately to be seeking and possibly qualifying for international protection.[125]

In the specific case, Italy insisted on the circumstance that the illegal migrants made no requests for asylum. However, the credibility of such a justification totally depended on the factual conditions in which operations of interception at sea were carried out. A number of questions could be asked in this regard. Were the migrants ever given the opportunity to be in a condition to present their asylum application, if any? The answer was a negative one:

> Nevertheless, the Italian Government has affirmed that no migrant has ever expressed his/her intention to apply for asylum and that, consequently, there has been no need to identify these persons and establish their nationality. Even if what is affirmed were to correspond to reality, it must be borne in mind that persons surviving a sea voyage are often not in a condition in which they should be expected to declare immediately their wish to apply for asylum.[126]

122 'In the application of this Convention, the Committee and the competent national authorities of the Party concerned shall co-operate with each other'.

123 'A Party shall provide the Committee with the following facilities to carry out its task: … other information available to the Party which is necessary for the Committee to carry out its task. In seeking such information, the Committee shall have regard to applicable rules of national law and professional ethics'.

124 'The CPT considers that the shortcomings outlined …, when taken together clearly indicate that the Italian authorities have not been engaging with the Committee in a co-operative spirit in relation to the issue addressed during the visit' (Council of Europe, *Report to the Italian Government on the visit to Italy carried out by the European Committee for the Prevention of Torture and Inhuman or Degrading Treatment or Punishment (CPT) from 27 to 31 July 2003*, CPT/Inf (2010) 14, 28 April 2010, para. 9).

125 Ibid., para. 13.

126 Ibid., para. 14.

> This is particularly the case when the circumstances are such that the persons concerned are not in a position to express such a request. In this regard, a Coast Guard Admiral responsible for a large Search and Rescue area stated to the delegation that persons surviving a sea voyage were clearly not in a condition in which they should be expected to declare their wish to apply for asylum. In particular, such persons were often dehydrated, physically and mentally exhausted and their sole preoccupation at the time of rescue was to be brought to safety.[127]

Were the Italian officials prepared to deal with potential asylum-seekers speaking languages different from Italian? The answer was a negative one:

> Further, information gathered through interviews held by the delegation would indicate that, even if a migrant were to request protection whilst aboard an Italian vessel, there is no procedure in place capable of referring him/her to a protection mechanism; nor have the competent authorities been instructed on how to identify and screen migrants. It should be noted, in this context, that intercepted migrants do not have access to linguistic or legal assistance on board the intercepting vessels, in order to express their needs.
>
> Indeed, representatives of both the Navy and the Coast Guard with whom the delegation spoke, clearly stated that they are not responsible in any way for the identification of migrants, the provision of information on how to apply for asylum, or the treatment of asylum requests; nor have they been instructed by the Ministry of the Interior in relation to these issues. The information gathered from representatives of the *Guardia di Finanza* [Italian Finance Police] also indicated that it did not proceed to individual identification of the migrants, though collective interviews may be carried out.[128]

Could a request for asylum be made in a situation where, as alleged, force is used in a disproportionate way? Again, the answer was a negative one:

> The delegation was unable to interview the migrants pushed back to Libya or, given the authorities' refusal to provide their names, the captains of the Italian vessels involved in the operation. However, reliable information collected by the delegation would indicate that, during the operation, which lasted around 12 hours, the 74 persons on the *Guardia di Finanza* vessel were provided insufficient water and no food or blankets; further, physical violence, in particular with kicks, punches and blows with an oar, was allegedly used against a number of

127 Ibid., para. 32.
128 Ibid., para. 13.

> migrants by Libyan police at the harbour in Tripoli, to force them to disembark from the two Coast Guard vessels.[129]

As regards the issues related to torture, the CPT recalled the peremptory norm of international law that prevents a state from sending a person to another state where there are substantial grounds for believing that he would run a real risk of being subjected to torture or other forms of ill-treatment.[130] It was the practice of the CPT to recommend to all parties to the ECPT

> that they ensure that migrants have ready access to an asylum procedure (or other residence procedure) which guarantees both confidentiality and an objective and independent analysis of the human rights situation in other countries. That procedure should involve an individual assessment of the risk of ill-treatment in case of expulsion of the person concerned to the country of origin or a third country.[131]

According to the CPT, states are obliged, in order to comply with the principle of *non-refoulement*, to screen intercepted migrants with a view to identifying persons in need of protection, assessing those needs and taking appropriate action.[132] In view of the specific circumstances, the alleged absence of requests for asylum could not be taken as a justification for returning people to states where their right not to be tortured could be violated.[133]

Considering also that Libya was not a party to the Refugee Convention and that it did not have asylum legislation or procedures in place, the view of the CPT was that

> there would appear to be a real risk ... that persons detained in Libya, including migrants, may be subjected to severe ill-treatment and/or be sent to a country where they are at risk of such treatment.[134]

---

129 Ibid., para. 18.

130 Ibid., para. 26.

131 Ibid., para. 27.

132 Ibid., para. 30.

133 'In any event, the absence of an explicit request for asylum does not necessarily absolve the Italian authorities of their *non-refoulement* obligations under Article 3 of the European Convention on Human Rights' (ibid., para. 32).

134 Ibid., para. 47. 'The CPT has not itself been in a position to verify, through an on-site visit, conditions of detention and the treatment afforded to persons detained in Libya. However, according to consistent accounts from a variety of sources, overcrowding, absence of beds, poor hygiene, inadequacy of food, lack of health care and sanitation, and rampant skin infections would appear to be commonplace in Libyan detention centres. The UNHCR has recently described the conditions of detention and treatment in such centres as "appalling"' (ibid., para. 42).

The conclusion of the CPT was that the Italian push-back policy did not meet the requirements 'to ensure that migrants are provided with appropriate treatment, are given an opportunity to apply for asylum and are not sent back to a country where they may be at risk of ill-treatment'.[135]

Yet the response given by Italy to the CPT report[136] was far from improving the Italian position. Beside insisting on state secrets[137] (in a case involving torture!), Italy put forward hardly convincing legal formalisms on who should first pronounce the word 'asylum':

> It is the opinion of Italian Authorities that, according to international and EU standards, there is no obligation during search and rescue operations to provide information on the possibility to apply for asylum. On the contrary, such information has to be ensured once the migrant expresses his/her willingness to apply for asylum. …
>
> To confirm such approach, Italian Authorities recall that when a migrant rescued at sea expresses the intention to apply for asylum or other forms of international protection on board of an Italian vessel, s/he is not returned to the country of departure/transit but s/he is brought to Italy. The same rule applies to all those who, after a medical visit, are in need of medical assistance.[138]

In fact, Italy was not able to explain how the interlocutors, namely the Italian officials and the migrants, who spoke different languages and were in a situation of danger and haste, could understand each other. Nor did Italy point out whether, before the operations, the applicable rules on refugees had ever been explained to the Italian officials involved.

The already mentioned judgment rendered on 21 February 2012 by the European Court of Human Rights (Grand Chamber) on the case *Hirsi Jamaa and others v. Italy* confirmed that the Italian push-back policy did not comply with the obligations arising from the European Convention on Human Rights. The case was filed by 11 Somalis and 13 Eritreans who were among a group of about 200 migrants intercepted at sea by Italian authorities and summarily returned to Libya. The applicants claimed violations of a number of provisions of the European

135 Ibid., para. 51.

136 Council of Europe, *Response of the Italian Government to the Report of the European Committee for the Prevention of Torture and Inhuman or Degrading Treatment or Punishment (CPT) on its Visit to Italy from 27 to 31 July 2009*, CPT/Inf (2010) 15, 28 April 2010.

137 'Once again, Italian Authorities recall that for security reasons, they are not in a position to provide the names of either the commanders of the Units involved or the physicians. Accordingly, neither logbooks nor relating documents can be provided since they should be considered as classified material' (ibid., para. A).

138 Ibid., para. D.

Convention on Human Rights, including Art. 3 (Torture) and Art. 4 of Protocol No. 4 (Prohibition of collective expulsion of aliens).

As regards the weight of bilateral agreements on the fight against illegal migration,[139] the Court observed that

> Italy cannot evade its own responsibility by relying on its obligations arising out of bilateral agreements with Libya. Even if it were to be assumed that those agreements made express provision for the return to Libya of migrants intercepted on the high seas, the Contracting States' responsibility continues even after their having entered into treaty commitments subsequent to the entry into force of the Convention or its Protocols in respect of these States.[140]

On the merits, the Court unanimously found that Italy was responsible for a violation of Art. 3 of the Convention, as, by returning the applicants to Libya, it had exposed them to the risk of being subjected to torture or inhuman or degrading treatment in Libya or in their countries of origin:

> During the period in question no rule governing the protection of refugees was complied with by Libya. Any person entering the country by illegal means was deemed to be clandestine and no distinction was made between irregular migrants and asylum seekers. Consequently, those persons were systematically arrested and detained in conditions that outside visitors, such as delegations from the UNHCR, Human Rights Watch and Amnesty International, could only describe as inhuman. Many cases of torture, poor hygiene conditions and lack of appropriate medical care were denounced by all the observers. Clandestine migrants were at risk of being returned to their countries of origin at any time and, if they managed to regain their freedom, were subjected to particularly precarious living conditions as a result of their irregular situation. Irregular immigrants, such as the applicants, were destined to occupy a marginal and isolated position in Libyan society, rendering them extremely vulnerable to xenophobic and racist acts.[141]

> … according to the UNHCR and Human Rights Watch, individuals forcibly repatriated to Eritrea face being tortured and detained in inhuman conditions merely for having left the country irregularly. As regards Somalia, in the recent case of *Sufi and Elmi* … the Court noted the serious levels of violence in Mogadishu and the increased risk to persons returned to that country of being forced either to transit through areas affected by the armed conflict or to seek

139 See *supra*, 'Italy and Libya'.
140 Para. 129.
141 Para. 125.

> refuge in camps for displaced persons or refugees, where living conditions were appalling.[142]

The situation existing in Libya was well-known to the Italian authorities or was easy to verify by them on the basis of multiple sources.[143]

According to the Court, irrespective of whether an intention to apply for asylum was manifested by the applicants – a circumstance that was disputed by the parties – Italy was under the obligation of not pushing the migrants back to Libya:

> In any event, the Court considers that it was for the national authorities, faced with a situation in which human rights were being systematically violated, as described above, to find out about the treatment to which the applicants would be exposed after their return ... Having regard to the circumstances of the case, the fact that the parties concerned had failed to expressly request asylum did not exempt Italy from fulfilling its obligations under Article 3.[144]

The Court unanimously found that Italy was also responsible for a violation of Art. 4 of Protocol No. 4, which prohibits the collective expulsion of aliens. In particular, the Court rejected the formalistic argument put forward by Italy that an expulsion can take place only if the aliens are inside the national territory. After having remarked that Art. 4[145] does not use the word 'territory',[146] the Court interpreted the Convention and its Protocols in a way 'which renders the guarantees practical and effective and not theoretical and illusory',[147] showing a particular consideration for the fate of migrants who risk their lives at sea:

> The Court has already found that, according to the established caselaw of the Commission and of the Court, the purpose of Article 4 of Protocol No. 4 is to prevent States being able to remove certain aliens without examining their personal circumstances and, consequently, without enabling them to put forward their arguments against the measure taken by the relevant authority. If, therefore, Article 4 of Protocol No. 4 were to apply only to collective expulsions from the national territory of the States Parties to the Convention, a significant component of contemporary migratory patterns would not fall within the ambit of that provision, notwithstanding the fact that the conduct it is intended to prohibit can occur outside national territory and in particular, as in the instant case, on the high seas. Article 4 would thus be ineffective in practice with regard to such situations, which, however, are on the increase. The consequence of that would

142 Para. 150.
143 Paras 131 and 156.
144 Para. 133.
145 'Collective expulsion of aliens is prohibited'.
146 Para. 173.
147 Para. 175.

> be that migrants having taken to the sea, often risking their lives, and not having managed to reach the borders of a State, would not be entitled to an examination of their personal circumstances before being expelled, unlike those travelling by land.[148]

Finally the Court unanimously found that there had been a violation of Art. 13 of the Convention (Right to an effective remedy), taken together with Arts 3 and 4 of Protocol No. 4, as the applicants were deprived of any remedy which would have enabled them to lodge their complaints with a competent authority and to obtain a thorough and rigorous assessment of their requests before the removal measure was enforced.[149]

Following, *mutatis mutandis*, the precedent of the *Hirsi Jamaa* case, the European Court of Human Rights has recently rendered the judgment of 21 October 2014 on the case *Sharifi and others v. Italy and Greece*, relating to the rejection to Greece in the years 2008 and 2009 of 35 illegal migrants who had clandestinely reached Italian ports. The Court, *inter alia*, found a violation by Italy of Art. 4 of Protocol 4 to the European Convention on Human Rights, that prohibits collective expulsion of aliens, as the practice followed by the Italian agents in immediately rejecting the applicants deprived the latter of any possibility to submit an application for asylum.[150] The Court also found violations by Italy of Art. 3 (Prohibition of torture) and Art. 13 (right to an effective remedy) of the same convention.

In the last years, also because of the worsening of the political situation in Libya and the consequent lack of control over the flow of illegal migrants, the number of unseaworthy boats that try to reach the other shore of the Mediterranean Sea has increased. This has aggravated the toll of thousands of human lives, including women and children, lost at sea. In the meantime, Italy radically changed its previous push-back policy. In October 2013, after 366 migrants drowned in the vicinity of the island of Lampedusa, it started the operation called *Mare Nostrum*, which engages units of the navy and police in facing the humanitarian emergency in the Channel of Sicily. Illegal migrants and asylum seekers found in unseaworthy boats, where they are often abandoned by smugglers, are rescued and transported to the Italian territory where applications for asylum are processed. *Mare Nostrum* is supposed to end in October 2014, when an operation, called *Triton*, should be launched by the European Union's border control agency. Given the lack of internal borders between many European states, support by the European Union is expected for this kind of operations.

---

148 Para. 177.

149 Para. 205.

150 Para. 215.

Conclusion

Migrations often have their roots in the suffering that too many individuals have to endure in the place where they live because of persecution, poverty, conflicts, natural disasters or other calamities. In the last years thousands among the poorest people of the world have put at risk and lost their lives in attempts to cross a border and reach a place where they would be safe and could hopefully spend a decent life.

Illegal migrants have the right to be treated humanely and not as criminals. If they are also in distress at sea, they have the right to be rescued and brought to a place of safety. If they are also refugees, they have the right not to be returned to a place where they are persecuted and to be put in the condition to apply for asylum. Like all human beings, they have the right not to be sent to a place where they could be tortured.

But many of the relevant facts show that illegal migrants are too often the victims not only of smugglers, but also of a number of states which try to evade their legal and moral duties by resorting to shows of strength against the weakest human beings or to hardly credible legal technicalities. The treaties so far concluded are not sufficiently clear to deal with all the problems posed by illegal migrations. The very invention of asymmetrical rights undermines the merits of international law in addressing the basic needs of illegal migrants and asylum seekers among them. This is the reason why, where different views are admissible, a clear position should be taken in favour of the weaker subject, that is the illegal migrant, and against the stronger subject, that is the state. If it appears that the international rules in force do not offer sufficient protection for the weaker party, the only conclusion to be drawn is that the present regime should be improved as soon as possible.

PART III
The Case for the Support of Asylum Seekers

Chapter 7
The Case for Asylum Seekers: Reverting to Human Rights

Laura Westra

Introduction

> Citizenship introduced a new type of privilege which was protected for some by excluding others. After the revolutions, nation-states are defined by territorial boundaries, which demarcate them from other states and exclude other people and nations. Citizenship shifted exclusion from class to nation, which became a disguised class barrier (Douzinas 2000: 103).

This work started by noting how the presence of migrants and asylum seekers put the very existence of human rights in question as so-called democratic countries have erected barriers both physical and bureaucratic against them, an unwarranted demonstration of hostility. In modern times, when class strife is no longer acknowledged (although surely some of its vestiges remain in the distinction between the 1 per cent and the 99 per cent), we need to question closely yet another causality, beyond the ones that clearly engendered the conditions that motivated the flight: what is the root of that hostility?

Douzinas sees the identity of the 'sovereign' individual citizen possessed of the same 'freedom of action and autonomy' as the sovereign state: both 'share decision-making and freedom from the power of others' (Douzinas 2000: 102). The citizen becomes the beneficiary of rights, within the ambit of national sovereignty:

> The declarations proclaim the universality of rights but their immediate effect is to establish the boundless power of the state and its law (Douzinas 2000: 101).

Nevertheless, the international human rights, guaranteed by the UN through its Declaration, are universal and cosmopolitan, and they are effectively dependent on and guaranteed by domestic legal regimes. These regimes transform the natural rights of man, into the rights of persons, both natural and legal, under the control of sovereign states. Thus the state's ultimate authority, it appears, supersedes universal rights, as the latter have lost their basis in natural law. They have been replaced by non-sacred rights of people, such as 'religious freedom and freedom of expression, the security of the person, due process of law and the presumption of innocence in criminal proceedings' (Douzinas 2000: 86). No longer based on and originating from natural law, the new rights simply represent 'desires expressed through free will':

> The proliferation of many desires destroyed the good, as it had done with the one truth. The emptied place of the good was filled by the (fear of) evil, symbolised by death and broadly interpreted as the non-achievement or frustration of desire (Douzinas 2000: 84).

The legitimacy of any individual desire, when it is 'writ large' in the legal regimes of the state, is guaranteed by the democratic vote, and it permits people to pursue their interests 'without consideration for substantive moral values' (Douzinas 2000: 92). These circumstances create a largely amoral society, as the best background for economic and trade transactions, no doubt, but they do not prepare morally sound state institutions, capable of acknowledging the universally valid human rights of refugees and asylum seekers.

Although 'overt racism ... [is] going out of fashion', and 'civil rights movements at home and anti-colonial movements abroad undercut the legitimacy of racial exclusion and discrimination' (Chomsky 2014: 2), 'global apartheid' is now imposed, separating 'the global North from the global south' (Chomsky 2014: 2). This separation is especially important as it affects refugees at all points in their saga: in the exposure to the conditions that render them asylum seekers; in the situation they find, when they are lucky enough to be able to flee; and even in the conditions of life they find when they reach their goal – life in another country.

The first aspect of this situation was emphasized in Chapters 2, 3 and 4 of this work. Juss puts it well:

> When one considers the root causes of flight in many developing nations, however, it is clear that a focus on narrow political interpretation of persecution excludes the bulk of the world's refugees today, thereby making such a definition wholly inappropriate for a global application. Thus the definition can exclude those suffering economic and social persecution. It can exclude those suffering from the effects of war. It can exclude the victims of natural disasters in countries where the state offers no protection. It can accordingly all too easily exclude the migration of people attributed to climate change. In short it excludes most of the world's humanitarian refugees (Juss 2006: 171).

It seems clear that the effort to render refugee law more relevant, thus ensuring a better fit between its regulations and the situation of those it is intended to protect, should be to switch the focus of relevant regimes to human rights. As well, the attempt to separate the conditions and the needs of asylum seekers from that of migrants is not conducive either to an understanding of the causes and conditions leading to the forced exodus of whole groups, or even to better knowledge of the situation of refugees who succeed in their flight, after their arrival in their chosen country.

For many reasons connected to the presence of 'global apartheid', the main issue regarding today's asylum seekers is the existence of multiple human rights breaches; we need to respect their dignity and their rights from the start. Their rights must be respected at their original location, at the start, as mass flights are better reduced by eliminating the causes than by attempting to redress the problems after they have occurred. In addition, their rights must be respected at the border, after they flee, if the harmful conditions that face them persist. Finally, their rights must be respected after their arrival.

The Rights of Asylum Seekers and the Role of the International Convention on the Elimination of All Forms of Racial Discrimination

> Conscious of their duty to achieve the total liberation of Africa, the peoples of which are still struggling for their dignity and genuine independence, and undertaking to eliminate colonialism, neo-colonialism apartheid, zionism, and to dismantle aggressive foreign military bases and all forms of discrimination, particularly those based on race, ethnic group, colour, sex, language, religion or political opinions (African Charter on Human and Peoples Rights, Preamble).

This paragraph could apply to any of the third world countries from which come the overwhelming majority of refugees: they are, in various measure, 'struggling for their dignity', as well as for their life, against different forms of aggression, all based upon the effects of ongoing discriminatory practices. In fact, all the circumstances that have been discussed in Part I as being causally determinant of the forced displacement of whole populations, start precisely with the discriminatory practice that underlies the harmful activities that force displacement.

Hence, there is a specific reason for choosing the African Charter to open this chapter's discussion. If we consider the origins of the disparate activities that result in (a) climate change, (b) famine and the illegal deprivation of peoples' natural resources and (c) the ongoing illegal conflicts, we note one common theme all these human rights breaches share: the total depreciation of the rights, hence the human dignity and value of those who are eventually affected by the consequences of the activities themselves.

I have argued that the commonality of all the phenomena discussed in Part I is manifested in the crippling poverty all refugees share (see Chapter 1). The additional common denominator that unites the activities that eventually make the flight inevitable is the discriminatory intent of those whose operations first create, then impose those conditions:

> Economists have focused on how best to provide incentives so that individuals and firms take into account their externalities: steel producers should be forced to pay for their pollution, and those who cause accidents should pay for the consequences. We embody these ideas for instance, in the 'polluter pays

> principle', which says that polluters should pay for the full consequences of their actions (Stiglitz 2012: 188).

Stiglitz adds that non-compliance is equivalent to rewarding the corporations involved by offering them a subsidy for their operations. For instance, 'nuclear power plants and offshore oil rigs are shielded from bearing the full costs should they explode' (Stiglitz 2012: 189). As we saw, at the time of Chernobyl (Ukraine), and we still see today after the Fukushima disaster in Japan, the question of possible malfunctions is only a small part of the ways in which these entities can impose harm. The gravest threat posed by nuclear power plants is the unsolved (and unsolvable) problem of radioactive waste, right from the start of their operations, that is, with the uranium mining that is also evidence of discriminatory intent, in the way such operations are located and staffed.

Another example of industrial harms can be found, for example, in uranium mining (Eichstaedt 1994). The history of uranium mining in the four-corner area (Utah, Colorado, Arizona and New Mexico, and the Navajo Reservation between the Grand Canyon and the Petrified Forest National Park) appears to have been written in blood.

The evidence of the narrative is unequivocal. It is consistently one group and one group alone that is targeted. I have termed this approach 'institutionalized ecological violence', and the author is correct in pointing out that this form of violence does more than destroy the unfortunate miners, working in hazardous unventilated 'dog holes', accumulating in one week multiple doses of the yearly maximum 'safe' radiation exposure in their bodies, and eventually succumbing to untreatable cancer and other diseases.

Some mill workers also had up to 60 micrograms of uranium in their urine samples. The yellowcake dust they inhaled and swallowed was making them radioactive from the inside out. This intolerable violence also destroys families who attempt to survive on the pitiful sums allotted to them, or with no compensation at all for surviving wives and children. Finally, this same violence, discriminating against Native Americans, also attacks their survival as people, hence the appeal to genocide in this case. Although we all depend on a healthy, non-toxic environment, Native people have a particular right and claim to the lands they inhabit and from which they assert their identity as a Nation.

Hence, when the Navajo miners, their families and supporters took on the 'fight for justice', requesting child support and simple compensation to survive, they were asking far less than what should have been theirs by right.

> … at the age of forty, Peter Yazzie knew the end was near and was driven to a hospital in Albuquerque. He died eight days later, on June 6, 1970. He left a home that was a simple adobe Hogan heated with wood, a wife Dolores, age thirty-six, and ten children ranging in age from two to eighteen. His wife began to collect $250.00 a month on which to raise a family (Eichstaedt 1994: 94).

The final injustices were disclosed in February 1993, when even the evident physical damages to the miners were shown to have been calculated improperly.

> (Dr. Louise) Abel demonstrated to the assembled doctors, lawyers and government officials that the medical tests are inadequate (Eichstaedt 1994: 151).

This resulted in hundreds of miners being excluded from 'compassion payments' ordered by the Radiation Exposure Compensation Act of 1990. When a group is singled out for special treatment that effectively eliminates most of their basic rights to life, health, and free information and consent, then all those involved are guilty of complicity in the crimes perpetrated against them. Through each sad interview describing the story of individual miners and their families (Eichstaedt 1994: 172–95), and through the appendices detailing the hearing on radiation exposure and finally the Radiation Exposure Compensation Act of 1990 (Eichstaedt 1994: 219–37), the story that unfolds is one that should fill everyone with shame. Nor is the United States the only country with that problem. A 2006 report from Australia, relates a similar story:

> Cancer cases among Aborigines near Australia's biggest uranium mine, according to a study by the Federal Government's leading indigenous research body, appear to be almost double the normal rate. The study also found there had been no monitoring in the past 20 years of the Ranger mine's impact on the health of local indigenous peoples. Yet since 1981 there have been more than 120 spillages and leaks of contaminated water at the mine located in the World Heritage listed Kakadu National Park (Minchin and Murdoch 2006).

Energy Resources of Australia (majority owned by Rio Tinto), which operates the mine, denied that the aboriginal peoples in the area were exposed to radiation, and in fact announced that the mine would continue to operate until 2020, despite the fact that,

> … [a] study compared Aborigines diagnosed with cancer in the Kakadu region with the cancer rate among all Aboriginal peoples in the Northern Territory from 1994 to 2003. It found the diagnosis rate was 90 per cent higher than expected in the Kakadu region (Minchin and Murdoch 2006).

In this case as well, neither the corporation(s) responsible for the extractive activities, nor the Australian government that allowed and, in fact, defended this operation, accepted responsibility for the harms they had perpetrated, or attempted to close the mine and redress the injustice for which they shared responsibility.

Examples can be multiplied, thus, it is neither the facts nor the science that are lacking, but the functionalist approach of industry and institutions that needs to accept the scientific reality and enact the required corrections.

Of course it is not only the internal stakeholder that is at risk from the nuclear industry. The whole world is under threat: after the 2011 earthquake and explosion and the Fukushima disaster in Japan:

> The Fukushima disaster in Japan has brought to the forefront the dangers of a worldwide nuclear radiation. The crisis in Japan has been described as 'a nuclear war without a war'. Nuclear radiation, which threatens life on planet earth, is not front page news (Chossudovsky 2012).

This reality speaks to the role and aim of the corporation, intended to serve the public good. As well, nuclear power workers at all levels contribute to the manufacture, stockpiling and use of nuclear weapons, with horrifying results for public health for decades following their use.

The most recent abuse of public health and human rights can be observed in the effects of so-called 'spent uranium' by the US in Iran, and Israel in Palestine (Fisk 2012). As there are no US official findings regarding the horrible fate of the children affected, so too there are no research data regarding the workers who assembled the ammunitions that used spent uranium.

All these facilities have been placed in remote areas that are far from the centres where wealthy white people live and congregate. The single exception may be Japan, a country where few, if any, unpopulated spaces exist, and here the population is largely homogenous. All these operations are inherently risky but corporations are inherently favourable to risk-taking, especially when the risks are eventually borne by others:

> The explosion aboard the Deepwater Horizon in April 2010 began a spill that spewed millions of barrels of British Petroleum Oil into the Gulf of Mexico. BP executives had gambled: skimping on safety increased immediate profits. In this case, they gambled and lost – but the environment and the residents of Louisiana and other Gulf States lost even more (Stiglitz 2012: 189).

Further difficulties are imposed upon these non-intended victims by the fact that large corporations, to a great extent, also control the regulatory bodies. Thus the legal outcomes of many of these disasters are often in their favour. Furthermore, their ability to employ expensive lawyers, who are given almost limitless means to countersue any and all groups daring to question their interpretation of 'the facts', also works in the favour of the corporate bodies (Westra 2012: ch. 6; Scovazzi 1991; Scovazzi 2012; Simons 2012).

Nevertheless, beyond corporate 'deep pockets', the basic disregard for human rights is clearly evident in the North American choice of locations as sites for hazardous operations, or for the ultimate disposal of hazardous waste (Westra and Lawson 2001; Mickelson and Rees 2003; Bullard 2001).

Stiglitz highlights the economic and political power of corporations, thus their connection to centres of power, especially in North America, where the touted 'public interest' orientation, originally intended to motivate corporate activities, is inexorably replaced by 'special interests' (Stiglitz 2012: 191), most often in direct conflict with the interests of citizens both near and far. In Part I, from the three chapters that indicate the causal nexus between corporate activities, government regulations and the influence of banking and loans on the stark division between North and South, it is clear that the shared interest of the harm-imposers is to promote their profit even at the cost of affected individuals.

Their practices, for the most part, enjoy success while the corporations enjoy impunity for the harms they impose, because the majority of the victims, eventually becoming 'refugees', are different, not fellow citizens of the same background, but 'others', viewed as less worthy of respect and consideration than those in the wealthy North who enjoy the profits. Stiglitz concludes this portion of his work, by saying:

> There is something to be said here for criminal prosecution against executives ... In such circumstances, we have to go beyond fining the company: it is people who make decisions and take actions and they should bear the responsibility for their actions (Stiglitz 2012: 205).

As stated in the African Charter, the starting point for a just treatment of human beings is the acceptance of their basic and equal dignity. Furthermore:

> Human dignity appears in the Preamble of the Charter of the United Nations as an ideal that 'we the peoples of the United Nations' are 'determined' to achieve ... the term dignity is also included in Article 1 of the Universal Declaration of Human Rights ... The Helsinki Accords, in Principle VII affirm that the participating states will promote the effective exercise of human rights and freedoms: all of which derive from the inherent dignity of the human person (Schacter 1983: 848).

Dignity refers to the intrinsic worth of all humans and that is what generates respect, as it possesses '... several nuanced meanings: "esteem", "deference", a "proper regard for", "recognition of". These terms have both a subjective aspect (how one thinks or feels about another), and an objective aspect (how one treats another)' (Schacter 1983: 848). Both subjective and objective aspects are foundational to the approach those in power, whether through economic or political organizations, take towards those affected by their operations.

Depriving people of their natural resources, or of a fair wage, or advancing one's interests without considering others' rights to health and safety, all implicitly, but clearly, deny 'esteem', 'deference' or 'a proper regard' for the other. The very recognition of the other as an equal is lacking: and that is the first step before further steps may be taken that lead to the victimization of others. However the denial of the dignity of others is in direct conflict with the International Convention on the Elimination of All Forms of Racial Discrimination (1965).

The Development of Refugee Protection: Discrimination and Politics Against Human Rights

> The experience of persecution during the Second World War and the emergence of human rights and justice as central themes of post-war institutions however had a significant impact on the response of states to victims of persecution. Reflecting the spirit of the age, Article 14(1) of the 1948 Universal declaration of Human Rights provided that 'everyone had the right to seek and enjoy in other countries asylum from persecution' (Betts, Loescher and Milner 2012: 12).

'Seek and enjoy' certainly implies that being an asylum seeker should not consign one to the category of undesirables, perhaps even borderline 'illegals', that appears to define today's asylum seekers, at least until proven otherwise. Nevertheless the initial international concern for refugees was actively opposed by the United States, who preferred the proposed Marshall Plan, that is, providing support to Europe, to a joint commitment with the international community to supply aid (Betts, Loescher and Milner 2012: 13). As well, the UN's policy after 1950 eventually turned toward attacking the Soviet Union and its allies, so that

> International refugee relief operations were curtailed, unilateral initiatives were encouraged, and international organizations unwilling to subordinate themselves to US foreign policy objectives were denied American aid (Betts, Loescher and Milner 2012: 13).

About that time the UNHCR was formed (UNHCR 2011). The UNHCR was established to serve two specific purposes: 'to protect refugees and to find permanent solutions to their plight, either through voluntary repatriation or through their assimilation within new national communities' (Betts, Loescher and Milner 2012: 15).

This mandate reflected the efforts of the US to limit both the authority and the functions of the new entity, as reflected in the Statute of the Office of the United Nations High Commissioner for Refugees (UNGA 1950). Particularly limiting was the original definition of 'refugees', according to the CSR, from the theoretical point of view, which served US and allied interests to 'stigmatize the fledgling Communist regimes as persecutors' while in paragraph 20 of the Statute itself, the UNHCR was clearly being limited in the practical sense, as the only planned financial support was intended for 'administrative expenditures' (Betts, Loescher and Milner 2012: 15).

All other activities were to be financed by voluntary contributions, thus negating the CSR's role as the arm of the UN's infrastructure for the protection of human and humanitarian rights, while reducing its work to that of an optional international 'charity'. The worst limit imposed was the decision of the participating states 'not to grant refugees a right to asylum, notwithstanding the provisions of the 1948 Universal Declaration of Human Rights (Betts, Loescher and Milner 2012: 16).

However, one major right of asylum seekers was respected, the right to '*non-refoulement*', which still remains the foundation of current regulatory regimes dealing with asylum seekers.

At any rate, the High Commissioner could use his authority to expand the role and function of his office to serve refugee needs, using high 'considerable moral authority' and a unique position (Betts, Loescher and Milner 2012: 20) in novel cases that might not fit precisely the CSR's definition. One such example was the presence of mass influx of refugees. The first major such case coincided with the Hungarian crisis of 1956:

> The invasion of Hungary by the Soviet Army precipitated the mass exodus of nearly 200,000 refugees to neighbouring Austria and Yugoslavia (Betts, Loescher and Milner 2012: 22).

The most important change to arise from this event was that High Commissioner August Lindt (1956–1960) argued that it was impossible to determine the status of Hungarian refugees on a case by case basis, during an emergency situation. Thus he approved 'all Hungarians in Austria and Yugoslavia as prima facie refugees' (Betts, Loescher and Milner 2012: 23).

Therefore, at this time, at least two major principles were established as foundational to the situation of mass influx of refugees after the advent of globalization on the one hand, and of climate change on the other. These were the High Commissioner's power to expand somewhat on the strict CSR definition of refugees, and his ability to change the requirement that each case was to be assessed on its own specific merits, a clearly impossible requirement in the case of mass influx of asylum seekers. These two novel additional acceptable mandates joined the right of refugees to *non-refoulement*.

In addition, a newly established 'good offices' formula, granted by the General Assembly, enabled the UNHCR 'to raise funds or to initiate assistance programs', beyond its traditional mandate (Betts, Loescher and Milner 2012: 25). Thus far, all the initiatives were primarily if not exclusively directed to Europeans in need of assistance, but in the mid-1950s, over 700,000 Chinese refugees flooded Hong Kong, desperately needing assistance. In 1957, the General Assembly 'declared the Chinese refugees to be of concern to the international community … without making a determination that the country of origin was persecuting its citizens' (Betts, Loescher and Milner 2012: 25).

Hence a third important principle was established, or at least a precedent was established: the lack of a specific persecutory origin to establish the status of refugees, as well as the extension of the expected geographical area from which refugees should receive assistance. In the 1960s the UNHCR

> … also progressively increased its range of programs for both refugees and host populations and governments. The Office's expansion in the developing world coincided with the growing postcolonial membership of the UN and the

> increasing recognition of the economic and political problems of the third world (Betts, Loescher and Milner 2012: 29).

The developing connection between UNHCR and the effects of the primacy of trade and 'development' that tends to govern the world today shows the importance of the three emerging new aspects of the CSR policies. These new aspects have led the UNHCR to initiate a new cooperation with other agencies, such as the International Labour Organization (ILO), the UN Development Program (UNDP) and others, through which a new emphasis is emerging on assistance to those in developing countries, a new policy indicating a departure from the original CSR mandate.

This new policy was confirmed in 1976 by ECOSOC which identified the objects of that office's concern as 'refugees and displaced persons, victims of man-made disasters, requiring urgent humanitarian assistance' (Betts, Loescher and Milner 2012: 32). In the 1980s the US confronted a grave asylum crisis, due to the arrival of 130,000 Cubans to Florida; 110,000 Haitians and the large number of Iranians, Nicaraguans and Ethiopians (Betts, Loescher and Milner 2012: 35).

Hence, starting from the last decades of the last century, the presence of mass influx of migrants has increasingly been viewed as a threat to the scarce jobs situation present especially in North America.

One of the results of this situation has been the persistence of refugee camps, where even the victims of persecution, that is, those who fit the basic definition of status refugees, continue to languish, awaiting asylum and a real solution to their plight. Often those who are 'contained' in this manner also include those who have been forcibly displaced for various reasons, including the victims of extreme environmental events:

> Western governments today are less interested to accept large numbers of refugees. Instead they are focussed on the need to provide protection and assistance for those displaced within their own communities. Indeed containment would appear to be the hallmark of contemporary refugee policy … (Juss 2006: 153).

At any rate, the 1970s to the early 1980s saw the intrusion of political issues that precluded the successful application of the UNHCR's 'three traditional solutions … (that is) repatriation, local integration and resettlement' (Betts, Loescher and Milner 2012: 39). Funds were easily available, primarily from the US, for the support of such camps, as other, more permanent solutions, appeared less and less viable. However, the fall of the Berlin Wall changed the political landscape especially in Europe, but with the additional collapse of the Soviet Union, the UNHCR was in a position to effect voluntary repatriation for many:

> … up to one million refugees returned to Ethiopia and Eritrea after the change of government in Addis Ababa in 1991. In 1992 and 1993 approximately 370,000 Cambodians repatriated from camps in Thailand … Between 1992 and 1996,

> some 1.7 million Mozambican refugees returned to their homeland from Malawi and other neighbouring states (Betts, Loescher and Milner 2012: 51).

At any rate, the UNHCR was clearly taking steps to expand its mandate and responsibilities to deal with mass influx of refugees, while the new international issues it faced included the increasing number of IDPs, already numbering 24 million by 1992 (Betts, Loescher and Milner 2012: 53; Report of the Representative of the Secretary-General on Internally Displaced Persons 2003). These changes prompted the President of the Security Council to note, in 1992, that

> … the non-military sources of instability in the economic, social, humanitarian and ecological fields have become threats to international peace and security (UN Security Council 1992).

However it was not the presence of pure humanitarian concerns that were driving new security initiatives for the protection of refugees, but the interests, once again, of Western powers (Betts, Loescher and Milner 2012: 59). In fact, the major changes were initiated precisely by Western powers after 2001 and the attacks on the US, events that led to a new phenomenon: the emergence of the so-called 'war on terror' (Westra 2013; Cassese 2006) creating the newly formed confusion between refugees and terrorists:

> Politicians and the media began to portray all border crossers, whether migrants or refugees, as potential terrorists and security threats (Betts, Loescher and Milner 2012: 62).

The 'securitization' of refugees emphasized the already latent racial discrimination present in several decisions informing the development of the UNHCR and its policies. Thus, rather than seeing an incremental expansion of protection and consideration for refugees, as asylum seekers and IDPs, consonant with the ongoing development of the mandate of earlier times, we are faced instead with

> … a series of migration control measures to deter new arrivals, by increasing pre-arrival screening, routinely detaining asylum seekers and deporting refugees to so-called safe third countries … (Betts, Loescher and Milner 2012: 63).

The discriminatory roots of current approaches include the US's treatment of migrants from Mexico and Central and South America. They are particularly obvious as we consider the plights of US supported camps established in Gaza and in the general housing of Palestinian victims of Israeli aggression and colonization, and other forms of ethnic/racial and religious discrimination, which are consonant with the ongoing treatment of persons of Arab origins, also evident in the ongoing presence of 'no-fly' lists, based on names, origins and, at most, allegations.

The Changing Nature of Forced Migrations and the Political Context of the UNHCR

> Significantly, in 1976, only 7 per cent of the UN's 150 Member States viewed their immigration rates as too high; by 1993 the percentage had jumped to 35 per cent – a five-fold increase in less than three decades. Today, 40 per cent of the UN'S 193 Member States have policies aimed at reducing immigration (Bimal 2007: 97).

To support these statistics we can simply review the costs of border control to the '25 richest countries', which amounts to between US$25–30 billion per year (Pecoud and de Guchteneire 2007: 4). The proposed 'scenario' counsels border openness, rather than the ongoing harsh trends in border control, in the context of globalization, and trade openness; and the need for 'new people to produce goods' which the authors believe demand such openness (Pecoud and de Guchteneire 2007: 4–5).

In contrast, I propose to view the desperate efforts, often unsuccessful despite their high costs, to block out refugees as a manifestation of the ongoing presence of racism and discrimination based on ethnic, religious and ideological preferences. The scenario of 'migrations without borders' advocates migrations to be viewed and considered together with immigration. In that case, the distinction between the voluntary and involuntary movement of peoples would be eliminated. In some sense this scenario might be best: it emphasizes human rights in a specific, cosmopolitan sense, as 'individuals are protected on the basis of personhood, not of nationality or citizenship'.

This means that civil society, human rights groups and NGOs can contest government measures, and they have indeed sometimes opposed them in the courts: in other words, control is controlled and states are limited in their initiatives (Pecoud and de Guchteneire 2007: 5).

However the international 'controls', based as they are on timehonoured theory and principle, are still to a great extent subject to economic and other interests of the most powerful nations, especially the US. Of course this point could also be made about the appeal to discrimination's prevention: a *jus cogens* norm that is not always observed by these countries, as their actions and inactions are based upon the goal of solidifying their power and influence, as well as supporting their own ideology. Hence the principles of respect for individual rights, let alone group rights, do not motivate its decisions.

The US was the first country to oppose protests, based on principles and the defence of human rights, such as the Occupy Movement, environmental movements and those who intend to defend social, economic and environmental rights (Westra 2014). Nevertheless, the human right to free movement is a basic right and as such it should be independent of the UNHCR and should not need to be included in the rights protected by that organization.

Despite all the walls erected and the funds expended to control migrations and the influx of refugees, it seems that all measures remain inadequate. These migrations include both voluntary and forced migrations, but it seems wrong to collapse both into one category. It is a misleading approach, as it treats as one the victims of harmful practices and various disasters that give rise to large migrations, and the movements of those who want to migrate because of a legitimate desire to better their lives. Both are, in some sense, voluntary, but the economic incentive of the latter is far from the desperate urgency of the former – whether they are victims of a sinking island state, of a violent weather event, or of an illegal ongoing conflict.

Still, the right to open borders and freedom of movement does not conflict with the present argument. It might be best to continue our brief overview of the history and activities of the UNHCR, particularly as we consider the full range of its responsibility against the background of the expanding refugee situation:

> In addition to its responsibilities for ensuring refugee protection, UNHCR is also mandated to work with States and other actors to ensure that refugees find a solution to their plight. In theory refugee situations should involve not only activities to provide protection for refugees, but initiatives to ensure that refugees do not remain in exile indefinitely (Betts, Loescher and Milner 2012: 86).

The question that arises is just whether UNHCR can actually deliver on its responsibilities, given the increasing problems it faces, not only with the quantity, but also with the quality of refugees, who now include large numbers of 'protracted Refugee situations' (PRS), which means 'refugees who have been in their situation for 5 years or more' (UNHCR 2009: Preamble). In fact, in 2008 it was found that '7.2 million refugees are in protracted situations, representing over two-thirds of the world's refugees' (Betts, Loescher and Milner 2012: 89).

A clear example is the presence of '4 million registered Palestinian refugees in longstanding exile in the Middle East' (these refugees fall under the mandate of the UN Relief and Works Agency) (Betts, Loescher and Milner 2012: 89).

The Statute of the UNHCR expects the organization to engage in humanitarian and non-political activities, but it is clear that its work can only take place in a political context (Betts, Loescher and Milner 2012: 93):

> The causes and consequences of displacement, and responses to refugees and other populations of concern to UNHCR are all intertwined with aspects of politics in different ways (Betts, Loescher and Milner 2012: 93; Betts and Gil 2011).

We noted in Part I that the connection between '*the causes* of human displacement' and the geopolitical situation, including 'great power rivalries, patterns of resource exploitation, and the legacy of colonialism' (Betts, Loescher and Milner 2012: 93), is a major aspect of the refugee situation.

Hence the UNHCR is forced into an involvement in situations it has little or no power to control, and which it is often even unable to control the outcome of, as states most often do not comply with their international legal obligations (Betts, Loescher and Milner 2012: 94). Yet the states that refuse to cooperate with the UNHCR are also the states who prefer to implement their own policies in dealing with refugees (Betts, Loescher and Milner 2012: 95). In addition, as noted, the UNHCR has no independent permanent funding, thus it is dependent on the 'top ten donors' for its operating funds (Betts, Loescher and Milner 2012: 97).[1]

Of all the top donors, the US's contributions are the most considerable (see Figure 7.1), thus ensuring the US dominance of UNHCR's policies.

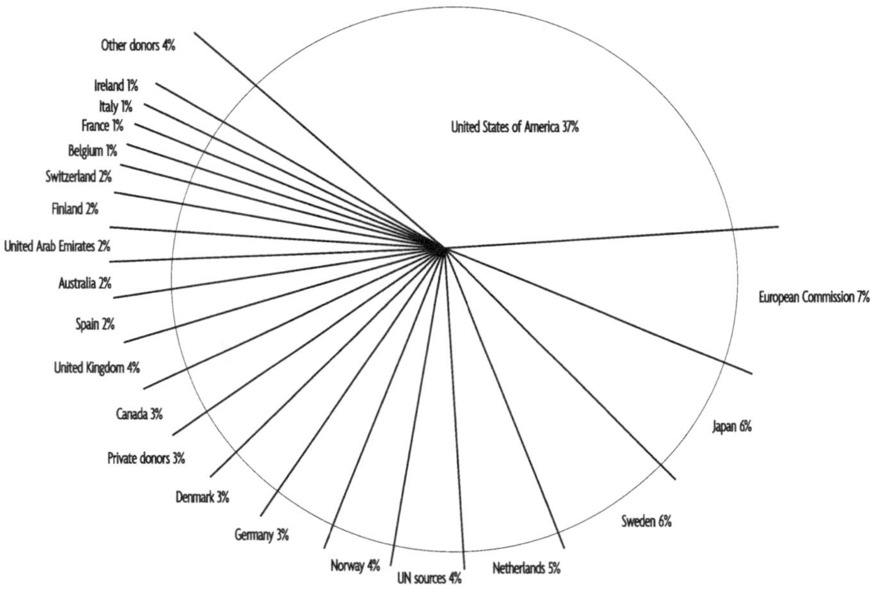

Figure 7.1 Major donors to UNHCR in 2009
Source: UNHCR, *Global Report 2009* (2010: 60)

Hence the UNHCR needs voluntary contributions, it needs to expand its mandate and – most of all – it needs to abide by its own principles and those of the UN, in order to retain its high moral position in the global community. But the political interests of the most powerful states, especially the US, clearly have

1 In 2009 the United States, the European Commission, Japan, Sweden, the Netherlands, Norway, the UK, Germany, Denmark and Canada accounted for 78 per cent of the total budget of the UNHCR.

a disproportionate power to influence policies and outcomes according to states' own interests. These interests, it bears repeating, represent the state's economic advantage, its power and influence and, underlying it all, its basic disrespect for certain 'others', certain ideologies, certain religions and ethnic traditions, not basic human and humanitarian rights.

Although the political impediments are probably the most serious ones encountered by the UNHCR, there are others that have undermined both its authority and its ability to pursue its important goals. For instance, as stated in the first paragraph of its Statute (UNGA 1950: ch. 1, para. l), the UNHCR must operate under the authority of the General Assembly, that is, it must report annually to the Economic and Social Council (ECOSOC), and its activities must be approved by both organizations. Further, its mandate was originally set for three years, renewable since 1950. It was only in 2003 that the General Assembly

> passed a resolution that finally removed the temporal limitation on the continuation of UNHCR and confirmed the office as a program of the UN ... until the refugee problem is solved (Betts, Loescher and Milner 2012: 106; UNGA 2003).

Nevertheless, the UNHCR is facing and in fact accepting new challenges, arising from current trends in world politics:

> The causes and consequences of forced migrations and the responses it requires are closely related to broader trends in the international system. 'Mega Trends' such as climate change, international migrations, urbanization, food insecurity, state fragility, terrorism, and the changing nature of conflict, all shape the context of the UNHCR's work challenging it to re-think both who is in need of international protection, and how best to protect and assist those people (Betts, Loescher and Milner 2012: 133).

The next section considers some of the new, expanding activities of the UNHCR, prompted by the new 'clients' with whom it must deal, such as IDPs, the victims of environmental displacement and other natural disasters, and the refugees forced, due to multiple causes, to move to urban centres.

Refugees, Displaced, Rejected: From Africa to Palestine, from Melia to Lampedusa

> The world of exile legislation on refugees (as individuals) or stateless minorities (as collectives) applied categories of identity that arose from the rejection that these individuals experienced from the nation state. The creation of the stateless meant recognizing the nation state's inability to integrate these individuals and groups, from the double standpoint of protection (legal, security, social) and recognition (political rights) (Agier 2012: 16).

We noted the discriminatory intent that underlies the very generation of refugees, IDPs and asylum seekers, even in the case of officially designated sources for their protection. As they are no longer living in the territory that has defined their identity in the past, they lose to a great extent what they are as a people. Agier refers to that as 'the problematic of a dispersed people in search of a state territory' (Agier 2012: 16), which, however, seems to eliminate the difference between land-based Indigenous communities and others.

Without diminishing the plight of those he terms 'displaced, rejected', I am not sure that territoriality is indispensable to establish or retain one's political and cultural identity: one of the states that has most contributed to create refugees and asylum seekers is the Zionist state of Israel. Its citizens claim the *right* to citizenship in what amounts to stolen lands, although they originate primarily from various European countries, each with its own culture and traditions.

In contrast, land-based Indigenous communities indeed have a legal and moral right to their own cultural integrity, which is closely tied to their environment, that is, the geographical locations of their lands, with traditional and religious ties to their specific ethnicity (Westra 2007: ch. 2). Hence it seems simplistic to ascribe the same need for a territorial component for their 'communal identity', for all other displaced persons. Most of the time migrants do retain their religious and ethnic traditions, perhaps they do so more freely in some countries, like Canada, less so in others, like the US. But, it must be admitted, the retention of one's cultural traditions is only enjoyed by those who are accepted and welcomed, mostly those corning from European countries.

The UNHCR is the highest authority for asylum seekers, but we have noted the various subtle and not so subtle pressures applied to that institution, intended to politicize its work, in direct conflict with its purely humanitarian, non-political mandate, originating from the United Nations. Essentially, those who are desperately seeking help – refugees, displaced, asylum seekers, in general considered 'illegals' – are asking for security, starting with their right to life, but their situation is, for the most part, viewed as a police question, a question of public order (Agier 2012: 17). They are displaced and expelled, and their condition is one of 'human superfluity',

> … in the sense in which total dehumanization (i.e. the suppression of life) is already historically and politically prepared by the suppression of rights (Agier 2012: 18).

They are the 'undesirable', and the great number of those who need to be 'managed' include 'around 50 million persons [who] are qualified by the UNHCR as "victims of forced displacement"' (Agier 2012: 19). They include 4 million Palestinians, and 'between 25 and 30 million [who] … are internally displaced persons (IDPs) (Agier 2012: 19).[2]

There is no desire to welcome or assist these people to help them remake their lives, although some European countries (especially Sweden, the Netherlands and Germany) have given asylum to many. But the main effort by the UNHCR has been to allocate funds to 'externalization', that is, to accommodate and control all those refugees and others who are the result of globalization practices, and those who are the result of 'a new form of war, conceived as a police operation on a world scale', which promoted the reversal of the rights of refugees (Agier 2012: 21).

The UNHCR is and has been the only higher authority to which refugees can appeal; but even in European countries, the arrival of asylum seekers was not greeted with interest and concern, they were at best 'tolerated', as was the case with Chechen refugees in Poland, while in France, in 2008, illegals were termed 'retenus' (retained), if not 'detained' in special centres of 'administrative detention' for up to 18 months (Agier 2012: 22). In fact, the agents whose work was intended to assist their agencies to determine the reasons for the flight of asylum seekers, as well as their specific conditions, conducted their activities, including 'limited time for face-to-face interviews, … incomprehension due to translation and cultural gaps' (Agier 2012: 23), with quite another goal in mind:

> … it is well known how the agents of OFPRA in France have personal quotas of rejection to attain, in the absence of which they risk non-renewal of their one-years contracts! But this constraint … actually generalizes the reversal of procedural logic that has taken place: on the one hand, arbitrary rates of rejection of asylum requests can be seen in many other countries European and American, on the other hand, whatever the particular case, the procedure consists in an examination taking between a few minutes and a few hours by officials who have only local means of investigation (Agier 2012: 23).

Hence, based on these observations and on comparable studies in other European countries, the procedure of evaluation of asylum seekers seems to aim to meet the requirements of a public policy (Valluy 2005: 23), resulting in Europe in a rejection rate of over 90 per cent. A similar situation occurs routinely in Colombia regarding the 'desplazados', displaced by war, thus technically IDPs, and in Australia with the well-known Tampa case.

For refugees, the right not to be returned is well-established in international law, and this fact supports the position of all asylum seekers. Goodwin-Gill states:

> … one of the measures employed by States to:
> (i) prevent embarkation of persons on an international journey;

2 The Palestinian refugees have been managed since 1948 by the United Nations Relief and Work Agency for Palestinian Refugees (UNRWA).

> (ii) prevent further onward international travel by persons who have commenced their journey; or
> (iii) assert control of vessels where there are reasonable grounds to believe the vessel is transporting persons contrary to international or national maritime law;
> where in relations to the above, the person or persons do not have the required documentation or valid permission to enter (UNHCR 2003).
> … is their practice of interception at sea of any vessel suspected of carrying migrants before it can reach the country intended (Goodwin-Gill 1996).

Other interception practices include the imposition of sanctions on carriers that attempt to carry refugees who are improperly documented (European Union Council 2001). This is another manoeuvre often practised in order to avoid 'asylum overload' (Brewer and Kumin 2003: 11). The practice of 'maritime interception', or 'interdiction' is often based on the same rationale. The US intercepts vessels coming from the Caribbean, and Australia, those originating from Indonesia; other countries such as Greece, Italy, Malaysia, Spain and Turkey practise interception both on their contiguous waters and on the high seas. Often interceptions are carried out disguised as 'anti-smuggling' or 'anti-trafficking' operations.

Essentially,

> The security strategy of considering every refugee as a policing problem, removed any hope of citizenship, and reduced them to a stigmatized identity that was reinforced by every police act of rejection (Agier 2012: 27).

No matter what the reasons for the departure of migrants, refugees, asylum seekers or IDPs, they are not respected as human beings, possessed of rights; they are for the most part viewed as encumbrances, undesirables, and they are eventually 'imprisoned outdoors' in refugee camps (Agier 2012: 46–59). Those who are victims of conflict situations are least likely to fit within the official categories that might 'gain' them a place in one of the storage units that are refugee camps, the specific 'spaces of confinement' (Agier 2012: 39), a situation many others can't even aspire to achieve.

The defining characteristic of these refugees is the causal link between the activities that created the situation that forced their flight. In contrast, too many others – IDPs and others – are the victims of legal activities such as those described in Chapters 2 and 3. Those victims are not clearly recognized as refugees or asylum seekers, and there is no jurisprudence on their cases, although in 2014 there has been one exception: the first successful case of a climate refugee.

Climate Refugees: The Undeniable Causal Connection and the Courts

> A Tuvalu family has been granted New Zealand residence after claiming it would be affected by climate change if it returned home. It is the first successful

> application for residence on humanitarian grounds in which climate change has featured, but the Immigration and Protection Tribunal said the family had strong ties to New Zealand (Maas 2014).

When we consider climate refugees we have an anomalous situation compared to other causes of forced displacement: on the one hand, what causes the flight is clear and obvious, as is the human responsibility for the problem, in a general way (a responsibility that does not include activity by those affected); on the other hand, only in certain specific circumstances does the usual racial motivation for which we have argued emerge. The most obvious case is that of the Inuit, so that such environmental cases are actually quite close to the letter and the intent of the CSR, albeit with the infliction of newer and specific forms of persecution (which have not been fully defined).

However, in the Inuits' case, there is no question of deliberate choice or intent on the part of those contributing to the conditions in the Arctic, but only one of negligence, together with the denial of the Inuits' dignity as human beings, and the respect due to those populations.

> The first form of disenfranchisement within the scope of refugee law is that based on race. While the drafters of the Convention did not specifically define the term, the historical context makes clear that the intent was to include those Jewish victims of Nazism who had been persecuted because of their ethnicity, whether or not they actively practiced their religion (Hathaway 1991: 141).

Racial and ethnic backgrounds are most often the basis for the persecution of large groups (Goodwin-Gill 1996: 43; Grahl-Madsen 1966: 217–18). Recent history provides a number of examples, such as those of Rwanda or Darfur. Indigenous groups are – almost by definition – distinct communities, identifiable as visible minorities, and belonging to separate ethnic groups, not to be confused with the majority of a country's citizens. And herein lies the most difficult aspect of treating refugees and IDPs as groups possessing, for the most part similar problems and similar goals for the solutions for those problems.

For instance, if we consider the problem of apartheid in South Africa or of racial discrimination in the US (Bullard 2001), we notice that in these cases, the persons involved were suffering because they were treated in a substantially different way than other citizens, who were white. Their aim was to regain equality with the other, dominant, racial majority. Parity was (and is) sought in housing, schooling, health care and, very often, in environmental exposures. Bill Clinton's Executive Order 12898 of 11 February 1994 (EPA 1994) is a case in point: the same prompt assistance to communities of colour that it used to provide to white communities. So, equality is the aim of racial minorities, vis-à-vis a different racial majority.

But the case of Indigenous peoples is completely different: protection in their case, cannot mean simple equality, as that would also imply assimilation: if successful that approach eventually eliminates them as a people. Hence the difficult problem that arises: how to ask for international protection on the basis of racial discrimination, on the one hand, yet to demand special treatment, consonant with the group's *sui generis* status, on the other.

The recent Inuit Petition presented to the US Supreme Court, and Spearheaded by Sheila Watt-Cloutier, is a case in point (Petition to the Inter American Commission on Human Rights Seeking Relief from Violations Resulting from Global Warming Caused by Acts and Omissions of the United States).[3] The Inuit of the Circumpolar Conference, ably represented by several lawyers including James Anaya, argued that they had been unfairly targeted, because of their ethnicity and the unique relationship to their territories, as the latter increasingly succumbed to global warming.

The Inuit are by no means the only population affected by climate change. But the citizens of coastal cities, Sub-Saharan Africa island states and other affected locations may find the conditions of their lives becoming brutally harsh, but not all of them are in the position of losing entirely their existence *as peoples*, if they could be helped to relocate, the way the Inuit are.

Their existence can be supported and re-established elsewhere in most cases. The different status of Indigenous peoples is revealed by considering other regions and continents, such as the Pygmies of Congo, or the former inhabitants of Chagos, in the Indian Ocean, and most other Aboriginal communities (Westra 2006: ch. 6). The Inuits are presently presenting once again their plight to the European Court of Human Rights, requesting redress under CERD (International Convention on the Elimination of All Forms of Racial Discrimination (1965)). Their argument is not that the conditions of their lives are becoming increasingly intolerable, and therefore they seek refuge elsewhere, to seek a better life. They are essentially saying that those who impose the intolerable conditions must cease and desist, that those activities are in breach of major human rights instruments, hence they should be punished, and ought to be forced to offer compensation and mitigation for the present circumstances of the Circumpolar peoples.

This is probably the best approach to the problem of all IDPs (and environmental refugees), but it is absolutely necessary for Indigenous peoples. The whole Earth is presently affected by both climate change and various industrial toxic exposures. Even if it were feasible, moving populations from one site to another would be difficult at present, and probably impossible in the future. Analogously populations moving westward at the time of the arrival of the first Europeans in North and South America eventually had no place to which to migrate, there was no territory left to conquer and colonize.

Hence, the threats presented by climate change and toxic industrial exposures have rendered most of the Earth hazardous to all life, including humans. Mitigation is possible only in wealthy nations, and that will simply postpone the inevitable,

---

3 Submitted 7 December 2005, see http://earthjustice.org/sites/default/files/library/legal_docs/petition-to-the-inter-american-commission-on-human-rights-on-behalf-of-the-inuit-circumpolar-conference.pdf (accessed 28 January 2015).

ongoing ecological collapse. But for Indigenous peoples, living on and off the land and water, the present hazardous conditions, imposed by so-called 'development', represent a form of biological genocide (Lamkin 1944). Also, perhaps they could be termed conditions of persecution, imposed because of the vulnerability of these peoples, based on their ethnicity, which precludes equal access to the centres of power, a problem we will return to in the Epilogue.

For now we need to focus on the role of 'race' once again. On the one hand, Indigenous groups may join with other refugee groups pleading a well-founded fear of persecution on the grounds of race. On the other, they must demand special treatment, special protection precisely on the basis of their race and ethnicity, which render their situation unlike that of any other group of refugee or IDPs. They key concept in their case is that of the environment, and their relationship to it.

That relationship is more direct and more necessary than that of other groups, and as well provides the basis for their uniqueness, their special ethnicity and their 'cultural integrity'. Theirs is not simply a valuable historical situation of academic interest to some scholars. It represents the basis of a respectful interaction with the Earth that most modern citizens of other communities can no longer sustain (Westra 2006: ch. 9; Earth Charter 2000).

That said, it is clear that Indigenous peoples represent far more than a tradition in our past history. They also indicate and instantiate in their traditional cultures the principles upon which the future of humanity must be based. To disrespect, let alone persecute, those who proudly live that specific ethnicity and culture is not only to impose irreparable harm on aboriginal communities, but also to ignore at our own grave risk the lessons we should learn to help us protect and ensure our future (Westra 2006; Westra 2007).

The original drafters of the Convention and of the UNHCR certainly did not have Indigenous peoples in mind, as Hathaway clearly indicates (Hathaway 1991). He cites their recommended definition as follows:

> Race, in the present connexion has to be understood in its widest sense to include all kinds of ethnic groups that are referred to as 'races' in common usage. Frequently it will entail membership of a specific social group of common descent forming a minority within a larger population (UNHCR 1979).

Then, he adds:

> This UNHCR-derived interpretation has been explicitly adopted into Canadian law in a series of decisions, commencing with *Boleslaw Dytlow*, as well as immigration policy guidelines. The relevant case law has equated race with ethnic background (*Pierre Katanku Tshiabut Tshibola* 1985), 'heritage' (*Ganganee Janet Permanand* 1967), and 'distinct minority' status (*Boleslaw Dytlow* 1987; Hathaway 1991: 142).

Yet the situation of the Tuvalu family is significantly different: it is simply evidence of a widespread negligence on the part of those who have been termed 'the 1 per cent' (Stiglitz 2012), or those whose connection to corporate interests is so intimate that no other moral or justice-related consideration interferes with the pursuit of their interests.

However, one can argue that to proceed with activities of one's choice with total disregard for the rights, and the very humanity of those who will be negatively affected by such activities is even worse than to act in a way that is deliberately discriminatory toward a specific ethnic group. The latter is a position that, minimally, accepts the existence of a group, a community, as a real entity, actual human beings, hated or despised perhaps, but a real presence nonetheless.

In contrast, those who continue to practise whatever is in their interest with full knowledge of the consequences that will ensue view those who are eventually harmed as unworthy of consideration, at most as impediments to the achievement of one's goals, at worst as non-entities. Perhaps this is not part of the definition of discrimination in international law instruments, but it represents a reality that grounds the attitude that allows the victimization of people, many of whom suffer the ultimate indignity of becoming asylum seekers (Ratner, Abrams and Bischoff 2009: 126).[4]

The clearest example of discriminatory disregard for climate change refugees played itself out in front of the whole world, after Hurricane Katrina struck New Orleans, a country which promoted itself as the richest country and the one with most freedom and respect for human rights. In contrast, its own citizens, African-Americans for the most part, were neglected, ignored and even mistreated when they became IDPs, refugees in their own country. The government officials of Louisiana did not ensure that the city would be protected from the increasing threat of climate change, preferring to listen to climate change deniers, thus to protect business interests instead.

Those interests and that very attitude are and have been more than 'business first', they were and are inherently racist, given the general composition of the most affected citizens of that area of Louisiana. Racism, however, is not always so evident in environmental refugees' cases; as noted above, in a general sense, the activities causative of climate disasters tend to ignore not only the rights, but the very existence, the simple humanity of whole nations and populations that will suffer the consequences.

Ioane Teitiota moved to New Zealand with his family in 2007, but despite numerous appeals to the courts, he had no legal status there until 2009. His two children, aged 3 and 5, were born in New Zealand and he was employed as a maintenance worker for a fast food chain – his work visa application had

4 The 1966 Racial Discrimination Convention defines, in Article 1, racial discrimination as 'any distinction, exclusion, restriction or preference based on race, colour, descent, or national or ethnic origin that denies equal enjoyment of human rights'.

been rejected repeatedly, so he could not practise his profession as a teacher (Marks 2014).

Thus his situation is unusual, despite the fact that his circumstances reflect a danger that is all too real for many populations of low-lying island and coastal areas. Justice John Priestly, who ruled in this case, noted that there are millions of people who face the immediate and medium-term consequences of extreme weather events who might qualify as climate refugees. This situation appears impossible to rectify at this time. But, it must be emphasized, this situation does not reflect discriminatory intent or negligence directed against a specific population: it fits instead the model of activities harming those considered both negligible and undesirable in general.

Perhaps the general, dehumanizing characteristic they all share might be that of belonging to the impoverished masses of the world, as the wealthy are not affected in the same manner. For instance, sea rises in the Netherlands do not generate effects similar to those occurring in Tuvalu or in New Orleans. Thus we can conclude that in the case of climate change refugees, the activities that force the displacement, seem to be based more on class lines than they are on race and ethnicity. However, since the world's povertystricken peoples tend to reflect racial and ethnic aspects, perhaps even this distinction remains somewhat blurred.

At any rate, as we saw, the UNHCR has expanded its protection beyond the refugees who fit the CSR definition, and has certainly included IDPs within its purview. It is difficult to separate climate or environmental refugees from other categories and, in most cases, they remain within the country of origin; unfortunately the considerable funds necessary for the assistance required are not easily found and no specific organization is charged with their support (Juss 2006: 177). The inability of states to fulfil their obligation to those who are affected by major climate events is not surprising, given that the events that are causative of those events are not the result of actions by the same states.

The Commissioner for Human Rights ought to be monitoring the protection of human rights in states that, although they have assumed international obligations, 'are not prepared to submit to international judicial scrutiny' (Cassese 2006: 388). As noted, the UNHCR deals with highly sensitive political issues, although its humanitarian work is not expected to deal with such issues. Hence the High Commissioner's main function is 'to play an active role … in preventing the continuation of human rights violations throughout the world (Cassese 2006: 388).

However, that role does not include taking an accusatory approach,

> … as they prefer not to engage in the attribution of responsibility to individual governments. Rather they opt for public exposure and pressure (Cassese 2006: 388).

This approach reduces the eventual responsibility of states to a voluntary one, and we are well aware of the largely non-existent response to problems that this approach generates. Consider for instance corporate voluntary 'compliance' to the expectation of human rights protection in its operations, especially when they take place in the third world (Ratner 2001; Ruggie 2007).

At any rate, nothing in the treatment (or the generation) of climate/environmental refugees disproves the presence of racial or ethnic bias that I have proposed as basic to all situations that involve asylum seekers or IDPs. This bias is even more obvious as we consider the existence of 'camps' as the ongoing 'solution' to the mass influx of refugees today.

Discrimination after Arrival and the Role and Background of Refugee Camps

> The calamity of the rightless is not that they are deprived of life, liberty and the pursuit of happiness, or of equality before the law and freedom of opinion – formulas which were designed to solve problems within given communities – but they no longer belong to any community whatsoever (Arendt 1966: 295–6).

New arrivals, whether by land or by sea, especially when they are part of a mass influx, are for the most part directed to some camp, perhaps intended as a temporary measure but, most often, as at least a semi-permanent 'solution', under an unyielding regime of exceptionalism, especially after 9/11 (Lipset 1996). As Agier remarks,

> The experience of refugees literally underlies the question of what human rights people effectively have access to if they lose the use of their national citizenship? (Agier 2012: 149)

One needs to consider some aspects of the history of camps and their operation, in order to understand fully the extreme exclusion they represent. Refugee camps have a long history in the twentieth century, starting with the 'concentration camps' initially connected with colonial occupation, hence based precisely on racial/ethnic discrimination on the part of the colonizers toward the population of the occupied territories. Not only were the victims of the occupations the first to be consigned to concentration camps, but it was also the most vulnerable among them who were first confined: the women and the children.

> The English term 'concentration camp' was first used to describe camps operated by the British in South Africa during this conflict. The camps had originally been setup by the British Army as 'refugee camps' to provide refuge for civilian families who had been forced to abandon their homes for one or other reason related to war ('Second Boer War').

Thus the British initiated the ongoing tradition of forcibly moving women and children to concentration camps. To add to the injury of forcible removal from their homes, their practice included the 'Scorched Earth Policy', or the systemic destruction of crops and slaughtering of their livestock, as well as 'the poisoning of wells and salting of fields'. These 'refugees' were interned either in black or in white camps ('Second Boer War'). Eventually, '[o]ver 26,000 women and children were to perish in these concentration camps' ('Second Boer War').

The conditions in the camps were brutal; and the health of the children suffered greatly, because 'poor hygiene' and malnutrition were rampant. The wives and children of the men who were still fighting, received reduced rations of food, compared to those given to the wives and children of those who did not fight. In addition, due to poor shelter and living conditions, contagious diseases such as 'measles, typhoid and dysentery' affected especially the camp children, who mostly perished as medical supplies and facilities were also limited.

One British woman, Emily Hobhouse, tried to change the appalling conditions in the camps, by reporting them in England, but she was viewed as a 'troublemaker' and a 'sympathizer' for the enemy by the conservatives in power. In fact, these latter attempted to convince the public that the 'interned Boers were "contented and comfortable"' ('Second Boer War'). Hobhouse wrote a report which she published in June 1901 to contradict the government's claims, describing the government's 'policy of extermination directed against the Boer population', as the death rates in the camps were particularly high for the children ('Second Boer War'):

> A report after the war concluded that 27,927 Boers (of whom 24,074 (50% of the Boer child population) were children under 16), had died of starvation, disease and exposure in concentration camps. In all, about one in four (25%) of the Boer inmates, mostly children, died ('Second Boer War').

The very need for international intervention in refugee issues depends on the actions of the state involved. There is the state from which the person or group is fleeing, and the responsibility they may bear for allowing, or not mitigating, the conditions that make life unlivable for individuals and groups, in various ways. Then there is the state at which the individuals or groups first arrive on the way to their desired destination. Finally there is the state they are attempting to reach.

Even at their final destination refugees may be detained, put in special camps or held in various jail-like receiving areas:

> Most disturbingly, asylum seekers can be detained for failing to arrive with the necessary travel documents, and can remain in detention for the entire length of the asylum process. And while many states have established special holding centres for asylum seekers and irregular migrants, in other countries they are detained in regular jails, alongside common criminals (UNHCR 2006: 43).

Hathaway and Neve's lengthy study of the realities of the refugees' situation clearly demonstrates the urgent need for reform (Hathaway and Neve 1997).

In 2000, the UN enacted a Protocol against trafficking in persons (Protocol to Prevent, Suppress and Punish Trafficking in Persons 2000), which is intent upon criminalizing those who extort large sums from desperate refugees for their passage to Europe. These traffickers do not expect the presence of appropriate travel documents from the 'clients'. No doubt that is a crime. But they do not 'sell' their passage seekers to anyone, and even if this 'service' were to be eliminated, it is unclear what the UN proposes in its place to offer refuge and safety to those who cannot find either on their home lands: at best this protocol is necessary, but it is certainly not sufficient to eliminate the mounting numbers of asylum seekers, as those who *cause* the unlivable conditions that necessitate the flight remain unnamed and unpunished.

Refugees' situations have not changed much in the last 200 years. Beyond the ugly origin of concentration camps, there has also been the existence of the infamous Nazi concentration camps, which were the prelude to a barbaric death for their inmates. The extreme exceptionalism of Hitler's Germany is somewhat diluted in the current camps, but the fact remains that research from the late 1990s can speak of 'janus-faced humanitarianism' (Agier 2012: 83), as the 'public face' does not always compare with the reality on the ground. The UNHCR is indeed a part of the UN and a representative of the international community yet, together with representatives of NGOs, such as the Lutheran World Federation, their camps in Africa were a sad example of what humanitarian protection should *not* be. That NGO had a representative in the camp, responsible for distributing goods, food and other necessities to the new arrivals, who came in dire need of assistance, tired, hungry and often sick (Agier 2012: 82). This example refers to the Makeba camp in Zambia.

The representative had substantive power over the camp inhabitants because of over 20 years' service in that capacity. His power included the right to decide which refugees could stay together, who was treated well, and who was deprived of any rights that might be available to the inmates of the encampment. Without supervision, both greed, brutality and sexual attacks went unpunished:

> The refugee camps are not zones of non-rights but rather zones of exceptional rights and power where everything seems possible for those in control (Agier 2012: 82).

In this case, other volunteers from Médecins Sans Frontières and the Jesuit Refugee Service alerted the UNHCR of the abuses, which included illegal disposal of food and money. But no legal action was ever taken, although both the man in charge and others responsible admitted their responsibility, and left or resigned. In addition though, all funding and aid available to the UNHCR

> is strictly conditional on their segregation in camps, which is contrary to the 1951 Geneva Convention on refugees (Agier 2012: 84).

Hence, we can conclude that despite the commitment to 'integration in the host country, resettlement in a third country or repatriation', what actually happens most of the time, especially outside of Europe, is long-term 'encampment [which] really is the UNHCR fourth solution' (Agier 2012: 84). Clearly, one example does not characterize the operations of all UNHCR camps. But what remains constant is the lack of any applicable law and monitoring, in what remains an exceptional situation, that is, the encampment is a place where neither are the inmates citizens of the country where the camp is located, thus subject to that country's laws, nor do they enjoy the rights due to the citizenship of their country of origin. What is left is international law and the protection of humanitarian and human rights instruments, at best.

Racism from Ferguson, MO and the Mexico/US Border Wall, to the Wall in Israel and the 'Protective Edge' Operation in Gaza

> While … [a] state-centred model has been eroded in international criminal law developments that eliminate the state action requirements, nationality remains central to personal identity within the international system (Castellino 2008: 504).

Castellino's position echoes that of Juss regarding the importance of citizenship (Juss 2006), or rather its lack, in the case of refugees (Agier 2012: 183–90). The discriminatory intent is clear when certain 'citizens' are routinely allowed to take the law into their own hands. In many ways, the ongoing illegality and criminality in Israel and its apartheid wall is vastly different from the hidden but equally ongoing racism prevailing in the US: the former is in a position of illegality from the start, given its occupation of territory and non-response to UN demands in several of its resolutions.

However, US racism is visible and obvious in the Mexico/US border wall, and it also obvious in the conduct of recent wars and in the conduct of counter-terrorism campaigns, especially but not exclusively after 9/11 (Westra 2012). It also manifests itself in its complicity with Israel's policies, which are completely at odds not only with international law, but also with the US Constitution itself.

From the standpoint of asylum seekers, we saw the hidden interests that controlled and directed the economics of the only official authority whose task is and was the protection of refugees, not the advancement of donors interests, that is, the UNHCR.

The prevailing 'us' and 'them' approach to others' ethnicity, religion or ideology is what underlies all policies and decisions taken on behalf of the US, and a brief overview of current events confirms this analysis.

In 2012 we saw in Florida an unarmed African-American boy, Trayvon Martin, killed in an 'enclosed' white development, where he had come simply to look around. The vigilante who shot him was absolved by US courts, despite President Obama's own words: 'he could have been me'. Possibly the policeman who shot more than six times Michael Brown in Ferguson, MO will not be so lucky. This time, rather than a generally approving mainly white populace, the Missouri crime was met with protests, first peaceful, then erupting into violence, by the two-thirds majority of African-American citizens in that state (Zagier 2014).

The resulting outrage continued, although the White House stepped in with an unprecedented federal autopsy, followed by the arrival in Ferguson of the US Attorney General, Eric Holder (Zagier 2014). The episode was widely reported in the international media, and *The Guardian* published a particularly powerful piece:

> We've had enough of the police brutality, of the colorblind mythologies and post-racial rhetoric, of the sweet-talk; of the calls for non-violence; of mass incarceration and systemic poverty, of trigger-happy cops and crying black mothers …. Dr. Martin Luther King jr said in 1968: 'A riot is the language of the unheard'. Today, nearly 50 years later, black America demands to not only be heard, but heeded by any means necessary (Fort 2014).

The connection between police power and illegality is noted by Yuli Tamir, in the case of the Israeli forces:

> In a normal country, criminals and security forces are on opposite sides of the fence and do not coordinate their activities (Tamir 2003).

In both cases, right and justice are and have been on the side of the victims, whereas the so-called 'forces of order' were acting both illegally and with criminal intent, particularly in the case of Israel. Brown argues that although the 'Israeli case is indeed extreme':

> … this kind of coordination has become increasingly 'normal' at the site of walls, where the familiar binaries of law/lawlessness, inside/outside, and military/civilian do not hold (Brown 2010: 85).

The Israeli case is particularly troubling as it is part of an ongoing policy of apartheid practised with impunity, supported by powerful lobbies intent on vilifying and attacking those who dare to cite facts and criticize those policies, including the UN Rapporteurs (Richard Goldstone and, more recently, William Schabas). These practices have been noted by Desmond Tutu ('Desmond Tutu Likens Gaza Crisis to Apartheid', *Daily Star* 2014), and Richard Falk's plea has been signed on by legal scholars worldwide, and a further plea by philosophers and political scholars, also signed on by many worldwide asking for boycott, divestment and non-cooperation with Israeli academics.

Finally Israel and the US have joined together to put pressure on the ICC, an organization created in 1998 precisely to eliminate impunity, demanding that it continue to turn a blind eye to the international crimes committed in Gaza in 2014 (Borger 2014). Such an inquiry could also bring attention to the ongoing abuse of refugees in the open air concentration camp that is Gaza.

Both these crimes and the refugee situation are quite distinct and different from what takes place in the US: what connects the two are the loud claims of democratic governance and respect for human rights in both countries, coupled with the reality of deeply embedded racism and the belief in their own exceptionalism. One cannot deny the great work and the heroism of the US Civil Rights movement (Westra 2014: ch. 2), but the latest occurrences place even those great undertakings in peril.

We started this work with a discussion of walls, starting with Israel's apartheid wall, and the US/Mexico border wall. What underlies both is a deep discriminatory intent that is echoed in the treatment of populations in the many encampments intended at first as places of temporary refuge, but eventually becoming, all too often, their final ongoing holding places, where a permanent state of exception reigns. In fact, aside from the presence of discrimination, both enclosures and walls indicate the presence of another basic and dangerous situation: the blurring between the actions of the forces of law and those of illegality.

Particularly obvious is the 'Israeli Defense Forces' protection of illegal Israeli settlements and settler aggression against their Palestinian neighbours' (Brown 2010: 85). These circumstances persist, together with Israel's illegality and the right to self-defence on the part of the Palestinians attempting to achieve self-determination:

> If the history of camps displays on a world scale a control of movements and a distancing of certain populations treated differently, most often foreigners – if it thus displays a *police* mentality of confinement and separation – today's humanitarian organizations have made a specialty for themselves of 'managing' these spaces and populations apart (Agier 2012: 4).

Populations Apart in a New Land: A Goal Achieved?

> … 'multiculturalism' is a policy of supporting polyethnicity within the national institutions of the English and the French cultures. Since 'multicultural' invites this sort of confusion, I will use the terms 'multinational' and 'polyethnic' to refer to the two forms of cultural pluralism (Kymlicka 1997: 17).

This clarification helps to define the state's relation with the new groups of arrivals and their status within it. Kymlicka refers primarily to the situation in Canada, a country which is already home to diverse ethnicities: English, French and its First Nations. But, although today many countries contain different ethnic groups, not all are prepared to accept with equal respect polyethnicity and the related multiculturalism, where the latter is understood as something that 'arises from national and ethnic differences' as Kymlicka understands it. He adds,

> … a 'culture' as synonymous with a nation or a 'people', that is as an intergenerational community, more or less institutionally complete, occupying a

> given territory or homeland, sharing a distinct language and history (Kymlicka 1997: 18).

In contrast, the current US usage of referring to multiculturalism as an approach that includes different groups such as 'the disabled, gays and lesbians, women' (Kymlicka 1997: 18) and others is quite different from the terminology that will be used here, following Kymlicka, instead. In fact, the United States has a long history of ignoring the cultural dimensions of its own first native inhabitants, that is, the people who were displaced by European immigrants.

At least on paper, and even most often in the courts, the Canadian aboriginals fare much better, as they are defined as First Nations, and the Canadian courts tend to decide on the side of the FNs *sui generis* rights, and the 'fiduciary duty' of the Crown in their regard (*R. v. Sparrow* 1990; *R. v. Van der Peet* 1996; *Delgamuukw v. British Columbia* 1997; Westra 2007: ch. 6).

In contrast, although much of the cultural diversity of the 'New World' originates from immigration from the 'Old World', and even aside from the presence of American Indians, the United States does not encourage, or perhaps even recognize as equal, other cultures, because of their own insistence on the value of a 'melting pot' approach instead. It seems that this position

> … reflects and perpetuates a long history of denying the rights, even the very existence of national minorities throughout North and South America on the ground that these countries are 'immigrant countries' (Kymlicka 1997: 21).

The UN wanted to protect minorities (ICCPR, Article 27), but countries such as the US, Brazil, New Zealand and Australia insisted that Article 27 only applied to countries where minorities existed, and therefore did not apply to them (Kymlicka 1997: 21). Europeans shared some of these feelings, that is, considering Indigenous peoples as 'subject races', thus considering themselves superior to other cultures. In Europe the case of the Roma is particularly obvious, especially in France, whereas countries like Belgium and Switzerland accept and respect the different ethnicities that comprise them.

But this acceptance contrasts clearly with the virtual walls that separate minorities from the mainstream. We saw that these 'walls' are particularly strong in the case of African-Americans in the US, long after the institutionalized and enforced racism of overt discrimination, segregated schools and public places, and Jim Crow laws dominated the relations between white and black (Black 1960; Blank 2007; Rustin 2003).

At any rate, adopting a polyethnic model of citizenship does not necessarily lead to 'the tribalization of society, and the loss of a common identity' (Kymlicka 1997: 179), it promotes integration with respect and equality, rather than fostering a demand for 'blending in' with the majority that may well be uncomfortable, or even threatening to some. Perhaps, however, it is the economists that perceive the biggest threat arising from mass migrations. For instance, Paul Collier (2013) who promotes the ideal of national identity as a substantive value, not only for citizens but also for migrants, states:

> Whether or not host populations have the moral right to manage migrations in their own interests, they currently have the legal right to do so (Collier 2013: 60).

Collier views the issue of refugees, asylum seekers and migrants as a unitary one, based primarily on economic motivations. He also sees the 'income gap' (Collier 2013: 37) as the main reason for the acceleration of migrations. The role played by conflicts and climate change are not seen as particularly significant, and neither is the causality that forces rather than simply suggests displacement. His main focus is the effect of migrations on host societies, which ought to define the approach taken by host governments:

> The social consequences of migration depend upon how immigrants relate to their host societies. At one extreme they are treated purely as workers and are permitted to enter the society on any other basis. A few host societies adopt this approach and for them the effects are indeed purely economic. But in most countries immigrants become part of the society as opposed to merely members of its labour force, and so engage with other people in a variety of ways. Migrants increase the diversity of society (Collier 2013: 61).

Nevertheless Collier sees diversity as problematic in several ways, hence he understands, and to some extent he justifies the call of 'too many immigrants' that often erupts in many otherwise welcoming host countries, such as Switzerland and the Netherlands, in recent times. But this flattened, particularized view of immigrants remains helpful to some extent, as it supports a qualified 'right to movement' for all; but it also emphasizes the economically positive effects that may follow, especially in the host country.

However, as he deplores the loss of trained and desirable citizens leaving their country of origin, he simply ignores the desperate position of the multitudes we have considered in this work together with the most pressing reasons for displacement. Their aim is most often simple survival, rather than economic advancement. Collier also ignores to some extent the noneconomic aspect of the interaction between migrants and local populations in most affluent Western countries.

A study of these complex interactions is well beyond the scope of the present work. It might be sufficient to say that a wholesale acceptance of polyethnicity, such as the one present in Canada, would tend to prevent the occurrence of obvious discriminatory practices, thus perhaps prepare if not a warm welcome, at least a respectful acceptance of diversity. However, the presence of a conservative government at this time is frustrating for those who in years past held Canadian justice in some regard.

Does this discussion advance the quest for new and better regimes for the protection of both refugees and IDPs? Perhaps not. But at least it proposes an approach based on principles that are already entrenched in law, through an international legal instrument, the International Convention on the Elimination of All Forms of Racial Discrimination (adopted and opened for signature and ratification by General Assembly Resolution 2106 (XX) of 21 December 1965, into force 4 January 1969, in accordance with Article 19), which would demand compliance with an important existing instrument, rather than (or even together with) an open search for a new version of the CSR, or at least the addition of appropriate language to that document.

Concluding Thought on an Accepted and Non-Derogable Norm

> Protection from racial discrimination is the fourth example of obligation *erga omnes* given in the *Barcelona Traction* case. A convenient starting point to examine this obligation is the principle that all human beings are equal. This principle was proclaimed in the solemn declarations that belong to the foundations of modern democracies (Ragazzi 1997: 118).

Ragazzi further points out that the principle of protection from racial discrimination is fundamental to the Universal Declaration of Human Rights, which he terms 'the "Magna Carta" of equality among human beings' (Ragazzi 1997: 119), and that this 'international custom belongs to *jus cogens*' (Ragazzi 1997: 120). Finally, Ragazzi also cites the Chief Prosecutor for the International Criminal Court for Yugoslavia, affirming that 'discrimination of any kind, anywhere, contains the seeds of genocide' (Ragazzi 1997: 121).

Perhaps we do not need to add any more of the copious available evidence to reiterate the fundamental importance of this principle. We might simply use this certainty as the starting point to affirm that we have seen those 'seeds' of discrimination from the very start of the saga of refugees and asylum seekers. They were not seriously considered when powerful states and corporations pursued goals and instituted practices that resulted in the grave harms that eventually led to the forced displacements.

The same 'seeds' were present when harms produced by those in power forced the displacements, and the refugees arrived at new locations, or found themselves displaced within their own country. The walls, virtual or real erected to restrain them, their treatment as 'undesirables', their placement in containment camps, all have been and are practices born of the unequal consideration of human rights and represent forms of discriminatory intent.

To my knowledge, this principle is not mandatory in the treatment of refugees and asylum seekers, according to the CSR. Perhaps, rather than seeking new formulae or additional instruments, incorporating openly this non-derogable norm might lead to a more human treatment of asylum seekers, perhaps even to a reduction of their numbers through the elimination of the discriminatory practices that lead to their displacement.

References

African Charter on Human and Peoples Rights, adopted 27 June 1981, OAU Doc. CAB/LEG/67/3 rev. 5, 21 ILM 58 (1982), entered into force 21 October 1986.

Agier, Michel, 2012, *Managing the Undesirables*, 2nd edition, Polity Press, Cambridge.

Arendt, Hannah, 1966, *The Origin of Totalitarianism*, Harcourt, New York.

Betts, Alexander and Loescher, Gil, eds, 2011, *Refugees in International Relations*, Oxford University Press, Oxford.

Betts, Alexander, Loescher, Gil and Milner, James, 2012, *UNHCR: The Politics and Practice of Refugee Protection*, 2nd edition, Routledge Global Institutions Series, London.

Bimal Gosh, 2007, 'Managing Migration: Towards the Missing Regime', in Pecoud, Antoine and de Guchteneire, Paul, eds, *Migration Without Borders*, UNESCO Publishing, Berghahn Books, New York, pp. 97–118.

Black, Charles, L. Jr., 1960, 'The Lawfulness of the Segregation Decisions', Faculty Scholarship Series, Paper 2586, http://digitalcommons.law.yale.edu/cgi/viewcontent.cgi?article=3590&context=fss_papers (accessed 28 January 2015).

Blank, Ishai, 2007, 'Spheres of Citizenship', *Theoretical Inquiries in Law*, 8, 411–47.

Boleslaw Dytlow, Immigration Appeal Board Decision V87–6040X, 7 July 1987.

Borger, Julian, 2014, 'Hague Court under Western Pressure not to Open Gaza War Crimes Inquiry', *The Guardian*, 18 August 2014, http://www.theguardian.com/law/2014/aug/18/hague-court-western-pressure-gaza-inquiry (accessed 28 January 2015).

Brewer, Andrew and Kumin, Judith, 2003, *Refugee*, 21.4 (December).

Brown, Wendy, 2010, *Walled States, Waning Sovereignty*, Zone Books, New York.

Bullard, R., 2001, 'Decision Making', in Westra, Laura and Lawson, Bill, eds, *Faces of Environmental Racism*, Rowman Littlefield, Lanham, MD, pp. 3–28.

Cassese, Antonio, 2006, *International Law*, 2nd edition, Oxford University Press, Oxford.

Castellino, M. Joshua, 2008, 'Territorial Integrity and the Right to Self-Determination: An Examination of the Conceptual Tools', *Brooklyn Journal of International Law*, 33(2), 503–68.

Chomsky, Aviva, 2014, *Undocumented: How Immigration Became Illegal*, Beacon Press, Boston, MA.

Chossudovsky, Michel, 2012, 'The Fuel Pools of Fukushima: The Greatest Short-term Threat to Humanity', 9 April 2012, Washington's Blog Global Research, http://www.globalresearch.ca/the-fuel-pools-of-fukushima-the-greatest-short-term-threat-to-humanity/30207 (accessed 28 January 2015).

Collier, Paul, 2013, *Exodus*, Oxford University Press, Oxford.

Delgamuukw v. British Columbia [1997] 3 SCR 1010.

'Desmond Tutu Likens Gaza Crisis to Apartheid', *The Daily Star* (Lebanon), 18 July 2014, http://www.dailystar.com.lb/News/Middle-East/2014/Jul-

18/264333-desmond-tutu-likens-gaza-crisis-to-apartheid.ashx (accessed 3 February 2015).

Douzinas, Costas, 2000, *The End of Human Rights*, Hart Publishing, Oxford.

Earth Charter, finalized 29 June 2000, http://www.earthcharterinaction.org/content/pages/Read-the-Charter.html (accessed 28 January 2015).

Eichstaedt, Peter H., 1994, *If You Poison Us: Uranium and Native Americans*, Red Crane Books, Santa Fe, NM.

Environmental Protection Agency (EPA), 1994, Executive Order 12898, 'Federal Actions to Address Environmental Justice in Minority Populations and Low-Income Populations', 11 February 1994, Federal Register, vol. 59, no. 32.

European Union Council, 2001, Council Directive on the Schengen Agreement, 2001/51/EC, 28 June 2001, Supplementing the Provisions of Article 26 of the Convention Implementing the Schengen Agreement of 14 June 1985 (OJ L 187/46, 10 July 2001).

Fisk, Robert, 2012, 'The Children of Fallujah: Sayef's Story', *The Independent*, 25 April 2012, http://www.independent.co.uk/voices/commentators/fisk/robert-fisk-the-children-of-fallujah--sayefs-story-7675977.html (accessed 28 January 2015).

Fort, Nyle, 2014, 'White Supremacy Is the Real Culprit in Ferguson: The Excuses Just Prove It', *The Guardian*, 20 August 2014, http://www.theguardian.com/commentisfree/2014/aug/20/white-supremacy-ferguson-black-excuses (accessed 28 January 2015).

Ganganee Janet Permanand, Immigration Appeal Board Decision T87–10167, 10 August 1967.

Goodwin-Gill, 1996, *The Refugee in International Law*, 2nd edition, Oxford University Press, Oxford.

Grahl-Madsen, Atle, 1966, *The Status of Refugees in International Law*, Vol. 1, A.W. Sijthoff, Leiden.

Hathaway, James, 1991, *The Law of Refugee Status*, Butterworths, Toronto.

Hathaway, James C. and Neve, Alexander, R., 1997, 'Making Refugee Law Relevant Again: A Proposal for Collectivized and Situation-Oriented Protection', *Harvard Human Rights Journal*, 10, 115–211.

International Convention on the Elimination of All Forms of Racial Discrimination, UNGA, res. 2106 (XX), 21 December 1965, into force on 4 January 1969.

Juss, Satvinder, 2006, *International Migration and Global Justice*, Ashgate, Aldershot.

Kymlicka, Will, 1997, *Multicultural Citizenship*, Clarendon Press, Oxford.

Lamkin, Raphael, 1944, *Axis Rule in Occupied Europe*, Carnegie Endowment for International Peace, Washington, DC.

Lipset, Seymour Martin, 1996, *American Exceptionalism*, Norton and Co., New York.

Maas, Amy, 2014, 'Tuvalu Climate Change Family Wins NZ Residence Appeal', *New Zealand Herald*, 3 August 2014, http://www.nzherald.co.nz/nz/news/article.cfm?c_id=1&objectid=11303331 (accessed 28 January 2015).

Marks, Kathy, 2014, 'World's First Climate Change Refugee Has Appeal Rejected: "When Kiribati Disappears, We're Going to Die with Our Kids"', 12 May 2014, http://beforeitsnews.com/environment/2014/05/worlds-first-climate-change-refugee-has-appeal-rejected-when-kiribati-disappears-were-going-to-die-with-our-kids-2501012.html (accessed 28 January 2015).

Mickelson, Karin and Rees, William, 2003, 'The Environment: Ecological and Ethical Dimensions', in Hughes, E., Lucas, A.R. and Tilleman, W.A., eds, *Environmental Law and Policy*, 3rd edition, Emond Publishers, Toronto, pp. 1–40.

Minchin, Liz and Murdoch, Lindsay, 2006, 'Aboriginal Cancer Doubles near Uranium Mine', *The Age*, 23 November 2006, http://www.theage.com.au/news/national/aboriginal-cancer-doubles-near-uranium-mine/2006/11/22/1163871482163.html (accessed 28 January 2015).

Pecoud, Antoine and de Guchteneire, Paul, 2007, 'Introduction: The Migration Without Borders Scenario', Pecoud, Antoine and de Guchteneire, Paul, eds, *Migration Without Borders*, UNESCO Publishing, Berghahn Books, New York, pp. 1–32.

Pierre Katanku Tshiabut Tshibola, Immigration Appeal Board Decision M84–1074, 30 May 1985.

Protocol to Prevent, Suppress and Punish Trafficking in Persons, Especially Women and Children, Supplementing the United Nations Covenant Against Transnational Organized Crime, Palermo 2000.

R. v. Sparrow [1990]1 SCR 1075.

R. v. Van der Peet, 137 DLR 4th 289, 9 WWR 1 (Can 1996).

Ragazzi, Maurizio, 1997, *The Concept of International Obligations Erga Omnes*, Clarendon Press, Oxford.

Ratner, Steven, R., 2001, 'Corporations and Human Rights: A Theory of Legal Responsibility', *Yale Law Journal*, 111.3, 443–545.

Ratner, Steven, Abrams, Jason S. and Bischoff, James L., 2009, *Accountability for Human Rights Atrocities in International Law*, 3rd edition, Oxford University Press, Oxford.

Report of the Representative of the Secretary-General on Internally Displaced Persons, submitted pursuant to Commission on Human Rights Resolution 2002/56, 21 January 2003.

Ruggie, John Gerars, 2007, *Business and Human Rights: The Evolving International Agenda*, June, Working Paper 38, John F. Kennedy School of Government, Harvard University.

Rustin, Bayard, 2003, 'From Protests to Politics: The Future of the Civil Rights Movement', in *Time on Two Crosses: The Collected Writings of Bayard Rustin*, ed. Devon W. Carhado and Donald Weise, Clair Press, San Francisco, CA, pp. 116–29.

Schacter, Oscar, 1983, 'Human Dignity as a Normative Concept', *American Journal of International Law*, 77.4, 848–54.

Scovazzi, Tullio, 1991, 'Industrial Accidents and the Veil of Transnational Corporations', in Francioni, Francesco and Scovazzi, Tullio, eds, *International Responsibility for Environmental Harm*, Graham and Trotman, Kluwer Academic, pp. 395–427.
——, 2012, 'Brevi Considerazioni sulle Responsabita d'Imprese in Materia di Tutela dei Diritti Umani', in Cutillo, M., Faugno, R. and Scovazzi, Tullio, eds, *La Responsibilita' Sociale delle Impresa in Temi di Diritti Umani e Protezione dell'Ambiente*, Giuffrè, Milan, pp. 3–24.
'Second Boer War', http://en.wikipedia.org/wiki/Second_Boer_War (accessed 28 January 2015).
Simons, Penelope, 2012, 'International Law's Invisible Hand and the Future of Corporate Accountability for Violations of Human Rights', *Journal of Human Rights and the Environment*, 3.1, 5–43.
Stiglitz, Joseph, 2012, *The Price of Inequality*, Norton and Co., New York.
Tamir, Yuli, 'Protection of the Territories', *Ha'aretz*, 18 March 2003.
UNGA, 1950, Resolution 428(V), Statute of the Office of the United Nations High Commissioner for Refugees, 14 December 1950.
——, 2003, Resolution 58/153, *Implementing Actions Proposed by the United Nations High Commissioner for Refugees to Strengthen the Capacity of His Office to Carry out Its Mandate*, 22 December 2003.
UN Security Council, 1992, 'Statement by the President of the Security Council', S/PRST/1992/5, 31 January 1992.
United Nations High Commissioner for Refugees (UNHCR), 1979, *Handbook on Procedures and Criteria for Determining Refugee Status* (reissued 2011), Geneva.
——, 2003, *Conclusion on Protection Safeguards in Interception Measures*, Executive Committee Conclusions, No. 97 (LIV), 10 October 2003.
——, 2006, *The State of the World's Refugees 2006: Human Displacement in the New Millennium*, Oxford University Press, Oxford.
——, 2009, *Conclusion on Protracted Refugee Situations*, Executive Committee Conclusions, No. 109 (LXI), 8 December 2009.
——, 2010, *Global Report 2009*, http://www.unhcr.org/gr09/ (accessed 28 January 2015).
——, 2011, *Global Trends 2010*, June 2011, UNHCR, Geneva, http://www.unhcr.org/cgi-bin/texis/vtx/home/opendocPDFViewer.html?docid=4dfa11499&query=Global%20Trends,%20June%202010 (accessed 28 January 2015).
Valluy, Jérôme, 2005, 'La Nouvelle Europe politique des camps: génése d'une source élitaire de phobie et de repression des étrangers', *Cultures and Conflits*, 57, 13–69.
Westra, Laura, 2006, *Environmental Justice and the Rights of Unborn and Future Generations*, Earthscan, London.
——, 2007, *Environmental Justice and the Rights of Indigenous Peoples*, Earthscan, London.
——, 2012, *Faces of State Terrorism*, Brill, Leiden.

——, 2013, *The Supranational Corporation*, Brill, Leiden.
——, 2014, *Revolt Against Authority*, Brill, Leiden.
Westra, Laura and Lawson, Bill, 2001, *Faces of Environmental Racism*, Rowman Littlefield, Lanham, MD.
Zagier, Alan Scher, 2014, 'Pathologist Can't Tell if Teen Had Hands Up', *The Toronto Star*, 10 August 2014, A1.

Epilogue

Satvinder Juss

Who are the voices of reform? Where do they come from? And, does it matter if they do not come from our governments and politicians? If the voices of reason come from elsewhere, if they come from a place far removed from our daily lives, should we worry that they are not from somewhere more immediate? Somewhere more familiar that we can directly relate to? If the voices of humanity come from somewhere far removed from us, like the religion of a place we do not share in, just like a place we no longer inhabit, should we worry that we no longer have a sense of ourselves? No longer a sense of our lost humanity? A belief in our civilization? How much longer can we, in contemporary liberal democracies, remain comfortable with a life lived in a moral vacuum? This final chapter briefly sets out to consider these questions.

In 2014, the British author, Hanif Qureshi, himself of an immigrant parent, argued that 'it is becoming impossible to speak up for the immigrant', and that the immigrant figure in today's public conversation is like an 'unslayable zombie in a video game'. As he explains, 'in the current public conversation, this figure [the immigrant] has not only migrated from one country to another, he has migrated from reality to the collective imagination where he has been transformed into a terrible fiction'. In this way, 'he is an example of the undead … If the 20th century was replete with uncanny, semi-fictional figures who invaded the decent, upright and hardworking – the pure – this character is rehaunting us in the guise of the immigrant'. Accordingly, immigrants have 'no face, no status, no protection and no story'. The immigrant 'is impossible to kill or finally eliminate not only because he is already silent and dead, but also because there are waves of other similar immigrants just over the border coming right at you'.[1] If he is right, this may explain why there are so few voices to speak up for the immigrant. He is already dead. Or, at any rate, it does not matter whether he is or is not – there are many more like him or her, just over the border coming in at you.

By a cruel irony, such horrors are not wholly unfounded. The year 2014 will be remembered for the United Nations being forced to consider establishing refugee holding centres in North Africa and the Middle East. This is because of the spiralling numbers of migrants attempting perilous journeys across the

1 Brown, Mark, 2014, 'The Migrant Has No Face, Status or Story', *The Guardian*, 30 May, http://www.theguardian.com/books/2014/may/30/hanif-kureishi-immigrants-debate-fiction-european-elections (accessed 25 February 2015).

Mediterranean in a desperate effort to reach Europe. According to the UNHCR, the UN's refugee agency, for the first time the large-scale processing of migrants and refugees outside Europe, in countries such as Egypt, Libya or Sudan, may be necessary as frontline authorities claim they have been abandoned by Brussels in the face of a 'colossal humanitarian catastrophe'.[2] This is a significant development because campaigners for refugee rights had up to now rejected the idea of large processing camps outside Europe. They feared that refugees would be at the mercy of states with poor records on human rights and justice. The cases discussed in this book under Dublin II, discussed in his contribution by Satvinder Juss, have highlighted precisely these problems in relation to Greece, Hungary and Italy. Tullio Scovazzi's contribution in this book refers to how 'the waters of some semi-enclosed seas, such as the Mediterranean or the Red Sea, have become the graveyard of thousands of human beings', and to the failure of 'rescue treaties' to provide proper protection, such that 'illegal migrants are too often the victims not only of smugglers, but also of a number of States which try to evade their legal and moral duties'. His firm conclusion is that 'the treaties so far concluded are not sufficiently clear to deal with all the problems posed by illegal migrations'. This is why he refers to the 'invention of asymmetrical rights' which undermine international law. Clearly, a much better system is called for to avoid the deaths of thousands more.

This is why the UNHCR's European director, Vincent Cochetel, explained in 2014, 'we would not be totally against external processing if certain safeguards were in place: the right to appeal, fair process, the right to remain while appeals take place'. There must still be misgivings under current arrangements for such an initiative. But the alternative at present is the prospect of more deaths at sea. As Vincent Cochetel lamented, the EU had not found effective mechanisms to prevent migrants dying at sea. In the circumstances, instead of focusing on ever tougher border controls, the EU needed to establish safe routes. The enormous rise in numbers is one reason. The inability of frontline states, like Greece and Italy, to cope with the problem is another reason. In 2013 there were only 3,362 arrivals by the end of April. Compare this to 42,000 people attempting to cross the Mediterranean to Italy by June 2014, according to the EU border agency, Frontex. The rise in numbers is due to the large numbers of Syrian refugees seeking to escape the civil war. This has displaced millions of people in the past three years, so that some 7,000 refugees from Syria arrived on the Italian coast in the first nine months of 2013, compared with only 350 in the whole of 2012.

---

2 Sherwood, Harriet, Smith, Helena, Davies, Lizzy and Grant, Harriet, 2014, 'Europe Faces "Colossal Humanitarian Catastrophe" of Refugees Dying at Sea', *The Guardian*, 2 June, where it is argued that the, 'UN considers Africa holding centres as "boat season" is expected to bring sharp increase in migrants making treacherous crossing', http://www.theguardian.com/world/2014/jun/02/europe-refugee-crisis-un-africa-processing-centres (accessed 25 February 2015).

By 2014, they had become the second largest group to arrive by sea in Italy in 2014, after Eritreans, so that the majority of people making boat journeys to Greece are Syrian refugees, many of whom include women and children. Amnesty International has condemned the EU's inaction, stating: 'with virtually no safe and legal routes into Europe, people are increasingly pushed into the hands of smugglers and traffickers, and are forced to risk their lives on unseaworthy vessels'.[3] This is what EU policies are now foisting upon the most vulnerable and destitute people in the world. Yet, there are no voices of reform from the EU itself. There are virtually none from politicians of mainstream parties. No one from government is speaking out in support of 'the undead', the 'unslayable zombie', in the words of Hanif Qureshi. This will remain until governments and politicians everywhere realize that the toxic nature of the immigration debate is poisoning our political discourse in the West. Until and unless they reject the abject and cynical politics, which place domestic electoral battles over the decency and principles which they otherwise purport to espouse, the voices of reform will come not from our national leaders. Real change will be difficult to achieve. The chapters by Laura Westra in this book have demonstrated the poverty of international instruments in the protection of refugees. They have demonstrated how the plunder of their resources in their home countries has driven them to go into exile in search of a more secure and stable future. And, they have demonstrated how limited are their legal rights to seek redress. Appeal to human rights norms, as her contributions here show, are no more effective in bringing real change.

Fortunately, the empty moral vacuum is being populated by ideas from elsewhere, and it is all the more effective for that, and all the more shaming for governments. It is possible to end the discourse in this book on a positive note. The shift in public attitude is beginning to take place. Policy changes must now only be a matter of time. Most casual observers of the European scene will remember the remarkable speech of Pope Francis to the European Parliament, at the end of 2014, when he highlighted his vision for Europe. It was memorable both for what it said and for the fact that it was a quarter of a century after St John Paul II travelled to Strasbourg to address a continent still divided by the Iron Curtain. It was memorable because the pontiff was greeted with a lengthy standing ovation at the start and finish of his speech. But most of all, it was memorable because Pope Francis said he wanted to bring a message of hope to Europeans distrustful of their institutions, burdened by economic crisis and spiritually adrift in a culture that, he said, no longer values the dignity of human beings. His ringing words that, 'a Europe which is no longer open to the transcendent dimension of life is a Europe which risks slowly losing its own soul' will act as a talisman in Europe for many years to come for those who so choose it.[4] This is especially true of his

---

3 Ibid.

4 'Pope Urges Fair Immigration Policy', *The Independent*, 25 November 2014, http://www.independent.ie/world-news/pope-urges-fair-immigration-policy-30772818.html (accessed 25 February 2015).

call for leaders to work together to protect immigrants from human traffickers and establish a Europe that 'revolves not around the economy but around the sacredness of the human person'.[5]

By the end of 2014, no less than 31 leading non-governmental organizations, including Oxfam, Amnesty International, ActionAid, Save the Children and Islamic Relief, had called on rich countries to accommodate tens of thousands of refugees who had been forced to flee their homes, so that tens of thousands of Syrian refugees could be resettled within their borders.[6] But the problem lies not just with the worst crises of displaced people since the Second World War, involving mostly women and children in the Syrian exodus, because by the end of 2015, other countries would need to start admitting at least 5 per cent of around 3.6 million people who have been forced to flee their homes, according to these humanitarian and human rights organizations. This is important given the current disparities in affording international protection. The sobering truth is that since the spring of 2011 those fleeing Syria have been hosted by just five countries in the region, namely Turkey, Lebanon, Jordan, Iraq and Egypt, leading to their resources being stretched to breaking point by the influx. Yet, Amnesty International has calculated that only 1.7 per cent of the total number of refugees have been offered sanctuary by the rest of the international community.

Germany and Sweden in Europe received some 100,000 asylum applications from Syrian refugees. But even within Europe the disparities are great because the UK, France, Italy, Spain and Poland pledged to admit just 2,000 refugees between them, and Britain then declined to join the UN's resettlement programme, setting up instead its own Vulnerable Persons Relocation Scheme for Syrian Refugees.[7] By mid-2014 only 50 Syrians had been resettled in the UK, according to the

5 Molloy, Antonio, 2014, 'Pope Francis Calls on European Parliament to Accept Migrants: "We Cannot Allow the Mediterranean to Become a Vast Cemetery"', *The Independent*, 25 November, which notes how, 'the leader of the Catholic Church compared the continent to a grandmother who has lost her vibrancy', http://www.independent.co.uk/news/world/europe/pope-francis-calls-on-european-parliament-to-accept-migrants-we-cannot-allow-the-mediterranean-to-become-a-vast-cemetery-9881858.html (accessed 25 February 2015).

6 Sherwood, Harriet, 2014, 'Take in Syrian Refugees, Aid Agencies Tell Rich Countries' *The Guardian*, 8 December, http://www.theguardian.com/world/2014/dec/08/take-in-syrian-refugees-rich-countries (accessed 25 February 2015).

7 See Smith, Ben, Gower, Melanie and Bardens, John, 2014, 'Syrian Refugees and the UK', International Affairs and Defence Section, Home Affairs Section, 9 December, www.parliament.uk/briefing-papers/sn06805.pdf (accessed 25 February 2015). Also see, Brokenshire, James (Immigration and Security Minister), 2014, 'Vulnerable Persons Relocation Scheme for Syrian Nationals', Written Statement to Parliament, 25 March, https://www.gov.uk/government/speeches/vulnerable-persons-relocation-scheme-for-syrian-nationals (accessed 25 February 2015).

Refugee Council.[8] But even more shameful than this is that the Gulf states had not offered to take any refugees by this time, notwithstanding their shared linguistic and religious ties with those seeking sanctuary. This mattered because when, subsequently, Turkey, Lebanon and Jordan sought to impose restrictions at their borders with Syria, in an attempt to stem the flow of refugees, desperate families were unable to escape the war. The plight of refugees in the world now is such that the UN High Commission for Refugees, after setting a goal of 30,000 Syrian refugees to be accepted by the international community in 2014, had by the end of 2014 called on states to provide resettlement or other forms of admission for an additional 100,000 by the end of 2016.[9] According to Sherif Elsayed-Ali, Amnesty International's Head of Refugee and Migrants' Rights, 'it is time for world governments to take the courageous steps needed to share the responsibility for this crisis and help avert further suffering … The apathy we have witnessed from some of the world's wealthiest countries has been exacerbated by scaremongering over rising immigration levels across Europe. Those with the economic means to do so must play a greater role'.[10]

Small wonder then that Pope Francis also in September 2014 excoriated the European Union to demand a 'globalisation of charity' towards those fleeing warzones and poverty, adding that 'mere tolerance' toward migrants and asylum seekers is not enough.[11] In a message to mark the World Day of Migrants and Refugees for January 2015, the pontiff declared that, 'it is necessary to respond to the globalisation of migration with the globalisation of charity and cooperation, in such a way as to make the conditions of migrants more humane'. Following the catastrophic drowning in September 2014 of 500 migrants and asylum seekers, after their boat sank off Malta, the Pope reminded us how, 'large numbers of people are leaving their homelands, with a suitcase full of fears and desires, to undertake a hopeful and dangerous trip in search of more humane living conditions', The sinking of the boat left just 10 survivors. These survivors complained how the traffickers in charge of organizing the dangerous crossing from North Africa had intentionally sunk their boat. The Argentine-born pontiff explained how, 'Often, … such migration gives rise to suspicion and hostility, even in ecclesiastical communities, prior to any knowledge of the migrants' lives or their stories of

---

8 http://www.refugeecouncil.org.uk/latest/news/4144_uk_resettles_just_50_refugees_from_syria (accessed 25 February 2015).

9 'Governments at Geneva Meeting Agree to Take in 100,000 Syrian Refugees', News Stories, 9 December 2014, http://www.unhcr.org/548737926.html (accessed 25 February 2015). Also see, Nguyen, Katie, 2014, 'UN Says Rich Nations Pledge to Take 100,000 Syrian Refugees', 9 December, http://www.reuters.com/article/2014/12/09/us-syria-refugees-idUSKBN0JN1KQ20141209 (accessed 25 February 2015).

10 Sherwood, 2014.

11 See, 'Pope Says "Mere Tolerance" Towards Migrants Not Enough', *Newsmax*, 23 September 2014, http://www.newsmax.com/Newsfront/Vatican-religion-pope-immigration/2014/09/23/id/596302/ (accessed 25 February 2015).

persecution and destitution'. The Pope, who has made the protection of the poor and the marginalized the hallmark of his papacy, stated that, 'achieving mere tolerance that respects diversity and ways of sharing between different backgrounds and cultures is not sufficient'. What was needed today was the creation of 'a universal network of cooperation' to fight trafficking and enslavement.[12]

But another back-drop to the Pope's comments was the growing euro-scepticism and anti-immigrant feeling across Europe, which has in turn fuelled the rise of right-wing parties, as he made two back-to-back speeches to the European Parliament and Council of Europe in the French city Strasbourg. The idea of Europe as a beacon of hope in a world of chaos was no longer true. It needed 'fair, courageous and realistic policies' when it came to immigrants and the countries from which they migrated. These policies should help in resolving the conflicts that fuel migration 'rather than adopting policies motivated by self-interest, which increase and feed such conflicts', he said. Whilst pointing out that, 'we cannot allow the Mediterranean to become a vast cemetery', since 'the boats landing daily on the shores of Europe are filled with men and women who need acceptance and assistance', whereby more than 3,200 refugees died trying to reach Europe in 2014 alone, this Argentine Jesuit was critical of the lack of fresh ideas coming out of Europe.

In compelling language, he declared how 'Europe seems to give the impression of being somewhat elderly and haggard, feeling less and less a protagonist in a world which frequently regards it with aloofness', so that today's reality is that, 'we encounter a general impression of weariness and ageing, of a Europe which is now a "grandmother", no longer fertile and vibrant'. For the Latin America-born Pope, from where the most progressive immigration and refugee policies today abound, the absence of a coherent EU migration policy 'contributes to slave labour and continuing social tensions' across Europe.[13] In the UK, the Archbishop of Canterbury, Justin Welby, has also expressed concern about the language of immigration, pointing out that 'with some people we have a duty of care' and that 'what we're seeing is an upsurge in minor racist, anti-semitic, anti-Islamic, anti-foreigner xenophobia – not major things – just comments being made, things being said which are for people who come in those backgrounds seriously uncomfortable, really quite frightening'.[14]

---

12 Ibid.

13 'Pope Attacks "Haggard" Europe over Immigration', msn news, 26 November 2014, http://www.msn.com/en-sa/news/world/pope-attacks-haggard-europe-over-immigration/ar-BBfOXGQ (accessed 25 February 2015).

14 White, Michael and Syal, Rajeev, 2014, 'Archbishop of Canterbury: "Don't Demonise Immigrants": Justin Welby Says He Is Worried about the Language Used to Debate Immigration after Michael Fallon's "Swamped" Comment', *The Guardian*, 27 October, http://www.theguardian.com/uk-news/2014/oct/27/archbishop-canterbury-justin-welby-warns-not-demonise-immigrants-michael-fallon-swamped (accessed 25 February 2015). Also see, Hardman, Isabel, 2014, 'Justin Welby: I Worry about Damage Caused

The Pope's devastating condemnation of how immigrants and refugees have now started to be treated, following the first decade of the twenty-first century, was not lost on thoughtful observers from across the world. Judy Dempsey[15] of the Carnegie Endowment for International Peace observed in relation to Pope Francis' impression of an 'elderly and haggard grandmother' that, 'old is something that Europeans are becoming at such a pace that many countries are in desperate need of a young and educated workforce to finance the ever-aging population. But Europe doesn't yet have an enlightened policy toward immigration. If anything, there is a dangerous backlash against immigrants, with the UK leading the way'. In her view, 'governments are losing sight of what made Europe prosper after World War II' where 'immigrants and refugees played a role in Europe's economic recovery'.

It is quite forgotten that, 'a part of Europe's identity was about being open to both' so that as recently as 20 years ago, 'Germany, among other EU countries, took in tens of thousands of refugees during the Yugoslav Wars of the 1990s'. But European leaders today are loathe to open their doors to refugees and immigrants because they fear this would strengthen far-right and far-left parties. Even those immigrants from within the EU are today despised by such parties – from Britain's UK Independence Party (UKIP) to Hungary's Jobbik – but that 'pandering to these parties … is despicable'.[16] Fraser Nelson in the UK pointed out how with respect to Iraq and the persecution of the Christian Yazidis there, 'France and Australia are taking in persecuted religious minorities, but Britain has remained strangely silent on the issue'.[17]

Another commentator, Finian Cunningham,[18] remarked that, 'the pope would have been more to the point if he had condemned the EU for creating this crisis in the first place', because although 'some parliamentarians were disgruntled that a religious leader was permitted to address what is supposed to be a secular institution', and that 'the Catholic pontiff was interfering in political matters' the 'truth is, however, that the pope was not being political enough'. He notes how the UN High Commission for Refugees reckons that over 160,000 people have tried in 2014 to sail across the Mediterranean to European shores, an increase of 60,000

---

by Language on Immigration', *The Spectator*, 27 October, http://blogs.spectator.co.uk/coffeehouse/2014/10/justin-welby-immigration-is-not-a-deep-menace-to-the-uk/ (accessed 25 February 2015).

15 Dempsey, Judy, 'The Pope and Fortress Europe', Carnegie Endowment for International Peace, 27 November, http://carnegieendowment.org/2014/11/27/pope-and-fortress-europe/hvib (accessed 25 February 2015).

16 Ibid.

17 Nelson, Fraser, 2014, 'Why Are We Not Offering Asylum to the Iraqi Refugees?' *The Telegraph*, 15 August, http://www.telegraph.co.uk/news/worldnews/middleeast/iraq/11034532/Why-are-we-not-offering-asylum-to-the-Iraqi-refugees.html (accessed 25 February 2015).

18 Cunningham, Finian, 2014, 'Papal Fallacy on EU Immigration Crisis', nsnbc international, 2 December, http://nsnbc.me/2014/12/02/papal-fallacy-eu-immigration-crisis/ (accessed 25 February 2015).

from the previous year. But the increase 'has resulted in a surge of deaths at sea, from boats capsizing or running adrift'. Most are heading to the Sicilian island of Lampedusa, which is only 113 kilometres from Tunisia, earning the nickname, 'the gateway to Europe' among the migrants. This is not without cost to human life.

In 2013, when their vessel foundered off Lampedusa 366 people died, prompting the Italian authorities to mount an ongoing sea-rescue operation known as '*Mare Nostrum*' (Our Sea), which then saved as many as 100,000 people distressed at sea. The operation had a financial cost of €100 million a year. So, barely a year later in November 2014, the Italian government faced the prospect of closing down the naval rescue mission, resulting in renewed fears that the death toll in the Mediterranean will rise again quite dramatically as a result. The fault lay not with the Italian government. It had embarked on a noble venture. The fault lay with the EU which failed to provide funds to keep the salvage operation running. The Italian economy was already in dire straits. So naturally *Mare Nostrum* was at risk of being discontinued.

Amongst the most unsympathetic of EU governments was Britain. According to the new Foreign Office minister, Lady Anelay: 'We do not support planned search and rescue operations in the Mediterranean', because the government believed there was 'an unintended "pull factor", encouraging more migrants to attempt the dangerous sea crossing and thereby leading to more tragic and unnecessary deaths'.[19] So, their chances of safely crossing the Mediterranean were being greatly enhanced by the Italian Navy's presence. This warped logic was denounced by humanitarian critics as 'callous'. Even though, to its credit, the Italian Navy immediately announced it would continue with the rescue operation, this is only because, 'the 'phasing out' of the current programme, announced by the government, could take many years …'.[20] Ian Birrell's account of how one wealthy couple set out to make a difference is telling of what is possible in the face of callous government inaction.[21] In 2013, Regina and Christopher Catrambone were cruising in the Mediterranean. They saw a jacket float past their yacht. The captain told them the owner was probably dead. He was probably one of thousands of desperate people who drown each year trying to get to Europe.

---

19 Travis, Alan, 2014, 'UK Axes Support for Mediterranean Migrant Rescue Operation', *The Guardian*, 27 October, referring to how, 'Refugees and human rights organisations react with anger as minister says saving people encourages others to risk voyage', http://www.theguardian.com/politics/2014/oct/27/uk-mediterranean-migrant-rescue-plan (accessed 25 February 2015).

20 Nelson, Arthur, 2014, 'Italian Navy Says It Will Continue Refugee Rescue Mission Despite Plan to Scrap It', *The Guardian*, 28 October, which reports that confusion surrounds future of Mare Nostrum programme as UK is condemned for 'morally shocking' withdrawal from rescues, http://www.theguardian.com/world/2014/oct/28/italian-navy-refugee-rescue-mission-mare-nostrum (accessed 25 February 2015).

21 Birrell, Ian, 2014, 'Britain's Refusal to Save Migrants Is an Act of Inhumanity', *The Guardian*, 29 October, http://www.ianbirrell.com/britains-refusal-to-save-migrants-is-an-act-of-inhumanity/ (accessed 25 February 2015).

After their holiday, and inspired both by this glimpse of tragedy and by Pope Francis's appeal to help migrants, the wealthy couple spent £3m on a rescue ship for refugees. Birrell's account explains how this couple's 40-metre vessel is equipped with a sick bay, drones to spot migrants adrift in the sea, and fast boats to pluck them from the waters. Their first trip was in August 2014, at the height of the 'Boat Season' in the Mediterranean. Their ship picked up 227 migrants crammed on to a floundering fishing boat. These were, Birrell tells us, 'just a few of those thousands of human beings fleeing carnage in Syria, chaos in Iraq, civil war in Libya, conflict in Nigeria and cruel repression in the horn of Africa' and 'another 300 were saved' again in October 2014. We are reminded to 'contrast this compelling display of Christian values with the shameful position of our government' where 'in response to the greatest refugee crisis in more than half a century, a foreign office minister', in his words, 'the little-known Lady Anelay justified this act of despicable inhumanity on the entirely spurious grounds that such missions might end up encouraging migrants to make a dangerous sea crossing'.

But this inhumanity does not end there because, 'we must not ignore that Britain was militarily involved in collapsed countries such as Iraq and Libya, while idiotic aid policies foster conflict and repression in swaths of sub-Saharan Africa'.[22] For Birrell, 'mainstream politicians fail to confront the myths and misinformation of misanthropes' and instead they are 'playing on people's insecurities'. This is 'the tragic inevitability of a politics fuelled by fear and pessimism'. Yet, what is lost is the 'terrible irony' of our governments making 'such play of being forces for good in the world, whether through military interventions against despotism or maintaining those aid budgets, but the same politicians treat human beings fleeing in search of tolerable lives like flotsam and jetsam to be discarded in the seas'. In his contribution in this Book, Donald A. Brown has called for the label 'refugee' to be applied to individuals more broadly 'to include all people who are forced to leave their communities .... Without regard to whether they leave their nation and cross national boundaries'. Whilst this makes sense, the same problems in securing redress faced by 'climate refugees' will undoubtedly also be faced by the 'conflict-induced refugees' (to coin a phrase). As Brown has explained, when 'climate refugees' have brought legal actions in America, the 'US courts have usually dismissed these actions on the grounds that climate change is a political rather than a legal issue'. The same will surely be said of 'conflict-induced refugees'.

The answer must lie in re-configuring international refugee law as a compensation scheme just as much as a human rights protection scheme. The Rome Statute of the International Criminal Court, which entered into force on 1 July 2002, lists as a war crime, 'intentionally launching an attack in the knowledge that such attack will cause ... long term severe damage to the natural environment'.[23] Yet, it is a perversion, barely unfathomable to the human mind, that we treat

22 Ibid.

23 Juss, Satvinder, 2006, *International Migration and Global Justice*, Ashgate, Aldershot, pp. 170–71. This is Article 8(2)(b)(iv). See http://www.icc-cpi.int/nr/rdonlyres/

'intentionally launching an attack' on a human population 'in the knowledge that such attack will cause' loss of civilian life, as 'collateral damage'. A compensatory scheme is needed, within the constructs of refugee law itself, to avoid poor people having to face the consequences of someone else's military adventures. If we can give monetary compensation for tortious acts, there is no reason why we cannot give refugee status in the same way. The chapter by Satvinder Juss refers to the possibility of refugee law being operated in this way. This what the 31 leading non-governmental organizations, including Oxfam, Amnesty International, ActionAid, Save the Children and Islamic Relief, have in mind when they have called on rich countries to resettle tens of thousands of refugees who have been forced to flee their homes. It is what Sherif Elsayed-Ali, Amnesty International's Head of Refugee and Migrants' Rights, has in mind when he demands that, 'it is time for world governments to take the courageous steps needed to share the responsibility for this crisis and help avert further suffering …'. There is already a *de facto* practice in place to compensate victims by giving them sanctuary. Some countries observe it better than others. That is why a legal obligation is now required to do so.

Finian Cunningham also believes that, 'the EU has largely created this immigration disaster, and it is the EU that is now scandalously turning its back on the human catastrophe of its own making' and that in fact, 'this central point was completely misunderstood or ignored by Pope Francis in his remonstration with the Strasbourg Parliament'. This is because 'the main national groups that are piling onto leaky boats and desperately seeking refuge in Europe are from Syria and Libya, according to monitors'. With remorseless logic, Finnian Cunningham presses on that, 'this flow of refugees is correlated with the spate of armed conflicts that have erupted in these countries over the past three years'. He argues that, 'Britain and France are the two main European governments that have been most responsible for fuelling the conflict in Libya when they led the NATO bombing of that country during 2013 and the eventual toppling of the Gaddafi government', although in his view other European members of NATO also bear responsibility for unleashing the humanitarian and political chaos prevailing in Libya. So, 'this is the crux of the matter', where 'the European Union is being assailed by a crisis of illegal immigrants from North Africa and the Middle East' and where 'thousands of these desperate people are being exploited by heartless modern-day slave traders and thousands are dying in watery graves – while the EU bureaucracy and member governments like Britain and France erect fortress-like barriers'. Finnian Cunningham concludes: 'Now if the pope had excoriated the real EU cause-and-effect of the immigration crisis during his address at Strasbourg then he really would have weighed into politics with a virtue'.[24]

---

ea9aeff7-5752-4f84-be94-0a655eb30e16/0/rome_statute_english.pdf (accessed 25 February 2015).

24 Cunningham, 2014.

On the other hand, it is fair to point out that not all have agreed with this perspective. Writing in *The Spectator*, Nicholas Farrell was of the view that 'foolishly' in October 2014, 'Italy's left-wing government became the first European Union country to decriminalise illegal immigration and deploy its navy at huge expense to save "illegal" migrants crossing the narrow Sicilian channel' and that 'the decision to open the floodgates came in a moment of national moral panic after 366 people drowned in a single boat … a stone's throw from an idyllic beach on the island of Lampedusa'. With almost embarrassing bathos, whilst on the one hand he refers to how 'the dead included a mother who had given birth during the voyage and was still attached to her newborn child when divers found their bodies trapped inside the sunken vessel', on the other hand, he is firmly of the view that, 'the policy change, driven by a perverted mix of human decency and political correctness, was pure folly: it has acted as a green light to wannabe boat people everywhere, whose numbers soar as the chaos in Africa and the Middle East escalates. The result is an exodus of biblical proportions out of Africa into Italy'. Farrell begins nonchalantly: 'the next time you eat a fish from the Mediterranean, just remember that it may well have eaten a corpse. As the Italian author Aldo Busi told the press just the other day: "I don't buy fish from the Mediterranean any more for fear of eating Libyans, Somalis, Syrians and Iraqis. I'm not a cannibal and so now I stick with farmed fish, or else Atlantic cod". Personally, I prefer my fish natural, fattened on drowned human flesh, but there you go'. For him, it is lamentable that 'Italy's boat people used to originate mostly from sub-Saharan Africa; but – thanks to '*Mare nostrum*', as the new policy is called – they now also come from the Horn of Africa, Syria, Palestine, Afghanistan, Bangladesh and Iraq'.[25]

Why this is a bad thing is not necessarily clear. In December 2014, just after the UK government had announced plans to toughen up its immigration policy yet again, the 34-nation Organization for Economic Cooperation and Development announced in its latest report that countries needed to see migrants 'as a resource rather than a problem' and invest in integration policies to harness their skills.[26] Germany, it is said, was an 'oasis of prosperity' in a struggling Europe. It was

---

25 Farrell, Nicholas, 2014, 'Libya's Boat People, and Italy's Tragic Folly', *The Spectator*, 6 September, where he makes the point that 'the "mare nostrum" policy has acted as a magnet for boat people; the crisis is only growing', http://www.spectator.co.uk/features/9303722/italys-decriminalising-of-illegal-immigration-has-acted-as-a-green-light-to-boat-people/ (accessed 25 February 2015). Such comments have to be seen in the context of how rising numbers of refugees and migrants have fuelled support for right-wing politicians in Greece and Italy. The neo-fascist Golden Dawn party, which has focused on the issue, pulled off a surprisingly strong performance in local and European elections in Greece. The leader of the right-wing xenophobic Northern League party in Italy, Matteo Salvini, flew to Sicily to demand an end to the Mare Nostrum operation.

26 See, OECD, 2014, *International Migration Outlook 2014*, http://www.oecd-ilibrary.org/social-issues-migration-health/international-migration-outlook-2014_migr_outlook-2014-en (accessed 25 February 2015).

not only the most favoured location for immigrants on the continent, and also the world's largest recipient of new asylum seekers, but it had also benefitted the most. Given that 'there are many ways for migrants to contribute to economic growth', immigration had contributed to employment growth in Germany, which in 2013 had welcomed over 400,000 immigrants, whereas the lack of such growth was the key problem for many European nations.

The Migration Outlook report urged member states to harness the skills of immigrants, not least because 'today's migrants are better educated than their predecessors. The number of foreign-born who are highly-educated has grown by 70 per cent over the past decade to exceed 31 million in the OECD area' according to the report, such that 'the underutilization of immigrants' skills is a waste of resources that OECD countries can scarcely afford'.[27] One country that is currently thinking of doing so is Scotland, whose former First Minister, Alex Salmond, has said that record levels of immigrants would be admitted to an independent Scotland because he wanted to increase Scotland's net migration to around 24,000 a year, a population increase the equivalent of a city the size of Edinburgh every 20 years.[28]

This figure was chosen because the Office for National Statistics (ONS) predicts net migration for Scotland over the long term will only be 15,500 a year, but the Treasury has said that net migration of 24,000 would be needed for the state pension to remain as affordable in an independent Scotland. The reason is that Scotland's 'dependency ratio' – the number of workers paying taxes to fund each OAP's state pension – would be worse than the UK's.[29] Scotland can surely not be the only country in Europe that has to worry about the need to keep its state pension affordable in an era of aging populations. Clearly, therefore, the adoption of a rational immigration policy – even if it is unashamedly only in the national interest rather than broader considerations of humanity – remains very much an option for advanced Western democracies. They should seize it.

27 'Germany Top European Destination for Immigrants and Asylum Seekers: OECD', *Daily News*, 1 December 2014, http://www.hurriyetdailynews.com/germany-top-european-destination-for-immigrants-and-asylum-seekers-oecd.aspx?pageID=449&nID=75055&NewsCatID=359 (accessed 25 February 2015).

28 Johnson, Simon, 2014, 'Alex Salmond Sets 24,000 Annual Immigration Target', *The Telegraph*, 28 May, who reports that the First Minister sets the increased total for an independent Scotland despite warnings this would create border controls with England, http://www.telegraph.co.uk/news/uknews/scotland/10861160/Alex-Salmond-sets-24000-annual-immigration-target.html (accessed 25 February 2015).

29 Ibid.

Appendix 1
The 1951 Convention and 1967 Protocol Relating to the Status of Refugees

Protocol Relating to the Status of Refugees (1967)

THE STATES PARTIES to the present Protocol,

CONSIDERING that the Convention relating to the Status of Refugees done at Geneva on 28 July 1951 (hereinafter referred to as the Convention) covers only those persons who have become refugees as a result of events occurring before 1 January 1951,

CONSIDERING that new refugee situations have arisen since the Convention was adopted and that the refugees concerned may therefore not fall within the scope of the Convention,

CONSIDERING that it is desirable that equal status should be enjoyed by all refugees covered by the definition in the Convention irrespective of the dateline 1 January 1951,

HAVE AGREED as follows:

Article I

GENERAL PROVISION

1. The States Parties to the present Protocol undertake to apply articles 2 to 34 inclusive of the Convention to refugees as hereinafter defined.
2. For the purpose of the present Protocol, the term "refugee" shall, except as regards the application of paragraph 3 of this article, mean any person within the definition of article 1 of the Convention as if the words "As a result of events occurring before 1 January 1951 and ..." and the words "... as a result of such events", in article 1 A (2) were omitted.
3. The present Protocol shall be applied by the States Parties hereto without any geographic limitation, save that existing declarations made by States already Parties to the Convention in accordance with article 1 B (1) (a) of the Convention, shall, unless extended under article 1 B (2) thereof, apply also under the present Protocol.

Article II

CO-OPERATION OF THE NATIONAL AUTHORITIES WITH THE UNITED NATIONS

1. The States Parties to the present Protocol undertake to co-operate with the Office of the United Nations High Commissioner for Refugees, or any other agency of the United Nations which may succeed it, in the exercise of its functions, and shall in particular facilitate its duty of supervising the application of the provisions of the present Protocol.
2. In order to enable the Office of the High Commissioner or any other agency of the United Nations which may succeed it, to make reports to the competent organs of the United Nations, the States Parties to the present Protocol undertake to provide them with the information and statistical data requested, in the appropriate form, concerning:
(a) The condition of refugees;
(b) The implementation of the present Protocol;
(c) Laws, regulations and decrees which are, or may hereafter be, in force relating to refugees.

Article III

INFORMATION ON NATIONAL LEGISLATION

The States Parties to the present Protocol shall communicate to the Secretary-General of the United Nations the laws and regulations which they may adopt to ensure the application of the present Protocol.

Article IV

SETTLEMENT OF DISPUTES

Any dispute between States Parties to the present Protocol which relates to its interpretation or application and which cannot be settled by other means shall be referred to the International Court of Justice at the request of any one of the parties to the dispute.

Article V

ACCESSION

The present Protocol shall be open for accession on behalf of all States Parties to the Convention and of any other State Member of the United Nations or member of any of the specialized agencies or to which an invitation to accede may have been addressed by the General Assembly of the United Nations. Accession shall be effected by the deposit of an instrument of accession with the Secretary-General of the United Nations.

Article VI

FEDERAL CLAUSE

In the case of a Federal or non-unitary State, the following provisions shall apply:
(a) With respect to those articles of the Convention to be applied in accordance with article I, paragraph 1, of the present Protocol that come within the legislative jurisdiction of the federal legislative authority, the obligations of the Federal Government shall to this extent be the same as those of States Parties which are not Federal States;
(b) With respect to those articles of the Convention to be applied in accordance with article I, paragraph 1, of the present Protocol that come within the legislative jurisdiction of constituent States, provinces or cantons which are not, under the constitutional system of the Federation, bound to take legislative action, the Federal Government shall bring such articles with a favourable recommendation to the notice of the appropriate authorities of States, provinces or cantons at the earliest possible moment;
(c) A Federal State Party to the present Protocol shall, at the request of any other State Party hereto transmitted through the Secretary-General of the United Nations, supply a statement of the law and practice of the Federation and its constituent units in regard to any particular provision of the Convention to be applied in accordance with article I, paragraph 1, of the present Protocol, showing the extent to which effect has been given to that provision by legislative or other action.

Article VII

RESERVATIONS AND DECLARATIONS

1. At the time of accession, any State may make reservations in respect of article IV of the present Protocol and in respect of the application in accordance with article I of the present Protocol of any provisions of the Convention other than those contained in articles 1, 3, 4, 16(1) and 33 thereof, provided that in the case of a State Party to the Convention reservations made under this article shall not extend to refugees in respect of whom the Convention applies.
2. Reservations made by States Parties to the Convention in accordance with article 42 thereof shall, unless withdrawn, be applicable in relation to their obligations under the present Protocol.
3. Any State making a reservation in accordance with paragraph 1 of this article may at any time withdraw such reservation by a communication to that effect addressed to the Secretary-General of the United Nations.

4. Declarations made under article 40, paragraphs 1 and 2, of the Convention by a State Party thereto which accedes to the present Protocol shall be deemed to apply in respect of the present Protocol, unless upon accession a notification to the contrary is addressed by the State Party concerned to the Secretary-General of the United Nations. The provisions of article 40, paragraphs 2 and 3, and of article 44, paragraph 3, of the Convention shall be deemed to apply *mutatis mutandis* to the present Protocol.

Article VIII

ENTRY INTO FORCE

1. The present Protocol shall come into force on the day of deposit of the sixth instrument of accession.
2. For each State acceding to the Protocol after the deposit of the sixth instrument of accession, the Protocol shall come into force on the date of deposit by such State of its instrument of accession.

Article IX

DENUNCIATION

1. Any State Party hereto may denounce this Protocol at any time by a notification addressed to the Secretary-General of the United Nations.
2. Such denunciation shall take effect for the State Party concerned one year from the date on which it is received by the Secretary-General of the United Nations.

Article X

NOTIFICATIONS BY THE SECRETARY-GENERAL OF THE UNITED NATIONS

The Secretary-General of the United Nations shall inform the States referred to in article V above of the date of entry into force, accessions, reservations and withdrawals of reservations to and denunciations of the present Protocol, and of declarations and notifications relating hereto.

Article XI

DEPOSIT IN THE ARCHIVES OF THE SECRETARIAT OF THE UNITED NATIONS

A copy of the present Protocol, of which the Chinese, English, French, Russian and Spanish texts are equally authentic, signed by the President of the General

Assembly and by the Secretary-General of the United Nations, shall be deposited in the archives of the Secretariat of the United Nations. The Secretary-General will transmit certified copies thereof to all States Members of the United Nations and to the other States referred to in article V above.

Appendix 2
Other Relevant Instruments

Universal Declaration of Human Rights (1948)

PREAMBLE

Whereas recognition of the inherent dignity and of the equal and inalienable rights of all members of the human family is the foundation of freedom, justice and peace in the world,

Whereas disregard and contempt for human rights have resulted in barbarous acts which have outraged the conscience of mankind, and the advent of a world in which human beings shall enjoy freedom of speech and belief and freedom from fear and want has been proclaimed as the highest aspiration of the common people,

Whereas it is essential, if man is not to be compelled to have recourse, as a last resort, to rebellion against tyranny and oppression, that human rights should be protected by the rule of law,

Whereas it is essential to promote the development of friendly relations between nations,

Whereas the peoples of the United Nations have in the Charter reaffirmed their faith in fundamental human rights, in the dignity and worth of the human person and in the equal rights of men and women and have determined to promote social progress and better standards of life in larger freedom,

Whereas Member States have pledged themselves to achieve, in co-operation with the United Nations, the promotion of universal respect for and observance of human rights and fundamental freedoms,

Whereas a common understanding of these rights and freedoms is of the greatest importance for the full realization of this pledge,

Now, Therefore THE GENERAL ASSEMBLY proclaims THIS UNIVERSAL DECLARATION OF HUMAN RIGHTS as a common standard of achievement for all peoples and all nations, to the end that every individual and every organ of society, keeping this Declaration constantly in mind, shall strive by teaching and education to promote respect for these rights and freedoms and by progressive measures, national and international, to secure their universal and effective recognition and observance, both among the peoples of Member States themselves and among the peoples of territories under their jurisdiction.

Article 1

All human beings are born free and equal in dignity and rights. They are endowed with reason and conscience and should act towards one another in a spirit of brotherhood.

Article 2

Everyone is entitled to all the rights and freedoms set forth in this Declaration, without distinction of any kind, such as race, colour, sex, language, religion, political or other opinion, national or social origin, property, birth or other status. Furthermore, no distinction shall be made on the basis of the political, jurisdictional or international status of the country or territory to which a person belongs, whether it be independent, trust, non-self-governing or under any other limitation of sovereignty.

Article 3

Everyone has the right to life, liberty and security of person.

Article 4

No one shall be held in slavery or servitude; slavery and the slave trade shall be prohibited in all their forms.

Article 5

No one shall be subjected to torture or to cruel, inhuman or degrading treatment or punishment.

Article 6

Everyone has the right to recognition everywhere as a person before the law.

Article 7

All are equal before the law and are entitled without any discrimination to equal protection of the law. All are entitled to equal protection against any discrimination in violation of this Declaration and against any incitement to such discrimination.

Article 8

Everyone has the right to an effective remedy by the competent national tribunals for acts violating the fundamental rights granted him by the constitution or by law.

Article 9

No one shall be subjected to arbitrary arrest, detention or exile.

Article 10

Everyone is entitled in full equality to a fair and public hearing by an independent and impartial tribunal, in the determination of his rights and obligations and of any criminal charge against him.

Article 11

(1) Everyone charged with a penal offence has the right to be presumed innocent until proved guilty according to law in a public trial at which he has had all the guarantees necessary for his defence.
(2) No one shall be held guilty of any penal offence on account of any act or omission which did not constitute a penal offence, under national or international law, at the time when it was committed. Nor shall a heavier penalty be imposed than the one that was applicable at the time the penal offence was committed.

Article 12

No one shall be subjected to arbitrary interference with his privacy, family, home or correspondence, nor to attacks upon his honour and reputation. Everyone has the right to the protection of the law against such interference or attacks.

Article 13

(1) Everyone has the right to freedom of movement and residence within the borders of each state.
(2) Everyone has the right to leave any country, including his own, and to return to his country.

Article 14

(1) Everyone has the right to seek and to enjoy in other countries asylum from persecution.
(2) This right may not be invoked in the case of prosecutions genuinely arising from non-political crimes or from acts contrary to the purposes and principles of the United Nations.

Article 15

(1) Everyone has the right to a nationality.

(2) No one shall be arbitrarily deprived of his nationality nor denied the right to change his nationality.

Article 16

(1) Men and women of full age, without any limitation due to race, nationality or religion, have the right to marry and to found a family. They are entitled to equal rights as to marriage, during marriage and at its dissolution.
(2) Marriage shall be entered into only with the free and full consent of the intending spouses.
(3) The family is the natural and fundamental group unit of society and is entitled to protection by society and the State.

Article 17

(1) Everyone has the right to own property alone as well as in association with others.
(2) No one shall be arbitrarily deprived of his property.

Article 18

Everyone has the right to freedom of thought, conscience and religion; this right includes freedom to change his religion or belief, and freedom, either alone or in community with others and in public or private, to manifest his religion or belief in teaching, practice, worship and observance.

Article 19

Everyone has the right to freedom of opinion and expression; this right includes freedom to hold opinions without interference and to seek, receive and impart information and ideas through any media and regardless of frontiers.

Article 20

(1) Everyone has the right to freedom of peaceful assembly and association.
(2) No one may be compelled to belong to an association.

Article 21

(1) Everyone has the right to take part in the government of his country, directly or through freely chosen representatives.
(2) Everyone has the right of equal access to public service in his country.
(3) The will of the people shall be the basis of the authority of government; this will shall be expressed in periodic and genuine elections which shall be by

universal and equal suffrage and shall be held by secret vote or by equivalent free voting procedures.

Article 22

Everyone, as a member of society, has the right to social security and is entitled to realization, through national effort and international co-operation and in accordance with the organization and resources of each State, of the economic, social and cultural rights indispensable for his dignity and the free development of his personality.

Article 23

(1) Everyone has the right to work, to free choice of employment, to just and favourable conditions of work and to protection against unemployment.
(2) Everyone, without any discrimination, has the right to equal pay for equal work.
(3) Everyone who works has the right to just and favourable remuneration ensuring for himself and his family an existence worthy of human dignity, and supplemented, if necessary, by other means of social protection.
(4) Everyone has the right to form and to join trade unions for the protection of his interests.

Article 24

Everyone has the right to rest and leisure, including reasonable limitation of working hours and periodic holidays with pay.

Article 25

(1) Everyone has the right to a standard of living adequate for the health and well-being of himself and of his family, including food, clothing, housing and medical care and necessary social services, and the right to security in the event of unemployment, sickness, disability, widowhood, old age or other lack of livelihood in circumstances beyond his control.
(2) Motherhood and childhood are entitled to special care and assistance. All children, whether born in or out of wedlock, shall enjoy the same social protection.

Article 26

(1) Everyone has the right to education. Education shall be free, at least in the elementary and fundamental stages. Elementary education shall be compulsory. Technical and professional education shall be made generally available and higher education shall be equally accessible to all on the basis of merit.

(2) Education shall be directed to the full development of the human personality and to the strengthening of respect for human rights and fundamental freedoms. It shall promote understanding, tolerance and friendship among all nations, racial or religious groups, and shall further the activities of the United Nations for the maintenance of peace.
(3) Parents have a prior right to choose the kind of education that shall be given to their children.

Article 27

(1) Everyone has the right freely to participate in the cultural life of the community, to enjoy the arts and to share in scientific advancement and its benefits.
(2) Everyone has the right to the protection of the moral and material interests resulting from any scientific, literary or artistic production of which he is the author.

Article 28

Everyone is entitled to a social and international order in which the rights and freedoms set forth in this Declaration can be fully realized.

Article 29

(1) Everyone has duties to the community in which alone the free and full development of his personality is possible.
(2) In the exercise of his rights and freedoms, everyone shall be subject only to such limitations as are determined by law solely for the purpose of securing due recognition and respect for the rights and freedoms of others and of meeting the just requirements of morality, public order and the general welfare in a democratic society.
(3) These rights and freedoms may in no case be exercised contrary to the purposes and principles of the United Nations.

Article 30

Nothing in this Declaration may be interpreted as implying for any State, group or person any right to engage in any activity or to perform any act aimed at the destruction of any of the rights and freedoms set forth herein.

United Nations Declaration on Territorial Asylum (1967)

The General Assembly,

Noting that the purposes proclaimed in the Charter of the United Nations are to maintain international peace and security, to develop friendly relations among all nations and to achieve international co-operation in solving international problems of an economic, social, cultural or humanitarian character and in promoting and encouraging respect for human rights and for fundamental freedoms for all without distinction as to race, sex, language or religion,

Mindful of the Universal Declaration of Human Rights, which declares in article 14 that:

"1. Everyone has the right to seek and to enjoy in other countries asylum from persecution."

"2. This right may not be invoked in the case of prosecutions genuinely arising from non-political crimes or from acts contrary to the purposes and principles of the United Nations",

Recalling also article 13, paragraph 2, of the Universal Declaration of Human Rights, which states:

"Everyone has the right to leave any country, including his own, and to return to his country",

Recognizing that the grant of asylum by a State to persons entitled to invoke article 14 of the Universal Declaration of Human Rights is a peaceful and humanitarian act and that, as such, it cannot be regarded as unfriendly by any other State,

Recommends that, without prejudice to existing instruments dealing with asylum and the status of refugees and stateless persons, States should base themselves in their practices relating to territorial asylum on the following principles:

Article 1

1. Asylum granted by a State, in the exercise of its sovereignty, to persons entitled to invoke article 14 of the Universal Declaration of Human Rights, including persons struggling against colonialism, shall be respected by all other States.
2. The right to seek and to enjoy asylum may not be invoked by any person with respect to whom there are serious reasons for considering that he has committed a crime against peace, a war crime or a crime against humanity, as defined in the international instruments drawn up to make provision in respect of such crimes.

3. It shall rest with the State granting asylum to evaluate the grounds for the grant of asylum.

Article 2

1. The situation of persons referred to in article 1, paragraph 1, is, without prejudice to the sovereignty of States and the purposes and principles of the United Nations, of concern to the international community.
2. Where a State finds difficulty in granting or continuing to grant asylum, States individually or jointly or through the United Nations shall consider, in a spirit of international solidarity, appropriate measures to lighten the burden on that State.

Article 3

1. No person referred to in article 1, paragraph 1, shall be subjected to measures such as rejection at the frontier or, if he has already entered the territory in which he seeks asylum, expulsion or compulsory return to any State where he may be subjected to persecution.
2. Exception may be made to the foregoing principle only for overriding reasons of national security or in order to safeguard the population, as in the case of a mass influx of persons.
3. Should a State decide in any case that exception to the principle stated in paragraph 1 of this article would be justified, it shall consider the possibility of granting to the person concerned, under such conditions as it may deem appropriate, an opportunity, whether by way of provisional asylum or otherwise, of going to another State.

Article 4

States granting asylum shall not permit persons who have received asylum to engage in activities contrary to the purposes and principles of the United Nations.

United Nations Convention against Torture and Other Cruel, Inhuman or Degrading Treatment or Punishment (1984)

The States Parties to this Convention,

Considering that, in accordance with the principles proclaimed in the Charter of the United Nations, recognition of the equal and inalienable rights of all members of the human family is the foundation of freedom, justice and peace in the world,

Recognizing that those rights derive from the inherent dignity of the human person,

Considering the obligation of States under the Charter, in particular Article 55, to promote universal respect for, and observance of, human rights and fundamental freedoms,

Having regard to article 5 of the Universal Declaration of Human Rights and article 7 of the International Covenant on Civil and Political Rights, both of which provide that no one shall be subjected to torture or to cruel, inhuman or degrading treatment or punishment,

Having regard also to the Declaration on the Protection of All Persons from Being Subjected to Torture and Other Cruel, Inhuman or Degrading Treatment or Punishment, adopted by the General Assembly on 9 December 1975,

Desiring to make more effective the struggle against torture and other cruel, inhuman or degrading treatment or punishment throughout the world,

Have agreed as follows:

PART I

Article 1

1. For the purposes of this Convention, the term "torture" means any act by which severe pain or suffering, whether physical or mental, is intentionally inflicted on a person for such purposes as obtaining from him or a third person information or a confession, punishing him for an act he or a third person has committed or is suspected of having committed, or intimidating or coercing him or a third person, or for any reason based on discrimination of any kind, when such pain or suffering is inflicted by or at the instigation of or with the consent or acquiescence of a public official or other person acting in an official capacity. It does not include pain or suffering arising only from, inherent in or incidental to lawful sanctions.

2. This article is without prejudice to any international instrument or national legislation which does or may contain provisions of wider application.

Article 2

1. Each State Party shall take effective legislative, administrative, judicial or other measures to prevent acts of torture in any territory under its jurisdiction.
2. No exceptional circumstances whatsoever, whether a state of war or a threat of war, internal political instability or any other public emergency, may be invoked as a justification of torture.
3. An order from a superior officer or a public authority may not be invoked as a justification of torture.

Article 3

1. No State Party shall expel, return ("refouler") or extradite a person to another State where there are substantial grounds for believing that he would be in danger of being subjected to torture.
2. For the purpose of determining whether there are such grounds, the competent authorities shall take into account all relevant considerations including, where applicable, the existence in the State concerned of a consistent pattern of gross, flagrant or mass violations of human rights.

Article 4

1. Each State Party shall ensure that all acts of torture are offences under its criminal law. The same shall apply to an attempt to commit torture and to an act by any person which constitutes complicity or participation in torture.
2. Each State Party shall make these offences punishable by appropriate penalties which take into account their grave nature.

Article 5

1. Each State Party shall take such measures as may be necessary to establish its jurisdiction over the offences referred to in article 4 in the following cases:
(a) When the offences are committed in any territory under its jurisdiction or on board a ship or aircraft registered in that State;
(b) When the alleged offender is a national of that State;
(c) When the victim is a national of that State if that State considers it appropriate.
2. Each State Party shall likewise take such measures as may be necessary to establish its jurisdiction over such offences in cases where the alleged offender is present in any territory under its jurisdiction and it does not extradite him pursuant to article 8 to any of the States mentioned in paragraph 1 of this article.

3. This Convention does not exclude any criminal jurisdiction exercised in accordance with internal law.

Article 6

1. Upon being satisfied, after an examination of information available to it, that the circumstances so warrant, any State Party in whose territory a person alleged to have committed any offence referred to in article 4 is present shall take him into custody or take other legal measures to ensure his presence. The custody and other legal measures shall be as provided in the law of that State but may be continued only for such time as is necessary to enable any criminal or extradition proceedings to be instituted.
2. Such State shall immediately make a preliminary inquiry into the facts.
3. Any person in custody pursuant to paragraph 1 of this article shall be assisted in communicating immediately with the nearest appropriate representative of the State of which he is a national, or, if he is a stateless person, with the representative of the State where he usually resides.
4. When a State, pursuant to this article, has taken a person into custody, it shall immediately notify the States referred to in article 5, paragraph 1, of the fact that such person is in custody and of the circumstances which warrant his detention. The State which makes the preliminary inquiry contemplated in paragraph 2 of this article shall promptly report its findings to the said States and shall indicate whether it intends to exercise jurisdiction.

Article 7

1. The State Party in the territory under whose jurisdiction a person alleged to have committed any offence referred to in article 4 is found shall in the cases contemplated in article 5, if it does not extradite him, submit the case to its competent authorities for the purpose of prosecution.
2. These authorities shall take their decision in the same manner as in the case of any ordinary offence of a serious nature under the law of that State. In the cases referred to in article 5, paragraph 2, the standards of evidence required for prosecution and conviction shall in no way be less stringent than those which apply in the cases referred to in article 5, paragraph 1.
3. Any person regarding whom proceedings are brought in connection with any of the offences referred to in article 4 shall be guaranteed fair treatment at all stages of the proceedings.

Article 8

1. The offences referred to in article 4 shall be deemed to be included as extraditable offences in any extradition treaty existing between States Parties. States Parties

undertake to include such offences as extraditable offences in every extradition treaty to be concluded between them.
2. If a State Party which makes extradition conditional on the existence of a treaty receives a request for extradition from another State Party with which it has no extradition treaty, it may consider this Convention as the legal basis for extradition in respect of such offences. Extradition shall be subject to the other conditions provided by the law of the requested State.
3. States Parties which do not make extradition conditional on the existence of a treaty shall recognize such offences as extraditable offences between themselves subject to the conditions provided by the law of the requested State.
4. Such offences shall be treated, for the purpose of extradition between States Parties, as if they had been committed not only in the place in which they occurred but also in the territories of the States required to establish their jurisdiction in accordance with article 5, paragraph 1.

Article 9

1. States Parties shall afford one another the greatest measure of assistance in connection with criminal proceedings brought in respect of any of the offences referred to in article 4, including the supply of all evidence at their disposal necessary for the proceedings.
2. States Parties shall carry out their obligations under paragraph 1 of this article in conformity with any treaties on mutual judicial assistance that may exist between them.

Article 10

1. Each State Party shall ensure that education and information regarding the prohibition against torture are fully included in the training of law enforcement personnel, civil or military, medical personnel, public officials and other persons who may be involved in the custody, interrogation or treatment of any individual subjected to any form of arrest, detention or imprisonment.
2. Each State Party shall include this prohibition in the rules or instructions issued in regard to the duties and functions of any such person.

Article 11

Each State Party shall keep under systematic review interrogation rules, instructions, methods and practices as well as arrangements for the custody and treatment of persons subjected to any form of arrest, detention or imprisonment in any territory under its jurisdiction, with a view to preventing any cases of torture.

Article 12

Each State Party shall ensure that its competent authorities proceed to a prompt and impartial investigation, wherever there is reasonable ground to believe that an act of torture has been committed in any territory under its jurisdiction.

Article 13

Each State Party shall ensure that any individual who alleges he has been subjected to torture in any territory under its jurisdiction has the right to complain to, and to have his case promptly and impartially examined by, its competent authorities. Steps shall be taken to ensure that the complainant and witnesses are protected against all ill-treatment or intimidation as a consequence of his complaint or any evidence given.

Article 14

1. Each State Party shall ensure in its legal system that the victim of an act of torture obtains redress and has an enforceable right to fair and adequate compensation, including the means for as full rehabilitation as possible. In the event of the death of the victim as a result of an act of torture, his dependants shall be entitled to compensation.
2. Nothing in this article shall affect any right of the victim or other persons to compensation which may exist under national law.

Article 15

Each State Party shall ensure that any statement which is established to have been made as a result of torture shall not be invoked as evidence in any proceedings, except against a person accused of torture as evidence that the statement was made.

Article 16

1. Each State Party shall undertake to prevent in any territory under its jurisdiction other acts of cruel, inhuman or degrading treatment or punishment which do not amount to torture as defined in article 1, when such acts are committed by or at the instigation of or with the consent or acquiescence of a public official or other person acting in an official capacity. In particular, the obligations contained in articles 10, 11, 12 and 13 shall apply with the substitution for references to torture of references to other forms of cruel, inhuman or degrading treatment or punishment.
2. The provisions of this Convention are without prejudice to the provisions of any other international instrument or national law which prohibits cruel, inhuman or degrading treatment or punishment or which relates to extradition or expulsion.

PART II

Article 17

1. There shall be established a Committee against Torture (hereinafter referred to as the Committee) which shall carry out the functions hereinafter provided. The Committee shall consist of ten experts of high moral standing and recognized competence in the field of human rights, who shall serve in their personal capacity. The experts shall be elected by the States Parties, consideration being given to equitable geographical distribution and to the usefulness of the participation of some persons having legal experience.
2. The members of the Committee shall be elected by secret ballot from a list of persons nominated by States Parties. Each State Party may nominate one person from among its own nationals. States Parties shall bear in mind the usefulness of nominating persons who are also members of the Human Rights Committee established under the International Covenant on Civil and Political Rights and who are willing to serve on the Committee against Torture.
3. Elections of the members of the Committee shall be held at biennial meetings of States Parties convened by the Secretary-General of the United Nations. At those meetings, for which two thirds of the States Parties shall constitute a quorum, the persons elected to the Committee shall be those who obtain the largest number of votes and an absolute majority of the votes of the representatives of States Parties present and voting.
4. The initial election shall be held no later than six months after the date of the entry into force of this Convention. At least four months before the date of each election, the Secretary-General of the United Nations shall address a letter to the States Parties inviting them to submit their nominations within three months. The Secretary-General shall prepare a list in alphabetical order of all persons thus nominated, indicating the States Parties which have nominated them, and shall submit it to the States Parties.
5. The members of the Committee shall be elected for a term of four years. They shall be eligible for re-election if renominated. However, the term of five of the members elected at the first election shall expire at the end of two years; immediately after the first election the names of these five members shall be chosen by lot by the chairman of the meeting referred to in paragraph 3 of this article.
6. If a member of the Committee dies or resigns or for any other cause can no longer perform his Committee duties, the State Party which nominated him shall appoint another expert from among its nationals to serve for the remainder of his term, subject to the approval of the majority of the States Parties. The approval shall be considered given unless half or more of the States Parties respond negatively within six weeks after having been informed by the Secretary-General of the United Nations of the proposed appointment.
7. States Parties shall be responsible for the expenses of the members of the Committee while they are in performance of Committee duties.

Article 18

1. The Committee shall elect its officers for a term of two years. They may be re-elected.
2. The Committee shall establish its own rules of procedure, but these rules shall provide, inter alia, that:
(a) Six members shall constitute a quorum;
(b) Decisions of the Committee shall be made by a majority vote of the members present.
3. The Secretary-General of the United Nations shall provide the necessary staff and facilities for the effective performance of the functions of the Committee under this Convention.
4. The Secretary-General of the United Nations shall convene the initial meeting of the Committee. After its initial meeting, the Committee shall meet at such times as shall be provided in its rules of procedure.
5. The States Parties shall be responsible for expenses incurred in connection with the holding of meetings of the States Parties and of the Committee, including reimbursement to the United Nations for any expenses, such as the cost of staff and facilities, incurred by the United Nations pursuant to paragraph 3 of this article.

Article 19

1. The States Parties shall submit to the Committee, through the Secretary-General of the United Nations, reports on the measures they have taken to give effect to their undertakings under this Convention, within one year after the entry into force of the Convention for the State Party concerned. Thereafter the States Parties shall submit supplementary reports every four years on any new measures taken and such other reports as the Committee may request.
2. The Secretary-General of the United Nations shall transmit the reports to all States Parties.
3. Each report shall be considered by the Committee which may make such general comments on the report as it may consider appropriate and shall forward these to the State Party concerned. That State Party may respond with any observations it chooses to the Committee.
4. The Committee may, at its discretion, decide to include any comments made by it in accordance with paragraph 3 of this article, together with the observations thereon received from the State Party concerned, in its annual report made in accordance with article 24. If so requested by the State Party concerned, the Committee may also include a copy of the report submitted under paragraph 1 of this article.

Article 20

1. If the Committee receives reliable information which appears to it to contain well-founded indications that torture is being systematically practised in the territory of a State Party, the Committee shall invite that State Party to co-operate in the examination of the information and to this end to submit observations with regard to the information concerned.
2. Taking into account any observations which may have been submitted by the State Party concerned, as well as any other relevant information available to it, the Committee may, if it decides that this is warranted, designate one or more of its members to make a confidential inquiry and to report to the Committee urgently.
3. If an inquiry is made in accordance with paragraph 2 of this article, the Committee shall seek the co-operation of the State Party concerned. In agreement with that State Party, such an inquiry may include a visit to its territory.
4. After examining the findings of its member or members submitted in accordance with paragraph 2 of this article, the Commission shall transmit these findings to the State Party concerned together with any comments or suggestions which seem appropriate in view of the situation.
5. All the proceedings of the Committee referred to in paragraphs 1 to 4 of this article shall be confidential, and at all stages of the proceedings the co-operation of the State Party shall be sought. After such proceedings have been completed with regard to an inquiry made in accordance with paragraph 2, the Committee may, after consultations with the State Party concerned, decide to include a summary account of the results of the proceedings in its annual report made in accordance with article 24.

Article 21

1. A State Party to this Convention may at any time declare under this article that it recognizes the competence of the Committee to receive and consider communications to the effect that a State Party claims that another State Party is not fulfilling its obligations under this Convention. Such communications may be received and considered according to the procedures laid down in this article only if submitted by a State Party which has made a declaration recognizing in regard to itself the competence of the Committee. No communication shall be dealt with by the Committee under this article if it concerns a State Party which has not made such a declaration. Communications received under this article shall be dealt with in accordance with the following procedure;
(a) If a State Party considers that another State Party is not giving effect to the provisions of this Convention, it may, by written communication, bring the matter to the attention of that State Party. Within three months after the receipt of the communication the receiving State shall afford the State which sent the communication an explanation or any other statement in writing clarifying the

matter, which should include, to the extent possible and pertinent, reference to domestic procedures and remedies taken, pending or available in the matter;
(b) If the matter is not adjusted to the satisfaction of both States Parties concerned within six months after the receipt by the receiving State of the initial communication, either State shall have the right to refer the matter to the Committee, by notice given to the Committee and to the other State;
(c) The Committee shall deal with a matter referred to it under this article only after it has ascertained that all domestic remedies have been invoked and exhausted in the matter, in conformity with the generally recognized principles of international law. This shall not be the rule where the application of the remedies is unreasonably prolonged or is unlikely to bring effective relief to the person who is the victim of the violation of this Convention;
(d) The Committee shall hold closed meetings when examining communications under this article;
(e) Subject to the provisions of subparagraph (c), the Committee shall make available its good offices to the States Parties concerned with a view to a friendly solution of the matter on the basis of respect for the obligations provided for in this Convention. For this purpose, the Committee may, when appropriate, set up an ad hoc conciliation commission;
(f) In any matter referred to it under this article, the Committee may call upon the States Parties concerned, referred to in subparagraph (b), to supply any relevant information;
(g) The States Parties concerned, referred to in subparagraph (b), shall have the right to be represented when the matter is being considered by the Committee and to make submissions orally and/or in writing;
(h) The Committee shall, within twelve months after the date of receipt of notice under subparagraph (b), submit a report:
(i) If a solution within the terms of subparagraph (e) is reached, the Committee shall confine its report to a brief statement of the facts and of the solution reached;
(ii) If a solution within the terms of subparagraph (e) is not reached, the Committee shall confine its report to a brief statement of the facts; the written submissions and record of the oral submissions made by the States Parties concerned shall be attached to the report. In every matter, the report shall be communicated to the States Parties concerned.
2. The provisions of this article shall come into force when five States Parties to this Convention have made declarations under paragraph 1 of this article. Such declarations shall be deposited by the States Parties with the Secretary-General of the United Nations, who shall transmit copies thereof to the other States Parties. A declaration may be withdrawn at any time by notification to the Secretary-General. Such a withdrawal shall not prejudice the consideration of any matter which is the subject of a communication already transmitted under this article; no further communication by any State Party shall be received under this article after the notification of withdrawal of the declaration has been received by the Secretary-General, unless the State Party concerned has made a new declaration.

Article 22

1. A State Party to this Convention may at any time declare under this article that it recognizes the competence of the Committee to receive and consider communications from or on behalf of individuals subject to its jurisdiction who claim to be victims of a violation by a State Party of the provisions of the Convention. No communication shall be received by the Committee if it concerns a State Party which has not made such a declaration.
2. The Committee shall consider inadmissible any communication under this article which is anonymous or which it considers to be an abuse of the right of submission of such communications or to be incompatible with the provisions of this Convention.
3. Subject to the provisions of paragraph 2, the Committee shall bring any communications submitted to it under this article to the attention of the State Party to this Convention which has made a declaration under paragraph 1 and is alleged to be violating any provisions of the Convention. Within six months, the receiving State shall submit to the Committee written explanations or statements clarifying the matter and the remedy, if any, that may have been taken by that State.
4. The Committee shall consider communications received under this article in the light of all information made available to it by or on behalf of the individual and by the State Party concerned.
5. The Committee shall not consider any communications from an individual under this article unless it has ascertained that:
(a) The same matter has not been, and is not being, examined under another procedure of international investigation or settlement;
(b) The individual has exhausted all available domestic remedies; this shall not be the rule where the application of the remedies is unreasonably prolonged or is unlikely to bring effective relief to the person who is the victim of the violation of this Convention.
6. The Committee shall hold closed meetings when examining communications under this article.
7. The Committee shall forward its views to the State Party concerned and to the individual.
8. The provisions of this article shall come into force when five States Parties to this Convention have made declarations under paragraph 1 of this article. Such declarations shall be deposited by the States Parties with the Secretary-General of the United Nations, who shall transmit copies thereof to the other States Parties. A declaration may be withdrawn at any time by notification to the Secretary-General. Such a withdrawal shall not prejudice the consideration of any matter which is the subject of a communication already transmitted under this article; no further communication by or on behalf of an individual shall be received under this article after the notification of withdrawal of the declaration has been received by the Secretary-General, unless the State Party has made a new declaration.

Article 23

The members of the Committee and of the ad hoc conciliation commissions which may be appointed under article 21, paragraph 1 (e), shall be entitled to the facilities, privileges and immunities of experts on mission for the United Nations as laid down in the relevant sections of the Convention on the Privileges and Immunities of the United Nations.

Article 24

The Committee shall submit an annual report on its activities under this Convention to the States Parties and to the General Assembly of the United Nations.

PART III

Article 25

1. This Convention is open for signature by all States.
2. This Convention is subject to ratification. Instruments of ratification shall be deposited with the Secretary-General of the United Nations.

Article 26

This Convention is open to accession by all States. Accession shall be effected by the deposit of an instrument of accession with the Secretary-General of the United Nations.

Article 27

1. This Convention shall enter into force on the thirtieth day after the date of the deposit with the Secretary-General of the United Nations of the twentieth instrument of ratification or accession.
2. For each State ratifying this Convention or acceding to it after the deposit of the twentieth instrument of ratification or accession, the Convention shall enter into force on the thirtieth day after the date of the deposit of its own instrument of ratification or accession.

Article 28

1. Each State may, at the time of signature or ratification of this Convention or accession thereto, declare that it does not recognize the competence of the Committee provided for in article 20.

2. Any State Party having made a reservation in accordance with paragraph 1 of this article may, at any time, withdraw this reservation by notification to the Secretary-General of the United Nations.

Article 29

1. Any State Party to this Convention may propose an amendment and file it with the Secretary-General of the United Nations. The Secretary-General shall thereupon communicate the proposed amendment to the States Parties with a request that they notify him whether they favour a conference of States Parties for the purpose of considering and voting upon the proposal. In the event that within four months from the date of such communication at least one third of the States Parties favours such a conference, the Secretary-General shall convene the conference under the auspices of the United Nations. Any amendment adopted by a majority of the States Parties present and voting at the conference shall be submitted by the Secretary-General to all the States Parties for acceptance.
2. An amendment adopted in accordance with paragraph 1 of this article shall enter into force when two thirds of the States Parties to this Convention have notified the Secretary-General of the United Nations that they have accepted it in accordance with their respective constitutional processes.
3. When amendments enter into force, they shall be binding on those States Parties which have accepted them, other States Parties still being bound by the provisions of this Convention and any earlier amendments which they have accepted.

Article 30

1. Any dispute between two or more States Parties concerning the interpretation or application of this Convention which cannot be settled through negotiation shall, at the request of one of them, be submitted to arbitration. If within six months from the date of the request for arbitration the Parties are unable to agree on the organization of the arbitration, any one of those Parties may refer the dispute to the International Court of Justice by request in conformity with the Statute of the Court.
2. Each State may, at the time of signature or ratification of this Convention or accession thereto, declare that it does not consider itself bound by paragraph 1 of this article. The other States Parties shall not be bound by paragraph 1 of this article with respect to any State Party having made such a reservation.
3. Any State Party having made a reservation in accordance with paragraph 2 of this article may at any time withdraw this reservation by notification to the Secretary-General of the United Nations.

Article 31

1. A State Party may denounce this Convention by written notification to the Secretary-General of the United Nations. Denunciation becomes effective one year after the date of receipt of the notification by the Secretary-General.
2. Such a denunciation shall not have the effect of releasing the State Party from its obligations under this Convention in regard to any act or omission which occurs prior to the date at which the denunciation becomes effective, nor shall denunciation prejudice in any way the continued consideration of any matter which is already under consideration by the Committee prior to the date at which the denunciation becomes effective.
3. Following the date at which the denunciation of a State Party becomes effective, the Committee shall not commence consideration of any new matter regarding that State.

Article 32

The Secretary-General of the United Nations shall inform all States Members of the United Nations and all States which have signed this Convention or acceded to it of the following:
(a) Signatures, ratifications and accessions under articles 25 and 26;
(b) The date of entry into force of this Convention under article 27 and the date of the entry into force of any amendments under article 29;
(c) Denunciations under article 31.

Article 33

1. This Convention, of which the Arabic, Chinese, English, French, Russian and Spanish texts are equally authentic, shall be deposited with the Secretary-General of the United Nations.
2. The Secretary-General of the United Nations shall transmit certified copies of this Convention to all States.

United Nations Convention on the Rights of the Child (1989)

Preamble

The States Parties to the present Convention,

Considering that, in accordance with the principles proclaimed in the Charter of the United Nations, recognition of the inherent dignity and of the equal and inalienable rights of all members of the human family is the foundation of freedom, justice and peace in the world,

Bearing in mind that the peoples of the United Nations have, in the Charter, reaffirmed their faith in fundamental human rights and in the dignity and worth of the human person, and have determined to promote social progress and better standards of life in larger freedom,

Recognizing that the United Nations has, in the Universal Declaration of Human Rights and in the International Covenants on Human Rights, proclaimed and agreed that everyone is entitled to all the rights and freedoms set forth therein, without distinction of any kind, such as race, colour, sex, language, religion, political or other opinion, national or social origin, property, birth or other status,

Recalling that, in the Universal Declaration of Human Rights, the United Nations has proclaimed that childhood is entitled to special care and assistance,

Convinced that the family, as the fundamental group of society and the natural environment for the growth and well-being of all its members and particularly children, should be afforded the necessary protection and assistance so that it can fully assume its responsibilities within the community,

Recognizing that the child, for the full and harmonious development of his or her personality, should grow up in a family environment, in an atmosphere of happiness, love and understanding,

Considering that the child should be fully prepared to live an individual life in society, and brought up in the spirit of the ideals proclaimed in the Charter of the United Nations, and in particular in the spirit of peace, dignity, tolerance, freedom, equality and solidarity,

Bearing in mind that the need to extend particular care to the child has been stated in the Geneva Declaration of the Rights of the Child of 1924 and in the Declaration of the Rights of the Child adopted by the General Assembly on 20 November 1959 and recognized in the Universal Declaration of Human Rights, in the International Covenant on Civil and Political Rights (in particular in articles 23 and 24), in the International Covenant on Economic, Social and Cultural Rights (in particular in article 10) and in the statutes and relevant instruments of specialized agencies and international organizations concerned with the welfare of children,

Bearing in mind that, as indicated in the Declaration of the Rights of the Child, "the child, by reason of his physical and mental immaturity, needs special safeguards and care, including appropriate legal protection, before as well as after birth",

Recalling the provisions of the Declaration on Social and Legal Principles relating to the Protection and Welfare of Children, with Special Reference to Foster Placement and Adoption Nationally and Internationally; the United Nations Standard Minimum Rules for the Administration of Juvenile Justice (The Beijing Rules); and the Declaration on the Protection of Women and Children in Emergency and Armed Conflict,

Recognizing that, in all countries in the world, there are children living in exceptionally difficult conditions, and that such children need special consideration,

Taking due account of the importance of the traditions and cultural values of each people for the protection and harmonious development of the child,

Recognizing the importance of international co-operation for improving the living conditions of children in every country, in particular in the developing countries,

Have agreed as follows:

PART I

Article 1

For the purposes of the present Convention, a child means every human being below the age of eighteen years unless, under the law applicable to the child, majority is attained earlier.

Article 2

1. States Parties shall respect and ensure the rights set forth in the present Convention to each child within their jurisdiction without discrimination of any kind, irrespective of the child's or his or her parent's or legal guardian's race, colour, sex, language, religion, political or other opinion, national, ethnic or social origin, property, disability, birth or other status.
2. States Parties shall take all appropriate measures to ensure that the child is protected against all forms of discrimination or punishment on the basis of the status, activities, expressed opinions, or beliefs of the child's parents, legal guardians, or family members.

Article 3

1. In all actions concerning children, whether undertaken by public or private social welfare institutions, courts of law, administrative authorities or legislative bodies, the best interests of the child shall be a primary consideration.
2. States Parties undertake to ensure the child such protection and care as is necessary for his or her well-being, taking into account the rights and duties of his or her parents, legal guardians, or other individuals legally responsible for him or her, and, to this end, shall take all appropriate legislative and administrative measures.
3. States Parties shall ensure that the institutions, services and facilities responsible for the care or protection of children shall conform with the standards established by competent authorities, particularly in the areas of safety, health, in the number and suitability of their staff, as well as competent supervision.

Article 4

States Parties shall undertake all appropriate legislative, administrative, and other measures for the implementation of the rights recognized in the present Convention. With regard to economic, social and cultural rights, States Parties shall undertake such measures to the maximum extent of their available resources and, where needed, within the framework of international co-operation.

Article 5

States Parties shall respect the responsibilities, rights and duties of parents or, where applicable, the members of the extended family or community as provided for by local custom, legal guardians or other persons legally responsible for the child, to provide, in a manner consistent with the evolving capacities of the child, appropriate direction and guidance in the exercise by the child of the rights recognized in the present Convention.

Article 6

1. States Parties recognize that every child has the inherent right to life.
2. States Parties shall ensure to the maximum extent possible the survival and development of the child.

Article 7

1. The child shall be registered immediately after birth and shall have the right from birth to a name, the right to acquire a nationality and, as far as possible, the right to know and be cared for by his or her parents.

2. States Parties shall ensure the implementation of these rights in accordance with their national law and their obligations under the relevant international instruments in this field, in particular where the child would otherwise be stateless.

Article 8

1. States Parties undertake to respect the right of the child to preserve his or her identity, including nationality, name and family relations as recognized by law without unlawful interference.
2. Where a child is illegally deprived of some or all of the elements of his or her identity, States Parties shall provide appropriate assistance and protection, with a view to speedily re-establishing his or her identity.

Article 9

1. States Parties shall ensure that a child shall not be separated from his or her parents against their will, except when competent authorities subject to judicial review determine, in accordance with applicable law and procedures, that such separation is necessary for the best interests of the child. Such determination may be necessary in a particular case such as one involving abuse or neglect of the child by the parents, or one where the parents are living separately and a decision must be made as to the child's place of residence.
2. In any proceedings pursuant to paragraph 1 of the present article, all interested parties shall be given an opportunity to participate in the proceedings and make their views known.
3. States Parties shall respect the right of the child who is separated from one or both parents to maintain personal relations and direct contact with both parents on a regular basis, except if it is contrary to the child's best interests.
4. Where such separation results from any action initiated by a State Party, such as the detention, imprisonment, exile, deportation or death (including death arising from any cause while the person is in the custody of the State) of one or both parents or of the child, that State Party shall, upon request, provide the parents, the child or, if appropriate, another member of the family with the essential information concerning the whereabouts of the absent member(s) of the family unless the provision of the information would be detrimental to the well-being of the child. States Parties shall further ensure that the submission of such a request shall of itself entail no adverse consequences for the person(s) concerned.

Article 10

1. In accordance with the obligation of States Parties under article 9, paragraph 1, applications by a child or his or her parents to enter or leave a State Party for the purpose of family reunification shall be dealt with by States Parties in a positive, humane and expeditious manner. States Parties shall further ensure

that the submission of such a request shall entail no adverse consequences for the applicants and for the members of their family.
2. A child whose parents reside in different States shall have the right to maintain on a regular basis, save in exceptional circumstances personal relations and direct contacts with both parents. Towards that end and in accordance with the obligation of States Parties under article 9, paragraph 1, States Parties shall respect the right of the child and his or her parents to leave any country, including their own, and to enter their own country. The right to leave any country shall be subject only to such restrictions as are prescribed by law and which are necessary to protect the national security, public order (ordre public), public health or morals or the rights and freedoms of others and are consistent with the other rights recognized in the present Convention.

Article 11

1. States Parties shall take measures to combat the illicit transfer and non-return of children abroad.
2. To this end, States Parties shall promote the conclusion of bilateral or multilateral agreements or accession to existing agreements.

Article 12

1. States Parties shall assure to the child who is capable of forming his or her own views the right to express those views freely in all matters affecting the child, the views of the child being given due weight in accordance with the age and maturity of the child.
2. For this purpose, the child shall in particular be provided the opportunity to be heard in any judicial and administrative proceedings affecting the child, either directly, or through a representative or an appropriate body, in a manner consistent with the procedural rules of national law.

Article 13

1. The child shall have the right to freedom of expression; this right shall include freedom to seek, receive and impart information and ideas of all kinds, regardless of frontiers, either orally, in writing or in print, in the form of art, or through any other media of the child's choice.
2. The exercise of this right may be subject to certain restrictions, but these shall only be such as are provided by law and are necessary:
(a) For respect of the rights or reputations of others; or
(b) For the protection of national security or of public order (ordre public), or of public health or morals.

Article 14

1. States Parties shall respect the right of the child to freedom of thought, conscience and religion.
2. States Parties shall respect the rights and duties of the parents and, when applicable, legal guardians, to provide direction to the child in the exercise of his or her right in a manner consistent with the evolving capacities of the child.
3. Freedom to manifest one's religion or beliefs may be subject only to such limitations as are prescribed by law and are necessary to protect public safety, order, health or morals, or the fundamental rights and freedoms of others.

Article 15

1. States Parties recognize the rights of the child to freedom of association and to freedom of peaceful assembly.
2. No restrictions may be placed on the exercise of these rights other than those imposed in conformity with the law and which are necessary in a democratic society in the interests of national security or public safety, public order (ordre public), the protection of public health or morals or the protection of the rights and freedoms of others.

Article 16

1. No child shall be subjected to arbitrary or unlawful interference with his or her privacy, family, home or correspondence, nor to unlawful attacks on his or her honour and reputation.
2. The child has the right to the protection of the law against such interference or attacks.

Article 17

States Parties recognize the important function performed by the mass media and shall ensure that the child has access to information and material from a diversity of national and international sources, especially those aimed at the promotion of his or her social, spiritual and moral well-being and physical and mental health. To this end, States Parties shall:
(a) Encourage the mass media to disseminate information and material of social and cultural benefit to the child and in accordance with the spirit of Article 29;
(b) Encourage international co-operation in the production, exchange and dissemination of such information and material from a diversity of cultural, national and international sources;
(c) Encourage the production and dissemination of children's books;
(d) Encourage the mass media to have particular regard to the linguistic needs of the child who belongs to a minority group or who is indigenous;

(e) Encourage the development of appropriate guidelines for the protection of the child from information and material injurious to his or her well-being, bearing in mind the provisions of Articles 13 and 18.

Article 18

1. States Parties shall use their best efforts to ensure recognition of the principle that both parents have common responsibilities for the upbringing and development of the child. Parents or, as the case may be, legal guardians, have the primary responsibility for the upbringing and development of the child. The best interests of the child will be their basic concern.
2. For the purpose of guaranteeing and promoting the rights set forth in the present Convention, States Parties shall render appropriate assistance to parents and legal guardians in the performance of their child-rearing responsibilities and shall ensure the development of institutions, facilities and services for the care of children.
3. States Parties shall take all appropriate measures to ensure that children of working parents have the right to benefit from child-care services and facilities for which they are eligible.

Article 19

1. States Parties shall take all appropriate legislative, administrative, social and educational measures to protect the child from all forms of physical or mental violence, injury or abuse, neglect or negligent treatment, maltreatment or exploitation, including sexual abuse, while in the care of parent(s), legal guardian(s) or any other person who has the care of the child.
2. Such protective measures should, as appropriate, include effective procedures for the establishment of social programmes to provide necessary support for the child and for those who have the care of the child, as well as for other forms of prevention and for identification, reporting, referral, investigation, treatment and follow-up of instances of child maltreatment described heretofore, and, as appropriate, for judicial involvement.

Article 20

1. A child temporarily or permanently deprived of his or her family environment, or in whose own best interests cannot be allowed to remain in that environment, shall be entitled to special protection and assistance provided by the State.
2. States Parties shall in accordance with their national laws ensure alternative care for such a child.
3. Such care could include, inter alia, foster placement, kafalah of Islamic law, adoption or if necessary placement in suitable institutions for the care of children. When considering solutions, due regard shall be paid to the desirability of

continuity in a child's upbringing and to the child's ethnic, religious, cultural and linguistic background.

Article 21

States Parties that recognize and/or permit the system of adoption shall ensure that the best interests of the child shall be the paramount consideration and they shall:
(a) Ensure that the adoption of a child is authorized only by competent authorities who determine, in accordance with applicable law and procedures and on the basis of all pertinent and reliable information, that the adoption is permissible in view of the child's status concerning parents, relatives and legal guardians and that, if required, the persons concerned have given their informed consent to the adoption on the basis of such counselling as may be necessary;
(b) Recognize that inter-country adoption may be considered as an alternative means of child's care, if the child cannot be placed in a foster or an adoptive family or cannot in any suitable manner be cared for in the child's country of origin;
(c) Ensure that the child concerned by inter-country adoption enjoys safeguards and standards equivalent to those existing in the case of national adoption;
(d) Take all appropriate measures to ensure that, in inter-country adoption, the placement does not result in improper financial gain for those involved in it;
(e) Promote, where appropriate, the objectives of the present article by concluding bilateral or multilateral arrangements or agreements, and endeavour, within this framework, to ensure that the placement of the child in another country is carried out by competent authorities or organs.

Article 22

1. States Parties shall take appropriate measures to ensure that a child who is seeking refugee status or who is considered a refugee in accordance with applicable international or domestic law and procedures shall, whether unaccompanied or accompanied by his or her parents or by any other person, receive appropriate protection and humanitarian assistance in the enjoyment of applicable rights set forth in the present Convention and in other international human rights or humanitarian instruments to which the said States are Parties.
2. For this purpose, States Parties shall provide, as they consider appropriate, co-operation in any efforts by the United Nations and other competent intergovernmental organizations or non-governmental organizations co-operating with the United Nations to protect and assist such a child and to trace the parents or other members of the family of any refugee child in order to obtain information necessary for reunification with his or her family. In cases where no parents or other members of the family can be found, the child shall be accorded the same protection as any other child permanently or temporarily deprived of his or her family environment for any reason, as set forth in the present Convention.

Article 23

1. States Parties recognize that a mentally or physically disabled child should enjoy a full and decent life, in conditions which ensure dignity, promote self-reliance and facilitate the child's active participation in the community.
2. States Parties recognize the right of the disabled child to special care and shall encourage and ensure the extension, subject to available resources, to the eligible child and those responsible for his or her care, of assistance for which application is made and which is appropriate to the child's condition and to the circumstances of the parents or others caring for the child.
3. Recognizing the special needs of a disabled child, assistance extended in accordance with paragraph 2 of the present article shall be provided free of charge, whenever possible, taking into account the financial resources of the parents or others caring for the child, and shall be designed to ensure that the disabled child has effective access to and receives education, training, health care services, rehabilitation services, preparation for employment and recreation opportunities in a manner conducive to the child's achieving the fullest possible social integration and individual development, including his or her cultural and spiritual development.
4. States Parties shall promote, in the spirit of international co-operation, the exchange of appropriate information in the field of preventive health care and of medical, psychological and functional treatment of disabled children, including dissemination of and access to information concerning methods of rehabilitation, education and vocational services, with the aim of enabling States Parties to improve their capabilities and skills and to widen their experience in these areas. In this regard, particular account shall be taken of the needs of developing countries.

Article 24

1. States Parties recognize the right of the child to the enjoyment of the highest attainable standard of health and to facilities for the treatment of illness and rehabilitation of health. States Parties shall strive to ensure that no child is deprived of his or her right of access to such health care.
2. States Parties shall pursue full implementation of this right and, in particular, shall take appropriate measures:
(a) To diminish infant and child mortality;
(b) To ensure the provision of necessary medical assistance and health care to all children with emphasis on the development of primary health care;
(c) To combat disease and malnutrition, including within the framework of primary health care, through, inter alia, the application of readily available technology and through the provision of adequate nutritious foods and clean drinking-water, taking into consideration the dangers and risks of environmental pollution;
(d) To ensure appropriate pre-natal and post-natal health care for mothers;

(e) To ensure that all segments of society, in particular parents and children, are informed, have access to education and are supported in the use of basic knowledge of child health and nutrition, the advantages of breast-feeding, hygiene and environmental sanitation and the prevention of accidents;
(f) To develop preventive health care, guidance for parents and family planning education and services.
3. States Parties shall take all effective and appropriate measures with a view to abolishing traditional practices prejudicial to the health of children.
4. States Parties undertake to promote and encourage international co-operation with a view to achieving progressively the full realization of the right recognized in the present article. In this regard, particular account shall be taken of the needs of developing countries.

Article 25

States Parties recognize the right of a child who has been placed by the competent authorities for the purposes of care, protection or treatment of his or her physical or mental health, to a periodic review of the treatment provided to the child and all other circumstances relevant to his or her placement.

Article 26

1. States Parties shall recognize for every child the right to benefit from social security, including social insurance, and shall take the necessary measures to achieve the full realization of this right in accordance with their national law.
2. The benefits should, where appropriate, be granted, taking into account the resources and the circumstances of the child and persons having responsibility for the maintenance of the child, as well as any other consideration relevant to an application for benefits made by or on behalf of the child.

Article 27

1. States Parties recognize the right of every child to a standard of living adequate for the child's physical, mental, spiritual, moral and social development.
2. The parent(s) or others responsible for the child have the primary responsibility to secure, within their abilities and financial capacities, the conditions of living necessary for the child's development.
3. States Parties, in accordance with national conditions and within their means, shall take appropriate measures to assist parents and others responsible for the child to implement this right and shall in case of need provide material assistance and support programmes, particularly with regard to nutrition, clothing and housing.
4. States Parties shall take all appropriate measures to secure the recovery of maintenance for the child from the parents or other persons having financial responsibility for the child, both within the State Party and from abroad. In

particular, where the person having financial responsibility for the child lives in a State different from that of the child, States Parties shall promote the accession to international agreements or the conclusion of such agreements, as well as the making of other appropriate arrangements.

Article 28

1. States Parties recognize the right of the child to education, and with a view to achieving this right progressively and on the basis of equal opportunity, they shall, in particular:
(a) Make primary education compulsory and available free to all;
(b) Encourage the development of different forms of secondary education, including general and vocational education, make them available and accessible to every child, and take appropriate measures such as the introduction of free education and offering financial assistance in case of need;
(c) Make higher education accessible to all on the basis of capacity by every appropriate means;
(d) Make educational and vocational information and guidance available and accessible to all children;
(e) Take measures to encourage regular attendance at schools and the reduction of drop-out rates.
2. States Parties shall take all appropriate measures to ensure that school discipline is administered in a manner consistent with the child's human dignity and in conformity with the present Convention.
3. States Parties shall promote and encourage international co-operation in matters relating to education, in particular with a view to contributing to the elimination of ignorance and illiteracy throughout the world and facilitating access to scientific and technical knowledge and modern teaching methods. In this regard, particular account shall be taken of the needs of developing countries.

Article 29

1. States Parties agree that the education of the child shall be directed to:
(a) The development of the child's personality, talents and mental and physical abilities to their fullest potential;
(b) The development of respect for human rights and fundamental freedoms, and for the principles enshrined in the Charter of the United Nations;
(c) The development of respect for the child's parents, his or her own cultural identity, language and values, for the national values of the country in which the child is living, the country from which he or she may originate, and for civilizations different from his or her own;
(d) The preparation of the child for responsible life in a free society, in the spirit of understanding, peace, tolerance, equality of sexes, and friendship among all peoples, ethnic, national and religious groups and persons of indigenous origin;

(e) The development of respect for the natural environment.
2. No part of the present article or Article 28 shall be construed so as to interfere with the liberty of individuals and bodies to establish and direct educational institutions, subject always to the observance of the principles set forth in paragraph 1 of the present article and to the requirements that the education given in such institutions shall conform to such minimum standards as may be laid down by the State.

Article 30

In those States in which ethnic, religious or linguistic minorities or persons of indigenous origin exist, a child belonging to such a minority or who is indigenous shall not be denied the right, in community with other members of his or her group, to enjoy his or her own culture, to profess and practise his or her own religion, or to use his or her own language.

Article 31

1. States Parties recognize the right of the child to rest and leisure, to engage in play and recreational activities appropriate to the age of the child and to participate freely in cultural life and the arts.
2. States Parties shall respect and promote the right of the child to participate fully in cultural and artistic life and shall encourage the provision of appropriate and equal opportunities for cultural, artistic, recreational and leisure activity.

Article 32

1. States Parties recognize the right of the child to be protected from economic exploitation and from performing any work that is likely to be hazardous or to interfere with the child's education, or to be harmful to the child's health or physical, mental, spiritual, moral or social development.
2. States Parties shall take legislative, administrative, social and educational measures to ensure the implementation of the present article. To this end, and having regard to the relevant provisions of other international instruments, States Parties shall in particular:
(a) Provide for a minimum age or minimum ages for admission to employment;
(b) Provide for appropriate regulation of the hours and conditions of employment;
(c) Provide for appropriate penalties or other sanctions to ensure the effective enforcement of the present article.

Article 33

States Parties shall take all appropriate measures, including legislative, administrative, social and educational measures, to protect children from the illicit use of narcotic drugs and psychotropic substances as defined in the relevant international treaties, and to prevent the use of children in the illicit production and trafficking of such substances.

Article 34

States Parties undertake to protect the child from all forms of sexual exploitation and sexual abuse. For these purposes, States Parties shall in particular take all appropriate national, bilateral and multilateral measures to prevent:
(a) The inducement or coercion of a child to engage in any unlawful sexual activity;
(b) The exploitative use of children in prostitution or other unlawful sexual practices;
(c) The exploitative use of children in pornographic performances and materials.

Article 35

States Parties shall take all appropriate national, bilateral and multilateral measures to prevent the abduction of, the sale of or traffic in children for any purpose or in any form.

Article 36

States Parties shall protect the child against all other forms of exploitation prejudicial to any aspects of the child's welfare.

Article 37

States Parties shall ensure that:
(a) No child shall be subjected to torture or other cruel, inhuman or degrading treatment or punishment. Neither capital punishment nor life imprisonment without possibility of release shall be imposed for offences committed by persons below eighteen years of age;
(b) No child shall be deprived of his or her liberty unlawfully or arbitrarily. The arrest, detention or imprisonment of a child shall be in conformity with the law and shall be used only as a measure of last resort and for the shortest appropriate period of time;
(c) Every child deprived of liberty shall be treated with humanity and respect for the inherent dignity of the human person, and in a manner which takes into account the needs of persons of his or her age. In particular, every child deprived of liberty shall be separated from adults unless it is considered in the child's best interest not to do so and shall have the right to maintain contact with his or her family through correspondence and visits, save in exceptional circumstances;
(d) Every child deprived of his or her liberty shall have the right to prompt access to legal and other appropriate assistance, as well as the right to challenge the legality of the deprivation of his or her liberty before a court or other competent, independent and impartial authority, and to a prompt decision on any such action.

Article 38

1. States Parties undertake to respect and to ensure respect for rules of international humanitarian law applicable to them in armed conflicts which are relevant to the child.
2. States Parties shall take all feasible measures to ensure that persons who have not attained the age of fifteen years do not take a direct part in hostilities.
3. States Parties shall refrain from recruiting any person who has not attained the age of fifteen years into their armed forces. In recruiting among those persons who have attained the age of fifteen years but who have not attained the age of eighteen years, States Parties shall endeavour to give priority to those who are oldest.
4. In accordance with their obligations under international humanitarian law to protect the civilian population in armed conflicts, States Parties shall take all feasible measures to ensure protection and care of children who are affected by an armed conflict.

Article 39

States Parties shall take all appropriate measures to promote physical and psychological recovery and social reintegration of a child victim of: any form of neglect, exploitation, or abuse; torture or any other form of cruel, inhuman or degrading treatment or punishment; or armed conflicts. Such recovery and reintegration shall take place in an environment which fosters the health, self-respect and dignity of the child.

Article 40

1. States Parties recognize the right of every child alleged as, accused of, or recognized as having infringed the penal law to be treated in a manner consistent with the promotion of the child's sense of dignity and worth, which reinforces the child's respect for the human rights and fundamental freedoms of others and which takes into account the child's age and the desirability of promoting the child's reintegration and the child's assuming a constructive role in society.
2. To this end, and having regard to the relevant provisions of international instruments, States Parties shall, in particular, ensure that:
(a) No child shall be alleged as, be accused of, or recognized as having infringed the penal law by reason of acts or omissions that were not prohibited by national or international law at the time they were committed;
(b) Every child alleged as or accused of having infringed the penal law has at least the following guarantees:
(i) To be presumed innocent until proven guilty according to law;
(ii) To be informed promptly and directly of the charges against him or her, and, if appropriate, through his or her parents or legal guardians, and to have legal or other appropriate assistance in the preparation and presentation of his or her defence;

(iii) To have the matter determined without delay by a competent, independent and impartial authority or judicial body in a fair hearing according to law, in the presence of legal or other appropriate assistance and, unless it is considered not to be in the best interest of the child, in particular, taking into account his or her age or situation, his or her parents or legal guardians;
(iv) Not to be compelled to give testimony or to confess guilt; to examine or have examined adverse witnesses and to obtain the participation and examination of witnesses on his or her behalf under conditions of equality;
(v) If considered to have infringed the penal law, to have this decision and any measures imposed in consequence thereof reviewed by a higher competent, independent and impartial authority or judicial body according to law;
(vi) To have the free assistance of an interpreter if the child cannot understand or speak the language used;
(vii) To have his or her privacy fully respected at all stages of the proceedings.
3. States Parties shall seek to promote the establishment of laws, procedures, authorities and institutions specifically applicable to children alleged as, accused of, or recognized as having infringed the penal law, and, in particular:
(a) The establishment of a minimum age below which children shall be presumed not to have the capacity to infringe the penal law;
(b) Whenever appropriate and desirable, measures for dealing with such children without resorting to judicial proceedings, providing that human rights and legal safeguards are fully respected.
4. A variety of dispositions, such as care, guidance and supervision orders; counselling; probation; foster care; education and vocational training programmes and other alternatives to institutional care shall be available to ensure that children are dealt with in a manner appropriate to their well-being and proportionate both to their circumstances and the offence.

Article 41

Nothing in the present Convention shall affect any provisions which are more conducive to the realization of the rights of the child and which may be contained in:
(a) The law of a State Party; or
(b) International law in force for that State.

PART II

Article 42

States Parties undertake to make the principles and provisions of the Convention widely known, by appropriate and active means, to adults and children alike.

Article 43

1. For the purpose of examining the progress made by States Parties in achieving the realization of the obligations undertaken in the present Convention, there shall be established a Committee on the Rights of the Child, which shall carry out the functions hereinafter provided.
2. The Committee shall consist of ten experts of high moral standing and recognized competence in the field covered by this Convention. The members of the Committee shall be elected by States Parties from among their nationals and shall serve in their personal capacity, consideration being given to equitable geographical distribution, as well as to the principal legal systems.
3. The members of the Committee shall be elected by secret ballot from a list of persons nominated by States Parties. Each State Party may nominate one person from among its own nationals.
4. The initial election to the Committee shall be held no later than six months after the date of the entry into force of the present Convention and thereafter every second year. At least four months before the date of each election, the Secretary-General of the United Nations shall address a letter to States Parties inviting them to submit their nominations within two months. The Secretary-General shall subsequently prepare a list in alphabetical order of all persons thus nominated, indicating States Parties which have nominated them, and shall submit it to the States Parties to the present Convention.
5. The elections shall be held at meetings of States Parties convened by the Secretary-General at United Nations Headquarters. At those meetings, for which two thirds of States Parties shall constitute a quorum, the persons elected to the Committee shall be those who obtain the largest number of votes and an absolute majority of the votes of the representatives of States Parties present and voting.
6. The members of the Committee shall be elected for a term of four years. They shall be eligible for re-election if renominated. The term of five of the members elected at the first election shall expire at the end of two years; immediately after the first election, the names of these five members shall be chosen by lot by the Chairman of the meeting.
7. If a member of the Committee dies or resigns or declares that for any other cause he or she can no longer perform the duties of the Committee, the State Party which nominated the member shall appoint another expert from among its nationals to serve for the remainder of the term, subject to the approval of the Committee.
8. The Committee shall establish its own rules of procedure.
9. The Committee shall elect its officers for a period of two years.
10. The meetings of the Committee shall normally be held at United Nations Headquarters or at any other convenient place as determined by the Committee. The Committee shall normally meet annually. The duration of the meetings of the Committee shall be determined, and reviewed, if necessary, by a meeting of the States Parties to the present Convention, subject to the approval of the General Assembly.

11. The Secretary-General of the United Nations shall provide the necessary staff and facilities for the effective performance of the functions of the Committee under the present Convention.
12. With the approval of the General Assembly, the members of the Committee established under the present Convention shall receive emoluments from United Nations resources on such terms and conditions as the Assembly may decide.

Article 44

1. States Parties undertake to submit to the Committee, through the Secretary-General of the United Nations, reports on the measures they have adopted which give effect to the rights recognized herein and on the progress made on the enjoyment of those rights:
(a) Within two years of the entry into force of the Convention for the State Party concerned;
(b) Thereafter every five years.
2. Reports made under the present article shall indicate factors and difficulties, if any, affecting the degree of fulfilment of the obligations under the present Convention. Reports shall also contain sufficient information to provide the Committee with a comprehensive understanding of the implementation of the Convention in the country concerned.
3. A State Party which has submitted a comprehensive initial report to the Committee need not, in its subsequent reports submitted in accordance with paragraph 1 (b) of the present article, repeat basic information previously provided.
4. The Committee may request from States Parties further information relevant to the implementation of the Convention.
5. The Committee shall submit to the General Assembly, through the Economic and Social Council, every two years, reports on its activities.
6. States Parties shall make their reports widely available to the public in their own countries.

Article 45

In order to foster the effective implementation of the Convention and to encourage international co-operation in the field covered by the Convention:
(a) The specialized agencies, the United Nations Children's Fund, and other United Nations organs shall be entitled to be represented at the consideration of the implementation of such provisions of the present Convention as fall within the scope of their mandate. The Committee may invite the specialized agencies, the United Nations Children's Fund and other competent bodies as it may consider appropriate to provide expert advice on the implementation of the Convention in areas falling within the scope of their respective mandates. The Committee may invite the specialized agencies, the United Nations Children's Fund, and other

United Nations organs to submit reports on the implementation of the Convention in areas falling within the scope of their activities;
(b) The Committee shall transmit, as it may consider appropriate, to the specialized agencies, the United Nations Children's Fund and other competent bodies, any reports from States Parties that contain a request, or indicate a need, for technical advice or assistance, along with the Committee's observations and suggestions, if any, on these requests or indications;
(c) The Committee may recommend to the General Assembly to request the Secretary-General to undertake on its behalf studies on specific issues relating to the rights of the child;
(d) The Committee may make suggestions and general recommendations based on information received pursuant to articles 44 and 45 of the present Convention. Such suggestions and general recommendations shall be transmitted to any State Party concerned and reported to the General Assembly, together with comments, if any, from States Parties.

PART III

Article 46

The present Convention shall be open for signature by all States.

Article 47

The present Convention is subject to ratification. Instruments of ratification shall be deposited with the Secretary-General of the United Nations.

Article 48

The present Convention shall remain open for accession by any State. The instruments of accession shall be deposited with the Secretary-General of the United Nations.

Article 49

1. The present Convention shall enter into force on the thirtieth day following the date of deposit with the Secretary-General of the United Nations of the twentieth instrument of ratification or accession.
2. For each State ratifying or acceding to the Convention after the deposit of the twentieth instrument of ratification or accession, the Convention shall enter into force on the thirtieth day after the deposit by such State of its instrument of ratification or accession.

Article 50

1. Any State Party may propose an amendment and file it with the Secretary-General of the United Nations. The Secretary-General shall thereupon communicate the proposed amendment to States Parties, with a request that they indicate whether they favour a conference of States Parties for the purpose of considering and voting upon the proposals. In the event that, within four months from the date of such communication, at least one third of the States Parties favour such a conference, the Secretary-General shall convene the conference under the auspices of the United Nations. Any amendment adopted by a majority of States Parties present and voting at the conference shall be submitted to the General Assembly for approval.
2. An amendment adopted in accordance with paragraph 1 of the present article shall enter into force when it has been approved by the General Assembly of the United Nations and accepted by a two-thirds majority of States Parties.
3. When an amendment enters into force, it shall be binding on those States Parties which have accepted it, other States Parties still being bound by the provisions of the present Convention and any earlier amendments which they have accepted.

Article 51

1. The Secretary-General of the United Nations shall receive and circulate to all States the text of reservations made by States at the time of ratification or accession.
2. A reservation incompatible with the object and purpose of the present Convention shall not be permitted.
3. Reservations may be withdrawn at any time by notification to that effect addressed to the Secretary-General of the United Nations, who shall then inform all States. Such notification shall take effect on the date on which it is received by the Secretary-General.

Article 52

A State Party may denounce the present Convention by written notification to the Secretary-General of the United Nations. Denunciation becomes effective one year after the date of receipt of the notification by the Secretary-General.

Article 53

The Secretary-General of the United Nations is designated as the depositary of the present Convention.

Article 54

The original of the present Convention, of which the Arabic, Chinese, English, French, Russian and Spanish texts are equally authentic, shall be deposited with the Secretary-General of the United Nations.

In witness thereof the undersigned plenipotentiaries, being duly authorized thereto by their respective Governments, have signed the present Convention.

Constitution of the International Organization for Migration (1987)[1]

Preamble

THE HIGH CONTRACTING PARTIES

RECALLING the Resolution adopted on 5 December 1951 by the Migration Conference in Brussels,

RECOGNIZING that the provision of migration services at an international level is often required to ensure the orderly flow of migration movements throughout the world and to facilitate, under the most favourable conditions, the settlement and integration of the migrants into the economic and social structure of the country of reception,

that similar migration services may also be required for temporary migration, return migration and intra-regional migration,

that international migration also includes that of refugees, displaced persons and other individuals compelled to leave their homelands, and who are in need of international migration services,

that there is a need to promote the cooperation of States and international organizations with a view to facilitating the emigration of persons who desire to migrate to countries where they may achieve self-dependence through their employment and live with their families in dignity and self-respect,

that migration may stimulate the creation of new economic opportunities in receiving countries and that a relationship exists between migration and the economic, social and cultural conditions in developing countries,

that in the cooperation and other international activities for migration the needs of developing countries should be taken into account,

that there is a need to promote the cooperation of States and international organizations, governmental and non-governmental, for research and consultation on migration issues, not only in regard to the migration process but also the specific situation and needs of the migrant as an individual human being, that

---

1 The present text incorporates into the Constitution of 19 October 1953 of the Intergovernmental Committee for European Migration (former designation of the Organization), which entered into force on 30 November 1954, the amendments adopted on 20 May 1987 by the 55th Session of the Council (Resolution no. 724), which entered into force on 14 November 1989, and the amendments adopted on 24 November 1998 by the 76th Session of the Council (Resolution no. 997), which entered into force on 21 November 2013.

the movement of migrants should, to the extent possible, be carried out with normal transport services but that, on occasion, there is a need for additional or other facilities,

that there should be close cooperation and coordination among States, international organizations, governmental and non-governmental, on migration and refugee matters,

that there is a need for the international financing of activities related to international migration,

DO HEREBY ESTABLISH

the INTERNATIONAL ORGANIZATION FOR MIGRATION, hereinafter called the Organization, and

ACCEPT THIS CONSTITUTION.

CHAPTER I – PURPOSES AND FUNCTIONS

Article 1

1. The purposes and functions of the Organization shall be:
a) to make arrangements for the organized transfer of migrants, for whom existing facilities are inadequate or who would not otherwise be able to move without special assistance, to countries offering opportunities for orderly migration;
b) to concern itself with the organized transfer of refugees, displaced persons and other individuals in need of international migration services for whom arrangements may be made between the Organization and the States concerned, including those States undertaking to receive them;
c) to provide, at the request of and in agreement with the States concerned, migration services such as recruitment, selection, processing, language training, orientation activities, medical examination, placement, activities facilitating reception and integration, advisory services on migration questions, and other assistance as is in accord with the aims of the Organization;
d) to provide similar services as requested by States, or in cooperation with other interested international organizations, for voluntary return migration, including voluntary repatriation;
e) to provide a forum to States as well as international and other organizations for the exchange of views and experiences, and the promotion of cooperation and coordination of efforts on international migration issues, including studies on such issues in order to develop practical solutions.
2. In carrying out its functions, the Organization shall cooperate closely with international organizations, governmental and non-governmental, concerned with migration, refugees and human resources in order, inter alia, to facilitate the coordination of international activities in these fields. Such cooperation shall be carried out in the mutual respect of the competences of the organizations concerned.

3. The Organization shall recognize the fact that control of standards of admission and the number of immigrants to be admitted are matters within the domestic jurisdiction of States, and, in carrying out its functions, shall conform to the laws, regulations and policies of the States concerned.

CHAPTER II – MEMBERSHIP

Article 2

The Members of the Organization shall be:
(a) the States being Members of the Organization which have accepted this Constitution according to Article 29, or to which the terms of Article 30 apply;
(b) other States with a demonstrated interest in the principle of free movement of persons which undertake to make a financial contribution at least to the administrative requirements of the Organization, the rate of which will be agreed to by the Council and by the State concerned, subject to a two-thirds majority vote of the Council and upon acceptance by the State of this Constitution in accordance with its constitutional processes.

Article 3

Any Member State may give notice of withdrawal from the Organization effective at the end of a financial year. Such notice must be in writing and must reach the Director General of the Organization at least four months before the end of the financial year. The financial obligations to the Organization of a Member State which has given notice of withdrawal shall include the entire financial year in which notice is given.

Article 4

1. A Member State which is in arrears in the payment of its financial contributions to the Organization shall have no right to vote if the amount of its arrears equals or exceeds the amount of the contributions due from it for the preceding two years. However, the loss of voting rights shall become effective one year after the Council has been informed that the member concerned is in arrears to an extent entailing the loss of voting rights, if at that time the Member State is still in arrears to the said extent. The Council may nevertheless, by a simple majority vote, maintain or restore the right to vote of such a Member State if it is satisfied that the failure to pay is due to conditions beyond the control of the Member State.
2. Any Member State may be suspended from membership by a two-thirds majority vote of the Council if it persistently violates the principles of this Constitution. The Council shall have the authority to restore such membership by a simple majority vote.

CHAPTER III – ORGANS

Article 5

There are established as the organs of the Organization:
(a) the Council;
(b) the Administration.

CHAPTER IV – COUNCIL

Article 6

The functions of the Council, in addition to those mentioned in other provisions of this Constitution, shall be:
(a) to determine, examine and review the policies, programmes and activities of the Organization;
(b) to review the reports and to approve and direct the activities of any subsidiary body;
(c) to review the reports and to approve and direct the activities of the Director General;
(d) to review and approve the programme, the Budget, the expenditure and the accounts of the Organization;
(e) to take any other appropriate action to further the purposes of the Organization.

Article 7

1. The Council shall be composed of representatives of the Member States.
2. Each Member State shall have one representative and such alternates and advisers as it may deem necessary.
3. Each Member State shall have one vote in the Council.

Article 8

The Council may admit, upon their application, non-member States and international organizations, governmental or non-governmental, concerned with migration, refugees or human resources as observers at its meetings under conditions which may be prescribed in its rules of procedure. No such observers shall have the right to vote.

Article 9

1. The Council shall meet in regular session once a year.
2. The Council shall meet in special session at the request of:

(a) one third of its members;
(b) the Director General or the Chairman of the Council in urgent circumstances.
3. The Council shall elect, at the beginning of each regular session, a Chairman and other officers for a one-year term.

Article 10

The Council may set up such subsidiary bodies as may be required for the proper discharge of its functions.

Article 11

The Council shall adopt its own rules of procedure.

CHAPTER V – ADMINISTRATION

Article 12

The Administration shall comprise a Director General, a Deputy Director General and such staff as the Council may determine.

Article 13

1. The Director General and the Deputy Director General shall be elected by a two-thirds majority vote of the Council and may be re-elected for one additional term. Their term of office shall normally be five years but may, in exceptional cases, be less if a two-thirds majority of the Council so decides. They shall serve under contracts approved by the Council, which shall be signed on behalf of the Organization by the Chairman of the Council.
2. The Director General shall be responsible to the Council. The Director General shall discharge the administrative and executive functions of the Organization in accordance with this Constitution and the policies and decisions of the Council and the rules and regulations established by it. The Director General shall formulate proposals for appropriate action by the Council.

Article 14

The Director General shall appoint the staff of the Administration in accordance with the staff regulations adopted by the Council.

Article 15

1. In the performance of their duties, the Director General, the Deputy Director General and the staff shall neither seek nor receive instructions from any State or from any authority external to the Organization. They shall refrain from any action which might reflect adversely on their position as international officials.
2. Each Member State undertakes to respect the exclusively international character of the responsibilities of the Director General, the Deputy Director General and the staff and not to seek to influence them in the discharge of their responsibilities.
3. Efficiency, competence and integrity shall be the necessary considerations in the recruitment and employment of the staff which, except in special circumstances, shall be recruited among the nationals of the Member States of the Organization, taking into account the principle of equitable geographical distribution.

Article 16

The Director General shall be present, or be represented by the Deputy Director General or another designated official, at all sessions of the Council and any subsidiary bodies. The Director General or the designated representative may participate in the discussions but shall have no vote.

Article 17

At the regular session of the Council following the end of each financial year, the Director General shall make to the Council a report on the work of the Organization, giving a full account of its activities during that year.

CHAPTER VI – HEADQUARTERS

Article 18

1. The Organization shall have its Headquarters in Geneva. The Council may, by a two-thirds majority vote, change its location.
2. The meetings of the Council shall be held in Geneva, unless two thirds of the members of the Council have agreed to meet elsewhere.

CHAPTER VII – FINANCE

Article 19

The Director General shall submit to the Council an annual budget covering the administrative and operational requirements and the anticipated resources of the

Organization, such supplementary estimates as may be required and the annual or special accounting statements of the Organization.

Article 20

1. The requirements of the Organization shall be financed:
(a) as to the Administrative part of the Budget, by cash contributions from Member States, which shall be due at the beginning of the financial year to which they relate and shall be paid promptly;
(b) as to the Operational part of the Budget, by contributions in cash, in kind or in services from Member States, other States, international organizations, governmental or non-governmental, other legal entities or individuals, which shall be paid as early as possible and in full prior to the expiration of the financial year to which they relate.
2. Member States shall contribute to the Administrative part of the Budget of the Organization at a rate agreed to by the Council and by the Member State concerned.
3. Contributions to the operational expenditure of the Organization shall be voluntary and any contributor to the Operational part of the Budget may stipulate with the Organization terms and conditions, consistent with the purposes and functions of the Organization, under which its contributions may be used.
4. (a) All Headquarters administrative expenditure and all other administrative expenditure except that incurred in pursuance of the functions outlined in paragraph 1 (c) and (d) of Article 1 shall be attributed to the Administrative part of the Budget;
(b) all operational expenditure and such administrative expenditure as is incurred in pursuance of the functions outlined in paragraph 1 (c) and (d) of Article 1 shall be attributed to the Operational part of the Budget.
5. The Council shall ensure that the management is conducted in an efficient and economical manner.

Article 21

The financial regulations shall be established by the Council.

CHAPTER VIII – LEGAL STATUS

Article 22

The Organization shall possess full juridical personality. It shall enjoy such legal capacity, as may be necessary for the exercise of its functions and the fulfilment of its purposes, and in particular the capacity, in accordance with the laws of the State:
(a) to contract;
(b) to acquire and dispose of immovable and movable property;

(c) to receive and disburse private and public funds;
(d) to institute legal proceedings.

Article 23

1. The Organization shall enjoy such privileges and immunities as are necessary for the exercise of its functions and the fulfilment of its purposes.
2. Representatives of Member States, the Director General, the Deputy Director General and the staff of the Administration shall likewise enjoy such privileges and immunities as are necessary for the independent exercise of their functions in connection with the Organization.
3. These privileges and immunities shall be defined in agreements between the Organization and the States concerned or through other measures taken by these States.

CHAPTER IX – MISCELLANEOUS PROVISIONS

Article 24

1. Except as otherwise expressly provided in this Constitution or rules made by the Council, all decisions of the Council and all subsidiary bodies shall be taken by a simple majority vote.
2. Majorities provided for in this Constitution or rules made by the Council shall refer to members present and voting.
3. No vote shall be valid unless a majority of the members of the Council or any subsidiary body concerned are present.

Article 25

1. Texts of proposed amendments to this Constitution shall be communicated by the Director General to Governments of Member States at least three months in advance of their consideration by the Council.
2. Amendments involving fundamental changes in the Constitution of the Organization or new obligations for the Member States shall come into force when adopted by two thirds of the members of the Council and accepted by two thirds of the Member States in accordance with their respective constitutional processes. Whether an amendment involves a fundamental change in the Constitution shall be decided by the Council by a two-thirds majority vote. Other amendments shall come into force when adopted by a two-thirds majority vote of the Council.

Article 26

Any dispute concerning the interpretation or application of this Constitution which is not settled by negotiation or by a two-thirds majority vote of the Council shall be referred to the International Court of Justice in conformity with the Statute of the Court, unless the Member States concerned agree on another mode of settlement within a reasonable period of time.

Article 27

Subject to approval by two thirds of the members of the Council, the Organization may take over from any other international organization or agency the purposes and activities of which lie within the purposes of the Organization such activities, resources and obligations as may be determined by international agreement or by mutually acceptable arrangements entered into between the competent authorities of the respective organizations.

Article 28

The Council may, by a three-quarters majority vote of its members, decide to dissolve the Organization.

Article 29

This Constitution shall come into force, for those Governments Members of the Intergovernmental Committee for European Migration which have accepted it in accordance with their respective constitutional processes, on the day of the first meeting of that Committee after:
(a) at least two thirds of the Members of the Committee, and
(b) a number of Members whose contributions represent at least 75 per cent of the Administrative part of the Budget,
shall have communicated to the Director their acceptance of this Constitution.

Article 30[2]

Those Governments Members of the Intergovernmental Committee for European Migration which have not by the date of coming into force of this Constitution communicated to the Director their acceptance of this Constitution may remain Members of the Committee for a period of one year from that date if they

2 Articles 29 and 30 were implemented upon the entry into force on 30 November 1954 of the Constitution of 19 October 1953 (at that time Articles 33 and 34) of the Intergovernmental Committee for European Migration (former designation of the Organization).

contribute to the administrative requirements of the Committee in accordance with paragraph 2 of Article 20, and they shall retain during that period the right to accept the Constitution.

Article 31

The English, French and Spanish texts of this Constitution shall be regarded as equally authentic.

Declaration of States Parties to the 1951 Convention and/or its 1967 Protocol relating to the Status of Refugees (2001)

Preamble

We, representatives of States Parties to the 1951 Convention relating to the Status of Refugees and/or its 1967 Protocol, assembled in the first meeting of States Parties in Geneva on 12 and 13 December 2001 at the invitation of the Government of Switzerland and the United Nations High Commissioner for Refugees (UNHCR),
1. Cognizant of the fact that the year 2001 marks the 50th anniversary of the 1951 Geneva Convention relating to the Status of Refugees,
2. Recognizing the enduring importance of the 1951 Convention, as the primary refugee protection instrument which, as amended by its 1967 Protocol, sets out rights, including human rights, and minimum standards of treatment that apply to persons falling within its scope,
3. Recognizing the importance of other human rights and regional refugee protection instruments, including the 1969 Organization of African Unity (OAU) Convention governing the Specific Aspects of the Refugee Problem in Africa and the 1984 Cartagena Declaration, and recognizing also the importance of the common European asylum system developed since the 1999 Tampere European Council Conclusions, as well as the Programme of Action of the 1996 Regional Conference to Address the Problems of Refugees, Displaced Persons, Other Forms of Involuntary Displacement and Returnees in the Countries of the Commonwealth of Independent States and Relevant Neighbouring States,
4. Acknowledging the continuing relevance and resilience of this international regime of rights and principles, including at its core the principle of *non-refoulement*, whose applicability is embedded in customary international law,
5. Commending the positive and constructive role played by refugee-hosting countries and recognizing at the same time the heavy burden borne by some, particularly developing countries and countries with economies in transition, as well as the protracted nature of many refugee situations and the absence of timely and safe solutions,
6. Taking note of complex features of the evolving environment in which refugee protection has to be provided, including the nature of armed conflict, ongoing violations of human rights and international humanitarian law, current patterns of displacement, mixed population flows, the high costs of hosting large numbers of refugees and asylum-seekers and of maintaining asylum systems, the growth

of associated trafficking and smuggling of persons, the problems of safeguarding asylum systems against abuse and of excluding and returning those not entitled to or in need of international protection, as well as the lack of resolution of long-standing refugee situations,

7. Reaffirming that the 1951 Convention, as amended by the 1967 Protocol, has a central place in the international refugee protection regime, and believing also that this regime should be developed further, as appropriate, in a way that complements and strengthens the 1951 Convention and its Protocol,

8. Stressing that respect by States for their protection responsibilities towards refugees is strengthened by international solidarity involving all members of the international community and that the refugee protection regime is enhanced through committed international cooperation in a spirit of solidarity and effective responsibility and burden-sharing among all States,

Operative paragraphs

1. Solemnly reaffirm our commitment to implement our obligations under the 1951 Convention and/or its 1967 Protocol fully and effectively in accordance with the object and purpose of these instruments;

2. Reaffirm our continued commitment, in recognition of the social and humanitarian nature of the problem of refugees, to upholding the values and principles embodied in these instruments, which are consistent with Article 14 of the Universal Declaration of Human Rights, and which require respect for the rights and freedoms of refugees, international cooperation to resolve their plight, and action to address the causes of refugee movements, as well as to prevent them, *inter alia*, through the promotion of peace, stability and dialogue, from becoming a source of tension between States;

3. Recognize the importance of promoting universal adherence to the 1951 Convention and/or its 1967 Protocol, while acknowledging that there are countries of asylum which have not yet acceded to these instruments and which do continue generously to host large numbers of refugees;

4. Encourage all States that have not yet done so to accede to the 1951 Convention and/or its 1967 Protocol, as far as possible without reservation;

5. Also encourage States Parties maintaining the geographical limitation or other reservations to consider withdrawing them;

6. Call upon all States, consistent with applicable international standards, to take or continue to take measures to strengthen asylum and render protection more effective including through the adoption and implementation of national refugee legislation and procedures for the determination of refugee status and for the treatment of asylum-seekers and refugees, giving special attention to vulnerable groups and individuals with special needs, including women, children and the elderly;

7. Call upon States to continue their efforts aimed at ensuring the integrity of the asylum institution, *inter alia*, by means of carefully applying Articles 1F and 33(2) of the 1951 Convention, in particular in light of new threats and challenges;
8. Reaffirm the fundamental importance of UNHCR as the multilateral institution with the mandate to provide international protection to refugees and to promote durable solutions, and recall our obligations as States Parties to cooperate with UNHCR in the exercise of its functions;
9. Urge all States to consider ways that may be required to strengthen the implementation of the 1951 Convention and/or its 1967 Protocol and to ensure closer cooperation between States Parties and UNHCR to facilitate UNHCR's duty of supervising the application of the provisions of these instruments;
10. Urge all States to respond promptly, predictably and adequately to funding appeals issued by UNHCR so as to ensure that the needs of persons under the mandate of the Office of the High Commissioner are fully met;
11. Recognize the valuable contributions made by many non-governmental organizations to the well-being of asylum-seekers and refugees in their reception, counselling and care, in finding durable solutions based on full respect of refugees, and in assisting States and UNHCR to maintain the integrity of the international refugee protection regime, notably through advocacy, as well as public awareness and information activities aimed at combating racism, racial discrimination, xenophobia and related intolerance, and gaining public support for refugees;
12. Commit ourselves to providing, within the framework of international solidarity and burden-sharing, better refugee protection through comprehensive strategies, notably regionally and internationally, in order to build capacity, in particular in developing countries and countries with economies in transition, especially those which are hosting large-scale influxes or protracted refugee situations, and to strengthening response mechanisms, so as to ensure that refugees have access to safer and better conditions of stay and timely solutions to their problems;
13. Recognize that prevention is the best way to avoid refugee situations and emphasize that the ultimate goal of international protection is to achieve a durable solution for refugees, consistent with the principle of *non-refoulement*, and commend States that continue to facilitate these solutions, notably voluntary repatriation and, where appropriate and feasible, local integration and resettlement, while recognizing that voluntary repatriation in conditions of safety and dignity remains the preferred solution for refugees;
14. Extend our gratitude to the Government and people of Switzerland for generously hosting the Ministerial Meeting of States Parties to the 1951 Convention and/or its 1967 Protocol relating to the Status of Refugees.

Index

Page numbers in **bold** refer to figures.

FSC
www.fsc.org
MIX
Papier | Fördert gute Waldnutzung
FSC® C083411

Kolibri 360 GmbH
Ferdinand-Jühlke-Straße 7
99095 Erfurt, Deutschland
produktsicherheit@kolibri360.de